MULTILITERACIES

D0221986

'This is a unique effort, the effect of which is a very persuasive, coherent volume set within a well-thought out conceptual framework. The style is extremely readable.'

Nancy Hornberger, University of Pennsylvania

Multiliteracies considers the future of literacy teaching in the context of the rapidly changing English language. Questions are raised about what constitutes appropriate literacy teaching in today's world: a world that is both a global village yet one in which local diversity is increasingly important.

This is a coherent and accessible overview of the work of the New London Group, with well-known international contributors bringing together their varying national experiences and differences of theoretical and political emphasis. The essays deal with issues such as:

- the fundamental premises of literacy pedagogy
- the effects of technological change
- multilingualism and cultural diversity
- social futures and their implications on language teaching

The book concludes with case studies of attempts to put the theories into practice and thereby provides a basis for dialogue with fellow educators around the world.

Contributors: David Bond, Courtney B. Cazden, Bill Cope, Norman Fairclough, James Paul Gee, Mary Kalantzis, Gunther Kress, Joseph Lo Bianco, Carmen Luke, Sarah Michaels, Martin Nakata, Denise Newfield, Richard Sohmer, Pippa Stein

LITERACIES
Series Editor: David Barton
Lancaster University

Literacy practices are changing rapidly in contemporary society in response to broad social, economic and technological changes: in education, the workplace, the media and in everyday life. The *Literacies* series has been developed to reflect the burgeoning research and scholarship in the field of literacy studies and its increasingly interdisciplinary nature. The series aims to situate reading and writing within its broader institutional contexts where literacy is considered as a social practice. Work in this field has been developed and drawn together to provide books which are accessible, inter-disciplinary and international in scope, covering a wide range of social and institutional contexts.

SITUATED LITERACIES
Reading and Writing in Context
Edited by David Barton, Mary Hamilton and Roz Ivanič

MULTILITERACIES
Literacy learning and the design of social futures
Edited by Bill Cope and Mary Kalantzis

GLOBAL LITERACIES AND THE WORLD-WIDE WEB
Edited by Gail E. Hawisher and Cynthia L. Selfe

Editorial Board:

MULTILITERACIES

Literacy learning and the design
of social futures

Edited by Bill Cope
and
Mary Kalantzis

for the New London Group

London and New York

First published 2000
by Routledge
11 New Fetter Lane, London EC4P 4EE

Simultaneously published in the USA and Canada
by Routledge
29 West 35th Street, New York, NY 10001

Reprinted 2002

Routledge is an imprint of the Taylor & Francis Group

Typeset in Baskerville by
Keystroke, Jacaranda Lodge, Wolverhampton
Printed and bound in Great Britain by
TJ International, Padstow, Cornwall

British Library Cataloguing in Publication Data
A catalogue record for this book is available from the British Library

Library of Congress Cataloging in Publication Data
A catalogue record for this book has been requested

ISBN 0–415–21420–3 (hbk)
ISBN 0–415–21421–1 (pbk)

CONTENTS

About the authors   ix

PART I
Introduction   1

Introduction: Multiliteracies: the beginnings of an idea   3
BILL COPE AND MARY KALANTZIS

1 **A pedagogy of Multiliteracies designing social futures**   9
THE NEW LONDON GROUP

PART II
Changing times: the 'why' of Multiliteracies   39

Introduction   41

2 **New people in new worlds: networks, the new capitalism
   and schools**   43
JAMES PAUL GEE

3 **Cyber-schooling and technological change: Multiliteracies
   for new times**   69
CARMEN LUKE

4 **Multiliteracies and multilingualism**   92
JOSEPH LO BIANCO

5 **History, cultural diversity and English language teaching**   106
MARTIN NAKATA

6 **Changing the role of schools**   121
MARY KALANTZIS AND BILL COPE

PART III
Designs of meaning: the 'what' of Multiliteracies   149

   Introduction   151

  7 Design and transformation: new theories of meaning   153
     GUNTHER KRESS

  8 Multiliteracies and language: orders of discourse and
    intertextuality   162
     NORMAN FAIRCLOUGH

  9 Multimodality   182
     GUNTHER KRESS

 10 Designs for social futures   203
     BILL COPE AND MARY KALANTZIS

PART IV
Pedagogy: The 'how' of Multiliteracies   235

   Introduction   237

 11 A Multiliteracies pedagogy: a pedagogical supplement   239
     MARY KALANTZIS AND BILL COPE

 12 Taking cultural differences into account   249
     COURTNEY B. CAZDEN

 13 Narratives and inscriptions: cultural tools, power and powerful
    sense-making   267
     SARAH MICHAELS AND RICHARD SOHMER

PART V
Multiliteracies in practice   289

   Introduction   291

 14 The Multiliteracies Project: South African teachers respond 292
     DENISE NEWFIELD AND PIPPA STEIN

 15 Negotiating a pedagogy of Multiliteracies: the
    communication curriculum in a South African management
    development programme   311
     DAVID BOND

**16 Four innovative programmes: a postscript from
Alice Springs**   **321**
COURTNEY B. CAZDEN

References   333
Index   349

ABOUT THE AUTHORS

This book has been collectively written by the New London Group although Bill Cope and Mary Kalantzis have taken responsibility for editing the collection.

The following contributors to this book attended the original New London meeting in September 1994, and authored the 'Pedagogy of Multiliteracies' manifesto, published in the *Harvard Educational Review* in 1996 and which appears as Chapter 1 of this book: Courtney B. Cazden, Bill Cope, Norman Fairclough, James Paul Gee, Mary Kalantzis, Gunther Kress, Carmen Luke, Sarah Michaels, and Martin Nakata. Joseph Lo Bianco was unable to attend the September 1994 meeting. He has, however, attended subsequent New London Group meetings.

Following the publication of the 'Pedagogy of Multiliteracies' manifesto, David Bond, Denise Newfield, Richard Sohmer and Pippa Stein were invited by the New London Group to contribute to this book, adding their perspectives and experiences in using and evaluating the Multiliteracies concepts.

Courtney B. Cazden is the Charles William Eliot Professor of Education Emerita at the Harvard Graduate School of Education, USA. She is a member of the National Academy of Education and a past president of the Council on Anthropology and Education and the American Association of Applied Linguistics. Currently she is working on a revised edition of her highly acclaimed *Classroom Discourse*.

Bill Cope is Director of the Centre for Workplace Communication and Culture and a former Director of the Office of Multicultural Affairs in Australia's Department of the Prime Minister and Cabinet. He is co-author, with Mary Kalantzis, of *Productive Diversity* (Pluto Press, Sydney, 1997), *Mistaken Identity: Multiculturalism and the Demise of Nationalism in Australia* (Pluto, 1992; with Kalantzis, Castles and Morrissey), *The Powers of Literacy* (Falmer Press, London, 1993, edited with Kalantzis), *Cultures of Schooling* (Falmer, 1991, with Kalantzis, Noble and Poynting) and *Minority Languages and Dominant Culture* (Falmer, 1988, with Kalantzis and Slade).

Norman Fairclough is Professor of Language in Social Life in the Departments of Linguistics and Modern English Language at Lancaster University, UK. He is the author of *Discourse and Social Change* and *Media Discourse.*

James Paul Gee holds the Tashia Morgridge Chair in Reading in the Department of Curriculum and Instruction at the University of Wisconsin, Madison, USA. He is the author of *Social Linguistics and Discourses* and *The Social Mind.*

Mary Kalantzis is Dean of the Faculty of Education, Language and Community Services at Royal Melbourne Institute of Technology, Australia. Her publications include co-authorship of *Mistaken Identity: Multiculturalism and the Demise of Nationalism in Australia* with Castles, Cope and Morrissey (Pluto Press, Sydney, 1988/1990/1992); *Minority Languages and Dominant Culture* with Cope and Slade (Falmer Press, London, 1989); *Cultures of Schooling: Pedagogies for Cultural Difference and Social Access,* with Cope, Noble and Poynting (Falmer Press, London, 1990); and *Productive Diversity* (Pluto Press, Sydney, 1997).

Gunther Kress is Professor of Education at the Institute of Education at the University of London, UK. He is the author of numerous books, including *Learning to Write* and *Reading Images.*

Joseph Lo Bianco is Chief Executive of Language Australia: The National Languages and Literacy Institute of Australia. This is a network of thirty-one centres across Australia devoted to research, policy and professional development for all aspects of languages and literacy in the context of Australian multilingualism and globalisation. The Institute derives from the 1987 *National Policy on Languages,* Australia's first explicit language policy, authored by Lo Bianco. He has been actively involved in public advocacy, research and policy-making for cultural diversity, multilingualism, literacy and improved education. Lo Bianco is an economist, linguist and teacher by training and also holds the position of visiting professor at the University of Wollongong.

Carmen Luke teaches sociology, communications and cultural studies and feminist theory at the Graduate School of Education, University of Queensland. Her most recent book is *Feminisms and Pedagogies of Everyday Life* (State University of New York Press), and she is currently working on research projects on women in Asian higher education and on interethnic families.

Sarah Michaels is Senior Research Scholar of the Hiatt Center for Urban Education at Clark University, Massachusetts, USA. A sociolinguist by training, she has been actively involved in teaching and research in the area of language, culture, literacy, and schooling. Her current work involves research and development in an experimental after-school science program, The Investigators Club, for inner-city middle school students. She has also worked closely over the past ten years with teacher researchers interested in documenting talk, text, and learning in their own classrooms. She holds a Ph.D. in Education (Language and Literacy) from the University of California, Berkeley.

Martin Nakata teaches at the Aboriginal Research Institute, Faculty of Aboriginal and Islander Studies, at the University of South Australia, Adelaide.

David Bond teaches in the Graduate School of Business at the University of Cape Town, Rondebosch, South Africa.

Denise Newfield is a teacher educator based in the Department of English, University of the Witwatersrand, Johannesburg, South Africa. She is engaged in the preservice and in-service training of teachers of English, and in outreach programmes aimed at redress. She currently co-ordinates the MA in English Education programme, an inter-disciplinary degree. Special interests are media studies, pedagogy, multiliteracies, and curricular change, as reflected in Words and Pictures and other publications.

Richard Sohmer teaches at the Jacob Hiatt Center for Urban Education at Clark University, Massachussetts, USA.

Pippa Stein teaches language and literacy to teachers in the Department of Applied English Language Studies at the University of the Witwatersrand, Johannesburg. She has published articles in the Harvard Educational Review, Perspectives in Education, TESOL publications and is also a co-author of Level Best, a new English textbook series for multicultural and multilingual classrooms. She is also a founder member of Junction Avenue Theatre Company and has co-authored numerous published plays on the hidden history of South Africa.

The editors and the contributors wish to acknowledge Lorraine Murphy for her painstaking work in bringing this book to publication.

Part I

INTRODUCTION

INTRODUCTION

Multiliteracies: the beginnings of an idea

Bill Cope and Mary Kalantzis

In September 1994, a small group of people – mostly professional colleagues and friends who had worked with one another over the years – met for a week in the small town of New London, New Hampshire, to consider the future of literacy teaching; to discuss what would need to be taught in a rapidly changing near future, and how this should be taught.

As it turned out, there were multiple ironies in the very idea of New London. Now one billion people speak that difficult and messy little language, English, spoken four centuries ago by only about a million or so people in the vicinity of London, old London. The story of the language, and the story of the last few centuries, including its many injustices, is the story of many new Londons. This issue – how the language meets with cultural and linguistic diversity – was one of our main concerns. Then there was the irony of the postcard serenity of this particular New London, the affluent, post-industrial village which produces little more than its idyllic eighteenth-century postcard image. This, in a world where the fundamental mission of educators is to improve every child's educational opportunities – a world which, much of the time, is far from idyllic.

This seemed a strange place to be asking some of the hardest questions we now face as educators. What constitutes appropriate literacy teaching in the context of the ever more critical factors of local diversity and global connectedness? As educators addressing the difficult question of cultural and linguistic diversity, we do so against a background cacophony of claims and counterclaims about the canon of great literature, about grammar and about the need to get 'back-to-basics'. These debates seemed a long way from the calm hills of a tourist's New Hampshire but they were at the forefront of our minds during that fruitful meeting.

Ten people met and talked for that week in New London. Courtney Cazden, from the United States, has spent a long and highly influential career working on classroom discourse, on language learning in multi-lingual contexts, and, most recently, on literacy pedagogy. Bill Cope, from

3

Australia, has written curricula addressing cultural diversity in schools, and researched literacy pedagogy and the changing cultures and discourses of workplaces. Norman Fairclough, as a theorist of language and social meaning from Great Britain, is particularly interested in linguistic and discursive change as part of social and cultural change. James Gee, from the United States, is a leading researcher and theorist on language and mind, and on the language and learning demands of the latest 'fast capitalist' workplaces. Mary Kalantzis, from Australia, has been involved in experimental social education and literacy curriculum projects, and is particularly interested in citizenship education. Gunther Kress, from Great Britain, is best known for his work on language and learning, semiotics, visual literacy, and the multimodal literacies that are increasingly important to all communication, particularly the mass media. Allan Luke, from Australia, is a researcher and theorist of critical literacy who has brought sociological analysis to bear on the teaching of reading and writing. Carmen Luke, also from Australia, has written extensively on feminist pedagogy. Sarah Michaels, from the United States, has had extensive experience in developing and researching programmes of classroom learning in urban settings. Martin Nakata, from Australia, has researched and written on the issue of literacy in indigenous communities. Joseph Lo Bianco, Director of Australia's National Languages and Literacy Institute, was unable to attend but has joined the New London Group in subsequent meetings.

Our purpose for meeting was to engage in the issue of what to do in literacy pedagogy on the basis of our different national and cultural experiences and on the basis of our different areas of expertise. The focus was the big picture; the changing word and the new demands being placed upon people as makers of meaning in changing workplaces, as citizens in changing public spaces and in the changing dimensions of our community lives – our lifeworlds.

Creating a context for the meeting were our differences of national experience and differences of theoretical and political emphasis. For instance, we needed to debate at length the relative importance of immersion and explicit teaching; our differing expert interests in the areas of multimedia, workplace literacies, and cultural and linguistic diversity; and the issue of the extent to which we should compromise with the learning expectations and ethos of new forms of workplace organisation. We engaged in the discussions on the basis of a genuine commitment to collaborative problem-solving, bringing together a team with different knowledge, experiences, and positions in order to optimise the possibility of effectively addressing the complex reality of schools.

Being fully aware of our differences, we all shared the concern that our discussion might not be productive. Yet it was. These differences, combined with our common sense of unease, allowed us to agree on the fundamental problem we needed to address – that is, that the disparities in educational outcomes did not seem to be improving. We agreed that we should get back to the broad question of the social outcomes of language learning, and that we should, on this basis, rethink the fundamental premises of literacy pedagogy in order to influence practices that will give students the skills and knowledge they need to achieve their aspirations. We agreed that, in each of the English-speaking countries we came from, what students needed to learn was changing. Clearly the main element of this change was that there was no singular, canonical English that either could or should be taught any more. Cultural differences and rapidly shifting communications media meant that the very nature of the subject of literacy pedagogy was changing radically.

We decided that the outcomes of our discussions could be encapsulated in one word, 'Multiliteracies' – a word we chose because it describes two important arguments we might have with the emerging cultural, institutional, and global order. The first argument engages with the multiplicity of communications channels and media; the second with the increasing salience of cultural and linguistic diversity.

The notion of Multiliteracies supplements traditional literacy pedagogy by addressing these two related aspects of textual multiplicity. What we might term 'mere literacy' remains centred on language only, and usually on a singular national form of language at that, being conceived as a stable system based on rules such as mastering sound–letter correspondence. This is based on the assumption that we can actually discern and describe correct usage. Such a view of language must characteristically translate into a more or less authoritarian kind of pedagogy. A pedagogy of Multiliteracies, by contrast, focuses on modes of representation much broader than language alone. These differ according to culture and context, and have specific cognitive, cultural, and social effects. In some cultural contexts – in an Aboriginal community or in a multimedia environment, for instance – the visual mode of representation may be much more powerful and closely related to language than 'mere literacy' would ever be able to allow. Multiliteracies also creates a different kind of pedagogy: one in which language and other modes of meaning are dynamic representational resources, constantly being remade by their users as they work to achieve their various cultural purposes.

Two main arguments, then, emerged in our initial discussions. The first argument relates to the increasing multiplicity and integration of significant modes of meaning-making, where the textual is also related to the visual, the audio, the spatial, the behavioural, and so on. This is particularly important in the mass media, multimedia, and in an electronic hypermedia. Meaning is made in ways that are increasingly multimodal – in which written-linguistic modes of meaning are part and parcel of visual, audio, and spatial patterns of meaning. Take for instance the multimodal ways in which meanings are made on the World Wide Web, or in video

5

captioning, or in interactive multimedia, or in desktop publishing, or in the use of written texts in a shopping mall. To find our way around this emerging world of meaning requires a new, multimodal literacy. We may have cause to be sceptical about the sci-fi visions of information super-highways and an impending future in which we are all virtual shoppers. Nevertheless, new communications media are reshaping the way we use language. When technologies of meaning are changing so rapidly, there cannot be one set of standards or skills that constitutes the ends of literacy learning, however taught.

The second argument relates to the realities of increasing local diversity and global connectedness. The news on our television screens screams this message at us every day. And, in more constructive terms, we have to negotiate differences every day, in our local communities and in our increasingly globally interconnected working and community lives. As a consequence, something paradoxical is happening to English. At the same time as it is becoming a *lingua mundi*, a world language, and a *lingua franca*, a common language of global commerce, media and politics, English is also breaking into multiple and increasingly differentiated Englishes, marked by accent, national origin, subcultural style and professional or technical communities. Increasingly, the name of the game in English is crossing linguistic boundaries. Gone are the days when learning a single, standard version of the language was sufficient. Migration, multiculturalism and global economic integration daily intensify this process of change. The globalisation of communications and labour markets makes language diversity an ever more critical local issue. Dealing with linguistic differences and cultural differences has now become central to the pragmatics of our working, civic, and private lives. Effective citizenship and productive work now require that we interact effectively using multiple languages, multiple Englishes, and communication patterns that more frequently cross cultural, community, and national boundaries. Subcultural diversity also extends to the ever broadening range of specialist registers and situational variations in language, be they technical, sporting, or related to groupings of interest and affiliation. When the proximity of cultural and linguistic diversity is one of the key facts of our time, the very nature of language learning has changed.

These two developments have the potential to transform both the substance and pedagogy of literacy teaching not only in English but also in other languages around the world. No longer do the old pedagogies of a formal, standard, written national language have the utility they once possessed. In contrast, the Multiliteracies argument suggests the necessity of an open-ended and flexible functional grammar which assists language learners to describe language differences (cultural, subcultural, regional/national, technical, context-specific, and so on) and the multimodal channels of meaning now so important to communication.

Clearly these are fundamental issues concerning our future. In addressing these issues, literacy educators and students must see themselves as active participants in social change; as learners and students who can be active designers – makers – of social futures. We decided at our first meeting, therefore, to begin the discussion with this question of social futures.

Accordingly, the starting point of those discussions and now this book is the shape of social change – changes in our working lives; our public lives as citizens; and our private lives as members of different community lifeworlds. The fundamental question is what do these changes mean for literacy pedagogy? In the context of these changes we must conceptualise the 'what' of literacy pedagogy. The key concept we developed to do this is that of Design, in which we are both inheritors of patterns and conventions of meaning while at the same time active designers of meaning. And, as designers of meaning, we are designers of social futures – workplace futures, public futures, and community futures.

In our discussions we developed a theory in which there are six design elements in the meaning-making process: those of Linguistic Meaning, Visual Meaning, Audio Meaning, Gestural Meaning, Spatial Meaning, and the Multimodal patterns of meaning that relate the first five modes of meaning to each other. Only then can we translate the 'what' into a 'how'. We also considered four components of pedagogy: Situated Practice, which draws on the experience of meaning-making in lifeworlds, the public realm, and workplaces; Overt Instruction, through which students develop an explicit metalanguage of Design; Critical Framing, which interprets the social context and purpose of Designs of meaning; and Transformed Practice, in which students, as meaning-makers, become designers of social futures. And we decided that through the International Multiliteracies Project we would begin to set up collaborative research relationships and programmes of curriculum development that test, exemplify, extend, and rework the ideas we had tentatively explored in New London.

The outcome of the New London meeting was that, as the 'New London Group', we developed a jointly authored paper entitled 'A Pedagogy of Multiliteracies: Designing Social Futures', which was published in the spring 1996 edition of the *Harvard Educational Review* (New London Group, 1996). Already the paper has generated enormous international interest.

The structure of this paper, and now this book, evolved from the New London discussions. We began the discussions with an agenda that we had agreed upon in advance, which consisted of a schematic framework of key questions about the forms and content of literacy pedagogy. Over the course of our meeting, we worked through this agenda three times, teasing out difficult points, elaborating on the argument, and adapting the schematic structure that had been originally proposed. One team member typed key points, which were projected on to a screen so we could discuss the wording of a common argument. By the end of the meeting, we had developed the final outline of an argument, which has subsequently become the text of Chapter 1. The various members of the group then returned to their respective countries and institutions, and worked independently on the different sections; the draft was circulated and modified; and, finally, we opened up the paper to public discussion in a series of plenary presentations and small discussion groups led by the team at the Fourth International Literacy and Education Research Network Conference held in Townsville, Australia, in June–July 1995.

In Townsville, we again met as a group for three days, and began to plan this book. This planning continued when next we met, for three days before the Domains of Literacy Conference organised by Gunther Kress at the Institute of Education, University of London in September 1996. Meanwhile, other people had joined in the original discussions and the authorship of this book has now expanded to include Dave Bond from the University of Cape Town; and Denise Newfield and Pippa Stein from the University of Witwatersrand in Johannesburg. The group met for a fourth time in Alice Springs, Australia, at the Fifth International Literacy and Education Research Network Conference in October 1997 to finalise the book. This book, then, is more than ever a product of international collaboration now extending well beyond the small group who originally met in New London.

Despite being the result of three years' exhaustive discussions, this book is by no means a finished piece. We still present it here as a programmatic manifesto, which necessarily remains open and tentative. The book, however, does two major things. First, it provides a theoretical overview of the current social context of learning and the consequences of social changes for the content (the 'what') as well as the form (the 'how') of literacy pedagogy. In this sense, the book is intended as the basis for open-ended dialogue with fellow educators around the world; a framework which will spark ideas for possible new research areas and help frame curriculum experimentation attempting to come to grips with our changing educational environment. Second, it discusses our initial attempts to put the Multiliteracies ideas into curriculum practice. This second aspect of the book represents the work that is still in its early stages. In this process, we hope to set up further collaborative research relationships and programmes of curriculum development that test, exemplify, extend, and rework the ideas tentatively suggested in the initial *Harvard Educational Review* paper, and now this book.

1

A PEDAGOGY OF MULTILITERACIES

Designing social futures

The New London Group

If it were possible to define generally the mission of education, it could be said that its fundamental purpose is to ensure that all students benefit from learning in ways that allow them to participate fully in public, community, and economic life. Pedagogy is a teaching and learning relationship that creates the potential for building learning conditions leading to full and equitable social participation. Literacy pedagogy, specifically, is expected to play a particularly important role in fulfilling this mission. Traditionally this has meant teaching and learning to read and write in page-bound, official, standard forms of the national language. Literacy pedagogy, in other words, has been a carefully restricted project – restricted to formalised, mono-lingual, monocultural, and rule-governed forms of language.

In this book, we attempt to broaden this understanding of literacy and literacy teaching and learning to include negotiating a multiplicity of discourses. We seek to highlight two principal aspects of this multiplicity. First, we want to extend the idea and scope of literacy pedagogy to account for the context of our culturally and linguistically diverse and increasingly globalised societies; to account for the multifarious cultures that interrelate and the plurality of texts that circulate. Second, we argue that literacy pedagogy now must account for the burgeoning variety of text forms asso-ciated with information and multimedia technologies. This includes understanding and competent control of representational forms that are becoming increasingly significant in the overall communications environ-ment, such as visual images and their relationship to the written word – for instance, visual design in desktop publishing or the interface of visual and linguistic meaning in multimedia. Indeed, this second point relates closely back to the first; the proliferation of communications channels and media supports and extends cultural and subcultural diversity. As soon as our sights are set on the objective of creating the learning conditions for full

9

social participation, the issue of differences becomes critically important. How do we ensure that differences of culture, language, and gender are not barriers to educational success? And what are the implications of these differences for literacy pedagogy?

This question of differences has become a main problem that we must now address as educators. And although numerous theories and practices have been developed as possible responses, at the moment there seems to be particular anxiety about how to proceed. What is appropriate education for women; for indigenous peoples; for immigrants who do not speak the national language; for speakers of non-standard dialects? What is appropriate for all in the context of the ever more critical factors of local diversity and global connectedness? As educators attempt to address the context of cultural and linguistic diversity through literacy pedagogy, we hear shrill claims and counterclaims about political correctness, the canon of great literature, grammar, and back-to-basics.

The prevailing sense of anxiety is fuelled in part by the sense that, despite goodwill on the part of educators, despite professional expertise, and despite the large amounts of money expended to develop new approaches, there are still vast disparities in life chances – disparities that today seem to be widening still further. At the same time, radical changes are occurring in the nature of public, community and economic life. A strong sense of citizenship seems to be giving way to local fragmentation, and communities are breaking into ever more diverse and subculturally defined groupings. The changing technological and organisational shape of working life provides some with access to lifestyles of unprecedented affluence, while excluding others in ways that are increasingly related to the outcomes of education and training. It may well be that we have to rethink what we are teaching, and, in particular, what new learning needs literacy pedagogy might now address.

The changing present and near futures: visions for work, citizenship and lifeworlds

The languages needed to make meaning are radically changing in three realms of our existence: our working lives, our public lives (citizenship), and our personal lives (lifeworlds).

Changing working lives

We are living through a period of dramatic global economic change, as new business and management theories and practices emerge across the developed world. These theories and practices stress competition and markets centred on change, flexibility, quality, and distinctive niches – not the mass products of the 'old' capitalism (Cross, Feather and Lynch 1994;

10

Davidow and Malone 1992; Deal and Jenkins 1994; Dobyns and Crawford-Mason 1991; Drucker 1993; Hammer and Champy 1993; Ishikawa 1985; Lipnack and Stamps 1993; Peters 1992; Sashkin and Kiser 1993; Senge 1990). A whole new terminology crosses and recrosses the borders between these new business and management discourses, on the one hand, and discourses concerned with education, educational reform, and cognitive science, on the other (Bereiter and Scardamalia 1993; Bruer 1993; Gardner 1991; Lave and Wegner 1991; Light and Butterworth 1993; Perkins 1992; Rogoff 1990). The new management theory uses words that are very familiar to educators, such as knowledge (as in 'knowledge worker'), learning (as in 'learning organisation'), collaboration, alternative assessments, communities of practice, networks, and others (Gee 1994b). In addition, key terms and interests of various postmodern and critical discourses focusing on liberation, the destruction of hierarchies, and the honouring of diversity (Faigley 1992; Freire 1968, 1973; Freire and Macedo 1987; Gee 1993; Giroux 1988; Walkerdine 1986) have found their way into these new business and management discourses (Gee 1994a).

The changing nature of work has been variously called 'postFordism' (Piore and Sable 1984) and 'fast capitalism' (Gee 1994a). PostFordism replaces the old hierarchical command structures epitomised in Henry Ford's development of mass production techniques and represented in caricature by Charlie Chaplin in the film *Modern Times* – an image of mindless, repetitive unskilled work on the industrial production line. Instead, with the development of postFordism or fast capitalism, more and more workplaces are opting for a flattened hierarchy. Commitment, responsibility, and motivation are won by developing a workplace culture in which the members of an organisation identify with its vision, mission, and corporate values. The old vertical chains of command are replaced by the horizontal relationships of teamwork. A division of labour into its minute, de-skilled components is replaced by 'multiskilled', well-rounded workers who are flexible enough to be able to do complex and integrated work (Cope and Kalantzis 1997a). Indeed, in the most advanced of postFordist, fast capitalist workplaces, traditional structures of command and control are being replaced by relationships of pedagogy: mentoring, training, and the learning organisation (Senge 1990). Once divergent, expert, disciplinary knowledges such as teaching and management are now becoming closer and closer. This means that, as educators, we have a greater responsibility to consider the implications of what we do in relation to a productive working life.

With a new worklife comes a new language. A good deal of this change is the result of new technologies such as the iconographic, text, and screen-based modes of interacting with automated machinery – 'user-friendly' interfaces operate with more subtle levels of cultural embeddedness than interfaces based on abstract commands. But much of the change is also the result of the new social relationships of work. Whereas the old Fordist organisation depended upon clear, precise, and formal systems of command such as written memos and the supervisor's orders, effective teamwork depends to a much greater extent on informal, oral, and interpersonal discourse. This informality also translates into hybrid and interpersonally sensitive informal written forms, such as electronic mail (Sproull and Kiesler 1991). These examples of revolutionary changes in technology and the nature of organisations have produced a new language of work. They are all reasons why literacy pedagogy has to change if it is to be relevant to the new demands of working life; if it is to provide all students with access to fulfilling employment.

For fast capitalism is also a nightmare. Corporate cultures and their discourses of familiarity are frequently more subtly and more rigorously exclusive than the most nasty – honestly nasty – of hierarchies. Replication of corporate culture demands assimilation to mainstream norms, and this really works only if a person already speaks the language of the mainstream. For anyone who is not a comfortable part of the culture and discourses of the mainstream, it is even harder to get into networks that operate informally than it was to enter into the old discourses of formality. This is a crucial factor in producing the phenomenon of the glass ceiling; the point at which employment and promotion opportunities come to an abrupt stop. And fast capitalism, notwithstanding its discourse of collaboration, culture, and shared values, is also a vicious world driven by the barely restrained market. As we remake our literacy pedagogy to be more relevant to a new world of work, we need to be aware of the danger that our words become co-opted by economically and market-driven discourses, no matter how contemporary and 'post-capitalist' these may appear.

The new fast capitalist literature stresses adaptation to constant change through thinking and speaking for oneself; critique and empowerment; innovation and creativity; technical and systems thinking; and learning how to learn. All of these ways of thinking and acting are carried by new and emerging discourses. These new workplace discourses can be taken in two very different ways – as opening new educational and social possibilities, or as new systems of mind control or exploitation. In the positive sense, for instance, the emphases on innovation and creativity may fit well with a pedagogy that views language and other modes of representation as dynamic, constantly being remade by meaning-makers in changing and varied contexts. However, it may well be that market-directed theories and practices, even though they sound humane, will never authentically include a vision of meaningful success for all students. Rarely do the proponents of these ideas seriously consider them relevant to people destined for skilled and elite forms of employment. Indeed, in a system that still values vastly disparate social outcomes, there will never be enough room 'at the top'. An authentically democratic new vision of schools must include a vision of meaningful success for all; a vision of success that is not defined exclusively in economic terms and that has embedded within it a critique of hierarchy and economic injustice.

In responding to the radical changes in working life that are currently under way, we need to tread a careful path that provides students with the opportunity to develop skills for access to new forms of work through learning the new language of work. But at the same time, our role as teachers is not simply to be technocrats. It is not our job to produce docile, compliant workers. Students need also to develop the capacity to speak up, to negotiate, and to be able to engage critically with the conditions of their working lives.

Indeed, the twin goals of access and critical engagement need not be incompatible. The question is, how might we depart from the latest views and analyses of high-tech, globalised, and culturally diverse workplaces and relate these to educational programmes that are based on a broad vision of the good life and an equitable society? Paradoxically, the new efficiency requires new systems of getting people motivated that might be the basis for a democratic pluralism in the workplace and beyond. In the realm of work, we have called this utopian possibility 'productive diversity'; the idea that what seems to be a problem – the multiplicity of cultures, experiences, ways of making meaning, and ways of thinking – can be harnessed as an asset (Cope and Kalantzis 1997a). Cross-cultural communication and the negotiated dialogue of different languages and discourses can be a basis for worker participation, access, and creativity, for the formation of locally sensitive and globally extensive networks that closely relate organisations to their clients or suppliers, and structures of motivation in which people feel that their different backgrounds and experiences are genuinely valued. Rather ironically, perhaps, democratic pluralism is possible in workplaces for the toughest of business reasons, and economic efficiency may be an ally of social justice, though not always a staunch or reliable one.

Changing public lives

Just as work is changing, so is the realm of citizenship. Over the past two decades, the century-long trend towards an expanding, interventionist welfare state has been reversed. The domain of citizenship and the power and importance of public spaces is diminishing. Economic rationalism, privatisation, deregulation and the transformation of public institutions such as schools and universities so that they operate according to market logic are changes that are part of a global shift that coincides with the end of the Cold War. Until the 1980s, the global geopolitical dynamic of the twentieth century had taken the form of an argument between communism and capitalism. Fundamentally, this was a debate about the role of the state in society, in which the interventionist welfare state represented capitalism's compromise position. The argument was won and lost when the Communist Bloc was unable to match the escalating cost of the capitalist world's fortifications. The end of the Cold War, in this way, represents an epochal turning point. Indicative of a new world order is a liberalism that eschews the state. In just a decade or two, this liberalism has prevailed globally almost without exception (Fukuyama 1992). Those of us who work either in state-funded or privately funded education know all too well what this liberalism looks like. Market logic has now become a much bigger part of our lives than ever before.

In some parts of the world, once strong centralising and homogenising states have all but collapsed, and states everywhere are diminished in their roles and responsibilities. This has left space for a new politics of difference. In worst-case scenarios – in Los Angeles, Sarajevo, Kabul, Belfast, Beirut – the absence of a working, arbitrating state has left governance in the hands of gangs, bands, paramilitary organisations, and ethnonationalist political factions. In best-case scenarios, the politics of culture and identity have taken on a new significance. Negotiating these differences is now a life-and-death matter. The perennial struggle for access to wealth, power, and symbols of recognition is increasingly articulated through the discourse of identity and recognition (Kalantzis 1997).

Schooling in general, and literacy teaching in particular, were a central part of the old order. The expanding, interventionary states of the nineteenth and twentieth centuries used schooling as a way of standardising national languages. In the Old World this meant imposing national standards over dialect differences. In the New World, it meant assimilating immigrants and indigenous peoples to the standardised 'proper' language of the coloniser (Anderson 1983; Dewey 1916/1966; Gellner 1983; Kalantzis and Cope 1993a).

In this way, just as global geopolitics have fundamentally shifted, so has the role of schools. Cultural and linguistic diversity is now a central and critical issue and, as a result, the meaning of literacy pedagogy has changed as well. Local diversity and global connectedness mean not only that there can be no standard; they also mean that the most important skill students need to learn is to negotiate regional, ethnic, or class-based dialects; variations in register that occur according to social context; hybrid cross-cultural discourses; the code switching often to be found within a text among different languages, dialects, or registers; different visual and iconic meanings; and variations in the gestural relationships among people, language, and material objects. Indeed, this is the only hope for averting the catastrophic conflicts about identities and spaces that now seem ever ready to flare up.

The decline of the old, monocultural, nationalistic sense of 'civic' has vacated a space that must be filled again. We propose that this space be claimed by a civic pluralism. Instead of states that require one cultural and linguistic standard, we need states which arbitrate differences. Access to wealth, power, and symbols must be possible no matter what identity markers, such as language, dialect, and register, a person happens to have. States must be strong again, but not to impose standards; they must be strong as neutral arbiters of difference. So must schools. And so must literacy pedagogy. This is the basis for a cohesive sociality; a new civility in which differences are used as a productive resource and in which differences are the norm. It is the basis for the postnationalist sense of common purpose that is now essential to a peaceful and productive global order (Kalantzis and Cope 1993b).

To this end, cultural and linguistic diversity is a classroom resource just as powerfully as it is a social resource in the formation of new civic spaces and new notions of citizenship. This is not just so that educators can provide a better 'service' to 'minorities'. Rather, such a pedagogical orientation will produce benefits for all. For example, there will be a cognitive benefit to all children in a pedagogy of linguistic and cultural pluralism, including for 'mainstream' children. When learners juxtapose different languages, discourses, styles, and approaches, they gain substantively in metacognitive and metalinguistic abilities and in their ability to reflect critically on complex systems and their interactions. At the same time, the use of diversity in tokenistic ways – by creating ethnic or other culturally differentiated commodities in order to exploit specialised niche markets or by adding festive, ethnic colour to classrooms – must not paper over real conflicts of power and interest. Only by dealing authentically with diversity in a structural and historical sense can we create a new, vigorous, and equitable public realm.

Civic pluralism changes the nature of civic spaces, and with the changed meaning of civic spaces, everything changes; from the broad content of public rights and responsibilities to institutional and curricular details of literacy pedagogy. Instead of core culture and national standards, the realm of the civic is a space for the negotiation of a different sort of social order; an order where differences are actively recognised; where these differences are negotiated in such a way that they complement each other; and where people have the chance to expand their cultural and linguistic repertoires so that they can access a broader range of cultural and institutional resources (Cope and Kalantzis 1997a).

Changing personal lives

We live in an environment where subcultural differences – differences of identity and affiliation – are becoming more and more significant. Gender, ethnicity, generation, and sexual orientation are just a few of the markers of these differences. To those who yearn for 'standards', such differences appear as evidence of a distressing fragmentation of the social fabric.

Indeed, in one sense it is just this – an historical shift in which singular national cultures have less hold than they once did. For example, one of the paradoxes of less regulated, multi-channel media systems is that they undermine the concept of collective audience and common culture, instead promoting the opposite: an increasing range of accessible sub-cultural options and the growing divergence of specialist and subcultural discourses. This spells the definitive end of 'the public' – that homogeneous imagined community of modern democratic nation states.

Yet, as subcultural differences become more significant, we also witness another, somewhat contradictory development – the increasing invasion of private spaces by mass media culture, global commodity culture, and communications and information networks. Childhood cultures are made up of interwoven narratives and commodities that cross television, toys, fast-food packaging, video games, T-shirts, shoes, bed linen, pencil cases, and lunch boxes (Luke 1995). Parents find these commodity narratives inexorable, and teachers find their cultural and linguistic messages losing power and relevance as they compete with these global narratives. Just how do we negotiate these invasive global texts? In some senses, the invasion of the mass media and consumerism makes a mockery of the diversity of its media and channels. Despite all the subcultural differentiation of niche markets, not much space is offered in the marketplace of childhood that reflects genuine diversity among children and adolescents.

Meanwhile, private lives are being made more public as everything becomes a potential subject of media discussion, resulting in what we refer to as a 'conversationalisation' of public language. Discourses that were once the domain of the private – the intricacies of the sexual lives of public figures; discussion of repressed memories of child abuse – are now made unashamedly public. In some senses, this is a very positive and important development, in so far as these are often important issues that need a public airing. The widespread conversationalisation of public language, however, involves institutionally motivated simulation of conversational language and the personae and relationships of ordinary life. Working lives are being transformed so they operate according to metaphors that were once distinctively private, such as management by 'culture' teams dependent on interpersonal discourses, and paternalistic relationships of mentoring. Much of this can be regarded as cynical, manipulative, invasive, and exploitative, as discourses of private life and community are appro-priated to serve commercial and institutional ends. This is a process, in other words, that in part destroys the autonomy of private and community lifeworlds.

The challenge is to make space available so that different lifeworlds can flourish; to create spaces for community life where local and specific meanings can be made. The new multimedia and hypermedia channels can and sometimes do provide members of subcultures with the opportunity to find their own voices. These technologies have the potential to make possible greater autonomy for different lifeworlds – for example, multilingual television or the creation of virtual communities through access to the Internet.

Yet, the more diverse and vibrant these lifeworlds become and the greater the range of the differences, the less clearly bounded the different lifeworlds appear to be. The word 'community' is often used to describe the differences that are now so critical – the Italian-American community, the gay community, the business community, and so on – as if each of these communities had neat boundaries. As lifeworlds become more divergent in the new public spaces of civic pluralism, their boundaries become more evidently complex and overlapping. The increasing divergence of lifeworlds and the growing importance of differences are happening at the same time, blurring their boundaries. The more autonomous lifeworlds become, the more movement there can be with people entering and leaving; whole lifeworlds going through major transitions; more open and productive negotiation of internal differences; freer external linkages and alliances.

As people are simultaneously members of multiple lifeworlds, so their identities have multiple layers that are in complex relation to each other. No person is a member of a singular community. Rather, they are members of multiple and overlapping communities – communities of work, of interest and affiliation, of ethnicity, of sexual identity, and so on (Kalantzis 1997).

Language, discourse, and register differences are markers of lifeworld differences. As lifeworlds become more divergent and their boundaries more blurred, the central fact of language becomes the multiplicity of meanings and their continual intersection. Just as there are multiple layers to everyone's identity, there are multiple discourses of identity and multiple discourses of recognition to be negotiated. We have to be proficient as we negotiate the many lifeworlds each of us inhabits, and the many lifeworlds we encounter in our everyday lives. This creates a new challenge for literacy pedagogy. In sum, this is the world that literacy pedagogy now needs to address:

	Changing realities	Designing social futures
Working lives	Fast capitalism/ post Fordism	Productive diversity
Public lives	Decline of the civic	Civic pluralism
Personal lives	Invasion of private spaces	Multilayered lifeworlds

17

What schools do and what we can do in schools

Schools have always played a critical role in determining students' life opportunities. Schools regulate access to orders of discourse – that is, the relationship of discourses in a particular social space and to symbolic capital; symbolic meanings that have currency in access to employment, political power, and cultural recognition. They provide access to a hier-archically ordered world of work; they shape citizenries; they provide a supplement to the discourses and activities of communities and private lifeworlds. As these three major realms of social activity have shifted, so the roles and responsibilities of schools must shift.

Institutionalised schooling traditionally performed the function of disciplining and skilling people for regimented industrial workplaces, assisting in the making of the melting pot of homogenous national citizenries, and smoothing over inherited differences between lifeworlds. This is what Dewey (Dewey 1916/1966) called the assimilatory function of schooling, the function of making homogeneity out of differences. Now, the function of classrooms and learning is in some senses the reverse. Every classroom will inevitably reconfigure the relationships of local and global difference that are now so critical. To be relevant, learning processes need to recruit, rather than attempt to ignore and erase, the different subjectivities, interests, intentions, commitments, and purposes that students bring to learning. Curriculum now needs to mesh with different subjec-tivities, and with their attendant languages, discourses, and registers, and use these as a resource for learning.

This is the necessary basis for a pedagogy that opens possibilities for greater access. The danger of glib and tokenistic pluralism is that it sees differences to be immutable and leaves them fragmentary. In so far as differences are now a core, mainstream issue, the core or the mainstream has changed. In so far as there cannot be a standard, universal, national language and culture, there are new universals in the form of productive diversity, civic pluralism, and multilayered lifeworlds. This is the basis for a transformed pedagogy of access – access to symbolic capital with a real valency in the emergent realities of our time. Such a pedagogy does not involve overwriting existing subjectivities with the language of the domi-nant culture. These old meanings of 'access' and 'mobility' are the basis for models of pedagogy that depart from the idea that cultures and languages other than those of the mainstream represent a deficit. Yet in the emergent reality, there are still real deficits, such as a lack of access to social power, wealth, and symbols of recognition. The role of pedagogy is to develop an epistemology of pluralism that provides access without people having to erase or leave behind different subjectivities. This has to be the basis of a new norm.

Transforming schools and schooled literacy is both a very broad and a narrowly specific issue, a critical part of a larger social project. Yet there is a limit to what schools alone can achieve. The broad question is, what will count for success in the world of the imminent future, a world that can be imagined and achieved? The narrower question is, how do we transform incrementally the achievable and apt outcomes of schooling? How do we supplement what schools already do? We cannot remake the world through schooling but we can instantiate a vision through pedagogy that creates in microcosm a transformed set of relationships and possibilities for social futures; a vision that is lived in schools. This might involve activities such as simulating work relations of collaboration, commitment and creative involvement; using the school as a site for mass media access and learning; reclaiming the public space of school citizenship for diverse communities and discourses; and creating communities of learners that are diverse and respectful of the autonomy of lifeworlds.

As curriculum is a design for social futures, we need to introduce the notion of pedagogy as Design. As educators we need to discuss and to debate the overall shape of that design as we supplement literacy pedagogy in the ways suggested by the notion of Multiliteracies. Different conceptions of education and society lead to very specific forms of curriculum and pedagogy, which in turn embody designs for social futures. To achieve this, we need to engage in a critical dialogue with the core concepts of fast capitalism, of emerging pluralistic forms of citizenship, and of different lifeworlds. This is the basis for a new social contract, a new commonwealth.

The 'what' of a pedagogy of Multiliteracies

In relation to the new environment of literacy pedagogy, we need to reopen two fundamental questions: the 'what' of literacy pedagogy, or what it is that students need to learn; and the 'how' of literacy pedagogy, or the range of appropriate learning relationships.

Designs of meaning

In addressing the question of the 'what' of literacy pedagogy, we propose a metalanguage of Multiliteracies based on the concept of 'Design'. Design has become central to workplace innovations, as well as to school reforms for the contemporary world. Teachers and managers are seen as designers of learning processes and environments, not as bosses dictating what those in their charge should think and do. Further, some have argued that educational research should become a design science, studying how different curricular, pedagogical, and classroom designs motivate and achieve different sorts of learning. Similarly, managers have their own design science, studying how management and business theories can be put into practice and continually adjusted and reflected on in practice. The notion of design connects powerfully to the sort of creative intelligence the best practitioners need in order to be able continually to redesign their activities in the very act of practice. It connects as well to the idea that learning and productivity are the results of the designs (the structures) of complex systems of people environments, technology, beliefs, and texts.

We have also decided to use the term 'Design' to describe the forms of meaning because it is free of the negative associations for teachers of terms such as 'grammar'. It is a sufficiently rich concept upon which to found a language curriculum and pedagogy. The term also has a felicitous ambiguity; it can identify either the organisational structure (or morphology) of products, or the process of designing. Expressions like 'the design of the car', or 'the design of the text', can have either sense: the way it is – has been – designed, or the process of designing it. We propose to treat any semiotic activity, including using language to produce or consume texts, as a matter of Design involving three elements: Available Designs, Designing, and The Redesigned. Together these three elements emphasise the fact that meaning-making is an active and dynamic process, and not something governed by static rules.

This framework is based upon a particular theory of discourse. It sees semiotic activities as a creative application and combination of conventions (resources or Available Designs) that, in the process of Design, transforms at the same time as it reproduces these conventions (Fairclough 1992b, 1995a). That which determines (Available Designs) and the active process of determining (Designing, which creates The Redesigned) are constantly in tension. This theory fits in well with our view of social life and social subjects in fast-changing and culturally diverse societies.

Available Designs

Available Designs – the resources for Design – include the 'grammars' of various semiotic systems: the grammars of languages, and the grammars of other semiotic systems such as film, photography, or gesture. Available Designs also include 'orders of discourse' (Fairclough 1995a). An order of discourse is the structured set of conventions associated with semiotic activity (including use of language) in a given social space – a particular society, or even a particular institution such as a school or a workplace, or more loosely structured spaces of ordinary life encapsulated in the notion of different lifeworlds. An order of discourse is a socially produced array of discourses, intermeshing and dynamically interacting. It is a particular configuration of Design elements. An order of discourse can be seen as a particular configuration of such elements. It may include a mixture of different semiotic systems, for instance, visual and aural semiotic systems in combination with language constitute the order of discourse of television. For example, it may involve the grammars of several languages or the orders of discourse of many schools.

Order of discourse is intended to capture the way in which different discourses relate to (speak to) each other. Thus, the discourse of African-American gangs in Los Angeles is related to the discourse of the LA police in historical ways. They and other related discourses shape and are shaped by each other. For another example, consider the historical and institutional relations between the discourse of biology and the discourse of religious fundamentalism. Schools are particularly crucial sites in which discourses relate to each other – disciplinary discourses; the discourses of being a teacher (teacher culture); the discourse of being a student of a certain sort; community discourses, ethnic discourses, class discourses, and public-sphere discourses involving business and government, for instance. Each discourse involves producing and reproducing and transforming different kinds of people. There are different kinds of African-Americans, teachers, children, students, police, and biologists. One and the same person can be different kinds of people at different times and places. Different kinds of people connect through the intermeshed discourses that constitute orders of discourse.

Within orders of discourse there are particular Design conventions – Available Designs – that take the form of discourses, styles, genres, dialects, and voices, to name a few key variables. A discourse is a configuration of knowledge and its habitual forms of expression, which represents a particular set of interests. Over time, for instance, institutions produce discourses – that is, their configurations of knowledge. Style is the configuration of all the semiotic features in a text in which, for example, language may relate to layout and visual images. Genres are forms of text or textual organisation that arise out of particular social configurations or the particular relationships of the participants in an interaction. They reflect the purposes of the participants in a specific interaction. In an interview, for example, the interviewer wants something, the interviewee wants something else, and the genre of interview reflects this. Dialects may be related to region or age. Voice is more individual and personal, including, of course, many discursive and generic factors.

The overarching concept of orders of discourse is needed to emphasise that, in Designing texts and interactions, people always draw on systems of sociolinguistic practice as well as grammatical systems. These may not be as clearly or rigidly structured as the word 'system' suggests, but there are nevertheless always some conventional points of orientation when we act semiotically. Available Designs also include another element: the linguistic and discoursal experience of those involved in Designing, in which one moment of Designing is continuous with and a continuation of particular histories. We can refer to this as the intertextual context (Fairclough 1989), which links the text being designed to one or more series ('chains') of past texts.

Designing

The process of shaping emergent meaning involves re-presentation and recontextualisation. This is never simply a repetition of Available Designs. Every moment of meaning involves the transformation of the available resources of meaning. Reading, seeing, and listening are all instances of Designing.

According to Halliday (Halliday 1978), a deep organising principle in the grammars of human languages is the distinction among macrofunctions of language, which are the different functions of Available Designs: ideational, interpersonal and textual functions. These functions produce distinctive expressions of meaning. The ideational function handles the knowledge, and the interpersonal function handles the 'social relations'. As for orders of discourse, the generative interrelation of discourses in a social context, their constituent genres can be partly characterised in terms of the particular social relations and subject positions they articulate, whereas discourses are particular knowledges (constructions of the world) articulated with particular subject positions.

Any semiotic activity – any Designing – simultaneously works on and with these facets of Available Designs. Designing will more or less normatively reproduce, or more or less radically transform, given knowledges, social relations, and identities, depending upon the social conditions under which the Designing occurs.

But it will never simply reproduce Available Designs. Designing transforms knowledge by producing new constructions and representations of reality. Through their co-engagement in Designing, people transform their relations with each other, and so transform themselves. These are not independent processes. Configurations of subjects, social relations, and knowledges are worked upon and transformed (becoming The Redesigned) in the process of Designing. Existing and new configurations are always provisional, though they may achieve a high degree of permanence. Transformation is always a new use of old materials, a re-articulation and recombination of the given resources of Available Designs.

The notion of Design recognises the iterative nature of meaning-making, drawing on Available Designs to create patterns of meaning that are more or less predictable in their contexts. This is why The Redesigned has a ring of familiarity to it. Yet there is something ineluctably unique to every utterance. Most written paragraphs are unique, never constructed in exactly that way ever before and – bar copying or statistical improbability – never to be constructed that way again. Similarly, there is something irreducibly unique about every person's voice. Designing always involves the transformation of Available Designs; it always involves making new use of old materials.

It is also important to stress that listening as well as speaking, and reading as well as writing, are productive activities, forms of Designing. Listeners and readers encounter texts as Available Designs. They also draw upon their experience of other Available Designs as a resource for making new meanings from the texts they encounter. Their listening and reading is itself a production (a Designing) of texts (though texts-for-themselves, not texts-for-others) based on their own interests and life experiences. And their listening and reading in turn transforms the resources they have received in the form of Available Designs into The Redesigned.

The Redesigned

The outcome of Designing is a new meaning, something through which meaning-makers remake themselves. It is never a reinstantiation of one Available Design or even a simple recombination of Available Designs; the Redesigned may be variously creative or reproductive in relation to the resources for meaning-making available in Available Designs. But it is neither a simple reproduction (as the myth of standards and transmission pedagogy would have us believe), nor is it simply creative (as the myths of individual originality and personal voice would have us believe). As the play of cultural resources and uniquely positioned subjectivity, the Redesigned is founded on historically and culturally received patterns of meaning. At the same time it is the unique product of human agency: a transformed meaning. And, in its turn, the Redesigned becomes a new Available Design, a new meaning-making resource.

Through these processes of Design, moreover, meaning-makers remake themselves. They reconstruct and renegotiate their identities. Not only has the Redesigned been actively made, but it is also evidence of the ways in which the active intervention in the world that is Designing has transformed the designer.

Designs of Meaning	
Available Designs	Resources for Meaning; Available Designs of Meaning
Designing	The work performed on or with Available Designs in the semiotic process
The Redesigned	The resources that are produced and transformed through Designing

Dimensions of meaning

Teachers and students need a language to describe the forms of meaning that are represented in Available Designs and the Redesigned. In other words, they need a metalanguage – a language for talking about language, images, texts and meaning-making interactions.

One objective of the International Multiliteracies Project is to develop an educationally accessible functional grammar; that is, a metalanguage that describes meaning in various realms. These include the textual and the visual, as well as the multimodal relations between the different meaning-making processes that are now so critical in media texts and the texts of electronic multimedia.

Any metalanguage to be used in a school curriculum has to match up to some taxing criteria. It must be capable of supporting a sophisticated critical analysis of language and other semiotic systems, yet at the same time not make unrealistic demands on teacher and learner knowledge, or conjure up teachers' accumulated and often justified antipathies towards formalism. The last point is crucial, because teachers must be motivated to work on and work with the metalanguage.

A metalanguage also needs to be quite flexible and open-ended. It should be seen as a tool kit for working on semiotic activities, not a formalism to be applied to them. We should be comfortable with fuzzy-edged, overlapping concepts. Teachers and learners should be able to pick and choose from the tools offered. They should also feel free to fashion their own tools. Flexibility is critical because the relationship between descriptive and analytical categories and actual events is, by its nature, shifting, provisional, unsure and relative to the contexts and purposes of analysis.

Furthermore, the primary purpose of the metalanguage should be to identify and explain differences between texts, and relate these to the contexts of culture and situation in which they seem to work. The meta-language is not developed to impose rules, to set standards of correctness or to privilege certain discourses in order to 'empower students'. The metalanguage we are suggesting for analysing the Design of meaning with respect to 'orders of discourse' includes the key terms 'genres' and 'discourses', and a number of related concepts such as voices, styles, and any probable others (Fairclough 1992b; Kress 1990; Van Leeuwen 1993). More informally, we might ask of any Designing, 'What's the game', and 'What's the angle'?

'The game' points us in the direction of purpose, and the notion of genre. Sometimes the game can be specified in terms of a clearly defined and socially labelled genre, like church liturgy; sometimes there is no clear generic category. Semiotic activity and the texts it generates regularly mixes genres – for example, doctor–patient consultations, which are partly like medical examinations and partly like counselling sessions, or even informal conversations.

In trying to characterise game and genre, we should start from the social context, the institutional location, the social relations of texts and the social practices within which they are embedded. Genre is an intertextual aspect of a text. It shows how the text links to other texts in the intertextual context, and how it might be similar in some respects to other texts used in comparable social contexts as well as its connections with text types in the order(s) of discourse. But genre is just one of a number of intertextual aspects of a text, and it needs to be used in conjunction with others, especially discourses.

A discourse is a construction of some aspect of reality from a particular point of view, a particular angle, in terms of particular interests. As an abstract noun, discourse draws attention to use of language as a facet of social practice that is shaped by – and shapes – the orders of discourse of the culture, as well as language systems (grammars). As a count noun (discourses in the plural rather than discourse in general), it draws attention to the diversity of constructions (representations) of various domains of life and experience associated with different voices, positions, and interests (subjectivities). Here again, some discourses are clearly demarcated and have conventional names in the culture (for example, feminist, party-political, or religious discourses), whereas others are much more difficult to pinpoint. Intertextual characterisations of texts in terms of genres and discourses are best regarded as provisional approximations, because they are cultural interpretations of texts that depend on the analyst's fuzzy but operationally adequate feel for the culture, as well as for specialist knowledges.

Design elements

One of the key ideas informing the notion of Multiliteracies is the increasing complexity and interrelationship of different modes of meaning. We have already identified six major areas in which functional grammars, the metalanguages that describe and explain patterns of meaning, are required – Linguistic Design, Visual Design, Audio Design, Gestural Design, Spatial Design and Multimodal Design. Multimodal Design, however, is of a different order to the others as it represents the patterns of interconnection among the other modes. We are using the word 'grammar' here in a positive sense as a specialised language that describes patterns of representation. In each case, our objective is to come up with no more than approximately ten major Design elements.

Linguistic Design

The metalanguage we propose to use to describe Linguistic Design is intended to focus our attention on representational resources. This metalanguage is not a category of mechanical skills, as is commonly the case in grammars designed for educational use. Nor is it the basis for detached

25

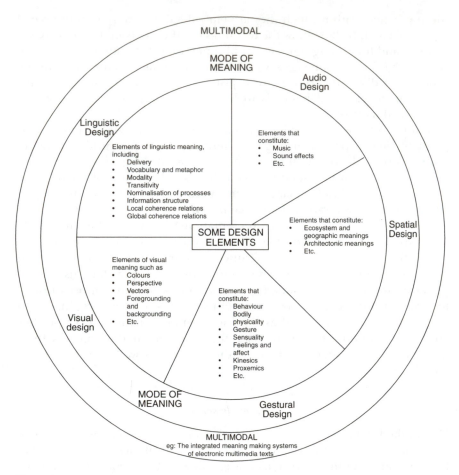

Figure 1.1

critique or reflection. Rather, the Design notion emphasises the productive and innovative potential of language as a meaning-making system. This is an action-oriented and generative description of language as a means of representation. As we have argued earlier, such an orientation to society and text will be an essential requirement of the economies and societies of the present and the future. It will also be essential for the production of particular kinds of democratic and participatory subjectivity. The elements of Linguistic Design that we foreground help describe the representational resources that are available; the various meanings these resources will have if drawn upon in a particular context; and the innovative potential for reshaping these resources in relation to social intentions or aims.

Consider this example: 'Lung cancer death rates are clearly associated with increased smoking', and 'Smoking causes cancer'. The first sentence can mean what the second means, though it can mean many other things as well. The first sentence is more explicit in some ways than the second (e.g. reference to lung cancer), and less explicit in other ways (e.g. 'associated with' versus 'cause'). Grammar has been recruited to design two different instruments. Each sentence is usable in different discourses. For example, the first is a form typical of much writing in the social sciences and even the hard sciences. The second is a form typical of public health discussion. Grammar needs to be seen as a range of choices one makes in Designing communication for specific ends, including greater recruitment of non-verbal features. These choices, however, need to be seen as not just a matter of individual style or intention, but as inherently connected to different discourses based on wider interests and relationships of power.

Our suggested metalanguage for analysing the Design of language is built around a highly selective checklist of features of texts, which our experience has shown to be particularly worthy of attention (see also Fairclough 1992b; Fowler *et al.* 1979). The following table lists some key terms that might be included as a metalanguage of Linguistic Design. Other potentially significant textual features are likely to be alluded to from time to time but we think that a facility in using the features on the check-list itself constitutes a substantive, if limited, basis for critical language awareness.

Some elements of Linguistic Design

Delivery	features of intonation, stress, rhythm, accent, etc.
Modality	the nature of the producer's commitment to the message in a clause
Transitivity	the types of process and participants in the clause
Vocabulary and metaphor	word choice, positioning, and meaning
Nominalisation of processes	turning actions, qualities, assessments, or logical connection into nouns or states of being (e.g. 'assess' becomes 'assessment'; 'can' becomes 'ability')
Information structures	how information is presented in clauses and sentences
Local coherence relations	cohesion between clauses, and logical relations between clauses (e.g. embedding, subordination)
Global coherence relations	the overall organisational properties of texts (e.g. genres).

We will now examine two of these key terms, nominalisation and transitivity, in order to illustrate our notion of Linguistic Design. Nominalisation involves using a phrase to compact a great deal of information, somewhat like the way a trash compactor compacts trash. After compacting, you cannot always tell what has been compacted. Consider the expression, 'Lung cancer death rates'. Is this 'rates' at which people die of lung cancer, or rates at which lungs die from cancer? You can't know this unless you are privy to what the discussion has been. Nominalisations are used to compact information – whole conversations – that we assume people (or at least 'experts') are up on. They are signals for those in the 'game' and thus are also ways to keep people out.

Transitivity indicates how much agency and effect one designs into a sentence. 'John struck Mary' has more effect on Mary than 'John struck out at Mary', and 'John struck Mary' has more agency than 'Mary was struck'. Since we humans connect agency and effect with responsibility and blame in many domains (discourses), these are not just matters of grammar. They are ways of Designing language to engage in actions like blaming, avoiding blame, or backgrounding certain things against others.

Designs for other modes of meaning

Now becoming increasingly important are modes of meaning other than Linguistic modes, including Visual Meanings (images, page layouts, screen formats); Audio Meanings (music sound effects); Gestural Meanings (body language, sensuality); Spatial Meanings (the meanings of environmental spaces, architectural spaces); and Multimodal Meanings. Of the modes of meaning, the Multimodal is the most significant, as it relates all the other modes in quite remarkably dynamic relationships. For instance, mass-media images relate the linguistic to the visual and to the gestural in intricately designed ways. Reading the mass media for their linguistic meanings alone is not enough. Magazines employ vastly different visual grammars according to their social and cultural content. A script of a sit-com would have none of the qualities of the programme if you didn't have a 'feel' for its unique gestural, audio and visual meanings. A script without this knowledge would allow only a very limited reading. Similarly, a visit to a shopping mall involves a lot of written text. However, either a pleasure or a critical engagement with a mall will involve a multiple reading that not only includes the design of language but also includes a spatial reading of the architecture of the mall and the placement and meaning of the written signs, logos and lighting. McDonald's has hard seats in order to keep you moving. Casinos do not have windows or clocks in order to remove tangible indicators of time passing. These are profoundly important spatial and architectonic meanings, crucial for reading Available Designs and for Designing social futures.

In a profound sense, all meaning-making is Multimodal. All written text is also a process of Visual Design. Desktop publishing puts a new premium on Visual Design and spreads responsibility for the visual much more broadly than was the case when writing and page layout were separate trades. So, a school project can and should properly be evaluated on the basis of Visual as well as Linguistic Design, and their Multimodal relationships. To give another example, spoken language is a matter of Audio Design as much as it is a matter of Linguistic Design understood as grammatical relationships.

Texts are designed using the range of historically available choices among different modes of meaning. This entails a concern with absences from texts, as well as presences in texts – for example, 'Why not that?' as well as 'Why this?' (Fairclough 1992a, 1992b) The concept of Design emphasises the relationships between received modes of meaning (Available Designs); the transformation of these modes of meaning in their hybrid and intertextual use (Designing); and their subsequent to-be-received status (The Redesigned). The metalanguage of meaning-making applies to all aspects of this process: how people are positioned by the elements of available modes of meaning (Available Designs); yet how the authors of meanings in some important senses bear the responsibility of being consciously in control of their transformation of meanings (Designing); and how the effects of meaning, the sedimentation of meaning, become a part of the social process (the Redesigned).

Of course, the extent of transformation from Available Designs to The Redesigned as a result of Designing can greatly vary. Sometimes the designers of meaning will reproduce the Available Designs in the form of The Redesigned more closer than at other times – a form letter as opposed to a personal letter. Or a classified as opposed to a display advertisement, for instance. Some Designing is more premeditated, more planned, deliberate, and systematised, than other instances – for example, a conversation as opposed to a poem. At times, Designing is based on clearly articulated, perhaps specialist, metalanguages describing Design elements (the language of the professional editor or the architect). Other Designing may be no more or less transformative, even though the designers may not have an articulated metalanguage to describe the elements of their meaning-making processes (such as the person who fixes up what they have just written or the home renovator). Notwithstanding these different relationships of structure and agency, all meaning-making always involves both.

Two key concepts help us describe Multimodal meanings and the relationships of different Designs of Meaning: hybridity and intertextuality (Fairclough 1992a; Fairclough 1992b). The term hybridity highlights the mechanisms of creativity and of culture-as-process as particularly salient in contemporary society. People create and innovate by hybridising, that is by articulating in new ways, established practices and conventions within and between different modes of meaning. This includes the hybridisation of established modes of meaning (of discourses and genres), and multifarious combinations of modes of meaning cutting across boundaries of convention and creating new conventions. Popular music is a perfect example of the process of hybridity. Different cultural forms and traditions are constantly being recombined and restructured. One example is where the musical forms of Africa meet audio electronics and the commercial music industry. And new relations are constantly being created between linguistic meanings and audio meanings (pop versus rap); and between linguistic/audio and visual meanings (live performance versus video clips).

Intertextuality draws attention to the potentially complex ways in which meanings, such as linguistic meanings, are constituted through relationships to other texts, either real or imaginary, to other text types (discourse or genres), to other narratives, and other modes of meaning (such as visual design, architectonic or geographical positioning). Any text can be viewed historically in terms of the intertextual chains (historical series of texts) it draws upon, and in terms of the transformations it works upon them. For instance, movies are full of cross-references, either made explicitly by the movie-maker or read into the movie by the viewer-as-Designer: a role, a scene, an ambience. The viewer takes a good deal of their sense of the meaning of the movie through these kinds of intertextual chains.

The 'how' of a pedagogy of Multiliteracies

A theory of pedagogy

Any successful theory of pedagogy must be based on views about how the human mind works in society and classrooms, as well as about the nature of teaching and learning. While we certainly believe that no current theory in psychology, education or the social sciences has 'the answers', and that theories stemming from these domains must always be integrated with the practical knowledge of leading practitioners, we also believe that those proposing curricular and pedagogical reforms must clearly state their views of mind, society and learning in virtue of which they believe such reforms would be efficacious.

Our view of mind, society and learning is based on the assumption that the human mind is embodied, situated, and social. That is, human knowledge is embedded in social, cultural and material contexts. Further, human knowledge is initially developed as part and parcel of collaborative interactions with others of diverse skills, backgrounds and perspectives joined together in a particular epistemic community, that is, a community of learners engaged in common practices centred on a specific (historically and socially constituted) domain of knowledge. We believe that 'abstractions', 'generalities', and 'overt theories' come out of this initial ground and must always be returned to it or to a recontextualised version of it.

This view of mind, society, and learning leads us to argue that pedagogy is a complex integration of four factors: Situated Practice based on the world of learners' Designed and Designing experiences; Overt Instruction through which students shape for themselves an explicit metalanguage of Design; Critical Framing, which relates meanings to their social contexts and purposes; and Transformed Practice in which students transfer and re-create Designs of meaning from one context to another.

Recent work in cognitive science, social cognition, and sociocultural approaches to language and literacy (Barsalou 1992; Bereiter and Scardamalia 1993; Cazden 1988; Clark 1993; Gardner 1991; Gee 1992; Heath 1983; Holland *et al.* 1986; Lave and Wegner 1991; Light and Butterworth 1993; Perkins 1992; Rogoff 1990; Scollon and Scollon 1981; Street 1984; Wertsch 1985) argues that if one of our pedagogical goals is a degree of mastery in practice, then immersion in a community of learners engaged in authentic versions of such practice is necessary. We call this Situated Practice. Recent research (Barsalou 1992; Eiser 1994; Gee 1992; Harre and Gillett 1994; Margolis 1993; Nolan 1994) argues that the human mind is not, like a digital computer, a processor of general rules and decontextualised abstractions. Rather, human knowledge, when it is applicable to practice, is primarily situated in sociocultural settings and heavily contextualised in specific knowledge domains and practices. Such knowledge is inextricably tied to the ability to recognise and act on patterns of data and experience, a process that is acquired only through experience, since the requisite patterns are often heavily tied and adjusted to context, and are, very often, subtle and complex enough that no one can fully and usefully describe or explicate them. Humans are, at this level, contextual and sociocultural 'pattern recognisers' and actors. Such pattern recognition underlies the ability to act flexibly and adaptably in context – that is, mastery in practice.

However, there are limitations to Situated Practice as the sole basis for pedagogy. First, a concern for the situatedness of learning is both the strength and the weakness of progressivist pedagogies (Kalantzis and Cope 1993a). While such situated learning can lead to mastery in practice, learners immersed in rich and complex practices can vary quite significantly from each other (and from curricular goals), and some can spend a good deal of time pursuing the 'wrong' leads, so to speak. Second, much of the 'immersion' that we experience as children, such as in acquiring our 'native' language, is surely supported by our human biology and the normal course of human maturation and development. Such support is not available in later school immersion in areas such as literacy and academic domains, since these are far too late on the human scene to have garnered any substantive biological or evolutionary support. Thus, whatever help biology and maturation give children in their early primary socialisation must be made up for – given more overtly – when we use 'immersion' as a method in school. Third, Situated Practice does not necessarily lead to conscious control and awareness of what one knows and does, which is a core goal of much school-based learning. Fourth, such Situated Practice does not necessarily create learners or communities who can critique what they are learning in terms of historical cultural, political, ideological, or value-centred relations. And, fifth, there is the question of putting knowledge into action. People may be able to articulate their knowledge in words. They could be consciously aware of relationships, and even able to engage in 'critique'. Yet they might still be incapable of reflexively enacting their knowledge in practice.

Thus, Situated Practice, where teachers guide a community of learners as 'masters' of practice, must be supplemented by several other components (see Cazden 1992). Beyond mastery in practice, an efficacious pedagogy must seek critical understanding or cultural understanding in two different senses. Critical in the phrase 'critical understanding' means conscious awareness and control over the intra-systematic relations of a system. Immersion, notoriously, does not lead to this. For instance, children who have acquired a first language through immersion in the practices of their communities do not thereby, in virtue of that fact, become good linguists. Vygotsky (Vygotsky 1978, 1987), who certainly supported collaboration in practice as a foundation of learning, argued also that certain forms of Overt Instruction were needed to supplement immersion (acquisition) if we wanted learners to gain conscious awareness and control of what they acquired.

There is, of course, another sense of 'critical', as in the ability to critique a system and its relations to other systems on the basis of the workings of power, politics, ideology, and values (Fairclough 1992b). In this sense, people become aware of, and are able to articulate, the cultural locatedness of practices. Unfortunately, neither immersion in Situated Practices within communities of learners, nor Overt Instruction of the sort Vygotsky (Vygotsky 1987) discussed, necessarily gives rise to this sort of critical understanding or cultural understanding. In fact, both immersion and many sorts of Overt Instruction are notorious as socialising agents that can render learners quite uncritical and unconscious of the cultural locatedness of meanings and practices.

The four components of pedagogy we propose here do not constitute a linear hierarchy, nor do they represent stages. Rather, they are components that are related in complex ways. Elements of each may occur simultaneously, while at different times one or the other will predominate, and all of them are repeatedly revisited at different levels.

Situated Practice

This is the part of pedagogy that is constituted by immersion in meaningful practices within a community of learners who are capable of playing multiple and different roles based on their backgrounds and experiences. The community must include experts, that is people who have mastered certain practices. Minimally, it must include expert novices, that is people who are experts at learning new domains in some depth. Such experts can guide learners, serving as mentors and designers of their learning processes. This aspect of the curriculum needs to recruit learners' previous and current experiences, as well as their extra-school communities and discourses, as an integral part of the learning experience.

There is ample evidence that people do not learn anything well unless they are both motivated to learn and believe that they will be able to use and function with what they are learning in some way that is in their interest. Thus, the Situated Practice that constitutes the immersion aspect of pedagogy must crucially consider the affective and sociocultural needs and identities of all learners. It must also constitute an arena in which all learners are secure in taking risks and trusting the guidance of others – both peers and teachers.

Within this aspect of pedagogy, evaluation, we believe, should never be used to judge, but should be used developmentally, to guide learners to the experiences and the assistance they need to develop further as members of the community capable of drawing on, and ultimately contributing to, the full range of its resources.

Overt Instruction

Overt Instruction does not imply direct transmission, drills, and rote memorisation, although unfortunately it often has these connotations. Rather, it includes all those active interventions on the part of the teacher and other experts that scaffold learning activities; that focus the learner on the important features of their experiences and activities within the community of learners; and that allow the learner to gain explicit information at times when it can most usefully organise and guide practice, building on and recruiting what the learner already knows and has accomplished. It includes centrally the sorts of collaborative efforts between teacher and student wherein the student is both allowed to accomplish a task more complex than they can accomplish on their own, and where they come to conscious awareness of the teacher's representation and interpretation of that task and its relations to other aspects of what is being learned. The goal here is conscious awareness and control over what is being learned – over the intra-systematic relations of the domain being practiced.

One defining aspect of Overt Instruction is the use of metalanguages, languages of reflective generalisation that describe the form, content, and function of the discourses of practice. In the case of the Multiliteracies framework proposed here, this would mean that students develop a meta-language that describes both the 'what' of literacy pedagogy (Design processes and Design elements) and the scaffolds that constitute the 'how' of learning (Situated Practice, Overt Instruction, Critical Framing, Transformed Practice).

Much assessment in traditional curriculum required replication of the generalities of Overt Instruction. As in the case of Situated Practice, evaluation in Overt Instruction should be developmental, a guide to further thought and action. It should also be related to the other aspects of the learning process – the connections, for example, between evolving metalanguages as they are negotiated and developed through Overt Instruction, on the one hand, and Situated Practice, Critical Framing, and Transformed Practice, on the other hand.

Critical Framing

The goal of Critical Framing is to help learners frame their growing mastery in practice (from Situated Practice) and conscious control and under-standing (from Overt Instruction) in relation to the historical, social, cultural, political, ideological, and value-centred relations of particular systems of knowledge and social practice. Here, crucially, the teacher must help learners to denaturalise and make strange again what they have learned and mastered.

For example, the claim 'DNA replicates itself' framed within biology is obvious and 'true'. Framed within another discourse in the following way, it becomes less natural and less 'true': Put some DNA in some water in a glass on a table. It certainly will not replicate itself, it will just sit there. Organisms replicate themselves using DNA as a code, but that code is put into effect by an array of machinery involving proteins. In many of our academic and Western discourses, we have privileged information and mind over materials, practice, and work. The original claim foregrounds information and code and leaves out, or backgrounds, machinery and work. This foregrounding and backgrounding becomes apparent only when we reframe, when we take the sentence out of its 'home' discourse and place it in a wider context. Here, the wider context is actual processes and material practices, not just general statements in a disciplinary theory (the DNA example is from Lewontin 1991).

Through Critical Framing, learners can gain the necessary personal and theoretical distance from what they have learned; constructively critique it; account for its cultural location; creatively extend and apply it; and eventually innovate on their own, within old communities and in new ones.

This is the basis for Transformed Practice. It also represents one sort of transfer of learning and one area where evaluation can begin to assess learners and, primarily, the learning processes in which they have been operating.

Transformed Practice

It is not enough to be able to articulate our understanding of intra-systematic relations or to critique extra-systematic relations. We need always to return to where we began, to Situated Practice, but now a re-practice, where theory becomes reflective practice. With their students, teachers need to develop ways in which the students can demonstrate how they can design and carry out, in a reflective manner, new practices embedded in their own goals and values. They should be able to show that they can implement understandings acquired through Overt Instruction and Critical Framing in practices that help them simultaneously to apply and revise what they have learned. In Transformed Practice we are offered a place for situated, contextualised assessment of learners and the learning processes devised for them. Such learning processes, such as pedagogy, needs to be continually reformulated on the basis of these assessments.

Situated Practice	immersion in experience and the utilisation of available Designs of meaning, including those from the students' lifeworlds and simulations of the relationships to be found in workplaces and public spaces
Overt Instruction	systematic, analytic, and conscious understanding of Designs of meaning and Design processes. In the case of Multiliteracies, this requires the introduction of explicit metalanguages, which describe and interpret the Design elements of different modes of meaning
Critical Framing	interpreting the social and cultural context of particular Designs of meaning. This involves the students' standing back from what they are studying and viewing it critically in relation to its context
Transformed Practice	transfer in meaning-making practice, which puts the transformed meaning (the Redesigned) to work in other contexts or cultural sites

35

In Transformed Practice we try to re-create a discourse by engaging in it for our own real purposes. Thus, imagine a student having to act and think like a biologist, and at the same time as a biologist with a vested interest in resisting the depiction of female things – from eggs to organisms – as 'passive'. The student now has to both juxtapose and integrate (not without tension) two different discourses, or social identities, or 'interests' that have historically been at odds. Using another example, how can a person be a 'real' lawyer and, at the same time, have his or her performance influenced by being an African-American? In his arguments before the US Supreme Court for desegregating schools, Thurgood Marshall did this in a classic way. And in mixing the discourse of politics with the discourse of African-American religion, Jesse Jackson has transformed the former. The key here is juxtaposition, integration, and living with tension.

The International Multiliteracies Project

Let us tie the 'what' and the 'how' of literacy pedagogy back to the larger agenda focusing on Situated Practices in the learning process, which involves the recognition that differences are critical in workplaces, civic spaces, and multilayered lifeworlds. Classroom teaching and curriculum have to engage with students' own experiences and discourses, which are increasingly defined by cultural and subcultural diversity and the different language backgrounds and practices that come with this diversity. Overt Instruction is not intended to tell; to empower students in relation to the 'grammar' of one proper, standard, or powerful language form. It is meant to help students develop a metalanguage that accounts for Design differences. Critical Framing involves linking these Design differences to different cultural purposes. Transformed Practice involves moving from one cultural context to another; for example, redesigning meaning strategies so they can be transferred from one cultural situation to another.

The idea of Design is one that recognises the different Available Designs of meaning, located as they are in different cultural contexts. The meta-language of Multiliteracies describes the elements of Design, not as rules, but as an heuristic that accounts for the infinite variability of different forms of meaning-making in relation to the cultures, the subcultures, or the layers of an individual's identity that these forms serve. At the same time, Designing restores human agency and cultural dynamism to the process of meaning-making. Every act of meaning both appropriates Available Designs and recreates in the Designing, thus producing new meaning as The Redesigned. In an economy of productive diversity, in civic spaces that value pluralism, and in the flourishing of interrelated, multilayered, complementary yet increasingly divergent lifeworlds, workers, citizens, and community members are ideally creative and responsible makers of meaning. We are, indeed, designers of our social futures.

Of course, the necessary negotiation of differences will be difficult and often painful. The dialogue will encounter chasms of difference in values, grossly unjust inequalities, and difficult but necessary border crossings. The differences are not as neutral, colourful, and benign as a simplistic multiculturalism might want us to believe. Yet as workers, citizens, and community members, we will all need the skills required to negotiate these differences.

Part II

CHANGING TIMES
The 'why' of Multiliteracies

INTRODUCTION

Literacy teaching and learning need to change because the world is changing. The chapters in this section address the 'why' of Multiliteracies: the reasons why we need to reconsider what literacy pedagogy does and how it does it.

In Chapter 2, James Paul Gee examines critical aspects of the new capitalism. He shows the way in which centralised command systems have been displaced by distributed systems in a wide range of areas – in automated machines, computers, organisational structures, the media and science, for instance. As specialised, disciplinary expertise instantly becomes out of date, learning needs to be oriented more towards flexibility and problem-solving. Some new forms of schooling are converging with the distributed logic of new capitalism, such as the idea that classrooms might be communities of practice centred upon experiential, situated knowledge. Examining the discourse of the self of two young women, Gee discusses the kind of consciousness that will be required in order to succeed in the new world of work – a world in which one of these two young women is more likely to succeed than the other. He concludes with a 'bill of rights' based on the four aspects of the Multiliteracies pedagogy – rights all students have to certain kinds of knowledge and instruction.

Carmen Luke extends this by examining in detail the implications of technological change for literacy language and learning. In Chapter 3, she takes us on a guided tour of the main issues raised by the new information technologies and computer-mediated communications. She examines, for instance, the impact of the Internet in the context of larger developments in the media and popular culture. Not only does the Internet pose an enormous challenge to education in the development of new kinds of classrooms; it also provides new tools for home-based learning. It has the potential, moreover, to create new forms of exclusion, raising the question of who has access, and the 'gendered' qualities of the medium. Luke concludes by discussing the possibility of developing Multiliteracies skills for all students, exploring new kinds of texts and developing new kinds of learning relationship.

Both the new capitalism discussed by Gee and the developments in information technology described by Luke are occurring on a global scale. In Chapter 4, Joseph Lo Bianco examines the linguistic consequences of this globalisation. Here, he notes a remarkable paradox. On the one hand, English is becoming a *lingua mundi,* or world language, at the expense of vastly reduced linguistic diversity. Indeed, thousands of small languages are simply facing extinction. On the other hand, however, English is fracturing into multiple Englishes. Meanwhile, globalisation of enterprise and labour markets, as well as the growth of supranational government such as the EU, makes multiculturalism a sheer necessity. Linguistically homogeneous nation states are now nearly impossible to create, and that objective is becoming less functional in the context of globalisation. This is why Lo Bianco argues that multilingualism is an important aspect of Multiliteracies.

In Chapter 5, Martin Nakata adds an indigenous or first-nation perspective to this discussion. He explains the reasons why the communities of the Torres Strait Islands often demand 'proper' education in English. It is certainly important that learning should begin with the students' situated experiences and culture. However, Nakata argues that, if Islanders are to deal effectively with the realities of globalisation and determine their own economic and political futures, they also need explicit, overt instruction in the English language. But, if this is not to repeat the mistakes of colonialism, it must not mean importing somebody else's 'correct usage' from the outside world. Rather, English language and literacy curriculum needs to be developed by indigenous researchers on the basis of an indigenous position.

Mary Kalantzis and Bill Cope conclude this section by discussing the broad dimensions of change across the domains of work, citizenship and public life. In this way Chapter 6 is an historical sketch of the shift over the course of the twentieth century from Fordist to postFordist and more recently towards Productive Diversity models of work and management; from models of citizenship based on the rigours of nationalism to a more recent decline in the civic, and perhaps in the near future to a genuine Civic Pluralism; and in personal life from the homogenising forces of mass culture to a prevailing sense of fragmented community, to a more optimistic vision which recognises and honours Multilayered Identities. The chapter discusses the role of education in general and literacy pedagogy in particular as we work towards the strategically optimistic possibilities of Productive Diversity, Civic Pluralism and Multilayered Identities.

2

NEW PEOPLE IN NEW WORLDS

Networks, the new capitalism and schools

James Paul Gee

We are living amidst major changes, changes creating new ways with words, new literacies, and new forms of learning. These changes are creating, as well, new relationships and alignments within, between, and among the spheres of family, school, business and science. This chapter seeks to place language, literacy, and learning in the broad context of these new alignments, alignments from which new 'kinds of people' are emerging. These issues are, as well, the backdrop against which the Multiliteracies Project has been carrying out its discussions and from which it is making its proposals.

The 'short story' behind the chapter is this. Networks and networking, within what I call 'distributed systems', are the master theme of our 'new times'. This theme is redefining what we mean by intelligence, as well as changing the shape of businesses and schools by setting up a new logic for a new capitalism. In fact, new businesses and new schools – fit for our 'new capitalism' – are progressively aligning themselves with each other and converging on such notions as 'communities of practice'. In this new world, social class works to create characteristic 'kinds of people' in characteristic 'worlds'; people and worlds differentially 'fit' for the new capitalism by their orientations in and to the world. The result is the emergence of one particular new kind of person on the historical stage: the 'portfolio person'. In opposition to this the Multiliteracies manifesto should be seen as a schooling Bill of Rights for all the children in this world.

This chapter is a bit unorthodox is two ways. First, it is written in a rather 'topic-associating' way, juxtaposing seemingly different topics, though arguing that, in our 'new times', they are becoming ever more deeply connected. Second, I engage in little overt critique, despite the fact that there is a great deal here to be critical about. I do this because I believe that critique can purchase little in this new world without first understanding the new connections at work in it. Furthermore, I believe that this world, with its seismic shifts of traditional political alliances, demands a new language of critique which is only beginning to be formulated (Gee *et al.* 1996).

Then, too, I trust that readers, from their own unique perspectives, will start to construct their own critique and begin for themselves the transformation of our critical languages. After reading this chapter, for instance, I hope readers will see that notions like 'community of practice' or Vygotsky's 'Zone of Proximal Development' – so often associated with 'liberal' and 'humanistic' approaches – are also examples of 'hard-headed' new capitalist thinking (Gee 1996d; Vygotsky 1978). Does this mean that the new capitalism is 'liberal' and 'humanistic', or does it mean that 'communities of practice' and Vygotsky are less so than we had thought and hoped? There is no easy answer here, only deep paradoxes that lie at the heart of a world not yet fully born.

But, enough of these preliminaries. Let's just jump directly into the 'flow' – to use one of the great many trendy terms that point to our need to master them.

A new theme: distributed systems

Today, all sorts of things are being talked about in new ways: genes, cells, molecules, fluids, concepts, bodies, brains, minds, eco-systems, species, weather, life, cultures, societies, businesses, organisations, schools, markets, computers, technology, media, and on and on. On all sides we hear words like: 'chaos', 'complexity', 'networks', 'emergent', 'flexible', 'fluid', 'dynamic', 'adaptive'. We are in the midst of a major shift in how we work on, and work out, our physical, biological, social, and mechanical worlds (e.g. see, among a great many sources, Castells 1996; Casti 1994; Kauffman 1991; Kelly 1994; Lash and Urry 1994; Lorentz 1993; Waldrop 1992).

Behind this new talk lies a new 'master theme'. Old-style systems based on authoritarian hierarchy, which we once found – and thought we wanted – in the mind, in nature, in society, and in organisations, are 'out'. Such systems involve a (small) top controlling a (bigger) middle controlling a (yet larger) bottom in a top-down, linear flow of hierarchical and pyramidal power and information. 'In' are 'distributed systems'. In these systems many small, efficient, and self-controlled local units act in fluid, flexible, and sometimes ephemeral combinations (networks, patterns) so as to adapt to and transform 'environments' (contexts) to which they are integrally linked.

Molecules in a flowing liquid are a clear example of such a system: ephemeral, but functional combinations of molecules arise fluidly and adaptably in response to environmental feedback and assistance from inside and outside the liquid system. The now oft-celebrated 'flattened hierarchies' in the 'new capitalism' are examples too: flexible, boundary-crossing teams, and even networks of businesses, form and reform project by project to adapt to and transform changing markets. Another example is the way in which cognitive science increasingly defines human intelligence as the flexible and context-sensitive manipulation of patterns (dynamic images), rather than in terms of following general decontextualised rules.

Distributed systems have become a *leitmotif* of late twentieth-century life because of an exponential growth in variety, variability, and diversity. Technological and social – for example, demographic – changes in a global world have caused us to focus on systems where variables, interactions, relationships, and complexity are nearly 'out of control', but where emerging patterns can sometimes be harnessed or leveraged for productive thought, work, and change.

Mobots: an example of distributed intelligence

Let me give a simple example of the sort of 'intelligence' and control found in distributed systems. Consider a 'Collection Robot' – actually it is called a 'mobot' – designed to collect empty soda cans in a lab at MIT (Kelly 1994, pp. 34–49). The mobot was designed by R. A. Brooks (see Brooks 1991) and has no central brain, but instead has 'intelligence' and decision-making capacities distributed throughout its mechanical body and, indeed, throughout its environment as well.

The mobot simply roams around until its video camera spots the shape of a soda can on a desk. This signal triggers the wheels of the mobot and propels it in front of the can. Rather than wait for a message from a central brain, the arm of the robot 'learns' where it is from the environment. The arm is wired so that it 'looks' at its wheels – if it 'sees' that its wheels are not turning, it 'knows' that it must be in front of a soda can – and the arm reaches out to pick up the can. If the can is heavier than an empty can, it is left on the desk; if it is light, the mobot – the arm? whose act is this anyway? – takes it. The mobot then roams until it runs across the recycle station, not bumping into furniture or walls because of its avoidance 'module'. Then, it stops its wheels in front of the station and the arm 'looks' at its hand to see if it is holding a can. If it is, it drops it; if there is no can in its hand, it begins to wander again through the offices until it spots another can.

This mobot is a very different sort of 'intelligence' from what we are used to defining. While it has 'smart parts' that interact, it has no 'central' boss or brain. This mobot is interesting not because it represents a very complex system in itself – because it doesn't – but because it demonstrates that distributing control across many parts, rather than in a central 'brain', leads to a system that behaves as if it has some centralised intelligence, when it doesn't. It also saves the immense cost in both money and weight of building a central brain.

Note, too, that the world itself serves as part of the mobot's 'intelligence'. The soda can on the desk, as well as its weight, and the recycling station all help structure the mobot's intelligence and behaviour. Since recyclable soda cans in the world are lighter than full ones, there is no need for the mobot to have a full theory of recycling in regard to soda cans. It need only have an arm that 'knows' heavy when it feels it. The rest comes 'free' by being represented (really, continually re-presented) in the world, not in any central brain. In a fast changing world, it is smart to let the world re-present itself and design learning to be adaptive and flexible.

The moral of the mobot story is that intelligence – control – in distributed systems leaks out of any 'head' – centre – and is distributed across relationships; relationships of parts 'inside' the system to each other as well as to the 'outside' environment or context. Furthermore, the system, in its 'urge' to 'get in sync', continually seeks to efface this 'inside'–'outside' boundary. The real system is the 'mobot-in-its-world' (see also Gee 1992).

The new logic of the new capitalism

Businesses in the new hyper-competitive global capitalism – so-called 'fast capitalism' – march to the drumbeat of distributed systems. Furthermore, this new capitalism is a siren song attracting other sorts of organisations, not the least of which are schools, to its values and perspectives The literature, both popular and scholarly, on the 'new capitalism' is vast. So much so that I will not cite it here. Castells's *The Information Age* (Castells 1996) is an excellent scholarly source and I hope *The New Work Order* (Gee *et al.* 1996) is, at least, a good one; *Workplace 2000* (Boyett and Conn 1992) is still the best of the popular sources, but see, too, *Productive Diversity* (Cope and Kalantzis 1997a) as well as *The Witch Doctors* (Micklethwait and Wooldridge 1996), which is a thoughtful and sometimes mildly critical popular source.

In the new high-tech-driven capitalism, products and services are created, perfected, and changed at ever faster rates. What makes a product distinctive is not the stuff of which it is made, nor even its function. After all, in a hyper-competitive world, everyone is producing high quality products or going out of business. What makes a product distinctive is its novelty and the way in which it is designed – customised – to serve the identity, lifestyle, or interests of a particular type of 'customer', whether this be a person or another business.

What businesses market now are not products; not even services; but knowledge. The knowledge it takes to design and create value, to produce it efficiently, and to market it effectively, becomes the premium in the new capitalism – the true 'value added' (Reich 1992). Brute strength and mechanical skills, especially in the face of new technologies, are worth little.

Old-style capitalism involved large corporations with many workers and many layers of hierarchical control, most of which existed to 'supervise' the lowest-level workers and 'tell them what to do'. They were perfect examples of authoritarian hierarchies. In the new capitalism the hierarchy is flattened, the business becomes a distributed system. Businesses and the units within become smaller, more efficient, more focused, more responsive, more flexible, quicker to change and adapt in a world with only moving targets. Workers, too, become parts of distributed systems – parts of networked teams devoted to temporary projects defined by meaningful, whole, and complex processes with which all team members must be familiar, whatever their current area of 'expertise'.

In the 'ideal' business, then, local units – both individuals and small business units – control their own actions, combining and uncombining in flexible ways project by project. Such networks of individuals, business units, and businesses are defined not by traditional boundaries – for example, engineering versus manufacturing versus sales – but by whole processes – for example, from design through implementation to sales and delivery.

Like a dynamically flowing liquid, teams and networks form and reform on demand in a symbiotic relation to the customer and the market. Leaders no longer 'boss'; they facilitate and mediate the relationship between the teams/networks so as to efface any sharp boundaries between business units, between associated businesses – for example, suppliers – and between the business and its customers – its market.

There is no centre. There are no discrete individuals. Only ensembles of skills stored in a person, assembled for a specific project, to be reassembled for other projects, and shared with others within 'communities of practice'. Individuals are not defined by fixed 'essential qualities', such as 'intelligence', 'a culture', or 'a skill'. Rather they are, and must come to see themselves as, an ever changing 'portfolio' of rearrangeable skills acquired in their trajectory through 'project space' – that is, all the projects they have been in. You are, in this way, your projects.

Thinking, learning, and the new capitalism

Distributed systems are changing how we think about thinking and learning, and, from there, how we think about schools and classrooms. Under the 'sign' of distributed systems as a master theme, our thinking about thinking, learning and schools is, in turn, coming to be aligned with our thinking about new capitalist businesses. So let us turn briefly to new views on the mind.

Not long ago educators worried about the disproportionate school failure of many lower socioeconomic and minority students. But this worry has been replaced by a wider concern. For it's not just minorities who fail; in actuality nearly all students do (Bruer 1993; Gardner 1991). Even those with good grades, we are told, do not 'really understand' what they are learning. This critique parallels the current critique of traditional workers in the old-style top-down hierarchically oriented capitalism, who could do what they were told, but who did not understand their jobs or the organisations in which they worked well enough to take proactive responsibility for true problem-solving or to feel truly committed to the organisation.

In 1991, Howard Gardner, a leading cognitive psychologist, diagnosed the problem with today's students and the solution to the problem in what had by then become canonical terms. The problem, as Gardner saw it, was that education does not remove or correct people's everyday 'folk theories'. People readily fall back on these folk theories even when they have been, or are being, exposed in school to 'correct', or, at least, 'better', disciplinary-based theories. Only people who 'really' understand these disciplinary theories, Gardner argued, can avoid this, and so, what schools must do is produce students who learn to think and act like disciplinary experts.

While Gardner's diagnosis of the problem fitted well with the spirit of the new capitalism, his solution did not. In the old authoritarian, hierarchical capitalism the expertise of the specialist was highly valued. Indeed, 'management' was itself a type of disciplinary expertise (Kotter 1995) created by and learned in business schools; themselves very much creatures of the old capitalism. But such expertise is best fit for supervising and disciplining others less knowledgeable than oneself in static times where knowledge has a long 'shelf life'. The new capitalism focuses on change, flexibility, speed, and innovation. In this context, disciplinary expertise goes out of date too rapidly and central controlling forms of intelligence are too big and too slow.

In line with this new capitalist spirit, current work on thinking and learning has progressively adapted its notion of 'expertise' away from 'disciplinary' or academic expertise to a broader notion more compatible with the new capitalist world view. For example, Carl Bereiter and Marlene Scardamalia, two cognitive scientists of Gardner's rank, have recently rendered the convergence of theories of mind and learning and the new capitalism closer and more overt.

Bereiter and Scardamalia (Bereiter and Scardamalia 1993, p. 6) distinguish between 'expertise' and 'specialisation' and clearly divorce the two. They see expertise as a process, not a product; a process involving a 'continual reinvestment of mental resources into addressing problems at higher levels' (Bereiter and Scardamalia 1993, p. 221). People, they say, 'must become expert at becoming experts' (Bereiter and Scardamalia 1993, p. 2) by developing the ability to work in non-routinised ways on ever more demanding problems in whatever domain they are confronted with.

Here we get a contrast very like that between the old-style capitalist worker engaged in the mindless routinised tasks of the Fordist economy versus the new 'fast capitalist' worker/partner engaged in a meaningful job and progressively learning and improving performance. It is also typical of the new capitalism to focus on processes and re-engineering processes rather than divisions, boundaries, and borders (e.g. Hammer 1996; Lipnack and Stamps 1993).

By the end of their book, Bereiter and Scardamalia connect their ideas directly to the new capitalism:

> As conceived by W. Edwards Deming and other gurus of the movement, quality bears a very close resemblance to the concept of expertise that we have been trying to develop here . . . So close is the resemblance of quality improvement to the process of expertise, that we might even characterise it as the process of expertise translated into a practical program for organisations.
>
> (Bereiter and Scardamalia 1993, pp. 242–3)

The same sort of progression can be seen also in the work of David Perkins (Perkins 1995), himself a renowned colleague of Gardner's at Harvard's *Project Zero*. In a discussion of schools, Perkins uses an analogy of a river-boat pilot, to state his view of intelligence:

> But the master river pilot benefits from much more than efficient information processing and knowledge of the landscape experience and disciplinary expertise. The master pilot stands alert to possible changes, takes a strategic view of time and weather, works through choices about route and schedule with the costs and benefits in mind. And it's the same with people who pilot their minds well – who, to use another common phrase, are good mental managers.
>
> (Perkins 1995, p. 99)

Perkins's view of intelligence is stated – albeit in what he intends as figurative language – in almost entirely business-oriented terms. His view of reflective, strategic intelligence as the goal of schooling is entirely in keeping with the goals of the new capitalism with its emphasis on efficient problem solving, productivity, innovation, adaptation, and non-authoritarian distributed systems.

The convergence is certainly not yet finished. In more recent work, Bereiter (Bereiter 1994) has begun to question the mental and individual focus of schooling. In the new capitalism, it is not really important what individuals know on their own, but rather what that they can do with others collaboratively to effectively add 'value' to the enterprise.

Remember, the focus of the new capitalism is on distributed systems. Knowledge and productivity should be distributed across teams and units and their accompanying technologies; they need not reside inside any one entity that uniquely controls the process. In fact, if they did reside too heavily inside individuals, those individuals could take their knowledge and 'walk', selling it to the highest bidder – a real fear in the new knowledge-driven capitalism. Whether we are talking about work teams or business units or even networked businesses, what matters is the knowledge – 'core competencies' – distributed across the whole system.

In light of the distributed nature of knowledge and work in the new capitalism, it is interesting, then, to watch Bereiter, in his recent work, distinguish between 'learning', where the goal is to worry about what is inside individual minds – the traditional goal of schooling – and 'knowledge building':

> [Knowledge building's] . . . objective is not to influence the contents of students' minds but to produce immaterial objects – explanations, theories, solutions, algorithms. Students are expected to learn something in the process, and this may well be evaluated at some time. But the actual work is not directed toward improving their minds but toward *improving the knowledge* that is being collectively created . . . The important point, however, is that their focus is outward, on the objects themselves and the world they relate to, rather than on their own mental states or social roles. They feel a kinship with scholars and scientists, but it is a kinship based on shared goals, not on similarities of practice.
>
> (Bereiter 1994, p. 23)

Here we see a movement away from schooling as reproducing the identities and practices of disciplinary experts; away even from schooling as producing individually 'smart people'. We see, rather, a movement towards people who can work collaboratively in teams to produce results and add value through distributed knowledge and understanding. Such students are much better fitted to be parts of a 'smart' mobot – better fitted to be better modules in a distributed non-authoritarian system – than are traditional students.

Classrooms as communities of practice

No educational trend better reflects the growing convergence between new classrooms and new businesses than the current focus on 'communities of practice'. Communities of practice are 'in', both in new workplaces and in new schools. In communities of practice, the romantic nostalgia associated with 'community' is recruited, while the primacy of sociotechnical engineering is masked. Communities of practice, I would argue, are the crucial node at which business, schools, and society are aligning and merging in the new capitalism.

Jean Lave (Lave 1988; Lave and Wegner 1991) – a leading theorist of socially situated cognition – centres her work on an analogy between 'apprenticeships' among traditional crafts people, for example tailors in West Africa, and classrooms as 'communities of practice'. Though Lave confines herself for the most part to educational issues, much of the new capitalist literature, in fact, celebrates the experiential, flexible, and situated knowledge of traditional craft groups as against the routinised work of the old industrial capitalist assembly line.

From Lave's perspective, learning is not best judged by a change in minds, which is the traditional school measure, but by 'changing participation in changing practices' (Lave 1996, p. 161). Most importantly, learning is a change not just in practice, but in identity. For Lave, 'crafting identities in practice becomes the fundamental project':

> Rather than particular tools and techniques for learning as such, there are ways of becoming a participant, ways of participating, and ways in which participants and practices change. In any event, the learning of specific ways of participating differs in particular situated practices. The term 'learning mechanism' diminishes in importance, in fact it may fall out altogether, as 'mechanisms' disappear into practice. Mainly, people are becoming kinds of persons.
>
> (Lave 1996, p. 157)

Lave's perspective fits perfectly with the team-and-project-based focus of the new capitalism. It fits, too, with the new capitalist idea that we all must see ourselves not in terms of a linear, progression up a 'career ladder', but as a 'portfolio' composed of the rearrangeable skills and identities we have acquired in our trajectory through diverse projects inside and outside of 'workplaces'. It fits also with the new capitalist stress on leveraging the tacit knowledge workers acquire 'on line' as they adapt to constant change.

In education, Lave's views on learning are best exemplified, perhaps, in the classrooms – called 'communities of learners' – designed by Ann Brown and Joseph Campione, who are two leading educational cognitive scientists (Brown and Campione 1994). Brown and Campione's classrooms use a wide variety of devices to ensure that knowledge and understanding are public, collaborative, and distributed. Two of these they call reciprocal teaching and the jigsaw method.

In reciprocal teaching (Brown and Palinscar 1989) the teacher and a group of students take turns leading a discussion about a reading passage. The leader begins by asking a question. The group rereads the passage and discusses possible problems of interpretation when necessary. Attempts to clarify any comprehension problems occur opportunistically. At the end of the discussion, the leader summarises the gist of what has been read. The leader also asks for predictions about future content. In this way the core components of successful reading comprehension, which is usually thought of as the preserve of 'private minds', are rendered public, overt, and distributable. Much like 'quality circles' in the new capitalism, people are made to display and share their knowledge publicly for the benefit of the group and, in fact, the system as a whole.

In the jigsaw method of co-operative learning (Aronson 1978) students are assigned a sub-part of a classroom topic to learn and subsequently teach to others via reciprocal teaching. In Brown and Campione's extrapolation of this method, the setting is a science classroom. Students do collaborative research in research groups, each devoted to a different sub-topic of a larger theme or overall topic like animal defence mechanisms, changing populations, or food chains. Then they redistribute themselves into learning groups where each student takes a turn teaching, by using the reciprocal teaching method, the sub-topic he or she has mastered in her previous research group (Brown and Campione 1994).

In the jigsaw method, each module or team is initially expert on only one part of the whole topic; no team is expert on the whole. But each team distributes its knowledge to the whole. There is no single 'leader' or teacher, but each member plays the role of researcher, student, and teacher in different configurations and contexts. There is no 'centre', only a flexible network of distributed roles and responsibilities.

There are many more features of Brown and Campione's classrooms, including a pervasive use of modern computer, telecommunications, and network technologies, that render them much like new capitalist work-places. However, all aspects of their classrooms are put in place to subserve what I take to be their most important tie to the new capitalism, namely the use they make of learning within a 'zone' of joint activity (Brown and Campione 1994).

Brown and Campione borrow from the Russian psychologist Lev Vygotsky (Vygotsky 1978) the concept of a 'zone of proximal development'. They define this zone as 'the distance between current levels of compre-hension and levels that can be accomplished in collaboration with people or powerful artefacts' (Brown et al. 1993, p. 191). The core idea is that novices, largely unconsciously, 'internalise' or accommodate to the goals, values, and understandings of those more expert than themselves through scaffolded joint activity with those others and their associated tools and technologies. The beauty of Brown and Campione's classrooms is that the other students, the various technologies in the classroom, and the very structure of the activities themselves take on the role of the scaffolding, structuring expert, not just the traditional classroom teacher.

The new capitalism seeks to leverage knowledge in a fast-changing world without having to explicate everything – in fast times knowledge is often out of date by the time it is explicated. It seeks, too, to train workers who can produce in collaborative practice, not just in isolated theory. And, finally, it seeks to empower workers while still ensuring that they 'buy into' the core goals, values, and understandings of the business – without being coerced to do so, which is bad for empowerment. When students or workers are 'in the zone' of joint, embodied practice within distributed systems, they create and transform knowledge in practice, not just in theory, and they often pick up values, attitudes, and understandings without much overt thought or, at least, critique.

Of course, Brown and Campione encourage reflective awareness in their classrooms, in addition to embodied joint activity (Brown and Campione 1994). So, too, do new capitalist businesses. The point is, however, that both students and workers working within communities of practice come to 'internalise' tacit goals, values, and understandings from whose perspective any overt reflective awareness operates. These tacit understandings are not themselves the subject of much conscious reflection and critique. Indeed, such reflection and critique would be 'dangerous', since these goals, values, and understandings define the often invisible limits within which schools and new capitalist businesses alike operate.

Communities of practice at large

Communities of practice – driven largely by businesses, which, in turn, influence their instantiation in schools – are beginning to take a distinctive shape, whether in classrooms or workplaces. Some salient features can be quickly mentioned here, before we move on. In this section I have been influenced by what I consider a seminal book, *Reflexive Modernisation* by Beck, Giddens and Lash (1994).

Members of the community of practice bond to each other primarily through a common endeavour and, only secondarily, through affective ties which are, in turn, leveraged to further the common endeavour. The implication is that affective ties and sociocultural diversity are dangerous if they transcend the otherwise good endeavour. The common endeavour is also organised around a whole process involving multiple but integrated functions, not single, discrete, or decontextualised tasks. The implication here is that there should be no rigid departments, borders, or boundaries.

Members of the community of practice must have extensive knowledge, not just intensive knowledge. By 'extensive' I mean that members must be involved with many or all stages of the endeavour; able to carry out multiple, partly overlapping, functions; and able to reflect on the endeavour as a whole system, not just their part in it. The implication is that there should be no narrow specialists and no rigid roles. Much of the knowledge in the community of practice is tacit, that is embodied in members' mental, social, and physical coordinations with other members and with various tools, and technologies. It is also distributed, that is spread across various members, their shared sociotechnical practices, and their tools and technologies, and dispersed so that it is not all on site but networked across different sites and institutions. The implication is that knowledge is not first and foremost either in heads, discrete individuals or books but in networks of relationships.

The role of leaders is to design communities of practice; to continually resource them; and to help members turn their tacit knowledge into explicit knowledge to be used to further develop that community of practice, while realising that much knowledge will always remain tacit and situated in practice. The implication is that only knowledge that can be extracted from situated sociotechnical practices can be spread and used outside the original community of practice.

In such communities of practice, people are committed through their immersion in practice, since it is the practice itself that gives them their identity and not some 'occupation', fixed set of skills, or culture apart from the practice. Diverse individual skills and cultures are recruited as resources for the community, not as identities that transcend the community of practice itself. Critique of the new capitalism has little purchase from within a practice much of whose knowledge is tacit, distributed, and dispersed, though innovation is still possible as an emergent property of the complex network. Further, criticism – like a lesion in a neural net – cannot disable the practice, which can simply shift responsibilities to other 'nodes' in the network and 'lesion' the critic.

Kinds of 'I's'

So far we have talked about 'society at large'. I have argued that the theme of distributed systems is reorganising how institutions of all sorts work and how they relate to each other. In particular, I have argued that new capitalist businesses and reformed schools are aligning themselves with each other around 'communities of practice' as distributed systems.

But what about individual everyday people leading their everyday lives? I want to argue that through the mediation of families, communities, and schools two broad types of people are emerging for our new world. One type is 'fit' for the new capitalism; the other type is not. Of course, I know that things are not really this simple and there is no clear dichotomy to be had here, but only a continuum of cases. But this rather gross over-simplification, none the less, makes a 'first cut' in what will, I argue, become progressively a more and more important issue for our schools and society at large.

In order to see what I am talking about in quite concrete terms, let me make what at first glance will seem a completely unrelated shift of gears from our earlier discussion. In the mid-1990s researchers at the Hiatt Center were interviewing teenagers about their lives and relationships with family and school. Here I want to consider just two of these teenagers – two teenage girls (Gee 1996c).

In the interviews, the girls speak as 'everyday people', not as specialists connected to institutions like schools, academic disciplines, or occupations. Of course, all of us have different ways of taking on the identity of an 'everyday person'; ways related to our various ethnic, cultural, gendered, class, age-based, and peer-based identities. Furthermore, in the interviews, each girl adapts and accommodates her language and attitudes, as much as she can or wishes to, to other identities she perceives as relevant at the moment. These may include school-based identities, or any identities she associates with her favoured activities, her family, local community, various role models, or the interviewer.

One of the girls, 'Sandra', is a fourteen-year-old working-class white girl from a 'post-industrial' and economically challenged city. The other girl, 'Emily', is a fifteen-year-old upper-middle-class white girl from a wealthy suburb of a major city. The girls, whose names have, of course, been changed, are different ages because, in certain respects – for example, relationships with boys – Sandra is about a year 'ahead' of Emily. Both girls are active and resilient participants in their environments, with no 'special' problems untypical of those environments.

The interviewer, Valerie Crawford, who is a graduate student in the Hiatt Center, is a middle-class white woman graduate student earning a Ph.D. in psychology. She is known to both girls to be interested in teenage girls' lives at home and at school. Thus, the interviewer potentially brings into play, as we intended, various school-based and 'public-sphere' identities – for instance, those connected to the university – to which the girls may or may not accommodate. The interviewer asked both girls the same sorts of questions; questions about their lives at home, in their communities, and at school.

These two girls are different kinds of teenagers, positioned differently in relation to other people and to schools. One of our main concerns in conducting our interviews was to better understand what these different 'kinds' of teenagers can tell us about how, in the United States, social class helps shape language and identity. One of the key points we have wanted to emphasise in this work is the way in which social class flows out of the material circumstances of one's life – where, how, and with whom we live, act, and move with quite different access to different sorts of activities, experiences, and forms of knowledge. Of course, these material circumstances, in turn, have deep implications for one's access to different social positions in the 'knowledge economy' of the new capitalism.

To analyse our interviews, we use three different tools, each giving a different 'snapshot' into the teenagers' 'ways with words'. The first tool looks at when the girls speak as an 'I', when they say things like 'I hope that . . .', 'I know that . . .', or 'I don't like it when . . .'. The second looks at key motifs that run through each interview and what they can tell us about each of the girl's crucial concerns. The third uses narrative analysis to uncover differences in how the girls 'make deep sense' of the world and themselves through stories. Here I want to consider just the first two of these tools.

Let's start with 'I'. Obviously, if we are interested in identity, it is particularly important when people speak in the 'first person' and say things like 'I want to go to college' or 'I don't like my family'. When Emily, the upper-middle-class girl from the suburbs, speaks as an 'I', she very often speaks as a knower and claimer, using such verbs as 'know', 'learn', 'think', 'am sure', 'imagine', and 'bet' (as in 'I know that . . .' or 'I am sure that . . .'). Thirty-one per cent of all the times Emily is speaking in the 'first person', she is speaking as such a knower and claimer. When Sandra speaks as an 'I', she much less commonly speaks as a knower and claimer: in fact she speaks as an 'I' only 13 per cent of the times.

When Sandra, the working-class girl from the inner city, speaks as an 'I', she is very often talking about how she feels, how things have affected her, or what she hopes, wants, and desires, using such verbs as 'care', 'feel', 'cry', 'want', 'hope', 'like', and 'hate'. Thirty-two per cent of the times Sandra does speak in the first person, she is making such statements. When Emily speaks in the first person, she much less commonly uses such affect and desire statements. In fact only 13 per cent of all the times she speaks in the first person involve such statements.

Emily and Sandra are, then, pretty much direct inverses of each other when it comes to making statements about knowing and thinking, on the one hand, and statements about affect and desire, on the other. These differences become clearer and more meaningful if we look at what the girls actually say.

What they make knowing-and-claiming – cognitive – statements about is totally different. The following are typical statements from Sandra, the working-class girl: 'I think it is good' [her relationship with her boyfriend]; 'I think I should move out [of the house]'; 'I didn't think it was funny' [something she had done that made others laugh]; 'I don't know how to explain it' [what's so good about her boyfriend]. Sandra's cognitive statements almost always assume a background of dialogue and interaction – for example, she makes clear elsewhere in her interview that others don't like her boyfriend and that there is a debate about who should move out of the house.

In contrast, here are some typical knowing-and-claiming statements from Emily, the upper-middle-class girl: 'I think no one . . . has bothered to talk to them' [African-American students bussed to her school]; 'I think it's okay for now' [living in her current town]; 'I think I have more of a chance of getting into college'; 'I think she's the coolest person in the whole world' [a trip leader she admired]. Emily's cognitive statements are explanatory claims within an explicit or assumed argumentative structure, rather than directly dialogic and interactional. They are, in fact, usually assessments or evaluations of things, events, state of affairs, or people.

When we turn to feeling, we see that Sandra's statements about how she feels deal, for the most part, with how she felt – usually negatively – as part and parcel of a particular social interaction. Emily, on the other hand, invests little in affect statements. What she feels bad about, when she does, as we will see again below, is the fact that she has used words to assess someone else negatively and in the act offended them.

As far as desire statements go – statements about wanting or liking, or not wanting and liking – Sandra uses such statements to talk about social interactions – for example, 'I get my way any time I want it', 'They give me the answer I want to hear', 'I don't want no relationship with them', 'I don't like my dad'. Emily, on the other hand, uses such statements to talk about pre-arranged activities and her life trajectory which, as we will see below, are related – for example, 'I wouldn't want to live [here] since I was born', 'Now I want to go to Europe', 'I want to go to MIT', 'I love rock climbing', 'I like backpacking and outdoor stuff'.

Of course, the girls talk about more than knowing, feeling, and desiring. But the other things they talk about simply reinforce the picture we already see emerging. Consider, for instance, when the girls talk about what actions they have done. When Sandra talks about things she has done, she is always talking about physical deeds and social interactions, things like getting up from bed, brushing and drying her hair, wearing a certain dress, listening to music, or fighting, pushing, helping, kissing, or working with various people. When Emily talks actions and interactions, she is almost always talking about achievements and specialised activities, things like 'challenging herself', 'trying harder', 'achieving' something, 'working hard' or 'spending time' at school, getting to and from activities like backpacking, rock climbing, music lessons, or trips in the USA or abroad.

Or consider when the girls talk about themselves as speakers, saying such things as 'I said . . .', 'I asked . . .', 'I blurted out', or 'I snapped at . . .'. Emily devotes a number of these sorts of statements to asocial and hostile speech acts ('get pissed at', 'get upset at', 'scream at', 'be mean to', 'yell at', 'snap at', 'say rude things to', 'jump down [someone's] throat', 'interrupt'). Speech is very often, for Emily, a form of control or regaining control. For her, speech is not really dialogic, even if others are involved. Rather it is a judgment of others' words or deeds or an emotionally charged response to a perceived (mis)judgment of herself.

Nearly all of Sandra's statements about her own speaking, on the other hand, are either her contributions to ongoing dialogue with one or more people or they are things she says or 'blurts out' inadvertently without control. For Sandra, speech is fully dialogic and interactional, though not always a space where the speaker is in control – for example, 'I didn't mean to say it, like it just came out of my mouth'; 'I'll mix up the words and stuff'.

After what we have seen thus far, it will come as no surprise to find out that Sandra's interview is much more heavily narrativised than Emily's. Sandra's interview contains twenty separate narratives and 65 per cent of all her transcript lines are involved in narratives. Emily's interview contains only three narratives and only 19 per cent of her lines are involved in narratives. This narrative difference is just the language-generic side of the contrast we have seen thus far: on the one hand, a world of social interaction; on the other, a world of assessments and claims to know subserving a biographical trajectory through what we might call 'achievement space'.

Much of Sandra's interview is negatively tinged, but it also contains much laughter and play. On the other hand, 'play' in Emily's interview is mostly made up of activities in her trajectory through 'achievement space', activities in which much about one's self and future is at stake. Emily's interview is 'biographical'; it is about the trajectory of self through space and time. She is often an actor, and, when a responder, she is usually 'correcting' other people. Sandra's interview is immersed in the physical and social world – it is, in fact, rather picaresque – and she is as often a responder (which is not to say 'passive') as an actor, if not more so.

Orientations in and to the world

Let us turn briefly to a second perspective on the girls' interviews, namely the key motifs that run, like threads, throughout their interviews. By 'motifs', I mean images or themes that recur throughout the interviews. There are three closely related motifs that run through Sandra's interview. Below, I list but a few of the many examples of each of these under the labels 'disconnection', 'not caring', and 'language and laughter':

Motif 1: Disconnection. Examples: Sandra's sister's fiancé says he hates her and then gives her a diamond ring; Sandra's boyfriend is blamed for things, but 'like nothing happens, he don't get punished'; Sandra tells her father to 'shove it', but 'I don't get punished' (there is 'no point since they are getting a divorce'); Sandra emotionally 'freaks out' at night, but doesn't really know why; Sandra wants no relationship with her parents because too good a relationship would be 'weird'; Sandra's friends laugh at her at a party, but she can't understand what's so funny, she doesn't 'get it at all'.

Motif 2: Not caring. Examples: Sandra's boyfriend swears and smokes and his 'mom doesn't care'; he was 'on house arrest and he went out anyway'; Sandra and her friends blame her boyfriend for everything, but 'he don't care'; Sandra 'doesn't care' that 'nobody likes him', nor that her father 'hates' him; if people say she's a 'slut', 'it doesn't bother her'.

Motif 3. Language and laughter. Examples: Sandra blurts out 'shut up, you fart smellers' at a wedding party when people are looking at her and she doesn't know what to say; Sandra often says things like 'pool pilter' instead of 'pool filter'; people she cares about give her 'the answer I want to hear, that sounds right, with my problem'; if someone says something to hurt her feelings, Sandra shakes until 'someone says something to make me feel better'; Sandra's boyfriend and grandmother hold her to make her feel better, but her mother 'says stupid things'; Sandra's oldest sister says something good 'and then ruins it'; Sandra likes her boyfriend because he's 'funny' and 'makes me laugh'.

What the key motifs above indicate, I believe, is that Sandra disavows – is uninterested and untrusting in – knowledge and language as the grounds of judgment, 'fact', and coherence.

In Motif 1, Sandra paints a social world in which disconnections and reversals are salient. Furthermore, in Motif 2, she indicates an affective disconnection (lack of caring) about these disconnections, both on the part of 'authority' figures (who might enforce such connections) and on the part of herself and her peers. In Motif 3, Sandra disavows the representational function between words and the world, the very language function that others (for example, schools) take to underlie the sorts of connections that Motifs 1 and 2 deny and undercut.

By 'representational function', I mean the idea that language connects directly and straightforwardly – objectively' – to the world 'out there'; that it 're-presents' it; and that this has little to do with how people feel; what their needs are; or what their personal opinions, based on their own lived experiences, are (Minnick 1993). Sandra sees words said only because they are 'true', or 'facts' backed up by some authority figure – for example, her sister, her mother, her father, or, by extension, her teacher – as 'stupid' and as a way to 'ruin' things. In turn, Sandra celebrates the social, bonding, and affective functions of language. Language that is silly or funny, but that 'feels right' and that is intended to make one feel good, is the only truly efficacious language.

We can sum up Sandra's motifs as a disavowal of 'authoritative representation', whether adult control or the authority of asocial 'factual' language, both in terms of how her world is and in terms of her ways of being in that world. This disavowal is coupled with a celebration of social interaction outside of, or opposed to, such authoritative representation.

There are also three main closely related motifs that run through Emily's interview, and these, too, are related. A few examples of each are listed below, labelled 'activities and achievement', 'assessments', and 'evaluative speech':

Motif 1. Activities and achievement. Examples of phrases used in the interview are magic lessons; getting into college; being productive; gymnastics; doing school work; horseback riding; go to Europe; career centre; push yourself; travelling; doing theatre; school trips; challenge self; play piano; learn a lot; rock climbing; outdoor stuff; marine biology; set goals; be well off; have a position; get where I am; achieve more.

Motif 2. Assessments. Examples are 'O god, you know these people are pretty weird'; 'They never like, bother to go out, see the rest of the world'; 'I think she's the coolest person in the whole entire world' [said of trip leader]; 'she just doesn't know like certain things, cos she hasn't experienced them' [said of best friend]; 'And then, like, you look at like my sister and like, anyone else in my school, like except like, a few of my friends . . . I think that I've like tried harder, than a lot of them'.

Motif 3. Evaluative speech. Examples are 'And I'll tell them, I'll be like, you know, "that's rude, don't say that, it's really offensive"' [reply to racist or homophobic remarks from her peers]; 'There's been times I've like jumped down people's throats. And, like sometimes I think they deserve it'; 'But I was like, I was like, you know, "that's so rude, and blah blah blah, and you don't know what you're talking about"' [to a friend who told a joke about gay people]; 'And I'd say like rude things not meaning it . . . like sometimes you just make a comment. And I'd be like "those kind of things are like bad"'; 'And I'm like, "Susie, you, you just don't understand that there are people like that"'.

In Motif 1, Emily uses words and phrases – and these are but a few examples of a great many more – that deal with what we earlier called 'achievement space'. Such achievements render one's life trajectory 'worthy' (or 'likely' or 'hopeful') of 'success' (in terms of 'position' and 'being well off'). In Motifs 2 and 3, we see that Emily is invested in *assessments* of acts and people. Her interest in thinking and knowing, in discursive relations and argumentation, which we pointed to earlier, is focused on assessment, not simply knowing 'facts'. However, we must immediately point out that, for Emily, 'knowing the world' and being knowledgeable about school-based sorts of things, are grounds for a positive assessment of self-worth and optimism about one's future trajectory (as her interview makes clear).

An investment in such assessment is, however, a double-edged sword: How can one be sure that one's own or others' words and deeds really do betoken inner worth and a likely future? Emily uses language to focus or refocus others on the 'correct' way of being in the world, but she, then, is herself potentially open to such correction – a theme that emerges strongly in her narratives, which we will not deal with here.

While Sandra disavows 'authoritative representation', Emily heavily invests in one form of it, namely, evaluative assessments of self and others. These assessments are 'authoritative' both in the sense that they are based on claims to know and understand, and in that they are often supported by activities and achievements rooted in public-sphere and adult-authorised systems – for example, schools, organisations, family and community supporting success in school and later in college.

People as portfolios

In the emerging world of the new capitalism, security, which people once sought in fixed identities, static localities, and permanent jobs, resides not in one's 'employment' but in one's 'employability'. One's 'employability' is a matter of the diverse skills and experiences one has had in the variety of 'projects' – both inside and outside workplaces – of which one has been a part. It is a matter, as well, of how adaptably and flexibly one can arrange and rearrange one's skills and experiences to 'shape shift' into the 'right' kind of worker-partner-team member required by ever new projects (communities of practice) in fast changing circumstances:

> If security no longer comes from being employed, it must come from being employable. Large organisations can no longer guarantee long-term employment, and few people would believe such a promise anyway. Now employability security – the knowledge that today's work will enhance the person's value in terms of future opportunities – is a promise that can be made and kept. Employability security comes from the chance to accumulate human capital – skills and reputation – that can be invested in new opportunities as they arise.
>
> (Kanter 1995, p. 157)

What the new capitalism requires is that people see and define themselves as a flexibly rearrangeable portfolio of the skills, experiences, and achievements they have acquired through their trajectory through project space as team members of communities of practice operating as distributed networks to accomplish a set endeavour which then terminates the community – see, in particular, though the theme is common, Crosby 1994; Handy 1989, 1994; Kanter 1995.

Emily, in her interview, represents herself as an actor enacting a trajectory through achievement space, building 'value' – and assessing such value – as she participates in various activities and projects. These activities and projects are never just 'play' in the 'lifeworld'. They are always hybrids of her lifeworld as a teenager and the interests and authority of public sphere, that is, professional/expert Discourses (Gee 1996d) – for example, trips sponsored by school or official organisations, music lessons, leadership workshops, school clubs, and so on. She is a new capitalist portfolio person in the making.

Sandra, in her interview, represents herself as responding to a chaotic social world, often resisting 're-presentational' authority rooted in people, language, and institutions, many of which happen – like the schools she has attended – to be mired in the backwaters of the old capitalism more than they are attuned to the new. She responds always from her lifeworld, unconnected to cosmopolitan and global concerns and networks connected to public-sphere Discourses:

> Where innovation, education, and collaboration flourish, and the links to global networks are clear, people's security increases. Where they are missing, economic marginality results. And concentrated marginality builds an underclass visible in inner cities everywhere.
>
> (Kanter 1995, p. 165)

It remains to be said only that in a world of distributed networks, simply intervening in schools, which is the typical educational reform strategy, will not work. The kinds of people that Emily and Sandra are becoming – and the many other kinds that a more subtle discussion of these matters would have to encompass – are mediated by an ensemble of family, peers, community, and schools, but not by any one of these alone. Some of these ensembles are networked with others in ways that enhance the possibility that people like Emily will move through them into a 'global world' – though not without grave risks of one's portfolio running dry. Others of these ensembles are not so networked. There will be no passages out.

Conclusions: language in and out of school

Poor children, like Sandra and many minority children, have historically failed in our schools. Once, their failure slotted them into the lower rungs of the old industrial capitalism; that is into jobs that in ever increasing numbers no longer exist. Today, as our schools change and realign themselves with the new capitalism, children like Sandra will, if we do not do something, fail again. They will, in turn, be slotted, at best, into the remaining backwaters of the old capitalism or into the massive service sector of the new capitalism, or, at worst, into complete economic marginality. Unfortunately, their schools and communities are ill equipped to produce them as the new 'portfolio people'.

At the same time, our reformed schools, with their new cognitivist curricula, are set to produce 'portfolio' people who can think 'critically', that is, engage in 'higher order thinking', but not 'critiquely', if I may coin a word, that is, unable to understand and critique systems of power and injustice in a world that they will see as simply economically 'inevitable'. They will be unable to understand or empathise with the plight of people like Sandra or to see that that plight may ultimately be the ruin of their 'new economic order'. They will be 'ideological dupes' of the new capitalism, just as much of the intelligentsia was of the old, but in a far more dangerous, because globally interconnected, world.

We, then, really have two school problems. The first concerns how to ensure that poor and minority children, really for the first time, get well educated enough to participate in building and transforming our societies. The second concerns how to ensure that advantaged children can get out of school able to think 'critiquely' about issues of power and social justice in the new global capitalist order.

The first issue confronts us directly with the traditional question about why so many minority and poor children fail in our schools. The answer to this often ran something like this. These children, like all of us, learn early in life how to use and understand language in the context of daily face-to-face interaction with people with whom they share lots of experiences and information. Such 'contextualised language' gets most of its meaning from the contexts in which it is used and the shared understandings on which it is based, not from the words uttered. However, many minority and poor children come to school unprepared for 'school language'. Such language, the language of lectures and books, is, it is held, 'decontextualised'. That is, such language is rendered meaningful not by the contexts in which it is used, nor on the basis of shared experiences, but solely on the basis of what the words and sentences uttered or written literally mean. Such language is 'explicit', while everyday 'contextualised language' is 'inexplicit'.

This view of 'decontextualised language' was a hallmark of schooling in the old capitalism. The Multiliteracies Project is based on a viewpoint that argues that the whole notion of 'decontextualised language' is deeply misleading and harmful. But, then, too, so do the sorts of contemporary school reforms we have looked at above, the sorts that are aligning themselves with the values of the new capitalism.

All language is meaningful only in and through the contexts in which it is used. All language is meaningful only on the basis of shared experiences and shared information. All language is 'inexplicit' until listeners and readers fill it out on the basis of the experiences they have had and the information they have gained in prior socioculturally significant interactions with others. This is precisely why both new schools and new businesses are so interested in communities of practice which can immerse newcomers in new collaborative practices and thereby build up new storehouses of shared tacit knowledge that actually works in practice.

There is, of course, no such thing as 'school language' or 'academic language' as single things. There are, rather, many different school languages, different styles of language used in different school practices. There are many different academic languages, different styles of language used in different disciplines and different academic practices. There are, too, many different sorts of public-sphere language, different styles of language used for a variety of civic, economic, and political purposes. None of these many styles of language is 'decontextualised'. They are all – just like 'everyday' face-to-face language – 'contextualised'.

But it is important here to see the word 'contextualised' as naming an active process: the process of a person 'contextualising', that is, of a person making and doing a context, not just passively registering one. What does it mean to say we humans actively 'contextualise' language? 'Context' is not just 'out there'. We do not just 'reflect' context when we speak or write. Rather, we always actively create 'context'. We make the world around us mean certain things.

If I come up to a female colleague and in 'everyday talk' say, 'You look great this morning', this means little or nothing until that colleague has actively construed the context in a certain way. It may be taken in the context of 'friendly banter between colleagues'; or as 'intended or unintended sexual harassment'; or as 'encouragement for someone who cares too much about her looks'; or as 'joking with someone who cares little about her looks'; or perhaps as 'irony meant to defuse a "politically correct" environment'. That colleague will consult what they know about me and about themselves, our mutual histories, where we are and what it means to be there here and now, and a myriad of other factors, in order to actively construe the context as being a certain way. In fact, they can go so far as to respond in ways that make me, the speaker, re-construe the context to be the way they want it to be (e.g. I realise that my remark wouldn't have been made to a male and see its sexual side). Or I can resist. Context is something, too, we negotiate over, fight over, and sometimes smoothly and harmoniously share (and, thus, forget how much work we are, in fact, doing to 'pull off' context).

This 'contextualising work' is something we do in all cases of language. But how do we manage it? We can only make a context mean a certain thing if we have the resources to make it mean that. And what are those resources? Quite simply they are that of having had experiences with others in construing contexts in that way – with others who, at least initially, know how to construe contexts that way better than we do. If a person does not know how to construe the context of 'You look great this morning' as 'intended or unintended sexual harassment', then they just haven't 'hung out' long enough with the right sort of 'feminists' or haven't had (or empathised with) the sorts of experiences many women have had. In this sense, learning to contextualise and contextualising are always 'social' and 'cultural' phenomena. A way of contextualising always belongs to some group or community of people with their own interests and practices, based on experiences they have had in the world.

One learns no variety of language without having fully and repeatedly participated in the typical experiences that render that form of language meaningful. All that I have said above is as true of any school-based, academic, specialist, or public-sphere variety of language as it is of everyday talk. To understand this consider a sentence I have taken at random from a 'popular' book called *Einstein's Moon*, written by the physicist, F. David Peat.

'Bell's theorem has spelled the end to hidden mechanical variables and local ideas of reality.' Remember, this is just the sort of language which is supposed to be 'decontextualised', that is, understandable when based on its words and sentence structure alone.

Consider what it takes to understand both this sentence or the book it is in. It takes having had the sorts of experiences that would allow you to construe a context or contexts in which this sentence would be meaningful. And what would those experiences have been? They would have been familiarity with certain texts, with certain issues and debates, with certain practices inside and outside laboratories, and with certain ways of talking and viewing the world. It is, by the way, very rare indeed that people understand this sort of language if all they have ever done is read books. Without having had the opportunity to engage in discussion with people who use this sort of language and without having experienced some of what they do and why they do it, it is very hard indeed to gain real understanding – just as hard as it is to learn French only by reading French books.

Sometimes people, instead of drawing the 'contextualised'/ 'decontextualised' distinction, draw a related distinction between language that is heavily 'deictic' and language that is not. 'Deictic' is a fancy word that means 'pointing'. Things like 'pronouns' and 'demonstratives' are 'deictics' because they 'point' outside the utterances they are in to the larger context. For example, in a sentence like 'He's funny because he does things like that', 'he' and 'that' point to things outside the utterance itself. Everyday speech is, indeed, full of such deictics that 'tie' it to its context.

But our sentence from the physics book is full of pointers of a different sort. 'Bell's theorem' points to an earlier discussion of a particular piece of mathematical physics and, thus, too, to your previous experiences with both physics and mathematics. 'Hidden mechanical variables' points via 'variables' to your previous experience with experimentation inside and outside physics. It points via 'mechanical' to your experiences with both machines and machine metaphors and the whole Western history of mechanistic explanations of nature. It points via 'hidden' to your previous experiences of explanations, inside and outside physics proper, that appeal to not easily observable or even invisible entities in order to offer a 'causal' explanation of observable phenomena. 'Local ideas of reality' points via the word 'local' to a contrast between 'local' and 'non-local' and, thereby, to your experiences of 'causes' that are far removed and seemingly unconnected to their 'effects' – experiences few of us, in fact, have had, so this bit is hard even for people who have had enough experiences to imagine contexts for the other bits of the sentence. The moral is that all language is heavily deictic, though different types of language point in different ways to different sorts of experiences.

It is the scandal of many so-called 'developed countries' today that the doors, not just to physics but to the most central sorts of 'school-based' and public-sphere language, the sorts connected to power in our society and virtually taken by those in power as constituting intelligence and full humanity, do not exist for a great many children, either early in life or later. When these children fail in school we ask why they have failed. This situation, where we can attribute failure to the children, rather than to our society, works because we systematically hide what experiences and how many of them are necessary to develop the ability to construe and imagine contexts that render school-based, academic, specialist, and public-sphere forms of language really and deeply meaningful. We pretend that it is easy to make up for a lack of these experiences late in the game, although, to use a sports metaphor, no one thinks many of us could make the college basketball team if we had never played basketball before college. Some (lucky) people can do it (though they usually have to cover up their gaps), but it is a sin to make people feel they are a failure when, late in the game, they don't 'make the team' in competition with others who have played the game all their lives.

There is some sense to the notion of 'decontextualised language', but not the sense most people who use the term intend. School-based, specialist, academic, and public-sphere languages, while always requiring acts of active contextualising, are decontextualised from people's 'lifeworlds'. By 'lifeworlds' I mean the culturally distinctive (different cultures have different lifeworlds) ways of being, acting as, and talking as an 'everyday', non-specialist person. School-based, specialist, academic, and public-sphere forms of language often require us to exit our lifeworlds and construe contexts based on experiences we have had outside the lifeworld, experiences in classrooms, laboratories, concert halls, academic discussions, research projects, civic institutions, businesses, and so forth.

When we exit our lifeworlds, that is the worlds we all live in when we are being 'everyday people' and not speaking out of some specialist domain or another, we leave 'home', in a sense. For many advantaged children, this trip is not really very treacherous. They are not asked to deny and denigrate their lifeworlds in the process. In fact, from the outset their induction into specialist domains has been built via rich bridges to their lifeworlds. Their lifeworlds have, in fact, incorporated from early on some of the practices and values of specialist domains, though, of course, in attenuated forms, for example the early reading of 'children's literature' provides a bridge to the specialist domain of 'literature' proper. For many minority and poor children, on the other hand, no such bridges exist or are built. We rarely build on their experiences and on their very real distinctive lifeworld knowledge. In fact, they are very often asked, in the process of being exposed to specialist domains, to deny the value of their lifeworlds and their communities in reference to those of more advantaged children.

The only real solution, of course, is to change the game, that is, to change our society. The only real solution is to imagine and begin to implement a society in which success in school and having access to specialised forms of knowledge are not markers of class and race and, in some cases, gender. But we can do much better in school while we are waiting for the 'revolution'. For one thing, we have seen above that even the new capitalism is demanding that people with specialist knowledge be able to put it into action (not just store it as 'facts') and that they be able to relate it to other sources of knowledge with an appreciation of the overall system within which they work.

First, we can tell the truth; which means the truth about the distribution of experiences in our society. We can be honest with people about where they have entered the game and how much work it is going to take to 'catch up'. We can be honest with people about the fact that 'catching up' may not always be possible. After all, the elites don't just stop having experiences, so that other strategies may be necessary, as well. We can be honest, too, about the fact that minority and poor children need more than just better schools than they currently have. They need even better schools than the schools we typically give to the elites, who, after all, have experiences outside school that compensate for what are often, in fact, mediocre schools, despite the price of the houses in their neighbourhoods.

The Multiliteracies Project suggests a set of pedagogical principles that I believe ought to be stated as a 'Bill of Rights' for all children, but most especially for minority and poor children. These principles seek to produce people who can function in the new capitalism, but in a much more meta-aware and political fashion than forms of new-capitalist-complicit schooling. Every child – but most especially those children who have heretofore been excluded from the experiences that would allow them to contextualise school-based, specialist, academic, and public-sphere forms of language – has a moral right to four forms of integrated instruction:

They have a right to lots of Situated Practice. By 'Situated Practice' I mean 'hands-on', embodied experiences of authentic and meaningful social practices involving talk, texts, tools, and technologies of the sort that help one imagine contexts that render what is being taught meaningful. If children are learning science, they have a right to see, feel, hear, and practice meaningful and authentic science with all its linguistic, techno-logical, cognitive, and social accoutrements – I've seen seven-year-olds doing it. And they have a right to have this sort of Situated Practice in a way that, far from denigrating their lifeworlds, makes bridges to them.

They have a right to Overt Instruction. By 'Overt Instruction' I mean all forms of guidance and scaffolding, within and outside Situated Practice, that focus the learner's attention, in a reflective and meta-aware way, on the important parts of the language and practice being taught. 'Overt instruction', in this sense, foregrounds the cognitively, socially, and historically important patterns and relationships in the language and practices being taught. For example, Western physics makes an important distinction

67

between 'underlying realities' and 'superficial appearances'. Children learning physics have a right to be made overtly aware that this is important, to know why it is important, and to know what sorts of language and practices follow from its importance.

They have a right to Critical Framing. By 'Critical Framing' I mean ways of coming to know where in the overall system you stand. How does what you are learning relate to other domains? Where in the overall system of knowledge and social relations does the language and knowledge you are learning stand? For example, the distinction physicists make between 'underlying realities' such as fundamental particles and 'superficial appearances' such as the solidity of objects has been imported to many other domains and in some of these it has been used for pernicious purposes – underlying racial characteristics, genetic determinism, or a single underlying mental variable called 'intelligence'.

They have a right to be allowed to produce and transform knowledge, not just consume it. Children should, indeed, master the standard 'genres' of many school-based, specialist, academic, and public-sphere forms of language and social practices, but they should also know how to transform them, break them, and innovate new ones for their own social, cultural, and political purposes. In fact, they should know that even in using the standard genres they are, or at least should be, always actively adapting them to their own purposes; customising them to the contexts they as actors are trying to create – construe, imagine, creatively reflect, whatever way you want to put it.

Ultimately, our failure of minority and poor children in school is rooted in our unwillingness or inability to give them the forms of instruction that are theirs by right and that are necessitated by the doors that have and continue to be closed to them. The advantages of advantaged children lie primarily in Situated Practice, although ironically these sorts of experiences are often provided by their families in out-of-school sites, as we have seen in our discussion above of 'portfolio people'. The other forms of instruction can begin to help disadvantaged children 'catch up' and, given the meta-knowledge and political awareness implied by Critical Framing and Transformed Practice, move beyond those who have attempted to keep the game to themselves. At the same time, the sorts of meta-knowledge and political awareness implied by these may help solve our other school problem, namely, the need to ensure that the advantaged are not so duped by new capitalist schooling that they are willing to leave children like Sandra in their dust.

3

CYBER-SCHOOLING AND TECHNOLOGICAL CHANGE

Multiliteracies for new times

Carmen Luke

Introduction: technological innovation and dissemination

In the last few years, talk about the information superhighway has saturated the media, the marketplace, and the public imagination. Social critics and commentators tell us we are in the midst of a technological and information revolution which will change for ever the way we communicate and conduct our everyday affairs. But what is the information revolution? How do the new technologies impact on our lives now and what might these changes mean for the future? What might all this mean for education, for teachers and students, for teaching and learning?

My aim in this chapter is to provide a guided tour of a range of issues currently being raised about new information technologies (IT) and computer mediation communications (CMC), in relation to schooling and literacy. What is interesting in current debates is that researchers and social commentators are looking at much broader and more long-term social and cultural consequences of the impact of CMC. Even among educators, concerns are not confined exclusively to pedagogical and curriculum issues. It seems that questions about the significant and permanent social change seeping into every crevice of our everyday work and private lives are on everyone's mind. Many of the issues that are being raised today, and which I will sketch out here, deal with abstract notions about the virtual and 'real'; about time and space; about 'body-less' interactions and communities of learners; about global access, global culture, and so forth. But despite what appears to be a highly abstract debate, it none the less has concrete implications for schooling as we know it and all the traditional industrial model precepts and practices developed within that model. And yet the radical technological changes we now hear about in the media

– most of which are framed in either a technophobic 'crisis' or else pro-technology 'panacea' rhetoric – have been with us for quite some time.

Of all the innovations in communications technologies over the past two decades, the video cassette recorder (VCR), computer, and now the global network of the Internet have had the most profound effect on home entertainment, education, and workplace practice. The VCR permanently changed the way viewers access broadcast television. No longer tied to network schedules, viewers now take for granted the flexibility of pre-programmed videotaping and delayed viewing. With close to 100 per cent of Australian households owning televisions, and about 80 per cent owning VCRs, the traditional patterns of Australia's favourite leisure pastime have irrevocably changed.

The computer has brought about the most profound changes in communication, information storage, retrieval, and dissemination. The effects of the computer on workplaces, on international money markets, and on education are incalculable. Not only have ways of doing business and handling information changed, but our everyday social relations, also increasingly electronically mediated, are undergoing profound changes. Yet change has been so rapid that the rate of technological innovation continually outstrips the rate of research output on the social, cultural, and educational consequences of electronic and global communication systems.

What began in the mid 1970s as a relatively slow trickle into the marketplace of home microcomputers had been transformed by the 1980s into the global and hugely successful phenomenon of the video game, video arcade, and home entertainment packages for the microcomputer. At the same time, Automatic Teller Machines (ATMs) proliferated in all major urban centres and rapidly proliferated around the globe. Cable television expanded exponentially in the USA throughout the 1980s but debate about 'pay-TV' hit Australian shores only in the early 1990s. The accelerated speed of technological developments, and the proliferation of increasingly cheaper electronic commodities and services in the private consumer marketplace, have seemingly made the public reel from one set of responses to the next – from fears of children's 'joystick arthritis' from too much video gaming to concerns over Big Brother surveillance through the electronic trail gathered by ATMs and other electronically monitored financial transactions. In many ways, these concerns parallel public fears over the advent of television in the 1940s, silent pictures at the turn of the century, or the coming of the book in the late 1400s.

Today, the internet is generating equally profound changes in the way we communicate, and how we access, produce, and distribute information and knowledge. Yet the Internet too is generating virulent responses from the public and social critics about its 'anarchic' nature: the inability to control it, to censor it, to manage and limit it. The Internet gets a lot of bad press particularly in relation to that age-old concern over various forms of pornography, privacy and sexual harassment issues concerning 'electronic stalking', and questions of ownership, monopoly, and unequal access. By the same token, the huge educational (and entrepreneurial) potential of the Internet – popularised as the information superhighway – often gets lauded to the point of blind faith.

Literacy requirements have changed and will continue to change as new technologies come on the marketplace and quickly blend into our everyday private and work lives. And unless educators take a lead in developing appropriate pedagogies for these new electronic media and forms of communication, corporate experts will be the ones to determine how people will learn, what they learn, and what constitutes literacy. For instance, a quick look through any of today's most popular CD-ROM encyclopaedias (for example, Microsoft's *Encarta*) shows how limited entries on, for example, 'Australia' or 'Aborigines' are; how ideas are connected by lateral links and pathways which exclude other knowledge options; and how the software in fact 'teaches' the user-learner certain cognitive mapping strategies. Many of these bestselling American-authored encyclopaedias are in use in Australian schools and households. But even Australian-authored educational CD-ROMs reproduce the same old tired narratives on, for instance, bushrangers framed in mythologies of male heroes, and narratives of colonialism framed in mythologies of settlement instead of invasion. The point is that today's corporate software designers can easily become the literacy and pedagogy experts of tomorrow. This is not to say that many educational products on the market today are pedagogically unsound or lack innovative teaching-learning methods. But it is to suggest that educators need to become familiar with the many issues at stake in the 'information revolution' so that we know how and where we must intervene with positive and critical strategies for Multiliteracies teaching, and how to make the best and judicious use of the many multimedia resources available.

It is important that we can step back in this chapter and take a broader historical look at the debates that have surrounded such technological innovations; to consider how technologies in educational contexts have been defined, and how their social uses and consequences are always contextual. Only then can the current debates about the 'information superhighway' and the democratising of information access and distribution be properly understood. Clearly, the social and cultural implications of such 'body-less' communications and what this might mean for 'cyber-education' of the twenty-first century need to be confronted.

Multiliteracies

What today appear as hybrid and frontier media forms and content will be commonplace in the near future, and will generate new text-based social repertoires, communication styles, and symbolic systems for accessing and participating in new knowledge and cultural configurations. Consider, for instance, that just to get into any basic computer program requires facility with both print literacy and any number of symbolic languages so that we know where to click in order to move through menued choices. Already we take that kind of literacy for granted.

Much has been written on the theory and practice of critical literacy (e.g. Gee 1996b; Muspratt, Freebody and Luke 1996; New London Group 1996) and critical media literacy (e.g. Alvarado and Boyd-Barrett 1992; Buckingham 1990, 1993; Hart 1991; Luke 1994, 1996a, 1996b; Lusted 1991). However, scholarship on critical print-text and media literacy has barely taken the emergent digital domain of hypertextuality into consideration (Bigum and Green 1993). At the classroom level as well, 'teaching students about new technologies in their social and cultural work and leisure contexts has not been a high priority in curriculum development' (Kenway 1995). None the less, the basic principles of a critical literacy are as applicable to computer-mediated communication and hypertextuality as they are to traditional print and mass-media texts.

A rudimentary working definition of critical literacy entails three aspects. First, it involves a meta-knowledge of diverse meaning systems and the sociocultural contexts in which they are produced and embedded in everyday life. By meta-knowledge I mean having an understanding of how knowledge, ideas and information 'bits' are structured in different media and genres, and how these structures affect people's readings and uses of that information. Second, it involves mastery of the technical and analytic skills with which to negotiate those systems in diverse contexts. This refers to how the pragmatics of use of literacy are translated into practice in different contexts. Third, it involves the capacity to understand how these systems and skills operate in relations and interests of power within and across social institutions. This means an understanding of how and why various social groups have different and unequal access to literacy (and knowledge), and how access and distribution work in the interests of some groups and can disadvantage others.

Since all meaning is situated relationally – that is, connected and cross-referenced to other media and genres, and to related meanings in other cultural contexts – a critical literacy relies on broad-based notions of intertextuality. As I will argue throughout this chapter, negotiating computer-mediated communication, constructing new forms of identity (for example, the online 'personas' that people construct for themselves), and participating in new virtual communities, require an intertextual understanding of how meanings shift across media, genres, and cultural frames of reference. Whether one 'visits' the Louvre online; joins an international newsgroup of parents of Down Syndrome children; or visits the WWW site of an agricultural college in Kenya, cross-cultural understanding and 'netiquette' are increasingly crucial for participating effectively in global communications.

The Multiliteracies of digital electronic 'texts' are based on notions of hybridity and intertextuality. Meaning-making from the multiple linguistic, audio, and symbolic visual graphics of hypertext means that the cyberspace navigator must draw on a range of knowledges about traditional and newly blended genres or representational conventions, cultural and symbolic codes, as well as linguistically coded and software-driven meanings. Moreover, the lateral connectedness of hypertext information, which users access by clicking on buttons or hotlinks, immerses navigators in an intertextual and multimodal universe of visual, audio, symbolic, and linguistic meaning systems. In hypertext navigation, reading, writing, and communicating are not linear or unimodal (that is, exclusively language- and print-based), but demand a multimodal reading of laterally connected, multi-embedded and further hotlinked information resources variously coded in animation, symbols, print text, photos, movie clips, or three-dimensional and manoeuvrable graphics.

In the digital information environment, an understanding of the relations among ideas is as important as, if not more important than, mastery of the ideas themselves. Today, the expert is the one who sees and seeks the connection among related pieces of information, not the one who has the bare decontextualised facts. Hence, electronic reading and writing, a sense of intertextual connectivity, relational knowledge, and thinking laterally across associations are fundamental to Internet (or CD-ROM) navigation and information sourcing. At the 'textual' and interactive level of hypertext reading, writing and communication, then, linear and print-based literacy skills applied to a handful of traditional genres (for example, the CV, job application form, scientific text, or the storybook grammar) are no longer adequate. The dynamics of lateral and cross-linked information of hypertext requires and generates a cognitive orientation akin to what is often termed lateral thinking – the very skills educators aim to instil in students. The global cross-cultural information flow on the Internet and the international composition of many virtual communities mean that any critical technological literacy by definition entails intercultural communication. This means new ways of thinking about and interacting with others from culturally divergent backgrounds.

Critical Multiliteracies for effective information sourcing from, and participation in, the new digital datasphere provides not only the rudimentary and 'functional' skills of, say, keyboarding, file management, CD-ROM searching, or Internet browsing. It also involves analysis of the power relations of new institutions and worlds: the very issues raised in this chapter about the politics of virtual identity and community; about new forms of sociality and changing concepts of time and spatiality; the hybridisation of media forms; the economics of technological and corporate convergence;

and market and governmental discourses of 'technological enhancement' and democratisation. These new relations and corporate alignments operate in and on behalf of particular interests with implications for potentially unequal access and distribution of information, material wealth and resources. Critical Multiliteracies, then, requires student debate and understanding of the political and material consequences of technological change. How will IT change our lives? Who will benefit? Who will be disadvantaged? For example, students trained in a critical technological literacy that provides them with a balanced curriculum of 'cybercitizenship education' (Greenhill and Fletcher 1996, p. 23), as well as the more technical 'how-to' skills, tend to gain more from the electronic information economy than those trained exclusively in technical front-end user skills (Goldsworthy 1992). How can that disadvantage be overcome?

Technologies: histories, definitions, contexts

A commonly accepted explanation for the relationship between technologies and society has been the notion of technological determinism. This view holds that technologies determine human behaviour, social relations, and, indeed, social organisation itself. What this position implies is first that technologies operate in a contextual vacuum independent of human agents, and second that the effects or consequences of technologies on, for instance, literacy or social interaction are similar for everyone across class, geographic, or cultural differences. Yet, given the history of technologies, we can see that, as was the case with the printing press, effects are never uniform or even. Technological diffusion in the social sphere proceeds unevenly, and is mediated by a range of interlocking socio-demographic and cultural factors that variously make possible and limit access and participation.

The effects of technologies are never intrinsic to a particular medium, but are always mediated by the uses to which technologies are put and the contexts in which they are used. The television set in the classroom is invariably used for educational purposes. In that context students are expected to read the audiovisual text for educational, information-gathering purposes which are likely to be tested by a teacher. The television set in the home, by contrast, is principally used by household members for leisure and entertainment, for background noise or companionship. Television viewing in the home is less purpose-driven than in school contexts and certainly does not undergo the kind of testing for learning outcomes typical of teacher–student encounters over media texts.

The uses of technologies, then, vary with context and generate effects in terms of their uses. Computers, for instance, were first put to use in the service of the US military for what many would consider dubious ends. In the early 1970s, the economic need for market expansion and push towards electronic miniaturisation produced computers more suitable to the consumer market, principally businesses. International Business Machines (IBM) had long cornered the manual and electric typewriter market in business and industry, and was quick to develop, market and saturate the corporate and tertiary education sector with computer software and hardware. As market competition and penetration increased, computer hardware and software costs decreased and by the 1980s a massive marketing shift from the corporate sector to the home and family market was under way.

As with all technological innovations, it is usually affluent groups who are the first to purchase new technologies: from electricity, telephones, electric washing machines, or cars early this century to televisions, mobile phones, VCRs, video cameras, or computers today. The use of ATMs is a similar case in point. People with limited financial resources – that is, those without credit cards or bank accounts – have no need for ATMs. Those living in rural areas where ATM penetration is still patchy have similar limited access to this technology. Furthermore, some cultural groups may see little value in Western technology or the narratives produced by television or computer video games. Finally, there are always individuals, groups, or entire communities who refuse to 'buy into' new technologies for a host of reasons ranging from lifestyle choices in favour of a more 'organic' and non-technologically mediated way of life to religious commitments (e.g. Amish communities), or personal choices which many families make against the household invasion of television, phones, or computers. In short, then, the social spread and uses of technologies are never uniform and predictable because of structural inequalities of access and participation, and various choices of resistance to technologies and the lifestyles and ideologies that accompany them.

Given the intrinsically social nature of technologies – at the levels of invention, production, dissemination, and uses – we can begin to formulate a definition of technology on at least three levels, all of which involve various dimensions of the social. According to sociologist of technology Judy Wacjman: 'at the most basic level technology refers to a set of physical objects . . . [but] to see these objects as nothing other than inanimate items . . . ignores the fact that they are developed, manufactured and marketed as part of economic and social activity' (Wajcman 1994, p. 6).

The car, Wajcman notes, is more than an 'arbitrary lump of matter, because it forms part of a set of human activity' (Wajcman 1994, p. 6), much as a computer is meaningless without programs, programmers, and users. The car is implicated in many layers of social activity from the discourse of road rules and the legal consequences of breaking those rules, to the textual domain and social and economic activity surrounding insurance and licensing; driver training and testing; school-based road safety curricula; new car product research, development, and marketing;

advertising; and, not least, the multiple unintended social uses to which vehicles are put. Recall, for example, O.J. Simpson's famous and globally televised getaway vehicle – the Ford Bronco; alternatively, most people have anecdotes of a first date or first kiss in somebody's car. The second level of meaning, then, refers to the social activities that derive from and shape the social context around particular technologies. The domestic washing machine, for instance, is located in a radically different (commonly gendered) social context and use patterns from, say, the gendered (and social class) contexts of use of military or commercial flight simulators.

Third, in Wajcman's view, technologies imply knowledge connected to social activities and relations, and to technological objects. The knowledge base within which technologies are situated include research and development; market research and testing; educational knowledge and testing; critical research into social uses and consequences; the informal sharing of knowledge among groups of users; and the popularisation of technology 'know-how' in the popular cultural realm of television, special interest and mass-audience magazines, cinema, and the Internet itself. To elaborate, consider the vast amount of knowledge and the human intellectual labour involved in technological innovations such as remote sensing apparatuses, supersonic aircraft, or the plethora of high-tech medical technology. Market research before and after product release includes not only the accumulation of vast amounts of data on consumer preferences and responses to new products but also involves the development and testing of (often global) advertising campaigns (for example, the launch of Microsoft Windows 95).

Critical research on the social and cultural impact of new technologies further generates a substantial knowledge base of which this very document is a part. Informal exchanges among technology users (whether teens in the video arcade or office workers in networked systems) create social networks and relations through the sharing of information and, often, 'insider knowledge' about how to 'beat a game', or how to bypass software protocols, or retrieve information at work for private use without 'getting caught'. On another level, workplace and educational training in new technological skills is based on and generates knowledge about appropriate curricula, pedagogy, and evaluation. This knowledge is also located in various policy documents which themselves are amalgams of various disciplinary and governmental discourses. In short, there are many social networks and levels of knowledge in which our understandings and uses of technology are embedded. Once we unravel the social relations in which technologies are embedded, we can begin to see the futility of any technological determinist arguments.

Finally, popular culture industries have a way of harnessing the public imagination and turning technology into narratives of consumption (for example, specialist consumer magazines), and narratives of the fantastic, the futuristic, and the anarchic, all of which generate their own social dynamics. Increasingly, technology features as a central plot device on which cinematic and television narratives are built. *Star Trek* is a prime example of a popular cultural text focused on futuristic space technology and the social relations, social organisation, and moral dilemmas faced by residual nineteenth-century humans on lost planets or spacecraft communities, and by humanoids, androids, and cyborgs of new high- or 'post'- tech societies. The immense popular interest in such programmes is evident in Star Trek spin-offs such as *Star Trek – Deep Space Nine, Star Trek – The Next Generation,* and *Star Trek – Voyager.*

These and the original *Star Trek* series (now called *Classic Star Trek*) have generated their own global (and online) communities of 'trekkies', fanzines, fan clubs and conferences which, together, generate a whole other level of sociality, and the production and exchange of specialised popular cultural knowledge. Popular cultural texts about technology which emanate from the public imagination generate knowledges, social exchanges, relationships, and communities (actual and virtual) on several levels which, in turn, are the object of academic interest, research, and knowledge production.

The Internet is another popular site for the formation of 'virtual' communities. Thousands of newsgroups or e-mail 'bulletin boards' have formed around technology-specific interests, some for general non-specialist users, others for the computer whiz-kids and high-tech specialists. Seen as a total entity, the diversity of electronic newsgroups can encompass millions of people logging on from around the globe to discuss their special interest topics. The Internet itself has generated countless magazines in the last few years dedicated to the techno-lifestyle of cyberculture as well as to the more technical aspects of computing and hypertext navigation. Most of these magazines are also available online to subscribers, but, whether in print or electronic versions, these emergent discourses are a whole other level of popular culture derivative of and constituting the social, cultural and technical dimensions of new forms of communications technology.

In short, technologies emerge in specific historical contexts, and become part of the diverse social fabric of everyday life where they shape and are shaped by the social practices through which uses are mediated. In the sections that follow I will outline some aspects of computer-mediated communication that are producing radically different – blended, merged, and reshaped – social practices and conceptions of community, subjectivity, time, space, textuality, and communication from those formulated in traditional print-based models. These changes and differences point to the need to consider an expanded definition of literacy to take account of multiple forms of textual, graphic, and symbolic languages, as well as the culturally diverse virtual communities of the global mediascape.

The global village: democratising information?

Three decades ago, communications theorist Marshall McLuhan coined the phrase 'the global village' in response to the advent of television, which he considered was bringing the diversity of global nations and communities together in a shrinking, electronically mediated global culture. Much like the telephone, television promised immediate and instantaneous communication across time zones, national boundaries, and geographic distances. Today, the phenomenon of global, electronic, and digital communications systems, the global 'mediascape', is said once again to erase traditional boundaries of nation, economies, and social organisation, thereby making global communications among all peoples a more democratic process (e.g. Rheingold 1994).

The global mediascape of the recent past was characterised by shifts in mass culture and consumerism wrought by the global diffusion of television and the global saturation of primarily American television programming and mass advertising. The contemporary mediascape is substantially different in form and content. For instance, television is prepackaged, non-interactive, and broadcast to millions within nations and globally across borders (e.g. Olympics, Miss Universe, Academy Awards, World Cup soccer). The Internet, whilst it is also potentially accessible to the global community, differs in several ways. First, it is interactive in the sense that users decide which databases, newsgroups, or World Wide Web sites they wish to 'visit'. Second, it requires a still relatively expensive set of hardware and software and, third, it requires more sophisticated skills than those required for switching on a television. The new mediascape may well, in theory, democratise communication and access to a global library of diverse information sources and knowledge bases. However, access is still fundamentally tied to economic privilege and, given that well over half of the world's population has only limited or no access to electricity (let alone private telephone line access), claims of global audience and of the Internet's role in democratising access to communications, information, and knowledge may be somewhat premature (Holderness 1993; McKie 1994; Schiller 1995).

Arguments about the democratisation potential of new communication technologies accompany most pro-technology claims, many of which are woven into federal and state technology policies, as well as corporate marketing narratives. Techno-utopia visions of the global digital village tend to assume a shared consciousness and understanding among groups and societies differently situated in what is still a world of profoundly hierarchised political and economic orders of power and control over knowledge and resources. Information-rich and information-poor societies, and groups within those societies, still tend to be demarcated along north–south and east–west axes as well as divides of social class, gender, and racialised differences. It is important, therefore, not to lose sight of differences in people's material conditions despite the formation of virtual cultural and social realms that hold the potential for new and different forms of community and material relations. Hence, arguments about the democratisation of information and global community access made possible by new communications technologies must be viewed with caution.

Space–time compression

Social geographer David Harvey (Harvey 1989, 1993) speaks of the 'space–time compression' of postmodern technological society. Communication technologies, he claims, have so substantially altered traditional, objective categories of place and time that 'we are forced to alter . . . how we represent the world to ourselves' (Harvey 1989, p. 240). The analogic real time of telephone or face-to-face communication, or the delayed time of communication through memo or letter writing is substantially different in digital electronic communications. For instance, it takes real time to type messages, search a disk, or access directories. Yet, if one has the correct address of a remote site, one can be 'there' in milliseconds; similarly, the transfer of vast amounts of data (depending on modem speed) can be almost instantaneous. This time-compressed relation to virtually any kind of information, coupled with the possibility of instant access and immediate downloading into hard copy, suggests a radically different orientation to text, information, and the organisation of time from when one had to think about getting organised to go to the local library, check out books, bring them home, hand-copy information or, in more recent years, make photocopies of the page one needed. Not only has time taken on new meaning in the ways in which we can now access almost any information instantaneously, but it also has meant a reduction in traditional forms of sociality. Computer-mediated access to other people at the end of online terminals, to information or consumer goods through teleshopping, means that we no longer have to leave the screen or our homes to conduct the business of much of everyday life.

As Harvey notes, changes in the ways in which 'we represent the world to ourselves' are already well under way. For instance, the concept of privacy has taken on new meanings (Benedikt 1991; Collins 1995); e-mail is both private and public, both inside and outside. Unlike paper envelopes, addresses of sender and receiver are not written as public text outside the private message, but are 'inside' as part of the private message body. And since all e-mail messages are assigned traceable number codes, any message can be tracked, encrypted, and made publicly accessible. An accidental wrong keystroke to 'send all' similarly unleashes the private note into the public domain. Many critics of the infomatic society are sceptical of the fading of traditional boundaries between public and private spheres and identities.

Bogard (Bogard 1996), for instance, suggests that when the subject is collapsed into what he calls 'telematic society', then private and public collapse into new forms of surveillance. 'When you no longer move', he says, when 'you make your home a world, without moving, by switching on the power . . . you become the ideal target, always there, always available to the apparatus, always locatable, isolatable, online' (Bogard 1996, p. 140). What this suggests is that 'when the world becomes our screen (or our bodies become our codes), privacy and publicity dissolve into one another . . . On the Net, in simulation, in virtual spacetime, everything and nothing is a secret, everything and nothing is seen' (Bogard 1996, pp. 140–1).

The collapse and ambiguity of public and private space, of activity and identity, are evident also in notions of place and spatiality (Robins 1996). Although we are in 'no place' on the Internet, we get a sense of the local, of community, of simultaneity, and of place when we log on to our newsgroups or visit World Wide Web sites. We refer to 'places' on the fibre optic cables: WWW sites claim to be 'under construction'; WWW sites or socially friendly newsgroups are referred to as 'nice places to visit'; some commentators talk about the superhighway as more of a 'dirt road', still 'under construction', rather than a superhighway. Students are encouraged to make their school's home page a 'nice place to visit', to provide a 'friendly community atmosphere' so that visitors stay and check out the resources.

Other virtual sites where people co-construct narrative and social interaction are what are called cyberspace cafés, or salons. Online pubs, cafés, or salons are like bulletin boards: you arrive, tell everyone hello, describe where you will sit, what you're going to drink, and then get into the prevailing discussion. Cyber-bar or cyber-café patrons organise birthday parties, bon-voyage or promotion parties; people collectively 'redecorate' or 'build' extensions to existing virtual space, and so on. These narrative collectives can include as many participants, sub-plots, characters, and 'spaces' as writer-participants can imagine. It is a 'place' where people from different geographic locations and time zones meet, where they conduct social exchange and engage in multilogues in real and delayed time. Many consider these communities 'safe' places to meet and socialise, where 'real' identities, looks, abilities, class, or professional status don't matter.

Out of the ether and back in 'real' time, the current vogue in the material world are actual cafés and bars that provide terminals and pay-per-hour online services so that Net surfing can be accompanied by a cappuccino on the mouse mat. These cyber-cafés are springing up in cities around the world, and they give many people who don't have Internet access a chance to try out virtual cyberspace. Virtual and actual cybercafés constitute a whole new cultural realm of 'play' and sociality which go beyond the phenomenal world: the materiality of place and the linearity of analogue time.

Cyberschool/industrial schooling: the romance of the book

Traditional classroom notions of schooling based on thirty desk-based kids with all eyes up front on the teacher will not be the model of schooling and learning in the near future. The single-file movement of students from class to class, from subject area to subject area, is a product of industrial model schooling, an outdated disciplinary regime both in terms of disciplining students and in accessing the disciplines as conceptually and physically separate knowledge domains. In a context where students literally walk to separate content areas headed by teacher specialists, learning is seen as possible (and assessable) only if students occupy physical spaces at desks in places called classrooms and schools. Place and print-bound learning and teaching have sedimented through ritualised massive group behaviours which apparently take twelve years of nine-to-three socialisation in places called school. These industrial-model, print- and book-based practices of schooling will become less relevant in the age of virtual classrooms, hyper-text, and online communities of learners. The shift from print and paper to electronic textuality, the proliferation of information resources and databases, global knowledge and social networks, require very different – multimodal and multimedia – social and literacy skills from those conceptualised on the basis of an essentially assembly-line, factory model of schooling, and the static linearity of print- and book-based models of literacy (Luke 1996a).

Consider one traditional feature of literacy: library skills. To access the material 'hard copy' of the world's knowledge base encased in books, located on shelves, and 'propertied' by libraries, requires physical presence in places (e.g., the Sorbonne, Harvard, Cambridge, the Library of Congress, etc.) most of us cannot access. It also requires requisite status and authorised credentials to gain entry, and most of us would not qualify for a swipecard at the Sorbonne. However, telecommuting and tele-presence erases the tyranny of distance and status. Instead of timetabling block periods for a class trip to the library during school hours, the virtual library is open twenty-four hours a day, 365 days of the year. Instead of place-bound architectures of reading rooms, checkout areas, shelves and stacks, school and world-class libraries (many of which are accessible only to scholars) are accessible any time to anyone connected to the infobahn.

But what about the romance narrative we have constructed around the sight, feel, and pleasure of owning, reading, and handling books and browsing along the shelves? And, on the other hand, what are the implications of the increasing cost of books and a range of environmental concerns which raise other issues about the long-term viability and sustain-ability of book publishing and the industry as a whole? As one commentator puts it:

81

> Those addicted to the look and feel of tree flakes encased in dead cow . . . would not have to kick the habit; elegant physical volumes could automatically be generated on demand. Nothing would ever be checked out, lost in somebody's else's carrel, or in the limbo of the reshelving cart. Old volumes could live out their days in safe and dignified retirement in climate-controlled book museums.
>
> (Mitchell 1995, p. 56)

In *City of Bits*, William Mitchell writes that schools and universities are designed to bring students and teachers together in age- and knowledge-differentiated spaces: where teachers speak knowledge to which students listen and respond. In an electronic digital and networked information environment, however, teaching spaces and practices must go undergo profound shifts. At the very least, the classroom or university lecture hall

> now needs a computer workstation integrated with the podium and a computer-connected video projector to supplement the old blackboards and slide projectors; the podium is no longer a place for reading from a book or lecturing from written notes, but a spot for directing and interpreting a stream of bits. And instead of taking notes on paper, students use their laptop computers to capture and annotate these bits.
>
> (Mitchell 1995, p. 69)

Traditional schooling requires students to come 'inside' under the watchful eye of the teacher's dictum: 'all eyes up front'. In cyber-school, on the other hand, students can't wait to get inside in order to log on and get outside beyond the classroom walls into the borderless world of Internet resources.

The virtual workplace

Another important shift in social practice and relations is evident in the workplace. Already people are working from home as part of virtual organisations or offices – business around the corner, across town, or on the other side of the globe is in the next room on a screen and yet a world away, accessible in seconds. For those with childcare responsibilities and for people with limited physical mobility, telecommuting offers huge opportunities for new ways of workplace participation. This relocation of work is beginning to erode the old distinctions between the public sphere of work and the private sphere of home and household.

On another level of representation, these shifts are increasingly evident in the way computers and new computer-literate subjects are being marketed in the popular culture discourses of computing magazines. In advertisements sprinkled across a range of family computing and lifestyle magazines, for example, ads that show the computer as part of a new lifestyle orientation are not uncommon. In many of these ads, the computer is positioned within a happy family unit where family members are variously portrayed as pursuing educational, entertainment, work, or home management activities. The message is that the high-tech creative potential and portability of the technology can make 'work' easy and pleasurable. In some ads, the visual absence of computer users centres the technology as the focal and exclusive object of desire in its own right, embedded in signifiers of artistic creativity and imagination, affluence, European 'style', and 'class'.

This kind of analysis – a simple interpretative exposition without any high-theory technical jargon – could well serve as a starter exercise for the kind of critical 'cybercitizenship education' I referred to earlier. Questions students could address include: What market segment is being targeted by a particular ad? What information is excluded and included? What emotional appeals do the text and pictures make? What kind of a social environment is being created in an ad? Who are the technology users? Why are they predominantly white, Anglo-Saxon, and seemingly middle-class? How are women portrayed as technology users?

Much as the computer has become a new educational tool for use in home-based learning, uncoupling pedagogy, learning, and instruction from its traditional school base, so has work undergone a subtle relocation from traditional places and routines of the 'workplace' to the privacy of the home. But the blurring of traditional distinctions and difference has also affected the language with which we talk about and operate the new technologies. Language and conventional concepts of text, reading and writing – all of which are derived from print culture and print-based textual forms and practices – are changing and blending into new 'hybrid' terms, textual forms and practices.

Hybrid textualities

New forms of literate practice are not simply a matter of technology: a kind of hardware and software determinism that prescribes people's communications and information management skills. Rather, technologies always emerge as products of specific cultural practices, literate traditions, and the interests and desires of those groups who design and name them. Just as early mechanised print technology in the fifteenth century emerged in hybrid form as part scribal part print discourse, so computer mediation communications (CMC) is emerging as a blend of print text, sound and graphic imagery: a hybrid of the language of the book and the language of computer technology.

Consider the following hybrid forms of meaning that signify new forms of hypertextuality. In CMC, book-based practices and the naming of these practices are changing: 'click' or 'double-click' is replacing 'turn the page'. The term 'bookmark' is common menu currency for clicking on and recording a WWW site address – that is, putting an electronic bookmark where there is no book in the traditional sense of the term. The 'home page' refers to the opening screen display of a WWW site or 'document'. Yet the 'document' or hypertext, which consists of 'pages' and can be 'bookmarked', is itself paperless and pageless. The electronic 'desktop' is the interface between the phenomenal and the virtual, the material and the symbolic, from where we launch ourselves through our textual constructs from our 'desks' into an electronic realm of pure information.

Reading practices also are in flux: we don't read electronic text on-screen in the exclusively bookish direction from left to right but we scroll text vertically with increasing speed and visual acuity in order to identify the gist of a message and locate keywords on which to click. Or, consider the ubiquitous trash bin icon used to denote deletion of text and files, common in numerous text-processing software programs. The trash bin is a distinctively Western signifier because only in societies affluent enough to generate garbage can the concept of trash have any meaningful association with choice to discard excess. From the point of view of societies feeding off First World refuse – many of whom literally build communities on garbage dumps – the garbage can carries very different cultural meanings. The terms and language of use for negotiating electronically coded information, then, borrows from traditional (Western) print- and book-based culture which suggests new forms of cultural imperialism. These blended vocabularies and reading-writing practices require new multimodal and multimedia literacies that combine the horizontal linearity of print with the vertical scrolling and laterally connected (button 'hotlinks') features of electronic texts.

The discourse structures of e-mail combine aspects of face-to-face and written communication in new textual forms of conversational turn taking. E-mail writing is unlike any other form of writing, combining the immediacy of talk (the need to reply to a conversational turn) with the permanence of text. Yet electronic 'permanence' is ephemeral and unlike the durability and materiality of print text on paper. Unlike face-to-face or print-on-paper communication, e-mail writing tends towards more informal and conversational modes but also generates more abusive and opinionated textual productions (Miller 1993). Short messages, abbreviated writing, acronyms and emoticons – 'smilies' such as :–) ;–/ :–(– characterise e-mail writing which some critics consider detrimental to reflective language practice. However, e-mail communication, or navigating CD-ROMs or the Net do require writing and reading. In fact, rather than diminish the culturally valued practices of reading and writing, communication on e-mail, usenet and the Internet have generated 'an explosion of writing' (Kramarae 1995, p. 53), 'the biggest boom in letter writing since the 18th century' (Saffo 1993, p. 48).

Millions who write in online collaborative environments, such as e-mail-based chatgroups or bulletin boards, are constructing new writing and communication strategies developed through negotiating texts and meaning among a collective of often culturally diverse writers. In that regard the iconic language of emoticons can be seen as an artefact (and metaphor) of changing literacy and communication practices because they cut across linguistic and cultural differences, boundaries of geography or nation. The 'new' electronic writing is a different form of literacy – not an inferior or lesser form of some 'golden age' vision of literacy. The electronic typewriter was not a diminished form of literacy or handwriting, and nor was the advent of book culture and print literacy an inferior form of scribal culture and manuscript literacy. These, and the current shift to microchip culture and electronic literacy, are historically different media of communication which engender different forms of literacy, communication, knowledge production and dissemination.

Body and identity

In the social sciences it is axiomatic that the body – the social subject – is the fundamental unit of sociality and of social analysis. However, in digital hyperspace, bodily difference and the social values attached to visible differences are invisible and irrelevant. In the hypermedia realm of pure information – where we construct ourselves still primarily through text – distinctions of gender, ethnicity, body shape or impairment, accent or speech styles don't matter. We know from decades of research that the student with an accent or wearing a turban, the one with the lisp, the overweight or the indigenous student, is often treated differently from the mainstream 'ideal' student by teachers and peers. But in virtual communities, where one's social identity is wholly textually constructed, such differences vanish, which means that traditional categories of the social subject and social differentiation may no longer be useful. For instance, Bourdieu's concept of habitus as a site for the politics of difference may no longer be an adequate tool of analysis for investigating 'disadvantage' or 'difference' in pedagogical relations. What this means for pedagogy is that CMC eliminates a whole range of 'informal', often unconscious, assessments educators make of student ability based on visible cues of difference. On the one hand, then, cybersociality (or cyber-pedagogy for that matter) can free up a whole range of cultural and gender politics and yet the lack of embodied and gestural cues that accompany face-to-face communication (or pedagogy) can fail to alert us to the special circumstances or needs of the people we communicate with online.

Despite widespread claims that CMC democratises access to and participation in the information revolution by eliminating the visibility of and social values attributed to differences of gender, race, ethnicity, dialect, and other embodied features, the discourse of CMC is unmistakably male. The gendered register, style, imagery, and content of much of online communications, computer software language, CD-ROM entertainment, and the adjunct print discourse on cyberculture, computing, and Net surfing gear, is decidedly male (Cherney and Weise 1996; McKie 1994). Estimates vary, but it is generally agreed that about 80 per cent to 90 per cent of Internet users are white, male, and mostly between ages seventeen to forty-five (Baym 1995; Hayles 1993). On the Internet it's obvious that both pop cyberculture discourse (e.g. top-selling magazines such as *Wired*, *mondo*, *net*, *infobahn*) and the electronic frontier are overwhelmingly a male domain (Spender 1995; Stone 1995). The longest running and most popular of cyberculture magazines is the US publication *Wired* – 'the hottest, coolest, trendiest new magazine of the 1990s' (Borsook 1996, p. 24). Yet, according to Pauline Borsook, a former *Wired* staff writer, 'It seems that women, even the techno-initiated, generally do *not* like *Wired* because it basically has very little to offer women although 20 per cent of its readership is comprised of women' (Borsook 1996, p. 27). Anyone who has ever taken even a few minutes to leaf through the generally hefty volumes of *Wired* and other cyberculture magazines will readily spot the similarity to top-selling men's lifestyle magazines such as *GQ*, *Playboy*, *Penthouse*, or even *Sports Illustrated*, which is less about sports per se but, as Karen Coyle (Coyle 1996) says, more about 'balls', 'guy things', and affirmations of WASP American and African-American cultures and icons of masculinity. *Wired* has the

> same glossy pictures of certified nerd-suave things to buy – which, since it's the nineties, includes cool hand-held scanners as well as audio equipment and cars – and idolatrous profiles of (generally) male moguls and muckymucks whose hagiography is not that different from what might have appeared in *Fortune*. It is the wishbook of material desire for young men.
>
> (Borsook 1996, p. 26)

Despite the sense of anonymity assumed in the 'body-less' realm of virtual sociality, where actual material and bodily differences remain invisible or can be interpreted into almost any fictional virtual identity, cyberspace remains a realm that women navigate with caution (Balsmao 1994; Spender 1995). However, this is not to suggest that all women are put off by nerdy Net crawlers or intimidated by potential e-mail stalkers, abusive flaming, or electronic cross-dressers. There are indeed hundreds of women's newsgroups, bulletin boards, and WWW sites that are safe, friendly and 'nice places to visit and chat' (Cherney and Weise 1996; Kramarae and

Taylor 1993). Moreover, hundreds of thousands of women worldwide are part of cyberpunk virtual subcultures (Herz 1995). Much feminist political work gets done on the Internet among women who see cyberspace as a place to be heard, for free speech, and as means to share information and gain support. Women have been vocal on the Internet for years bringing to the attention of the world issues that do not always get taken up by the popular press. For example, during the breakup of the Baltic states, the conflict in Chiapas, Mexico, and the year leading up to the 1995 Fourth UN Conference on Women in Beijing, women were active online alerting the West about issues including human rights violations, rape as a widespread weapon of war and, in the case of the Beijing UN Conference, Chinese efforts to exclude Tibetan women. In short, the overwhelmingly male population of cyberspace, the distinctively gendered dimension of cyberculture discourse, the body-less and ostensibly genderless presence on the Internet have not precluded women's very vocal and 'visible' presence (Cherney and Weise 1996; Kramarae and Taylor 1993).

Pedagogy

Students connected to an online site can work with classmates down the hall, across the country, or from around the world. Students and teachers working in networked classrooms consistently report that computers encourage group learning and collaborative problem-solving (Becker 1992; Berston and Moont 1996). Unlike the solitary student at her desk in the traditional teacher-centred classroom, students in networked classrooms tend to prefer working together to pool their knowledge and skills in the search for information, navigating WWW sites and data bases (Gruber, Peyton and Bruce 1995). The ability to import, download, drop and drag text and imagery from an inexhaustible global library of information creates new skills, processes and multimodal forms of 'textual' production that encourage interdisciplinarity, creativity and imagination, collaborative authorship, editing, reading and writing, and problem-based learning. Anecdotal and empirical research evidence (e.g. Becker 1992; Gruber, Peyton and Bruce 1995) suggests that unlimited technology in the classroom – that is, fully networked laptop schools rather than schools with locked computer labs containing a handful of desktop PCs – 'leads to better problem solving ability, less truancy and greater collaboration between students', and teachers report feeling 'more like guides and less like lecturers' (Berston and Moont 1996, p. 43).

The multimodal and iconographic nature of the World Wide Web and CD-ROMs appeals to learners of all ages by mediating the difficulty and apprehension many first and second language learners often have. For LOTE learners, for example, the multilingual WWW, the possibility of international e-mail exchanges, and the countless international chatgroups or bulletin boards provide ideal opportunities for 'authentic' language experiences (Felix and Askew 1996). According to Ron Watts of the Open Net,

> some of the biggest advantages are going to come in language training. Once you start to put image and voice together – and you can do it right now – you can give students very good examples of speech and foreign languages along with images associated with the words, which we know is a very powerful way of language training.
>
> (Watts 1995, p. 73)

For second language learning or adult literacy instruction, the interactive and visually dynamic nature of networked CMC has tremendous potential to minimise the difficulties many students experience in language and literacy learning that is exclusively print- and book-based and augmented by static pictures, illustrations, or pre-recorded audio tapes. Setting students up with e-mail partners, for instance, is one simple way to encourage reading and writing. Many primary schools have used first-year university English students as e-mail partners with primary school students to 'talk' about the books they are reading in and out of school.

In one study of e-mail partnerships organised around the concept of peer tutoring, teachers found that the primary students couldn't wait to hear from their university partners, they always wrote back immediately, and the more frequent the responses, the longer and more detailed each e-mail post became (Curtiss and Curtiss 1995). The primary students enjoyed the experience because they discovered how to use a computer while also engaging in 'real-life' communication with 'adult' students who took the children's writing seriously. In response to one child's message: 'I rote a book called The 4 People football team and Its a real story', a university e-mail partner commented: 'I learned that children don't need to learn to read before they learn to write. I now know that it is a simultaneous process' (Curtiss and Curtiss 1995, p. 63). What this illustrates is that using CMC as a teaching–learning device doesn't just have to rest on the teacher's shoulder. There are many pedagogical resources available – including university students in this case – that can be used in peer tutoring contexts which can benefit all those involved. But it also illustrates one important principle which applies to beginning reader-writers of all ages: the simultaneity and fluid overlap of reading and writing development. As the e-mail partnership project shows, the use of computers as a different medium of classroom communication which made possible different ways of writing (i.e. keyboarding), and the use of community resources such as university students, served as a powerful motivational device and learning tool for the primary school students.

The pedagogical key for learners of all ages is to start with student resources: their skills, interests and contexts. This might mean logging in with other classes in other cities, states or countries, guiding some students to Web sites on car remodelling, volcanoes, 'X-File' trivia, whale watching, or devising group projects on topics of their choice where students search and collect information from virtual museums, libraries, movie studios, or tourist offices from around the world. Unlike the traditional library, the virtual library is open twenty-four hours a day, 365 days of the year. One doesn't need a swipe card or proof of enrolment to get into the best libraries in the world at any time of day.

For instance, imagine that we are conducting a group project with senior secondary or adult literacy students on, for instance, a hypothetical class trip to Thailand. Our Thai students probably will be able to provide a lot of local information on their home communities, but we also would want the class to visit the best libraries in the world to get more detailed and general information. In addition, we would suggest that a group of students find their way to the Thailand Tourist Office website for information on roads, weather, shopping, and vaccination requirements. Another group should visit some airline websites to get flight schedule and air fare information, and those who want to backpack should probably consult the website of Harvard Let's Go guide on backpacking hints. We also would want to know about cultural customs, foods, religion, and some general history. As a problem-based learning project, our hypothetical class trip to Thailand requires that students work in collaboration; that they organise and delegate various information gathering tasks among themselves; that they use a range of Internet and other media resources, and prepare individual or small group presentations: perhaps a little booklet or a series of brochures augmented by posters, video and oral presentations, and various displays. All these tasks require reading and writing, keyboarding and Internet (and CD-ROM) searching skills, as well as co-operative teamwork skills. Moreover, students apply Multiliteracies skills and are engaged in interdisciplinary learning, connecting diverse content areas related to the general topic of 'A Trip to Thailand'. A 'virtual class holiday' can be as focused or elaborate as teachers and students can imagine.

Navigating the Net requires writing and reading, but the interactivity and ease of button click hypertext navigation, coupled with the blending of graphics and print, eliminates reliance on the abstract and static nature of print-only text. Moreover, since computer-mediated learning tends to generate group rather than solitary learning, it encourages collective risk taking ('let's click here and see what happens'), collaborative problem-solving and information sharing. Collaborative learning can substantially minimise student performance anxiety associated with teacher demands for individual responses so common in the traditional Initiation–Response–Evaluation sequence of most classroom pedagogies (Becker 1992; Worthen, Van Dusen and Sailor 1994).

The virtual classroom will not replace the teacher or classroom but it certainly challenges traditional concepts of teacher authority, timetabling, disciplinary divisions, curriculum, and pedagogy founded on the linearity of print-based textbook learning. Cyber-pedagogy eliminates the teacher 'talking head' and puts an end to collection code curriculum wherein each content area comprises a collection of discrete facts and skills disconnected from other related disciplinary domains. Education at all levels, from primary to tertiary, is at a crossroads. Information technology is no longer an option for schools or teachers and traditional notions of schooling, pedagogy and literacy will inevitably be transformed into hybridised forms of place-bound and virtual schooling, face-to-face and cyber-pedagogy, and multimodal print-electronic-multimedia literacies. As Dale Spender comments:

> No aspect of education will remain untouched by electronic information. The emphasis will move (and has already moved) from the teachers and what they are teaching, to the students and what they are doing . . . computer mediated education will be a whole new world to teachers; one where teaching is subordinated to learning.
>
> (Spender 1995, p. 115)

Rather than having threatening implications for teachers' work, learning and teaching in cyberspace have the potential to enhance and expand teacher repertoires by taking tremendous pressure off their shoulders to be the sole source of classroom knowledge and interpretation. Once teachers are freed from the 'batch processing' of students through a 'mass-market basic curriculum', they will be in better positions to guide students 'to manage the pace of their online learning [which] will inevitably change the speed at which they progress through their education' (Petre and Harrington 1996, p. 107). Letting go of long-cherished tenets of teacher authority and control over all aspects of student learning may not be easy for many teachers trained in chalk-and-talk pedagogy, even in its 'student-centred learning' variant. But cyber-education benefits not only students. The networked teacher – the 'infonaut' charting a course with her students across the vast terrain of Internet communities, databases, and WWW sites – can connect with other teachers in online professional communities and thereby mediate the sense of isolation inherent in teachers' work (Williams and Bigum 1994).

The 'information revolution' is here and it's here to stay. It is therefore incumbent upon educators to be informed about the many issues at stake in order to take informed positions on IT implementation, on the development of supportive teacher professional development, and on the theoretical and practical development of a Multiliteracies and multimedia cyber-pedagogy. Equally important is the need to give all students the critical analytic tools with which to assess the sociocultural and political consequences of technological change. As discussed earlier, not all groups will have ready access to the new technologies and, in consequence, many will be disadvantaged in an increasingly competitive and shrinking labour market where computing and a range of communication and technological skills are considered fundamental. In that regard, social justice issues become even more crucial. Schooling cannot compensate for the profound structural inequities in society. However, the provision for all students – regardless of social circumstance, age, geographic location, or ability – of the technological and Multiliteracies skills requisite for equitable workforce competition and meaningful participation in society is both a social responsibility and an entitlement of all students in the impending Information Age.

4

MULTILITERACIES AND MULTILINGUALISM

Joseph Lo Bianco

Multiliteracies

The Multiliteracies Project aims to develop a pluralistic educational response to trends in the economic, civic and personal spheres of life which impact on meaning-making and therefore on literacy. These changes call for a new foundational literacy which imparts the ability to understand increasingly complex language and literacy codes; the ability to use the multiple modes in which those codes are transmitted and put to use; and the capacity to understand and generate the richer and more elaborate meanings they convey (Lo Bianco and Freebody 1997).

To develop a pedagogy that is effective in imparting to learners confident control over the codes, modes and meanings of the new literacies is, for this reason, an important part of the Multiliteracies Project. In this way, Multiliteracies aims to make salient those notions of literacy competence which are actively pluralist. It seeks, therefore, to chart an original path, different from the skills family of thought which emphasises the perceptual and technical procedures of decoding and encoding written language; different from the growth and heritage family of thought about literacy which emphasise the private, personal, individual relationships with written language; and different again from critical–cultural schools which emphasise variability in literacy practices and how variation correlates with social and ideological categories (Christie *et al.* 1991; Gilbert 1989).

The challenge I want to consider here is whether Multiliteracies can address the more substantive diversity of cultural and language differences while accommodating diversity of modality such as e-mail and visual literacy alongside the book and the letter. For in the transformed work, civic and private domains which have stimulated the Multiliteracies Project, competent functioning requires not only a Multiliteracies pedagogy but also multilingual and multicultural policies.

Personal bilingualism and societal multilingualism are inevitable and insistent consequences of the same globalisation which generates the multiple modalities of communication within single languages. Perversely, the same almost total globalisation of the last decade of the twentieth century gives rise to a homogenising imperative that threatens to contract linguistic and cultural diversity in a dramatically escalating way and make the multilingualism of modern nations a transitional stage towards a vastly reduced linguistic repertoire.

Globalisation's effects

Processes of international integration have accelerated in recent years to the point where almost complete globalisation is imminent. Three principal forces generate this seemingly inexorable emergence of a unified world system. The first is the almost universal phenomenon of market deregulation; the second is the advanced integration of international financial markets; and the third is the critical facilitating force of instantaneous communications.

A linguistic consequence of this is intra-lingual diversification and cultural tension. As English assumes the function of *lingua mundi* (Jernudd 1992), absorbing the *lingua franca* role of other international languages, a complex dynamic of cultural politics emerges (Pennycook 1994). The solidarity effects of language forms become interrupted for native English speakers when stable but radically different Englishes serve global communication needs. In such tension *laissez-faire* traditions of language policy can be cast aside and policies of officialisation of English, of mandating native speaker norms as correct and of promoting monolingualism can take hold (Cameron 1996; Lo Bianco 1997).

In this tension the language of affect for English speakers is no longer English as such, but a variety, and solidarity functions in language are transferred to standard varieties of the language (Marenbon 1987). In this way polycentricity (many norms of correctness that differ within an easy or uneasy intelligibility) emerges and 'English' becomes a network of inter-related models; a 'single interdependent communication matrix' (Pattanayak 1986, p. 59). These intra-language tensions accompany inter-language tensions which result from the practical collapse of the goal of nation-state language policy which sought to enshrine single national standard languages as emblems of distinctiveness and national cultural identity. The sheer scale of human movement has made multiculturalism a global phenomenon with unprecedentedly large and differentiated population transfers in all parts of the globe.

Languages caught up in the multimodal environment of contemporary communication, which combine verbal linguistic meaning-making with the gestural, visual, spatial, and the radically altered writing and reading regimes of computer literacy, such as oral-like writing and writing-like oralism in voice instruction, complicate literacy practices with multicultural contexts as the modes, codes and cultural meanings interact with each other.

The effect, then, of these forces for change is to make every nation need to come to grips, in public policy and in educational practice, with polyglot populations. Languages serve functions of affect and solidarity as much as the more obvious communication function. Since languages are emblematic of group identity in plural societies they present a strong contest to nations founded on concepts of unilingualism. But nations which construe themselves as pluralist, accommodating to diversity, imagining it as a resource in a globalising and multipolar world, are a recent innovation. The state has traditionally been either neutral or neglectful of popular multilingualism. More commonly it has been hostile.

Paradoxically, in the same moment of cultural, civic and personal diversity brought about by globalisation, with its hybrid language and cultural forms emerging from new population mixes, there is also a massive contraction of diversity. The spread of consumer society, with its gradations of industrial to post-industrial structure and the interconnected world-system of production and distribution of goods and services, constricts the social and semantic space for language systems which order the world in pre-industrial ways and whose speakers organise their sociality in ways incompatible with industrialised order. Much of contemporary cultural diversity consists of national inflections of an underlying consumerist commonality. Diversity, for this reason, may be more illusory than real.

Even as the technological changes that accompany and make globalisation possible themselves multiply and diversify, and as communication becomes progressively multimodal, the universalising and homogenising force of absorption into a common underlying ethic and process of signification is obliterating language diversity. During this and the next decade there will be the greatest collapse of language diversity in all history. In parallel with natural ecology, where species diversity is being rapidly eroded, human linguistic diversity is also contracting dramatically. It is a sobering thought that a staggering 90 per cent of the world's presently spoken languages are on the verge of extinction.

What does globalisation replace?

In agrarian and preindustrial society – the pre-nation state – language diversity was normal and unthreatening. According to Edwards, 'In all parts of the world there was benign linguistic neglect on the part of rulers' and 'given linguistically diverse empires, peace and prompt payment of taxes were the major concerns linking rulers and ruled' (Edwards 1994, p. 130).

The agrarian and pre-industrial state allowed space for diversity; rulers did not seek community with their subjects, preferring horizontal attachments of culture with either the dynastic systems or religious systems of rule in other political entities. The state's authority and purpose rarely included the inculcation of the ruled into normative patterns of culture that identified them with the rulers (Gellner 1983; Hobsbawm 1993; Seton-Watson 1977).

The nation-state, on the other hand, is constructed on the idea of a symmetry between ethnicity, or peoplehood as expressed in and by language among other defining factors, and the organs and structures of the state. A long and complex process produced such a dramatic change in the notion of a polity. The seeds, at least, of the nation-state's hostility to multilingualism can be discerned in this pre-nation-state. In particular two developments had an impact: the emergence of standard languages and the notion of national languages, subsequently fused in the idea of national standard languages.

From the late medieval period, language academies had worked to cultivate prestige literary forms of vernaculars. They did this primarily in the interests of cultures as civilisation, not cultures as rivalrous identifications. Such language cultivation was not explicitly addressed towards replacing vernaculars and the large chains of spoken language forms that typically were the communication tools of primarily rural populations. Rather these standardised literary forms were to sit on top of the communication patterns as an elite peak to a deprecated, but largely ignored, multilingual and multidialectal base.

The second seed in the agrarian world that led to the nation-state's hostile position with regard to minority languages came partly from the ideas of Romantic philosophers. Reacting against the rationalism of science which, through descriptive examination, was theorising genetic links and universal or common properties among languages, Romantic philosophy asserted the distinctiveness of individual languages. Languages were claimed to express the essential qualities of peoplehood. Individual languages were claimed to be distinctive of the essence of groups, and therefore of their differences. For the Romantics, what science might uncover about the common features of languages could not diminish their expressive power as emblems of the soul and character of the 'races' who spoke them and who were in turn themselves made, by the languages, into peoples. In this way, while the beginnings of linguistic chauvinism may lie elsewhere, a strong impetus for it results from the idea that particular languages provided for the carriage of identity and national character.

Such thinking influenced the later view that nations were, essentially, groups of people speaking the same language. The formula was something like: 'A group speaking the same language is known as a nation and a nation ought to constitute a state' (Kedourie 1961).

The nation as state

Language names give effect to the link between peoplehood and linguistic behaviours. The selection of a variety of language was made from the many spoken chains of communication. Spoken communicative practice, rarely self-conscious as language, was interrupted by the selection of one variety for its elevation to the role and function of national standard. This involves the de-selection and disempowerment of other varieties.

Naming one variety for fulfilling functions of national identification over other claimants is accompanied by another process, 'officialisation'. Officialisation involves allocating privileged, hierarchical functions and status to some, while deliberately excluding others. National languages are claimed to unify the nation, often a disparate people of the horizontal domain, and then are called upon to fulfil the functions of the state, the vertical axis of public administration (Enloe 1981). Language standard-isation, initially generated for literary reasons, then serves, through the precision and predictability that codified norms allow, the practical tasks of running state apparatuses. National minorities around the world still struggle today with the legacies of this dual elevation of single varieties within nation-states.

It is the 'nationing' of peoples through unitary forms of language around the world that is contributing to the reduction of language diversity worldwide.

The academies and dictionary writers could hardly have imagined that the outcome of their work would, in the hands of industrialism and nineteenth-century nationalism, be such a powerful tool for the practical job of inculcating whole populations, whose main unity often was that they shared the same geopolitical space, into national administration.

These 'practical' needs require the precision and accuracy of standard languages: the taking of a census; fitting workers into the labour force by making them minimally literate; or the creating of a school system (Hobsbawm 1993). These needs of 'nations-become-states' enshrined the position of the standardised form of national languages.

The dysfunctional nation-state?

The nation as state, in its classic or canonical form, has now had to concede enormous ground. One reason has to do with the size and great diversity of modern states, especially those in the New World; another with the failure of most classic 'ethnically pure' nation states to eliminate internal diversity completely. Finally, of course, there has been the impact of processes of globalisation and of regionalism, usually for reasons of economic self-interest but often leading to substantial interdependency.

In clan life, in villages, or in small settings of any type, community is sustained materially through interdependent practices of life, such as subsistence farming; the common tending of property; mutual and manifest dependence on resources; or through the ritualised ways in which cultures re-present communality to their members. However, modern nations may be really too vast and populous to sustain community materially in such ways. Such nations are imagined communities (Anderson 1983).

The nation-state constructed on a unitary set of affiliations did not eliminate diversity and multilingualism; rather it marginalised them functionally. Interdependence in the economic realm and other conditions of possibility, such as instantaneous and uncontrolled communications, easy mobility, mass migrations and the new pluralisms such population transfers have produced, have led to the possibility of the transcendence of the nation-state as the exclusive organising structure for political affairs.

The emergence virtually everywhere of pluralistic nations necessitates new distinctions between the political nation and the cultural nation. An homogeneous, or rather a unitary, political nation, embodied in egalitarian citizenship, can be conceptualised as the common ground which allows diversity and heterogeneity in the cultural nation. Indeed it may be possible to secure cultural diversity only on the basis of uniformity in the political and economic realm. The defeat of the homogenising tendencies of the classic nation-state depends in large part on the idea of citizenship as the aggregating principle and the internal need, reinforced by external pressure and economic self-interest, for linguistic tolerance and cultural diversity.

The super-state and the micro-nation

Many of today's polities do not invoke ethnicity, culture, religion, or dynastic succession. NAFTA, EU, APEC, and ASEAN are acronyms that describe regionally derived economic–political and strategic units. Geographic regionalism for the conduct of economic affairs is burgeoning in all parts of the world. The world appears to be splitting into three gigantic trade blocs – a dollar-dominated American zone, a yen-dominated Asia and a Deutschmark-dominated Europe. Within such zones economic entities progressively manage, in a technicist, economically rationalist way, the macro affairs of vast populations.

Dual or multiple citizenships abound; passport control is shared if not conceded by individual nations to supranational authorities; population mobility is currently at unprecedented levels. National governments struggle to limit and circumscribe the depletion of their control over populations; controls that once appeared to be unassailable. Population mobility and facilitated communication are essential, requiring high levels of cultural adjustment.

As the super state is too large to meet the identity needs of its constituents so at its heart the micro-nation emerges. Supranational entities appear less likely to oppose regional and local minorities in their interest in language maintenance. It is no accident that in 1991–2 the European Union and the Council of Europe opened up funded education to exactly the same minority languages that the same member states had tried for generations to obliterate in the interests of national cohesion.

Political structures based on notions of economic co-operation are not as concerned with the persistence of local languages of identity as states based on ethnic homogeneity. The communicative function of language is more salient. In Europe proximal groups whose languages were divided by arbitrary political borders are regrouping across old barriers, as internal borders become narrower and lower, and reviving languages of affect and contact, even for local economy.

The Red Book

In February 1992, a group of linguistic experts was convened by a UNESCO programme which deals with the cultural heritage of the world to consider and report on the language diversity of the world. The experts called for 'world solidarity' to preserve 'the non-physical cultural heritage' of the world and its endangered languages (UNESCO 1992) and recommended the issuing of a *Red Book on Endangered Languages*. This alarm was generated by their finding that 90 per cent of the world's currently spoken languages are endangered and may become extinct within one or two generations. Depending on the exactitude of definition there are between five thousand and six thousand spoken languages today and at present rates of extinction there will remain only some five to six hundred by 2020, only a small handful of which will be spoken by sizeable numbers of people (Vines 1996).

For those nations or regions of the world that are excluded from the global integrated economy, and for those regions of countries that are otherwise part of the global economy but which themselves are not, a massive attrition of language and cultural diversity is currently under way. In the face of such relentless absorption of the world's societies into the web of consumer capital, 'experts' can offer only two (impotent and questionable) responses: either more research or a programme of human 'museumification'.

> On the basis of a feasibility study, a number of regional ecological language reserves to protect the endangered or dying languages can be set up. Their aim will be to keep the ecology of endangered languages intact or to reduce the risks of their irreversible extinction. These are experimental laboratories for the scientists and managers concerned, aimed at enabling them to find out the most effective means of preserving numerous expressions of the non-physical cultural heritage.
>
> (UNESCO 1992)

Phillipson and Skutnabb-Kangas (Phillipson and Skutnabb-Kangas 1986, p. 20) have labelled the advancement of languages of wider communication, and the subsequent death of indigenous languages, *linguicism*. By this they denote the crime of linguistic genocide and the reduction of the number of the world's languages. The major criminal in their scenario is English although there are a number of regional languages of wider communication in Africa, Asia and South America – sometimes through deliberate language planning but probably more commonly via the operation of linguistic 'market forces' – which are also restricting the domains and functional range of pre-existing languages and leading to their death.

Bilingualism: skill versus sedition

In the same breath that America's politicians seek to make English the official language – the language for which there are year-long waiting lists in some cities for access to places in adult programmes – they are also commending the study of foreign language as a skill (Zelasko 1993). In education debates, bilingual education is frequently deprecated as a 'cash cow' and claimed as an enemy of American civilisation (Gingrich 1995), yet at least '33 Federal agencies have over 34, 000 positions which require foreign language proficiency' (Lo Bianco 1997). These are in languages where proficiency is seen to be a skill, where the languages are desirable as Truly Foreign Languages or TFLs and thereby deemed capable of being able to 'add to or sustain a national competency' (Walton 1992).

Mastery of foreign languages, spoken far away 'in other countries', is something sufficiently divorced from daily life that it can be appreciated as a skill. Its mastery is likely to be less than the mastery and attachment to English, not thereby challenging presumed deep attachments of national allegiance. However, when the languages are less foreign, when emotional attachment and mastery may be high, their study, public use and maintenance 'threaten civilisation'. No longer a skill, but sedition.

Designing multilingual futures

The Multiliteracies Project seeks to create a metalanguage to unite disparate areas of communication and representation, multimodally as well as multiculturally, into a new pedagogy. Much of its justificatory logic is the potential for pluralism within globalisation. However, as argued above, this pluralism can be seen to be deeply ambiguous. At the same moment as globalisation is generating cultural diversity, technological sophistication and civic pluralism, the linguistic diversity of the globe is contracting dramatically and within new and established nation-states formal practices of statecraft valorise distanced, foreign skill in languages and neglect or deprecate domestic language diversity.

For this reason a Multiliteracies pedagogy must be able to adopt a wider vision and envisage a linguistically plural society and future. Unilingualism sits comfortably with, and gives credence to, ideas of naturalness and inevitability of world view. These can be made vulnerable only through the study of other languages and the interruption of the naturalness to which each predisposes its users. As the largest signifying system and set of practices available to humans, languages represent the embodiment of pluralist alternatives. Languages are potentially continually additive because there is theoretically no limit to the number which could be learned, and they are cumulative because their learning requires systematicity since knowedge and skill are built on necessary prior knowledge and skill. They are also embedded in wider cultural practice because they are systemically integral to the symbolic order of the culture of which they form a part. The maintenance and acquisition of additional languages, within a pedagogy of explicit attention to the surrounding sociocultural context, may generate intercultural skill and competence few other areas of education could aspire to; add rigour and academic substance few other curriculum domains could equal; and, because languages are performative, require the acquisition of rules of practice and implementation that only practical 'hands-on' subjects envisage.

Each of the dimensions of the 'what' of the Multiliteracies Project is capable of integrally accommodating bilingual competence. Designs of meaning in languages differ and reflect arbitrary constructs of 'reality'. Available Designs as resources for Design are discursive orders shaped by languages, and within them are the conventions of semiotic activity particular to different 'lifeworlds'. Their multiplication across languages strengthens the purpose of Multiliteracies in focusing on the grammars of semiotic systems to give students transportable knowledge and skill for participation in rapidly evolving communication environments. The process of Designing inherently carries the negotiating practice of languages, the pragmatics of meaning-making which allows pidgin languages to be created in a matter of hours. The proximity of languages without historical relationships produces original compromises for communication similar to the new Designs that emerge as the outcomes of Designing new meanings.

Integrally, then, the teaching and learning of other languages bolsters the purpose and practice of Multiliteracies, enabling each of its phases to de-naturalise communicative practice and thereby to render it more available to scrutiny. The policies of education systems in many countries, which seek continually to define the literacies and languages of immigrant minority and indigenous students as defective by assessment against established norms, could be subverted by attaching recognition to the potential articulacy of these same students. This squandered bilingualism is the direct result of the inability of education systems to comprehend the intellectualisation of a potential bilingual skill. Many children utilise complex literacy awareness and talent daily; literacies which invoke ethnic, ideological, religious, script, technical and nation-identity statuses (Saxena 1994) in a marketplace of authorised, traditional and hybrid forms. Like spoken language, diversity in the plural literacy practices of minority children is often relegated to the margins of their lives. Yet they have within them the power to open up new intellectual worlds which are, at the moment, linguistically and intellectually closed to us.

The Multilteracies team has set itself several tasks for development, one of which is the accommodation of the pedagogy to include true linguistic diversity. It is already evident from the trials of the Multiliteracies framework in South Africa (see Newfield and Stein, Chapter 14 below) that language diversity is perceived by students to be a crucial area for further development. It is critical to avoid the normalising, or 'naturalising', of English language and literacy with consumer capital society.

The challenge faced by the Multiliteracies Project is to develop a theory of communication and meaning making for a radically changing world. The challenge of language variation and variation in language attitudes and communication patterns are both internal to language and part of the wider linguistic ecology of which each language is a part. For instance, it is possible in certain languages to raise questions that are not typically encountered in other languages. Certainly some questions cannot be adequately comprehended within the English language. There is simply no linguistic provision for this to take place.

To explain this point I will use three separate examples. First, written Japanese, a language which consists of three interacting script forms: Kanji (adapted Chinese ideograms); a syllabic system of fifty-six items called Hiragana which is used mainly for grammatical particles; and a variation of Hiragana, also of fifty-six items, called Katakana.

Katakana is like a more sharp-edged form of the syllabic system of Hiragana but it is interesting mainly in relation to our concept of Multi-literacies because of the ideological work that it performs in Japanese writing. The social and literacy functions of Katakana in Japanese communication systems come from its exclusive use to render foreign words in written form. When a second language learner of Japanese encounters the required use of Katakana the effect is like a semiotic jolt. The practice of reading and writing anything encodes a constant reminder, that for a learner requires conscious attention to a dimension of language of which English speakers can be barely conscious. This is the boundary which marks the foreign from the indigenous; both the existence and the extent of loans within a language. Whatever pragmatic force impels borrowing mostly in the spoken form it becomes phonologised and nativised. Written Japanese requires, however, its constant elevation, keeping before the learner a theory about language and its emblematic function for its native users.

There is a slight parallel in English, which can be glimpsed in the 1981 edition of the *Macquarie Dictionary*, which represents the first dictionary of English from an Australian standpoint. This dictionary adopted the practice of giving Australian usages the unmarked form, with an asterix serving as a mark, both literally and linguistically, of foreign Englishes. If the effect of Katakana is a semiotic jolt for learners of the language it must be experienced differently, but no less significantly, by its native users. Mother-tongue readers and writers of Japanese may have a sort of recurring, underlying, practice of having to operationalise a national/ foreign boundary marking, via a distinctive script form which is like a sort of subliminal, habitual coding of loans. Kanji operates as an imported but nativised system for encoding Japanese words, while Katakana is a native system for encoding foreign words. There is both a practice – and a reason – for making salient a script alternation pattern around word origins. A theory of communication cannot but be influenced by coding practices that carry such depth of meaning.

My second, and perhaps more dramatic, example of script meaning-making of which there is no parallel in English comes from Vietnam. Vietnam has an ancient literary tradition. In the early eleventh century learned activity took place at the Temple of Literature in Hanoi. Exams were held to determine who was granted access to the Temple and to pursue a scholarly life. The exams were in Chinese, Chu Han, for Vietnam was at that time a colony of China.

For several centuries Vietnamese scholarship proceeded in Chinese using Chu Han, the Chinese ideograms. During the fourteenth century, however, the Vietnamese language itself evolved an indigenous writing form – Chu Nom – which used Chinese characters in combinations unintelligible to Chinese speakers. Ideograms are, of course, a radically different literary idea from the alphabetic script which the English language uses. The decoding of an ideogram involves instant access to an idea not mediated by the sound of letters or letter groups. Chu Nom further complicated ideogram-decoding by encoding both idea and grammar.

Chinese writing and its Vietnamese variant co-existed for centuries. Chinese was reserved for courtly affairs; for administration, education and government and other high-level tasks, even after Chinese colonial rule was over. Chu Nom, on the other hand, came to be used for vernacular or popular writing; for stories and poems about everyday life. Chu Han ruled and Chu Nom was for the ruled. This socially divided concept of literacy, or script hierarchy, remained until the seventeenth century when French priests devised a romanised representation of spoken Vietnamese, which came later to be called Quoc Ngu.

It is interesting to speculate about how we might regard these competing scripts within a Multiliteracies framework. Perhaps colonialism is an Available Design whose semiotics pervade script selection and use. In the long period of transition from colonial rule this goes through the process of being Redesigned, transforming its meanings into new Available Designs; Designs which will always carry the messages of the old system in the bruises and shape of the new forms. For the two centuries after Quoc Ngu emerged, Vietnamese literacy involved a series of struggles between Chu Han for ruling; Chu Nom for identity; and roman script for Catholicism and conversion. Quoc Ngu was despised by the users of Chinese, and resented by Chu Nom users.

As French colonial domination and rule took hold of the country, language policy became a critically important tool of its ruling, just as it had been for the Chinese rulers of Vietnam. There were several attempts to promote Quoc Ngu, as well as some attempts by French colonial elites to reinforce Chinese, since with this writing domination came a rigid hierarchy the French imagined would be easier to control than the possibly revolutionary effects of vernacularisation. French attempts to promote the French language both in spoken and written forms were, however, paramount; their attempts to promote Chinese were motivated only by the effort to remove Vietnamese from nationalist literature in Chu Nom, but resisted by the Confucian-loyal scholar class and independence-minded nationalists. Nobody desired, or even imagined possible, mass and popular literacy in any script.

During the twentieth century national opposition to French colonialism fused with communist politics. Literacy became an object and a means of fostering independence and rebellion. Quoc Ngu was reappraised from a European imposition to a practical tool for mass literacy. The complex history and struggle of Vietnam led eventually to the full adoption of Quoc Ngu – initially Catholic proselytising writing – as the national script, via successful mass literacy campaigns.

Vietnam thus became the only Confucian society to adopt alphabetic writing. Vietnamese society and history thus have available to them a tradition, a set of practices and meanings, an experience of literacy, of language literacy, and of scripts in language literacy, that can truly be called Multiliteracies. When Vietnamese read and write, these very acts invoke meanings which English does not know. Accretions of meaning built on to script in anciently sanctioned ways makes literacy more than some ecological process; it is a cultural achievement in which standards are sanctioned and carry deep messages.

In this way, even though the script battle has been resolved in favour of romanised writing, the designs available for literate practice in Vietnam have dimensions, complexities and resonances that a theory of communication and meaning-making such as that proposed by the Multiliteracies Project must acknowledge and incorporate.

Examples of this can be found in certain religious-based literacy practices – what might be called devotional reading. In some religious practices, reading holy books or holy words, which are often gendered and specified by age, requires motion such as rocking and other gestural practices. These are critical to the reading since the relation between reader and text involves transcendence. Committing sacred words to the body, that is infusing the body or embodying the word and its transcendent knowledge, is a meaning-making (or meaning-receiving) form of communication that is not readily identifiable in English or any other Western literary practice. I can think of some Christian mystic practices that indeed do involve literacy events and practices that are distinctive in some ways – for example, what Shakers practise – but there are few devotional reading and reciting practices whose meaning is dependent on motion or gesture.

There are, however, many mystical practices in many religions and typically words with powers of transcendence, which, after all, is what a mantra essentially constitutes, feature in these practices. These are Designs, if you like, available to participants, practitioners and believers. The process of Designing, and the Redesigned, both confirm and reproduce patterns from the culture and society and belief community. Invariably these are multimodal and much more ancient than any modality combinations that we accept as being multimodal.

My final example is more down to earth. Both the British national curriculum and the Australian curriculum frameworks and new literacy benchmarking activities have struggled with, but ultimately fail to accommodate, linguistic difference. Language diversity is either trivialised or confined to the outer spaces of a centre staked out exclusively for a monolingual literacy in standard English.

Mukul Saxena (Saxena 1994) has argued persuasively about the complex literacy awareness and practices of Panjabi families, and especially the children in Southall in England, who deal with script choices and their associated religious identities: Panjabi written in Gurmukhi script and associated with Sikhs; Hindi written in Devanagari script and associated with Hindus; and Urdu which is written in Perso-Arabic script and associated with Muslims. As Saxena explains, all three languages can be written in all three scripts, with everyday Hindi and Urdu being very similar in their spoken form and especially in their grammar. However in certain contexts these are made to diverge with the importation of either Sanskrit or Perso-Arabic origin words to mark Hindu or Muslim allegiance. Combined with English literacy, children in families with several generations have available to them literacies that mark Western/South Asian choices, Muslim-secular-Sikh-Hindu choices, and various nationalisms. Children from such backgrounds show impressive literacy skill and subtle awareness of the complex worlds of identity choices in the continuum of Hindi-Urdu-Panjabi language. According to the dictates of national curriculum initiatives, however, such children are deemed to be pre-literate because these assessments are based on English literacy alone, ignoring, or at worst not identifying, this complexity.

Similarly, the professional elaboration to the literacy benchmarks in Australia currently make no mention of English as a second language, bilingualism, or any of the non-prestige Englishes for that matter. It is as though schooled literacy in English in Australia can assume a native English community of learners. There is not one mention of traditional literacies in Australia; not one reference to the patterns of integration of signs, gestures, meaning in landforms and art which are an Australian literate tradition of great antiquity; let alone any mention of the spoken language differences from the assumed standard English norm which is seen to underlie all literacy learning in school. It is literacy issues such as these that the Multiliteracies Project must address in the future.

Within a pedagogy of Multiliteracies, languages other than English, foreign languages, individual and social bilingualism, and, more broadly, global language diversity justify their space. A Multiliteracies pedagogy cannot but be multilingual.

5

HISTORY, CULTURAL DIVERSITY AND ENGLISH LANGUAGE TEACHING

Martin Nakata

What does a tiny group of indigenous people in Australia have to do with the much broader problem in English language teaching of accommo-dating the recent recognition of changing and multifaceted aspects of language use in an the emerging technological and global marketplace? The short answer to this is that since the early 'contact' periods of European migration to the Australian continent over two centuries ago, both Islanders and Aborigines learned very early on that they had to live and work around emergent changes to their historical trajectories. The fact that modern language use may be technologically or globally changing thus is not something new to the first peoples of the Australian continent. However, facing the challenges together to renew a literacy pedagogy we have all become so familiar with is a new development.

While I am not a teacher of English, I am a researcher of literacy and pedagogy, and a Torres Strait Islander who has for a long time been advocating a more focused and urgent pursuit of English education in the Torres Strait Islands. Many people in the field find it hard to understand and accept that we do want English education; to do this requires an understanding of our history. Our needs are currently at risk from those who argue that the teaching of English undermines traditional language and culture, without understanding how that has developed in the recent past. The belief that English has relevance only for those Islanders who wish to pursue a life outside the Straits or for those in the sector of the marketplace that requires a higher education is quite wrong.

I want to emphasise at the outset that although I will be critical of the cultural agenda here, this is only because of its primacy in educational circles and because of the complacency of an attitude which asserts that a cultural agenda is all that is needed to address the wide range of issues and problems Torres Strait Islanders face in formal schooling in English. In no way am I wanting to suggest that we should abandon the cultural agenda. What I want to get across is that it would work more powerfully alongside a more focused approach to English language teaching. There will, however, be no prescriptions – no ABCs to a quick fix. In the complex area of indigenous education, especially in Australia, there is no longer room for such measures in language learning and teaching. Instead, it will take all of us, working together systematically as well as progressively and putting in huge efforts at a collaborative level, to make any impact. And at the very least, it will require that we first take a long hard look at what we have been doing thus far.

But first, who are the Torres Strait Islanders and what is our recent history? We are the first inhabitants of the islands in the Torres Strait, which lies between the tip of Cape York Peninsula, Australia, and the southern coastline of Papua New Guinea. We are predominantly of Melanesian origin but since the first days of missionary and pearling activity there has been considerable interracial mixing with South Pacific people, South-East Asians, and to a lesser extent with Europeans. The population of the Torres Straits is approximately five thousand but there is a much larger population on the Australian mainland; a migration which began in the 1960s for economic and political reasons by those Islanders who wanted to improve their living standards and life-chances and who were frustrated by the conditions of their lives in the Straits at that time. Islanders are recognised as first peoples of the Australian nation, alongside but distinct from Aboriginal people. They have always been traders (McCarthy 1938) and travellers (Haddon 1904) looking outward to the north that is Papua New Guinea and to the south that is Australia, as well as being on guard against any unwelcome intruders.

When the London Missionary Society first arrived in the Torres Strait in 1871 they were intending merely to use the Straits as a stepping stone to evangelise Papua New Guinea (McFarlane 1888). So the earliest experience of formal education for Islanders was an integral part of the missionary project to spread the Gospel. The pastors of the Mission believed that to be a Christian was to 'live a certain way of life' and so they systematically set about reorganising Islander ways of life; mostly with consent and persuasion but also with some brutal sanctions for those who infringed the new codes of conduct (Beckett 1987). Islanders thus were propelled upon a path that required both a certain level of literacy and numeracy and the pursuit of material possessions (McFarlane 1888). These things were to be had from our participation in the education process and through our labour in commercial activity. And we were almost continuously self-supporting until the 1960s (Imms 1961).

The missionaries achieved this physical reorganisation remarkably quickly and, by the time there was a settled government presence on Thursday Island in 1877, the missionaries held considerable sway over a number of Islands. As the cornerstone of the missionary project, the London Missionary Society founded the Papuan Institute on Murray Island and began taking willing Islanders from all over the Straits (Langbridge 1977). This Institute consisted of an industrial school, which taught boat building, forging and other building skills, as well as a seminary. Before entering the seminary the boys had 'to be able to read and write tolerably well . . . They then receive[d] a course of instruction in the English language, geography, practical arithmetic, object lessons, Bible history and indeed every subject which the portion of Scripture in hand suggests' (McFarlane 1888, p. 89). On the other islands, schools were established alongside the churches as well.

In 1885, John Douglas, a former Queensland Premier, was appointed as government magistrate in the Islands and remained in the islands until his death. He seems to have held Islanders in high regard and was quite liberal in his views. On 17 January 1900, he had this to say to the Royal Geographical Society of Australasia: 'The natives of the islands of the Torres Strait are capable of exercising all the rights of British citizens, and they ought to be regarded as such' (Douglas 1899–1900, p. 35). He made reference also to their desire for education and English:

> They are a growing and intelligent people, and they want to be educated. They want to be educated even more than our people. They show an inclination for education which often exceeds that of our own white population. This is not an extreme statement. It is a true statement, which I can prove by facts, and I am quite sure that anyone who saw these people would be quite convinced that what I have said is true.
>
> (Douglas 1899–1900, p. 35)

> There are nearly 100 children on Mabuiag Island. The people are very anxious that their children should learn English, and they desire them to learn English because they know their prospects will be materially assisted by their knowledge of English. I am trying to secure a volunteer, either male or female . . . A good school ma'am while teaching the young children would thereby obtain an influence upon the people.
>
> (Douglas 1899–1900, p. 33)

In 1892, Douglas began appointing teachers to some communities, although he seems to have had some trouble finding people to work in such isolated conditions. He also instituted a system of elected councillors to run village affairs and to liaise with him – an arrangement unparalleled in the colonial Pacific (Beckett 1964). It provided a counterpoint to the missionaries who managed village life and regulated moral standards through their church law. Though these elections fell rather short of democratic procedure, Islanders did engage somewhat with regard to their own internal affairs. However, a close reading of the texts, particularly of what was instituted as 'Island-law', shows that much of the 'law' was rooted in the church rather than traditional law, and much of it had no equivalent in Australian law (e.g. nine o'clock curfews; daily inspections of houses at breakfast time to ensure everyone was 'eating well'; and supervising personal habits and hygiene).

Perhaps Douglas's main achievement was to keep Islanders from being regulated under the Aboriginals Protection and Restriction of the Sale of Opium Act 1897. This he managed to do by arguing that Islanders were capable of running and managing their own affairs and acquiring citizenship rights – a position which was reversed unfortunately upon his death in 1904. J. W. Bleakley (Imms 1961), a Chief Protector of Aborigines in Queensland, in his recount of the events records the change as such:

> Because of their supposed superiority . . . the control of the Aboriginals protection laws had not been applied to them. A few seemed to manage their affairs quite satisfactorily, and some thrifty ones even had bank accounts. But ample evidence began to be seen that the majority were unable to protect themselves from unscrupulous dealers and, particularly, from the drink traffic.
>
> (Imms 1961, p. 255)

After Douglas's death, therefore, the Islanders moved into a new phase of their history. Although they were not removed from their land as were Aborigines in Queensland, and although families were not split up, the terms and the conditions of the Act were much the same. For Islanders, this period of Protection from 1904 until 1971 included complete control over their movements and their finances, their wages, their employment, and their labour as well as their communications, both within the Straits and outside (Beckett 1987; Campbell *et al.* 1958; Imms 1961).

During this period the administrative goal that emerged was to develop a self-sustaining community, separate and apart from the Australian community; a community that might eventually be able to have Home Rule, albeit under paternal supervision, should the Islanders aspire to it and show themselves to be capable of it (Imms 1961, p. 255). While the isolation of the Islands helped keep unwelcome intrusions out, and allowed Islanders to incorporate outside practices along customary lines – the legacy of which is a strong continuing Islander custom – it also denied Islanders communication with and knowledge of the outside world.

It was during this period also that the marine industry expanded, making huge profits for southern-based companies. This same industry had brought with it the need for earlier government regulation, as it was the enormous wealth of this industry that moved Queensland to annex our

Islands. With traditional life already interrupted by the missionaries, the incorporation of Islanders into the cash economy encouraged the pursuit of material improvements.

In the days of Protection, teachers were appointed not for their academic qualifications but for their 'common sense' and ability to perform administrative duties. Resources were limited and government financial input was minimal. By 1909, there were four hundred children enrolled in six schools, under six white teachers/administrators. To assist the teacher, intelligent pupils were selected to teach and monitor the lower classes and later a teacher training institution of some sorts was established for promising pupils. Promising pupils were also apprenticed to boat builders and engineering workshops. In 1927, following requests from Islanders, and from concerns that the gap between the schools and the requirement for the theological college was too great, a secondary school at one of the islands was proposed but never proceeded with. By 1938, there were fifteen schools with an enrolment of 1036 pupils and nine European teachers. The schools were not run by the Education Department but by the Department of Native Affairs – schools in the Torres Straits, excluding those on Thursday Island, the administrative centre, did not come under the control of the Education Department until 1985.

The most promising pupils, at this later stage, were now being channelled into administration and clerical roles, teaching, nursing, and the trades, generally at the assistant level. Government policy continued to aim 'not so much at raising standards of living as at preparing Islanders for even greater self-reliance' (Barrett 1946). No secondary schooling was forthcoming but, as a concession, the brightest pupils were selected for a further three years' schooling on Badu Island.

During the Second World War, the threat of Japanese invasion from the north resulted in the evacuation of everyone except the Islanders from the Islands. It brought the marine industry to a halt and it brought a military garrison to the area. And, in accepting Islander volunteers for the defence of the area, it opened up the outside world to the Islanders in a way that had never been possible before. More importantly, it introduced the Commonwealth government to Islanders as a higher authority than the state. What happened in many parts of the colonised world at this time in history also happened here. The Islanders were exposed to the discourse of freedom – the propaganda ideology that solicited a concerted effort from the Australian population to defend and fight for certain principles of freedom (Beckett 1987).

The Islanders, unfortunately, assumed that they were in fact fighting for their entitlement to be free. Exposed to the friendship of white soldiers, they learned considerably about their position in relation to white Australians. They learned that they were not equal citizens. They learned that they were not materially or educationally anywhere near the standards of white Australians. They learned that they did not receive equal pay. A couple of small protests were staged but, interestingly, they began to articulate their case through the discourse of citizenship, and equal rights, and freedom. They were led to believe that after the war everything would change and their frustrations would be over. But this was not to be, although they made quite specific demands, including 'proper' schooling, secondary education, equal pay, control over their finances, freedom of movement and the vote. In short, they were demanding an end to the Act (Beckett 1987).

After the war, Islanders went straight back under the Act and, though it was never enforced as stringently as in prewar times, it was administered until 1971, and in fact, there is still an Act just for us, the Community Services Act. It is in this postwar period we see the big Catch-22 for Islanders. The cry for citizenship which went up in the Straits, and indeed all around the colonised world, was met in the Torres Straits with a response from the government of caution and pacification. Were Islanders with their low levels of education ready for the entitlements of citizenship? Or should they wait until they were in a better position to understand the full responsibilities that went with citizenship? The demand was once again made for higher levels of education. However, the cry for freedom was quelled with a cautionary hose until even the most radical communities acquiesced by conceding that they were not ready for the responsibility. There was never again mass political action. Nevertheless, with the United Nations came the human rights discourse and outside forces began to exert an influence on Commonwealth and state governments. Islanders began to associate the Commonwealth government with freedom and the state government with control and oppression.

For me, the history of our struggle to mediate the effects of administrative control is reflected in the history of our calls for education and English. With discontent, dissatisfaction, scepticism about official explanations of these controls and ongoing frustration about their position, Islanders continued to pursue education as the means for meeting their desire for control. When grievances could not be accommodated by the administration and when concessions never fully satisfied Islanders, their response was always to renew their calls for a better education. This is not surprising when administrators rationalised their continuing control of Islander life on the grounds that Islanders were not in a position to look after themselves. The migration to the mainland that took place in the 1960s was considered by many to be a collective political statement about conditions in the Islands.

So what does this history tell us about what Islanders were doing?

Missionaries, pearlers and colonial administrators effected a rupture that could not and cannot be undone. Islanders have embraced change and have never retreated from this. Instead, we responded and engaged intelligently with it. As change rolls through our lives, Islander custom changes and adjusts but Islanders make it what it is. We have pursued formal education in English. Through individual and collective persistence we have migrated in the pursuit of equal living standards and better education without waiting for the Act to be abolished. We have experienced change and somehow realised that to mitigate the effects of that change required us to pursue English education.

It is often suggested that this pursuit of English education was a 'misplaced hope' that, even on the mainland, education in that period could not even raise the levels for the working white classes, let alone Islanders. Islanders, it is repeatedly argued, don't really understand what they are calling for when they call for English and Western education. Their aspirations are unrealistic and far beyond their needs. In fact, this couldn't be further from the truth.

We were actively engaged in a political way, within the very real constraints of the colonial order, with increasing our capacity to mediate and control outside forces and improve the conditions of our lives. In the face of constant denial of more freedom, we pursued education as a means to earning the rights of entitlement. This is the history of a people who are outward looking and progressive; embracing change and struggling to have some control of those changes. We have evolved a strong and vibrant Islander custom from the remnants of pre-contact culture; one which continues to centre our meaning-making system on traditional forms while adjusting ourselves to the external forms of capitalism for our own material and political benefit. An English education will enable us to negotiate our position in relation to these outside influences.

At present, when Islanders call for English literacy we are told we need literacy in one of our traditional languages first. Why do we need to read and write in our first language which is after all still a robust oral tradition? Simply because it works in French Canada! This standpoint assumes that learning English at school cancels out children's previously acquired and ongoing acquisition of their first language competencies and communicative patterns. On the contrary, our history shows forward and outward-looking Islanders successfully domesticating outside forms and practices into their own meaning-making systems. What about harnessing Creole in the teaching process as an oral aid? Why take the time to teach how to read and write it when it is a vibrant, changing oral language?

This same standpoint also assumes that our language is synonomous with our identity; that our culture is our identity. Having read the history, it is obvious that Islander identity is also a product of colonial rule, in part derived from our responses to colonial rule. Our identity has everything to do with our political struggle. Holding on to our languages and holding on to our cultures is an important part of that struggle, but clearly they are not the only defining elements of our identity.

Our group identity has been historically forged for political purposes, in the face of outside control. Moreover, it is not just 'the essence' of our culture that is so intrinsic to us but it is also our capacity to form and reform it as the contexts of our lives change. We don't need to stress cultural identity to compensate for a lack of self-esteem either. In fact Islanders actually have an overabundance of self-esteem. We think people who have to have red convertibles, designer clothing, mobile telephones, and expensive jewellery may need self-esteem programmes more than we do.

Children in the Torres Strait are born into a diverse language situation, and are most likely to be exposed to three languages. Two traditional languages are in use, one in the Eastern Islands and the other in the Western and Central Islands. Children in these outer islands will grow up in a household which uses one or the other. As well, they will acquire Torres Strait Creole, the *lingua franca* across the entire Straits and understood and spoken by all Islanders. This Creole varies according to the degree to which it incorporates each of the traditional languages and English. Furthermore, this Creole may also incorporate Malay, Filipino and South Pacific words. These traditional and Creole languages are oral languages, although they are being steadily documented by white linguists. The English language is also used on these islands for specific purposes, primarily as Islanders interact with Western institutions: government, schools, health services, and so on, as well as popular culture media and commerce. On Thursday Island, the administrative centre, Creole is likely to be a child's first language with the traditional language being the second language, but there is considerable variation between households and sometimes English is the second language. Moreover, there is considerable variation between households in children's exposure to English as well.

Children on the outer islands in the Torres Straits receive a primary education that is intended to reach comparable standards with mainland schools. Although some of the outer island schools have Islander principals, they are mostly run by white principals, who come for an average two-year period. Classroom teachers in the main are Islanders who have varying levels of qualifications. Some have no qualifications and have been selected from the community to fill vacancies. Some have been teaching for many years and have received training and extensive ongoing professional development. Many of these teachers are excellent, but many struggle to teach English because of their own inadequacies with the language, poor resources and inadequate professional support. As Creole speakers, they conduct a lot of teaching using Creole as the language of instruction. This facilitates communication and understanding and is a helpful pedagogical tool. The shortfall occurs when teachers' knowledge of English is not adequate to provide pupils with the means of understanding and developing competence with Australian English. For this reason a significant proportion of pupils in these schools enter secondary school as emergent readers.

The primary school children on Thursday Island also receive an education intended to produce comparable outcomes. However, there are significant differences. They are always taught by fully qualified white or Islander teachers. English is the language of instruction. The children are Creole speakers with teachers who in the main do not understand Creole. Communication and understanding are often difficult but at the end of the day these children are exposed to a lot more standard English, move through the curriculum faster, and generally enter the high school with much higher reading ages.

Across all these schools, the Torres Strait English Program is in use. This programme was developed for the outer islands to provide a comprehensive language teaching programme for Islander teachers. It is based on the whole language approach, uses as much local content as possible, and aims to maximise meaningful and relevant contexts for the learning of English. While teachers on Thursday Island use it, most innovate and supplement it with other activities and programmes, especially where they perceive shortfalls and weaknesses in the programme.

The secondary school on Thursday Island, which takes children from all these primary schools, streams children upon entry in response to their literacy levels. The task that high school teachers face is formidable. The situation the students find themselves in is daunting and in many cases demoralising. Teachers who are trained to teach the content of their subjects find themselves having to teach literacy as well. Most of them have little knowledge of the students' language and culture, even less understanding of the history and politics of the region, and even less of the processes of language learning and teaching.

The most recent response of the school has been to teach the English Language Across the Curriculum. All teachers receive some in-service training but still struggle to cover both the content of their subjects and the teaching of English. Many teachers innovate and adapt, preferring to capitalise on visual and aural modes which students find easier and are seen to prefer. Thus the difficulties of printed texts are to a certain degree bypassed. Evaluation provides its own dilemma. Should teachers assess students understanding and knowledge of the content, or should they as well take into account their level of English? The school employs an ESL teacher and also a support teacher for the emergent readers who have reading ages of six and seven years, but, as in all schools, these additional teachers and resources are rarely seen to be adequate and sufficient.

Teachers in the high school generally understand the urgency and need for English because they understand the needs of the workplace and of higher education. In part, they see the primary school as not preparing students properly for secondary school, and many call for a more co-ordinated effort between the two sectors. Primary school teachers, on the other hand, trained as they are to cater for individual differences, view it as counter-productive to push children along faster than they can cope with developmentally.

In all these schools there are committed and hard-working teachers, dedicated to the task of improving students outcomes by continually reflecting on what they do, and innovating and trialing different approaches. What many of these teachers don't always appreciate is that teachers have been doing this for a long time, coming and going every few years, trying different things, often feeling that they have good ideas and not realising that many things have been tried over and over. And generations of Islanders observe the process, trying to remain optimistic, often sceptical, and always, in the end, frustrated.

There are many people who would argue that educational standards generally have improved. However, it is hard to state definitively whether these standards can stand on their own in terms of academic achievement or whether they are statistically reflective of increased access to tertiary education through the extension of available local high school education to matriculation, the increase in quotas for indigenous students as well as the development of special courses and provision of ongoing tutorial assistance in tertiary institutions, and also the general increase in tertiary participation across the entire Australian community.

There are those also who would argue that the changes of the last twenty years have led to improvements in outcomes. But it is difficult to argue that the teaching of English in the Torres Straits has improved significantly when recent surveys show that a significant proportion of students in the secondary school are still emergent readers; that people in the work-place struggle to do the written components of their jobs and still require supervision by outside 'experts'; and when tertiary students continue to struggle with basic reading and writing and are thus unable to engage fully with the content of their courses and in many instances fail to complete them.

Islanders today still consistently call for 'proper' education in English and see it as necessary not just for the formal schooling process but as well for everyday living, for understanding the world, and for the wider political project of self-government which they see as being delayed because of their low levels of education.

Currently Islanders' views of how higher standards of English education are to be achieved vary. Older Islanders quite publicly deplore the use of Creole in schools, while younger teachers see it as a valuable tool for increasing understanding and a valuable language in its own right. White linguists tend to predominate in influence in the outer islands and reinforce a longtime call for bilingual education in schools. Education Department policy predominates in Thursday Island and reinforces the developing educational trends in mainstream education, for example, whole language and ESL. All approaches are underwritten by the cultural agenda, which emphasises cultural relevance and sensitivity, and acknowledgment of differences in traditions, values, and languages.

Amongst all this is an emerging division between those who continue to advocate English in schools and those who see it as destructive. The latter yearn for an increase in traditional and Creole languages in all aspects of life in the Torres Strait region. In this is advocated literacy in the written forms of traditional language and Creole supplanting as much as possible the need for English. This division is framed for Islanders by the oftentimes disparate and competing positions of white experts. Linguists are interested in the project of recording and preserving traditional languages but are not necessarily attuned to the current political and economic concerns of Islanders, nor guided by a wider view of the relationship between languages, literacy education, and educational outcomes. State educational policy and practice uphold the teaching of English, while at the same time being attentive to the issues of cultural sensitivity and accommodating Islanders' desires to be more active in the decision-making process. However they continue to fail to engage rigorously with the enormous complexity of our language situation. Many Islanders support both these positions. They understand the importance of English literacies in their lives but value their own languages and cultural practices and wish to retain them.

The emergence of these divisions is increasing the confusion which surrounds the issue of language in the Torres Strait, particularly with respect to how the issues are discussed. This is the complex linguistic and cultural situation that the Multiliteracies Project needs to address. Starting from the premise that recognises complexity, diversity, change, and the reality of global connectedness, the project already recognises the current tensions between immersion and explicit teaching. The old phonics approach to the teaching of reading, for instance, left generations of Islanders including mine, 'doing it' but not understanding what we were doing. We learnt to decode but didn't comprehend much. The current generation, which has been 'immersed' in local content and culturally sensitive teaching, has perhaps had more understanding and been able to participate more actively in the process but in the end this knowledge still cannot be given full expression in English and so they continue to be disadvantaged in the competitive world of higher education, the marketplace and politics.

The concept of Situated Practice allows for the inclusion of Islander lifeworlds and experiences, thus continuing the strength of the present cultural curriculum. However it recognises as well the complexities of these lifeworlds and their endless and changing intersections. Overt instruction introduces a missing element: the connection of the importance of contextualisation of learning experiences to conscious understanding of elements of language meaning and design. The development of metalanguage is crucial to unravelling the confusion that surrounds Islander students as they operate in English literacy programs.

Islander students already code-switch and negotiate meanings on a daily basis. What is our Creole language but a hybrid form, which the current generation continues to shape and reshape as they incorporate the language of technology and popular culture? But their skills are currently unrecognised, at least in any formal sense. They enrich and extend the Creole which gives them full expression and representation in their interactions with other Islanders, but, with lesser skills in English literacies, they have difficulty in full expression and representation of themselves as they face competent English speakers and their texts, whoever and wherever they may be and in whatever form.

For Islanders who had been the recipients of a pedagogy that did not even recognise them as second-language learners and that did not make any allowance for their cultural context in curriculum, a Multiliteracies pedagogy holds out the promise of better and more effective education. The development of a metalanguage appropriate to Islander classrooms and contexts to me is central to the project if it is to work for us. This is work that needs to be done, in context, in the Torres Strait – not researched in other classrooms and overlayered on to our context. I would argue that such a language needs to emerge from Islander needs and not from some academic schema of our perceived needs.

It almost goes without saying, given my central argument in this chapter, that I would consider crucial, as well, the other two elements to the model: Critical Framing and Transformed Practice. These elements are essential to understanding our position in relation to others and to exploring possibilities for our future, in both the individual and the collective sense.

One of the goals a Multiliteracies pedagogy needs to pursue is the articulation of an indigenous standpoint in relation to academic disciplines, and the importance of this is, in my mind, twofold. First, because it allows indigenous researchers and students a space to explore issues on their own behalf, to explore not just the academic disciplines but, as well, the relationship between the disciplines and knowledges they need to pursue and what it means for their own position as indigenous people in Australia. Second, because it will allow such an indigenous standpoint to effect a better dialogue with non-indigenous academics and, in this case, educators.

For if indigenous academics themselves, and there are increasing numbers of us, can articulate an indigenous position in relation to the educational issues then it must surely bring influence to bear on the many committed non-indigenous educational practitioners struggling to find better ways of teaching literacies to our children.

An indigenous standpoint, however, can be established only by indigenous people. It is not something that can be constructed by non-indigenous people as 'Other' to their own standpoint. And as indigenous people we should not establish a standpoint from which we are engaged only in our defence of ourselves as 'Other' because in any consideration of our position we are not 'Other'. We are at the centre of our own lives and our own history and we need to give primacy to that position. We stand in relation to the mainstream but we do not have to view that relationship as secondary to it, as it has been inscribed in the corpus.

To establish an indigenous standpoint we must give primacy to our experiences in our lifeworlds as we articulate our position in relation to the mainstream. If we don't establish an indigenous standpoint from which to articulate our position, then the dialogue concerning the indigenous position will continue to be between those who construct us as 'other' and the indigenous subject that has been constructed by them, even when the indigenous people, ourselves, are participants in that dialogue. And the experiences of indigenous peoples in their own lifeworlds will continue to be submerged, misrepresented and omitted in the process.

So what does this all mean overall in relation to the pedagogical issues of the Multiliteracies Project? In regards to Situated Practice, for instance, teachers will seek to immerse students in meaningful practices based on students' own experiences. For many years in the Torres Strait there has been a concerted effort to situate literacy and numeracy curriculum and pedagogy around contexts that are meaningful and relevant to students.

In terms of motivating and maintaining interest, it has been a successful strategy and it has encouraged a lot of creative and innovative practice on the part of many teachers – which I might add does not get enough recognition.

But the experiences of children living on remote islands in the Torres Strait are limited by their isolation, and one of the most important goals of education in the Torres Strait is to extend the students' knowledge of the world beyond the Islands and their competence and competitiveness in that world. Thus they have to confront a lot of foreign and seemingly irrelevant practices, many of which are not practised competently in their communities. In this situation teachers still struggle to make these practices relevant.

In terms of the Multiliteracies pedagogy the inclusion of an indigenous standpoint would free teachers to make use of, for instance, any non-Islander text or practice and make it more relevant by dealing with it in terms of its relation to the students and their position in the world.

Involved in Overt Instruction is the development of a metalanguage which assists students to articulate how their position is related to the practice. It might involve the awareness and the language with which to express that consciousness of, for example, why a text or practice is alien, or not much in evidence in their community, or confined to a particular domain or time or place etc. and of what significance it is to them. Or indeed how that practice or story or language has been transformed over time by Islanders as much of Outside practice has been transformed to take its place as 'Island custom'. Good teachers of course do this but often in no systematic or developmental way.

Critical Framing then becomes much more interesting because it will extend students' growing mastery of practice and conscious control and understanding into a further relation to the historical, social, political, cultural, ideological relations of particular systems of knowledge and social practice.

With this understanding indigenous students can begin to see themselves and their position in relation to the duality between those who construct and what they construct. Whether the text or practice is foreign, mis-representative, or remarkable for its omission of their position, they can at least see themselves in their relation to that text but independent of the construct.

As regards Transformed Practice I suggest that Torres Strait Islanders are masters at transforming practice. That is how we have survived all these years under colonial rule. In transforming practice, after all, students are surrounded by a community of experts. However, I think the effects on Transformed Practice, though, may lie in students being in a position to make more conscious decisions about what practices to transform, what and where and to which domains practices belong. And, importantly, how to switch between them.

The Multiliteracies approach starts from a premise that recognises complexity, diversity, change and the reality of global connectedness. It recognises the current tensions between immersion and explicit teaching and the place of both these elements. The concept of Situated Practice allows for the inclusion of Islander lifeworlds and experiences, thus continuing the strength of the current culturally inclusive curriculum by recognising the complexities of these lifeworlds and their endless and changing intersections. Overt Instruction introduces an often overlooked element – the connection of the importance of contextualisation of learning experiences to conscious understanding of elements of language meaning and design. The development of a metalanguage appropriate to Islander classrooms and contexts is crucial, for there is much confusion for Islander students as they code-switch between at least two and some-times three languages and in cross-cultural contexts, not to mention the requirements of various disciplines and genres. Clearly the inclusion of pedagogical strategies that develop at the same time a conscious awareness of their position as indigenous is very important if indigenous people are to develop a literacy pedagogy that in the first instances recognises the position of indigenous students in Australian classrooms.

I have struggled in the course of my academic work to connect the individual personal struggle to the collective historical struggle of the Torres Strait community. I have tried to use the disciplines and knowledges of the mainstream to elucidate an analysis that white Australians might understand, and that might open up possibilities for Islanders. If I could succeed in this I may well have contributed to the transformation of existing discourses which circumscribe the Islander and the emergence of new discourses which will better represent the position of Islanders and improve the conditions of our lives. But, in becoming articulate, English literacy skills have been my primary need and continue to be my biggest stumbling block. It is this which pushes me to drive home what continues to be a very unpopular point: English and English texts cannot be ignored or bypassed, and it is here that the Multiliteracies pedagogy could develop a way for Torres Strait students to give full expression to the context of their lives as they are articulated with the changing technological and global order. This, at least for me, is the principal challenge I want to address as my part of the International Multiliteracies Project.

6

CHANGING THE ROLE OF SCHOOLS

Mary Kalantzis and Bill Cope

Education, inclusion, and equity

When school buildings go up, they are a sign of progress, a promise for the future. Among all the other icons of modern times – roads, real estate developments, factories, or prisons – new schools engender less ambivalence and attract less protest. Education is something that modernising people almost unequivocally want.

Education promises change and improvement. It promises individuals a chance in the game of social mobility: more access to material resources through better-paid employment; a greater capacity to participate actively in the processes of government; and the dexterity that comes with knowing the world. To communities it promises improved employment prospects, more self-government and extended access to the wider world. If you have faith in the promise of education, you are quintessentially a modern person.

Literacy is at the heart of education's promise. Of all the functions and purposes of education, reading and writing have always been foundational. Literacy is the first major function of formal education both historically in the origins of modern, institutionalised education and in the life history of every child or adult learner as they enter the modern education process. Literacy represents a kind of symbolic capital in two senses: as the preeminent form of symbol manipulation that gets things done in modern times and as a symbolic marker of 'being educated'.

The problem for institutionalised education, and the problem for the teaching and learning of literacy, is that students bring with them different life experiences. What they know, who they feel themselves to be, and how they orient themselves to education varies because their lifeworlds vary; because life as they have subjectively experienced it varies so markedly. As a consequence, people experience education differently, and their outcomes are different.

As different lifeworlds engage with education, one thing is certain: the process is one of transformation, more or less intended, either a narrowly conceived 'to learn to . . .' or a more broadly conceived 'improving my prospects' or 'giving my child the best chance'. The problem is that the transformation by and large works better for some groups of people than for others. Undeniably, you get a better education if you are wealthier; if you speak the national language; if you belong to the most powerful ethnic group; if you live in the right neighbourhood or the right country; or if you are a male. There is something deep in the culture and purposes of institutionalised education which means that, mostly, it works better for some groups of people than others.

Yet the promise of education is universal. If we accept that the world is inevitably unequal, education is one of the key practical foundations to the systems argument that this inequality is not unjust. Through education everyone has opportunity, so the argument runs, to access material resources; the public realm in the form or participatory citizenship; and the symbolic realm of belonging. Education is one of everybody's main chances. And if everyone does not end up enjoying the same outcomes, it's not because they haven't been given the chance. Deeply embedded in modern education is the assurance of equity – a promise that the game of opportunity is fair and that its rules are even-handed. In short, education is one of the most important parts of the argument that, although unequal, everybody has the same chance. Whatever your lifeworld experience, your chance is still supposed to be there, somewhere. 'It's up to you to find your opportunity and to make the most of it.' That's what they say.

If education in its modern institutionalised form was to promise equality, that is, was to promise broadly similar outcomes for all, no one would believe it. The best it can do is promise equity. This is both a recognition of the variability of lifeworld experiences and a recognition that these experiences do affect outcomes. The reassurance of equity follows from this recognition of variation: if you are not from the 'right' lifeworld, if you do not have the mix of inherited or acquired attributes that already matches the one which has the preponderance of wealth, political power and symbolic presence, then education is your main chance. This is what makes education equitable. Although education cannot pretend to produce equality amongst individuals, it does pretend to produce equity between groups of people.

'Pretend' is the operative word here because certain educational orientations to the variability of lifeworlds cannot produce in theory, and have never produced in practice, results which could in any sense be said to be evidence of equity. The equity case can only be proved when one major group of students achieves a pattern of educational outcomes comparable to others. When blacks do as well and as badly as whites, or when women do as well and as badly as men, then the equity case is proved.

Different forms of education are defined by the way in which they engage with the variability of lifeworlds. The pattern of inequitable, not to mention unequal, outcomes is determined in part by the nature of that engagement. If education is a matter of transformation, a kind of cultural journey from one state of capacity and being to another, then while some people find it easy to get on to the through train, others can only get on to the all-stops; others can't get a ticket to go the whole way; and still others never manage to get on at all simply because there are no seats for them. The transition from lifeworld to education is fundamentally a process of varying degrees of inclusion – whether you are on the train in the first place, and how you're positioned if you are on it. The relation of education to lifeworld is in the nature of a subtle and more or less difficult dialogue between the culture of the institution and subjectively lived experience. From lifeworld to lifeworld, student to student, the dialogue differs, the form of inclusion differs and the outcomes differ.

Fundamentally, there are four archetypical forms of modern education: exclusion; assimilation; multiculturalism and pluralism.

Education as exclusion means not being able to contemplate trying to get in; not getting the marks to get in; or simply getting in and failing. There can be a variety of reasons for exclusion, and these all turn on the kind of distance existing between the lifeworld and institutionalised education: between the education you can afford; what you know you can realistically wish for from education; what you expect; and what you can slip into more or less comfortably. In the modern era, when education is compulsory and the promise of equity through education is universal, exclusion is powerfully a form of inclusion. Not being there as a form of being there; absence is presence. Missing the train – not getting an education or getting an education limited in certain ways – still means that you have a powerful relationship to education, the journey. Literacy understood narrowly, and the discourses of power or expertise understood broadly, are amongst the touchstones of exclusion; they are the acid test, both metaphorically and literally at points of 'assessment'. As a consequence of exclusion, you will do certain kinds of work, be a certain kind of citizen, have a certain kind of relationship to the icons of belonging. Your relationship to institutionalised education is a key determinant in larger patterns of inclusion. When exclusion dashes the promise of education, it is in order to establish a particular form of inclusion.

Education as assimilation means getting into institutionalised education and succeeding at it by crossing over, and by making yourself over in the process. You can leave the old self of your lifeworld as hitherto experienced, and get with the strength of those lifeworlds closest to the culture of education. For some, this is a short and comfortable journey. For others, it is long and painful. When you get there, you've become literate in the sense of being a living embodiment of the official word and the discourse of power.

Education as a superficial kind of multiculturalism means that, at a surface level, the system recognises, even honours, the variability of lifeworlds, but deep down, you've still got to make yourself over in the image of those life-worlds closest to the culture of institutionalised learning and 'mainstream' power. Different lifeworlds might be made an object of study or celebrated as folkloric colour, but only in so far as the fundamental framework of seeing, valuing and knowing remains singular and undisturbed. The margins are recognised as just that, and thereby framed as marginal. We can 'do' literacy, for instance, through reading about other people's cultures and developing special purpose strategies for 'access', but only in so far as these activities are no more than interim accommodations; and only as long as they contribute to transformation in the direction of the lifeworld of power, from the margins to the centre.

Education as pluralism means that you don't have to be the same to have similar opportunities: not identical opportunities, but the same kinds of opportunities measured in terms of access to material resources through employment, political participation and senses of belonging to a broader as well as a localised community. Pluralism involves a subtle but profound shift from a more superficial multiculturalism. Pluralism means that the mainstream – be that the culture of the dominant groups or institutional structures such as education – is itself transformed. Instead of representing a single cultural destination, a monolithic cultural position, it is a site of openness, negotiation, experimentation, and the interrelation of alternative frameworks and mindsets. Learning is not a matter of 'development' in which you leave your old selves behind; leaving behind lifeworlds which would otherwise have been framed by education as more or less inadequate to the task of modern life. Rather, learning is a matter of repertoire; starting with a recognition of lifeworld experience and using that experience as a basis for extending what one knows and what one can do. The pluralist process of transformation, then, is not a matter of vertical progress but of expanding horizons. These new horizons do have an impact on the lifeworld: learners still engage in and with their lifeworlds in new ways, but not necessarily in order to leave those lifeworlds behind in a kind of one-way trip.

The methods of transformation and inclusion are such that, despite the rhetorical pretences, equity cannot be achieved in any but the pluralist alternative. In fact, the first three forms of inclusion are simultaneously rationalisations of exclusion; the first explicitly so and the other two by way of practice. In all three, the pattern of those who are more likely to miss out on opportunities reflects the relative distances of lifeworlds to the culture of power and the culture of institutionalised education. The crossover is more possible for some than for others. Only pluralism is even-handed, because negotiating the variability of lifeworlds is the main game.

Pluralism is both an ambitious programme and a minimalist, unambitious programme. It is ambitious in the sense that it is based on the argument that the mainstream needs to be transformed. It is unambitious in that it does no more than take the limited equity argument at its word. To the question of what are the conditions of mere equity – not equality – the only answer can be: an educational system which does not favour and reward some lifeworld experiences over others. This is simply to take at its word the apologetic rhetoric of a society which does not pretend to equality of outcomes, just 'opportunity' for all. Pluralism is the only way the system can possibly do that; the only way it can possibly be genuinely fair in its distribution of opportunity, as between one group and another, one kind of lifeworld experience and another.

Pluralism, however, is more than just a matter of holding a society that is unequal to its word on equity. There are peculiar shifts in our moment of modern times that increasingly make the three other approaches to the process of inclusion redundant. Shifts in the forms of work, civics and the personal make pluralism increasingly functional – once again, both in the most unambitious of systems terms and in the most ambitious of strategic and political terms.

Education and changing patterns of work

'Work' refers to the undertaking of any socially purposeful task, paid or unpaid. In modern times, paid tasks are valued over unpaid tasks, because the material necessities of life must be purchased on the market, and because a person's level of access to material resources is fundamentally a function of purchasing power and accumulated capital. Education is one of the key elements in the nexus of work and material resources, most obviously as an entree into forms of work that pay more. The connection between education, work, and material resources is one of the great 'opportunity' or mobility promises of an unashamedly unequal society. If you don't inherit material resources, education is a critical path to mobility.

Going with the flow of the most conventional of arguments for the moment, we will consider work only in the restricted sense of paid employment – the sense that is privileged in our modernity – and how to get into it. There are some elementary constancies within this narrowly modern form of work: to undertake tasks or manipulate capital in order to earn the money income necessary to purchase what for that historical moment constitutes the material necessities of life; maybe also to consume beyond what is the norm for the historical moment; or perhaps to accumulate a surplus in the form of capital. This is what makes modern life different from other cultural moments in human history and other cultural spaces in the contemporary world. One fact of modern times rings true: for better or for worse, the modern money economy has inexorably spread across the globe over the past few centuries to the point where, at the end of the twentieth century, there is virtually no future in anything other than paid work. The alternatives are now little but bleak forms of marginalisation:

'underdevelopment' often to the point of near starvation, or minimal social security payments in lieu of paid work. The alternatives are so unattractive as to place enormous pressures on people to undertake even the most unpleasant and poorly paid forms of modern work. This is called the free market for labour.

To this background of fundamental constancy, there is a history of change in the forms of paid work in modern times, from Fordism to post-Fordism to productive diversity. Education has changed and continues to change, as it must and should, to function effectively in relation to these different forms of work.

Fordism takes its name form Henry Ford, an iconic as well as a truly influential figure in modern management and industrial production. Both in theory (Ford 1923) and in practice, Fordism is the high point of a certain form of work, which is characterised by a minimalist division of labour, strictly hierarchical relations of control and subordination, a culture of uniformity, and clear patterns of exclusion. Ford arranged his production line on the basis of a minutely dissected division of labour. Here, a factory of predominantly unskilled workers produced an item of unprecedented technological sophistication, with one worker putting this panel in place and the next tightening that nut. Which worker, which panel or nut, and where on the production line, were all determined centrally in both a technological sense by the engineers and an organisational sense by the managers. The worker was told what to do, or more likely shown what to do, given that the workers were predominantly immigrants and not necessarily competent speakers of English. From the point of view of the organisation, human beings were reduced to a physiological common denominator as unskilled working capacities: the stuff of time and motion studies. From the point of view of the organisation and the production process, all human beings were the same. The minimalism of the production line was a way of bracketing off, in short ignoring, differences in lifeworld experience.

Mass production, meanwhile, begat mass consumption, with parallel assumptions about the universal and homogeneous interests of modern people. 'Any colour you like as long as it is black', said the enlightened Mr Ford, who paid his workers five dollars a day so they could afford the five-hundred-dollar Model 'T'. The economies of scale of mass production made it possible to produce cheaply; certainly cheaply enough to create a mass market. Integral to inclusion in Ford's regime of paid work were certain forms of exclusion for most workers: exclusion from technical knowledge in a global or active sense; exclusion from power in the sense of organisational self-determination; and even exclusion from alternative forms of consumption, not just in terms of the colour of a car but also in terms of mobility as the United States entered an era in which the urban geography of roads increasingly meant you had to have a car to get around (Cope and Kalantzis 1997a).

From the point of view of teachers, schools, of course, are workplaces as well. In the era of Fordism, the state determined the syllabus; the teachers led their students through the textbooks; and the students were assessed against the correct answers, centrally determined. And from the point of view of students, the classroom is mock workplace, a site that prefigures the world of work. In the era of Fordism, the teacher took the systematically divided-up component parts of the curriculum, transmitted them to students bit by bit, and then assessed knowledge as 'discipline' (Kalantzis and Cope 1993a). If you didn't make the crossover into the world of disciplined order, you at least got the message that disciplined order ruled. If you failed in terms of the more powerful and prestigious outcomes of education and didn't get beyond basic literacy and into the discourses of power, you were included in the system of 'opportunity' by way of exclusion. So you ended up on a production line like Ford's, included there too by way of exclusion from an active or holistic relation to technology, through the denial of rights to organisational self-determination, and through the necessities of mass consumption.

Fordism was a brilliantly successful moment in modern times, not only as economics and technology but as culture. Fordism wrought a massive transformation in the lifeworlds of those people who migrated from the country to the city; from the Old World to the New World; from the world of production directly for needs to the world of paid work and market consumption. But, as a system, it was destined to be superseded, albeit slowly and unevenly. As soon as it is fully established, Fordism faces three, related crises of employment, of consumption, and of technology. In its initial moments, the lifeworld transition into the realm of mass production and mass consumption appears a desirable one, with the workers accepting demeaning conditions of work in order to consume the technological and aesthetic marvels of modernity. After a time, a generation perhaps, the allure of consumption, however, does not seem to outweigh the unpleasantries of work and there follows a crisis of motivation amongst the long-time residents of the modern world of paid work. This is accompanied by a parallel crisis of consumption, in which the charms of mass consumption themselves lose their shine. Demand becomes differentiated according to the critical and highly personalised eye of the consumer, infused with preferences for colour and style – the finer points of self-image as manifest in the sensuous form of the product. Meanwhile, what the crises of work and consumption make a matter of necessity, technology more than fortuitously makes a possibility with software-driven machines; cybernetic information systems that relate market variables to a process of flexible production; and distributed systems of knowledge and control (see Gee, Chapter 2 above). Information networking and just-in-time inventory mean that economies of large scale and mass production are replaced by economies of small scale and flexible specialisation: a network of small and closely connected organisations or semi-autonomous divisions works better under this new regime than a centrally controlled system of mass production. The massive bulk and inertia of fixed capital plant under Fordism is replaced by geographically dispersed, always reprogrammable, networked production units. Within the constant framework of paid work, the three crises of Fordism portend a fundamental shift.

This is a time in history when we appear to have no confidence in what we are. In fact, we seem to be more comfortable with what we are not and define our society as, for example, post-industrial or postmodern. So, what follows Fordism is often unimaginatively called postFordism – a system of 'multiskilling', worker 'empowerment' and cultural assimilation, or at best a superficial multiculturalism of niche marketing. Technologically, the multiskilled worker has to be able to adapt to constant change and undertake a broad range of tasks as the need arises. Organisationally, multiskilled workers to a significant extent have to be in control of their own work processes. So, for instance, total quality management means that production workers are responsible for monitoring quality and continuous improvement in the production process. This leads to a shift in the process of management from centralised and hierarchical command systems to 'empowered' workers. If workplaces are sites of governance and consent, postFordism fundamentally changes the organisational politics of work. The autarchy of Fordism is replaced by the guided democracy of post-Fordism in which 'empowered' workers assume the objectives of the organisation as a matter of their own volition – hence the postFordist rhetoric of vision, mission, identifying with the culture of the organisation, team building and shared values. Systems-structure-command talk is replaced by motivation-culture-responsibility talk. Then, the dynamics of inclusion and exclusion become a matter of cultural assimilation; you're in and you'll make it if you can or will clone to the culture of the organisation; personify the organisation as 'passion'; and maintain a semblance of authenticity as you project the corporate persona by saying 'have a nice day' to all the customers. At best, there's a superficial kind of multiculturalism, in which you might 'get close to the customer' to find out exactly what colour they want; what niche in the market they belong to, but the recognition of variability between lifeworlds is mostly no deeper than this. It is a coat of paint and really no more than a cynical ploy to sell a product or services that, when you scratch the surface, are still essentially generic (Cope and Kalantzis 1997a).

As much as postFordism speaks generously of inclusion, it is also a system of exclusion; a system of 'glass ceilings' for those who don't manage to clone to the dominant culture of management; or of user-friendly software which is so culturally embedded as to be baffling to all but those who are already friends in the culture that creates it. Its assimilationist cultural project works best for those lifeworlds closest to the culture of management, which in turn reflects the nature of the lifeworlds of those who happen to be in a position of managing. Even the anti-discrimination apparatuses of Equal Employment Opportunity, Affirmative Action, quotas and targets are no more than strategies for access – to give a few people the chance to assimilate against the terrible odds faced by people from more distant lifeworlds. The main game doesn't change, only the gate of assimilation is left slightly ajar.

PostFordism is also a system of exclusion in so far as Fordism remains comfortably alongside it in a relationship of uneven development. This symbiotic relationship means exclusion from the more advanced post-Fordist forms of work and consumption around enduring and systemic divisions between the First World and the Third World, the rust belt and the sun belt, higher-paid workers and lower-paid workers, and those who can afford to consume in fancy niche markets and those who can afford only generic, mass-produced goods.

Schools as both workplaces and mock workplaces have undergone a parallel transition as they have moved towards progressivist forms of pedagogy: starting 'where the student is at', building motivation, facilitating student-centred 'inquiry' or 'discovery' learning, establishing 'communities of practice', and developing the literate 'voice'. And all the same kinds of exclusions emerge: between those who slip most easily into the discourses of power, and those who slip in uncomfortably or not at all (see Gee, Chapter 2 above; Michaels and Sohmer, Chapter 13 below) Not to mention the places where older forms of learning relationships still survive: in the less developed world, in 'difficult' neighbourhoods, in schools which cannot afford the time and resources for student-centred learning.

The trouble with postFordism as a way of organising work is what it means by culture, and what it means to do with culture. So postFordism spawns the seeds of its own instability with its cultural crisis founded on what it does with lifeworld differences. Even though its deeply embedded project is to assimilate or to limit diversity to a superficial kind of multi-culturalism, postFordism faces the related challenges of local diversity and global connectedness: the differences manifest in local niche markets and migrant workforces; and the formerly distant differences brought close to home by the globalisation of markets and radically improved technologies of transport and communication. The cultural simplicities and simplifications of assimilation or superficial multiculturalism are no longer viable. Having to deal with the variability of lifeworlds becomes the main game.

Within the constant frame of reference of modern work, the logistics of negotiating differences leads the organisation of work into a new phase: Productive Diversity, which defines itself by what it is, as opposed to what it isn't. Instead of attempting to force cultural homogeneity upon people whose lifeworlds are diverse, the organisation attempts to 'capitalise on the talents of diversity'. Its approach to organisational culture and system is to ensure that the organisation is just as variegated internally as the local and global markets it serves. This is not only a matter of cultural match – having Vietnamese- and German-speaking workers if the organisation serves Vietnamese and German speakers in local ethnic or global export markets. It is also a matter of developing an organisational culture founded on habits of mind in which people are constantly prepared for the unpredictability of engagement with lifeworld differences; where people have the capacity to recognise those differences and negotiate them effectively. In its relations with clients the organisation attempts to set up relationships of customisation sufficiently reflexive to ensure that the needs and expectations of clients in different lifeworlds are incorporated into the design of products and services.

Here induction and transformation are processes of defining the extraneous as central and then constantly extending one's lifeworld horizons and cross-lifeworld negotiations repertoire. Groups recognise and use the irreducible and profound variety of lifeworld experiences; they establish relationships of complementarity on the basis of different lifeworld experiences; and they define group boundaries by their permeability – how easy it is to get involved with outsiders and for outsiders to get involved inside. The group's character and effectiveness are determined by the breadth and effective use of overlapping networks, multiple group memberships, and outside collaborations and alliances (Cope and Kalantzis 1997a).

Against the measure of equity, it is possible to interpret the shift towards Productive Diversity both optimistically and pessimistically. Optimistically, it creates the conditions for greater equity because people are valued in their difference for systemic reasons. When dealing with lifeworld, distances are the main game; lifeworld distance will not prejudice access to more privileged domains of work.

Pessimistically, however, in an inherently unequally system of work, Productive Diversity may be no more than another – if more sophisticated – technology of control; of inveiglement into the objectives of an economic system which always disproportionately benefits those in positions of ownership and control; of hyper-exploitation; and of culturally invasive market racketeering.

In the first instance, education needs to set its sights on the optimistic, if limited, version of Productive Diversity. This requires an epistemology and a pedagogy of pluralism – a particular way of knowing and learning a world in which local diversity and global proximity have become factors of such critical importance. In the area of literacy teaching in particular, it is the purpose of this book to outline the ways in which our conception of Multiliteracies is closer to what is needed to succeed in the most powerful, prestigious and best-paid forms of work today.

But in so far as lifeworlds pattern themselves in historically settled relationships to capital markets and labour markets, and in so far as there's an enormous inertia to privilege, it's unlikely that even this limited version of Productive Diversity will come easily. Indeed, the optimistic and limited version of Productive Diversity could well prove to be a dangerous friend, a trickster who promises that things are getting better (more equitable, comparable for groups), when for most people nothing is really happening (inequality in the overall distribution of material resources stays the same).

But, then again, if things are heading in the direction of equity, and even if in the first instance this shift is limited to what's possible within a systems point of view, this may well be the start of expanding expectations that go beyond what the system can provide without transforming itself fundamentally. The logic of equity, as anticipation and disappointment, leads people into wider expectations and to demand real results. With a gentle nudge, minimalist improvements within systems logic become a utopian imagination which reflects and acts in deeper systems terms. In education, this might mean more than assisting students to get into the new, reflexively pluralist world of locally responsive and globalised work. Yet at the same time it might also mean extending the ethics of equity beyond the logic of the modern system of paid work and structural inequality, to consider, for instance, how globalism, difference and the world of working-for-money relate to the larger questions of our human natures and habitation within the ecosystem. This is a larger, more ambitious objective for the educational programme of Multiliteracies.

Education for civic participation

Civics is the place where civil society relates to the state, where people participate in government.

In one sense, there is a fundamental constancy to the function of civics in the modern era: to establish a stable relationship of consent that preserves the fundamentals of the existing socioeconomic order while assisting in its intrinsic processes of self-transformation: its 'progress' and 'development'. The institutional structures through which this relationship of state to civil society is formed are also enduring and characteristic of the modern era. Legislatures, armies, legal systems, social welfare, education and the various agencies of strategic economic intervention and market assistance are all institutions which take uniquely modern forms and perform an invariable function. Consider the function of education, for instance. Universal schooling is a uniquely modern phenomenon and pre-eminently the domain of the state or, if private, subject to considerable state regulation. For the first time in human history, modern people entrust a large part of the socialisation of children to public or publicly regulated institutions.

Yet, in another sense, within the constancy of modern civics there have been transitions of great significance: from nationalism to a more recent retreat from the civic, to the possibility of a civic pluralism.

The impacts of these transitions reverberate through all our civic institutions. So, for instance, although the function and fundamental purposes of education in modern times stay the same, these civic transitions change the dynamics of education in some profound ways. As with work, we will trace these transitions both as historical narrative and political project. And as was the case with Productive Diversity, Civic Pluralism represents both an unambitious pragmatics and an ambitious strategic possibility. It represents both an appropriate response to the real world of change and a goal for education as a constructive social agent.

Nationalism is a story that creates, on three dimensions, a deeply personalised sense of belonging to the nation-state. On a time dimension, nationalism attempts to place the persons who exist within a nation into a distinctive historical narrative; a narrative of folk origins, of the establishment of the nation-state, of common cultural roots and of enduring traditions. On a space dimension, nationalism defines people geographically. Being-within-borders is a condition of political status (nationality), and one that is made crystal clear by the border police who check passports in order to establish precise geographical credentials (from citizen, to resident, to myriad categories of visitor and immigrant, to illegal immigrant). Also on the space dimension, nationalism builds an affective sense of place shaped in relation to the distinctive sensuous physicality of the land and the human environments within those borders. Nationalism creates a sense of being-at-home; a feeling of the attachment to place that develops with presence over time. On a structural dimension, nationalism is the story of the relation of citizen to the state in which the state assures citizens of universal and identical rights; or, when this seems implausible on the measure of outcomes, citizens are at least assured of 'opportunity' or 'equity' as a process.

The modern state can take various forms and relate to civil society on the basis of a variety of legitimating rationales. Being-at-home, in time, in place, and in the structures of governance is what all governments want to achieve for their citizens for a variety of reasons. The distinctiveness of nationalism is the unrelenting singularity of its story. On all three dimensions, there is just one story in nationalism; the three dimensions back up each other's story to the point where they become inseparably one. One history, one geography, one state. The foundational assumption of nationalism is that there is only one national lifeworld.

'Story' is a critical concept in the definition of nationalism, because on each of the time, space and structure dimensions it has all the truth of fiction. The fiction is that states are never homogeneous. On the time dimension, the people of the nation can never have lived the same historical experience. They are immigrants, or longer-established settlers, or indigenes who speak any number of ancestral heritages and tongues. The fiction of nationalism is to imagine that all the members of the nation share a sense of kinship rooted in a single communal-national past. On the geographical dimension, the people within the boundaries of the nation can be defined by their difference in any number of ways. Where they live within the nation for example, in ghettos, regions, frontiers, or mountains, is defined by ethnicity and language, region and dialect, religion, or affiliation and even those peculiarly local senses of space such as streets, neighbourhoods, valleys, cantons, or states within federal systems. Nor on the structural dimension are they ever equals for there are deep differences between lifeworlds. Access to the state's participatory rights, services and symbols of belonging is easier the closer your lifeworld is to the lifeworld of those who happen to hold power in the nation-state and who, by virtue of their accidental proximity, declare the national identity to be their own.

Yet nationalism is nevertheless a true story precisely because it is operative. Nationalism is a process; the process, more or less successfully, of making people the same; of homogenising them. In fact, the fiction of oneness is simply a method of dealing with difference. The details that make up the stories of nationalism may be largely nonsense: the dubious narratives of origins; the tendentious antiquity of parts of the narrative which were in reality remembered or re-invented only yesterday; the conveniently ignored shared histories and overlaps with other nations. The empirical veracity of these stories of nationalism, however, is in practical terms irrelevant. For the question of the truth or otherwise is no more than a diversion, as are the details of difference between one nationalist story and the next. The main point, indeed the only point, is their consistency and universality of operational purpose.

At the heart of this system of nationalism is what Gellner calls 'modular man': individuals have to be identical in order to be mobile and replaceable. Any worker has to be replaceable by another. This demands cultural homogeneity and the standardisation of the national language (Gellner 1983, 1994). As an homogenising process, in other words, nationalism admirably serves to support the modern labour market.

From outside the labour market, the modern state compensates for the disastrous irregularities of the market. In fact, the strongest of modern states are those deliberately created as an antidote to the failure of the market to provide the necessities of life: fascism, communism and the welfare state (Polanyi 1975). The redistributive mechanisms of these states are themselves soaked through with the principles of homogenisation; with services such as mass education and social welfare provided identically to every person and on the basis of universal principles.

As well as this compensatory and redistributive function, nationalist states also serve the function of creating solidarity outside the market; even in spite of the market and, in fact, as an antidote to the market. Although the unattractive reality of the market is that isolated individuals can be substituted for each other at any time, nationalism develops a narrative of kinship and national belonging; a story which says that there are millions of others who share the same sense of themselves by virtue of experiencing exactly the same things across time and space. Anderson calls these 'imagined communities' because they are real in the imagination, but not in their actual, temporal and spatial proximity (Anderson 1983).

The modern nationalist state has two ways of facing differences: either through direct exclusion or by requiring the assimilation of people defined as 'outsiders' in relation to the dominant lifeworld. Exclusion may be through codes of immigration restriction, apartheid, genocide, wars to redefine borders, or refugee movements. To explain these exclusions, nationalists draw on the ideology of racism, which speaks of the superiority of the official national 'us' and provides the ostensible reasons why it is undesirable to live with 'those others'. Alternatively, assimilation meets difference by demanding that people become the same by demanding that they make themselves identical and invisible by taking on the official language and national identity. The word 'identity' powerfully means what it says. So does the word 'naturalisation' which marks the crossover into a new statedness; as if you'd been born into that kin; as if you had been for ever there. Assimilation is, of course, a gentler racism than straight-out exclusion. Otherness here is not irredeemable for it is possible to cross over. Furthermore, the cultural and linguistic transformation entailed will be beneficial and can be rationalised for the best of reasons; the inherent virtues of 'our' progress or development in comparison to 'yours', 'our' level of 'civilisation' in comparison to 'yours'. Be it by means of exclusion or assimilation, however, the intended result of nationalism is always the same: to create a singular nation with one history, one geography, and one state (Kalantzis 1997).

More than any other place in the modern world, schools were the place in which 'modular man' and modern nationalism were created. For the first time in history, the nation-state took away a large part of the socialisation of children from families and communities. Families and communities were diverse; their lifeworld experiences varied. Schools were to socialise their children into national 'identity'. Education was the key to the creation of a culture of commonality with children singing the national anthem, saluting flags and making oaths of loyalty watched over by a picture of the head of state prominently displayed on the classroom wall. Right in the depths of the curriculum as well, there was always nationalism intrinsic in the teaching of literacy in the official, 'standard' language, the history of national origins, and the geography of borders. Against these measures students were passed or failed; assimilated or unassimilated. If the story didn't make sense to you or the language did not slip easily from your tongue or pen, you were failed, and thus perversely included within the framework of national homogeneity through a kind of internal cultural exile, a form of inclusion defined by exclusion and marginalisation (Cope and Kalantzis 1998; Phillipson 1992).

The heyday of nationalism is now over, splintered by two, related forces in late modern times: the politics of diversity at the local level, and globalisation. In nationalism's wake, we are experiencing a decline of the civic. The iconic moment in this transition was 1989; the symbolic moment when the Cold War ended. That was the year when the century-long argument about the redistributive role of the state reached its conclusion: an argument between unfettered capitalism and totally fettered communism, with all sorts of permutations of the modern nationalist state, principally the welfare state and fascism, holding the middle ground. Globally, there is now only one principal form of state: a state that primarily exists to facilitate the workings of the 'free market', as little fettered in its operation as possible and culturally agnostic. Working for the conservative US think tank the Rand Corporation, Fukuyama triumphantly calls this 'the end of history' (Fukuyama 1992). The unfettered capitalism side of the argument won. The Cold War, the interfering state, lost. Now there is no middle ground.

The consequences are both global and local. Locally, the state is vacating areas to which it had formerly been deeply committed; committed culturally as well as committed as an agent of redistributive justice. States everywhere in the world are busily privatising industries once considered national treasures and too important to be out of state control. They are deregulating and allowing industry sectors or professional interest groups to set their own standards. They are shrinking in size and reducing the services they provide; taking less of an obsessive interest in education and becoming agnostic about culture.

Globally, states are becoming less important as sites of citizenship and *loci* of community. They are being replaced by transnational corporations, globalised professional communities and geographically dispersed and perpetually shifting diasporas. The paradox of globalisation is that its universalisation sometimes produces diversification to the point of startling fragmentation. It's not just the transformed nature of locality when neighbourhoods are irreducibly diverse and their populations constantly changing. It's also the fact that, since 1989, global markets are such that there is no place in the world where you cannot sell your wares and no place in the world which cannot have its wares in your local market; no place in the world that is more than a twenty-four-hour journey away; and no place in the world that is not instantaneously there at the other end of a telephone line, or a fax, or the Internet, or a television reporter's camera. Global cultural diversity is a deeply localised phenomenon. The juxtaposition of divergent lifeworlds is immediate and striking, locally and globally. It is an unavoidable fact of our postnational existence. The story of nationalism is no longer plausible. Nor does it make operational sense any more.

As a consequence of these changes, the nation-state faces a new crisis of recognition; the voices of difference become louder, their 'denunciations of discrimination and refusals of second class citizenship' more vehement (Taylor 1994, p. 39). A politics of cultural difference has stepped into the space in political discourse now vacated by the Cold War argument about the form of the state. Sometimes this is called 'devolution'; other times 'deregulation'; still other times 'multiculturalism'. Breakaway communities also form, made possible through a system of media communications which is moving away from the common national culture created by broadcasting, towards the infinite variegation created by narrowcasting and pointcasting with its hundreds of television channels, thousands of newspapers and magazines, and an infinitely segmented Internet.

This is not to say that nationalism is dead – far from it. The virulent nationalisms of the former Yugoslavia, for instance, are belated attempts at the project of the modern, ethnically homogenous nation-state. This is a kind of catching-up with modernity, and the human cost is comparable to earlier attempts: attempts such as the grouping of disparate peoples within a single German Reich under Hitler, or the policies designed to assist the Aboriginal people to either assimilate or die out in Australia. Fascism and Aboriginal 'Protection' made a terrible kind of sense in the era of modern nationalism. But catching-up now by going back to the future means that the worst of today's nationalisms are being bypassed by another future that is already upon us: the future of globalisation.

Since schools were pre-eminent amongst the institutional children of modern nationalism, they face the same crises as their parent. The first is the withdrawal of the state, which takes many forms: 'self-managing' public schools with devolved budgets and school councils; the proliferation of private schools offering every kind of lifeworld promise from ruling-class disciplinarity to fundamentalist religious withdrawal; parents removing their children and undertaking home schooling; flexibly delivered, distance-mode, work-relevant training-as-education; and the sponsorships, the marketing and widespread commercialisation of education. As a consequence, the singularity of purpose existing within education has gone, as has its institutional coherence. The result is that the pretence to universalism, opportunity and equity has also dissolved. Instead subcultural withdrawal has taken its place.

So the rationale for education itself changes, and choice and diversity become the catch-cries. In reality, this means one of two things. The first is a veneer of tokenism in which it appears diversity is honoured – a spaghetti and polka multiculturalism – but in which nothing really changes in terms of patterns of educational outcomes. The second alternative is a kind of parting of company between lifeworlds: fracturing and fragmentation as educational institutions attempt to create self-enclosed communities. Children go to a fundamentalist religious school, run by their religious community, later to be employed in businesses run by their co-religionists. This is not just a function of lifeworld differences; it is a sign of a certain kind of politics of disappointment – a retreat that begins with the failed promise of modernity. There is a dreadful inexorable logic in this retreat: you were different to the lifeworld of power; the opportunities were not forthcoming; so you retreated.

And, of course, in the face of this fragmentation, there is just as much of a proliferation of back-to-the-future educational nostalgias as there is nationalist revivalism in the wider world of states and citizenries. Hence the sloganeering of the 'culture wars': sloganeering about the lost virtues of the 'Western canon', 'cultural literacy', 'the basics', and about a golden era before 'political correctness'. These nostalgias are no less anachronistic than nationalism, given the new realities of local diversity and global connectedness (Cope and Kalantzis 1997b). The fact that education has been the site of these 'wars' is evidence of its central importance in the project of nation. At the same time, they are also evidence of the momentousness of the broader transformation which portends the end of nationalism.

Civic Pluralism is a response to the changing shape of the state and its relationship to civil society. In some moments, Civic Pluralism is limited and pragmatic; in others optimistic and utopian. Either way, it is an attempt to come to grips with the changed dynamics of post-Cold-War times. Living after the Cold War is like moving to another part of the country. It seems the same at first, but the longer you are there, the more you realise it is different. This is particularly the case in the relation of civil society to the state.

How do you create a culture of civility amongst people existing in close local and global proximity but not of the same kin group? How do we face the challenges of the period of interregnum that we have called the moment of the decline of the civic? The answer is that we have to redefine the civic in terms of pluralism. On a time dimension, this requires new forms of historical recovery. Civic Pluralism's sense of time and history are relational. One angle on the relational story is about inequality of lifeworld experience, of privilege or discrimination and of insider or outsider status. But the character of each lifeworld is not defined in itself and for itself. Rather, it takes its character in relation to others, exclusion as a form of inclusion, inequality as a relationship. The populists in the culture wars call this 'black armband history'. The other angle is an upbeat story of collaboration. Each lifeworld could never have created itself in its own image. Each, rather, has been born in dialogue with 'others', and this is the source of its proudest self-attribution. These relationships and collaborations are of real value to civics, to the economy, and to the national community. The result is mutual influence, hybridity and cultural dynamism. From both angles, differences are now the narrative-in-time of Civic Pluralism. The nation now defines itself in history as the outcome of the dialogue of difference.

On the space dimension, differences are honoured by measures of regional and local self-government. And they are honoured aesthetically through the variable iconography of place. The phenomenal growth in tourism is a kitschy version of this honouring of differences, and it has had its noticeable effects to the extent that the bulldozers of abstract development are now halted with increasing frequency by those wanting to preserve environmental heritage values – the fabric of uniqueness and the value of difference in place.

And on a structural dimension, instead of centralised bureaucratic control, federalism and subsidiarity become guiding principles. Federalism means multiple and overlapping sites of self-government, whether geographically defined (federal, state, local); defined by culture and ethnicity (indigenous self-government, ethnic community groups); defined by expertise (professionals, hobbyists, volunteers); or defined by institution (educational, medical, corporate). Subsidiarity means that certain co-ordinating, negotiating and mediating roles are delegated out from the more particular and localised of these governments to the broader and more general. The power of the more general is founded on the commitment to delegation on the part of the more particular. This reverses the logic of delegation inherent in the modern nationalist state. With the decline of the civic, devolution often spells worrying fragmentation. Civic Pluralism, by contrast, forges more powerful cohesion through a process of subsidiarity that begins with differences and multiple sites of self-government and moves to more generalising and interconnecting – progressively more federal – levels of government. The result is an apparent paradox: cohesion-through-diversity.

As we move from more local and specific to more general and federal levels of government, ethnos or lifeworld particularity must be stripped from the processes of government – from indigenous community self-government to national government, for instance, or from an ethnic-community-run school to a national education system. Government needs to become a more and more neutral arbiter of differences.

Having a subsidiarity relation to more localised and particularised levels of government fundamentally transforms the character of federal government. The paradoxical universal of civic pluralism is openness to difference. This universal is achieved by customising public service provision to meet the particular needs of different lifeworlds. Varied lifeworlds will be included only by being recognised in their difference, and by having specialised services, such as education, health, or welfare, designed to meet universal ends. This means that, at more general, federalising levels, government must become neutral with respect to the details of cultural difference. It is a listener, a negotiator, a mediator, a broker. It customises all it does in order to meet effectively the needs of the varied communities it serves.

This is not to say that the state is uncommitted. On the contrary, it is deeply committed to pluralism and its procedures. The state remains infused with the symbolism and narratives of belonging but now they are narratives of diversity, inclusion, collaboration and cosmopolitanism. It remains committed to redistributive justice, but recognises that redistributive justice has to work with the raw material of varied lifeworld experiences. It strongly commits itself, in sum, to access to the material resources, social services and symbols of national belonging without prejudice to the differences between the lifeworlds of its citizens.

Education is one of the key areas of responsibility of the interfering federal state of Civic Pluralism; however, the principles and forms of inter-ference are now very different from those of the nationalist state. Unlike the education systems of nationalism, the federal state must be agnostic about lifeworld variations. However, the state does have a responsibility to ensure comparable outcomes, not of the exclusionary kind that had been measured by standardised tests, but by measuring comparabilities and customising its support to the school in order to provide outcomes for its students of the same order as those provided by other schools.

The cultural agnosticism of education in a state of Civic Pluralism also represents a deep commitment to a civic and ethical role. If the social contract is a moral act, a matter of belonging to moral community, and if civics is something that entails responsibilities as well as rights, then Civic Pluralism points us in the direction of a new commonwealth, a new social contract. This means that schools must teach new kinds of competence and new forms of civic morality in the era of Productive Diversity and Civic Pluralism. They must develop in students an ability to engage in the difficult dialogues that are an inevitable part of negotiating diversity. They must develop in students the morality of compromise in which parties to negotiations are willing to meet, on ground which they do not necessarily share in common; multiple citizenship in both the literal sense of being a participating member of more than one nation-state and the metaphorical sense of participating in a range of public and community forums. They must develop in students an ability to express and represent multilayered identity appropriate to the different lifeworlds, civic spaces, and work contexts that all citizens encounter; the extension of cultural repertoires appropriate to the range of contexts where difference has to be negotiated. They must develop in students a capacity to engage in collaborative politics which matches differences in relationships of complementarity; and dexterity with systems devolved according to the principle of federalism, where self-governing community and work activities are the social core, and more federal forms of government are subsidiary to these, rather than the other way around.

These generalities lead directly into the specifics of literacy teaching. The nationalist state had never taught literacy as mere skill. Literacy teaching has always been a civic act. In the case of the nationalist state this was to help students join an homogenous national community using official and standard forms of the language, or to appreciate a literature which captured the national essence. In this process, there were clear rights and wrongs, standards and non-standards, literatures and less-than-literatures. Civic Pluralism fundamentally transforms the civic purposes of literacy teaching. Now its purpose is to negotiate the increasing variability of the languages and discourses one encounters: interacting with other languages through interpreters or translations, using context-specific interlanguages, using English as *lingua franca*, and making sense of the plethora of dialects, accents, discourses and registers that one inevitably encounters. If the literacy curriculum of the nationalist state taught the rules of grammar as a standard, then the literacy curriculum of Civic Pluralism needs to tackle the issue of differences through a kind of comparative linguistics. For example, how can we account for the form of one text compared to another in terms of the peculiarities of its cultural location and the interests of writers and readers? How do we cross the border of language difference, to make a meaning that works? There are still rules in the language game and these need to be taught and learnt. These rules, however, are not located in language fixed to standards. Rather they are the rules of comparison, location and boundary crossing.

Education for personal life

Unlike other societies in human history, modern societies have separated work and civics from personal life. The personal occurs in its own spaces (the home, the family, grassroots community) and in its own times (after work, the weekend, holidays). Of course, in one sense, this separation of the private from the public is a kind of pretence, because work and civics always involve people in the most personal of ways. The public and the private profoundly shape each other. In an institutional sense, however, there is nevertheless a separation of the public realms of work and civics from the private realm of the personal. This is a constant frame of reference in modern times; one of the key features that distinguishes modern societies from others. Yet, within modern times, the nature of the mutual influence of private and public realms changes, from mass culture to fragmented community to multilayered identities.

In order to tell this story, we will trace changes in several aspects of personal life: changes in the aesthetics of consumption, in 'popular culture', in gender relations, and in language. These are important constituent parts of identity or who one senses oneself to be – the 'sources of the self' is Taylor's expression (Taylor 1994); 'structures of feeling' is the term Raymond Williams uses (Williams 1973, 1977, pp. 128–35; 1981).

Mass culture was one of the consequences of mass production and mass consumption as epitomised in Henry Ford's production line and sales philosophy ('. . . so long as it is black'). For the first time, all people in modern society had to work for money in order to purchase the necessities of life on the market. In its initial phase, this consumption was reduced to the barest, most minimal aesthetics. Human interests in this new modernity were reduced to generic demand and identical desires and the aesthetics of uniformity were celebrated even in the minimalist functionalism of modernist architecture and futurist design.

With the arrival of this modernity, something similar happens in the realm of popular culture. The narratives of the mass media increasingly galvanise people around a common identity. Major national newspapers, nationally broadcast radio, several television channels – the mass media drew people into a common cultural experience, the boundaries of which were substantially those of the nation-state and nationalism. Here, individualisation occurs as well as homogenisation. The mass media, by and large, speak in a kind of monologue to isolated individuals. These individuals, it is assumed, share identical interests in their 'imagined community'; the community of fellow readers and views they imagine as they read the daily press or watch the nightly news.

Meanwhile, gender relations took a new and ideally replicated form: the nuclear family, with dad working on the labour market, mum doing unpaid domestic work and looking after the two-point-however-many children. The radical novelty of this kind of family in modern times is not to be underestimated. Never before had the private realm been so dramatically separated from the public realm. This impacted on women particularly, perhaps in this sense the most radical frontierspeople of modernity: stuck in separate boxes, alone with the two-odd children and the generic domestic appliances (any colour you like, so long as they are white), they became isolated individuals working with little or no help and little or no community.

The dictates of mass culture also played themselves through in that most intimate of expressive domains, language. The express intent of the modern nation-state was to reduce language variety to a standard. The long-term consequence on a global scale has been an enormous drop in the number of languages (see Lo Bianco, Chapter 4 above), and the hundreds of millions of people who have lost ancestral languages from one generation to the next as they have moved into modern society. In one sense, this was a premeditated, imperialist, and even racist project – 'linguicism' is Phillipson's term (Phillipson and Skutnabb-Kangas 1986). In another sense, it was a kind of pragmatics: a project actively and sometimes enthusiastically undertaken by people entering modern society. Martin Nakata describes what he sees to be the sheer necessity for Torres Strait Islanders to take on forms of English that would get things done for them in the modern world (see Nakata, Chapter 5 above).

These, then, are just a few of the dimensions of mass culture. Of course, there was another realm of difference that endured in private life; in the form of folk life or ethnicity, for instance. But this was constantly under threat, either from modernity as a kind of explicit cultural imperialism, or as people internalised the pragmatics of modern life as their own cultural project. In their strongest moments, cultures of difference were a kind of resistance to modernity; a refusal of mass culture. There was, however, very little room for alternatives to the mass-produced goods that were available or affordable; the mass media that filled many of the available spaces of personal life; the housing that really worked only for nuclear families; the pragmatics of having to speak and read the national language to get ahead in school or in work. The cultural conversation of mass culture took the form of a monologue: an insistence so persistent that it easily slipped at times into propaganda and indoctrination.

Situated at one of the critical interfaces between the personal and the public, education was a decisive instrument of this insistence. Schools start with personal life as raw material, regardless of whatever oral language children have learnt in the private space of the home, and whatever their culturally situated interests and inclinations. They engage with these 'sources of the self' in order to transform them. Thus modern schools themselves become a formative source of the self. Take literacy teaching, for instance. Literacy is uniquely a schooled thing, and very different to oral language. It is not simply oral language transcribed; rather it is a radically different form of language which makes for a different kind of consciousness. The literacy of Fordism and nationalism privileged certain forms of writing. Business letters, internal memos and scientific reports, for instance, each spoke with an affected voicelessness. 'Don't use the first person, and certainly not the first person, singular', said the teacher in the grammar lesson. Persons in flesh and blood, with lives and histories, were spirited away to be replaced by abstract reason, instrumental rationality, authoritative systems-speak and ostensibly objective science-speak (Martin and Halliday 1993; Yates 1989). Literacy was formulaic, replicated from one modularised individual to the next; reducing as much as possible the variability that inevitably comes from different persons.

Schooled literacy was an assimilating business, in other words, which touched one's person in the most subtle and profound of ways. It was also exclusionary. Few individuals ever got to voice abstract authority through writing; most were included by exclusion, included to the extent that they were readers of the texts of command and the mass media, but excluded from forms of creation of the written word through which they might themselves have been one of the voiceless voices and thus have a real impact on their social environment.

Against the insistence of mass culture, personal life after Fordism and after the Cold War is increasingly moving towards a kind of fragmented community. Instead of mass consumption, we are experiencing increasing subcultural fragmentation around niche markets. At one end of the spectrum of consumption, a proliferation of 'boutique' products and services is emerging. At the other end of the spectrum, there is a broadening band of the working poor and welfare recipients who have no alternative but to purchase generic products which have none of the glossy novelty mass consumption items used to have, or to buy second-hand cast-offs.

There is just as much fragmentation in popular culture, too. Some of this is the result of new technological possibilities; narrowcasting on hundreds of television channels, pointcasting and the infinite variability of sites on the Internet. But fragmentation is not just a fiat of technological change. Some of the new, fragmented media also use older communication technologies, hence the proliferation of specialist magazines, niche radio stations and carefully targeted direct mail. It is subcultural fracturing, not technology, that is at the root of this customisation of communication with fracturing by ethnic group, by indigenous origins, by sexual orientation, by gender politics, by ethical concern, by domain of expertise, by hobbyist fetish, by proclivities in consumption, by fashion and fad, by taste and personal style. When not through a language of its own, each subculture speaks in its own specialised discourse. With the collapse of the homogenising processes of Fordism and nationalism, the discourses of subcultures are becoming progressively more divergent, and thus less mutually intelligible and harder for outsiders to get into. Yet, paradoxically perhaps, at the same time as this fragmentation is occurring, divergent subcultures find themselves juxtaposed in more intimate ways in workplaces, in neighbourhoods, in the media. The sense of fragmentation is palpable and ever-present.

Not only does this new media landscape indicate subcultural fragmentation. For many people, not being in the landscape is a part of the fragmentation. The 'mediascape' of the Internet, for instance, is more male than female, predominantly in English, and available only to those who have access to entry points or who are affluent enough to be able to buy the equipment and pay the service provider (see Luke, Chapter 3 above). Mapping the urban information landscape, geographers find 'wild zones' that are communication-dead (Lash 1994, p. 132). These are the zones inhabited by an excluded underclass: the ghettos in which migrants, the unemployed and the working poor live. And, within the household, women are frequently excluded: who holds the remote, surfs the Internet, plays the Nintendo?

The certainties of gender in the era of mass culture also fall to the fracturing of gender roles and identity. Women's magazines peddle myriad versions of womanhood – according to age, to style, to a domestic or a career focus. Men make themselves what they will, from 'sensitive New Age guys' to macho men, Volvo drivers to Harley-Davidson riders, careerists to gang members. And homosexuality emerges as a legitimate alternative – not one alternative, however, but many: from transvestites to body builders, and ultra-women to dykes on bikes.

These cultural shifts find their expression also in enormous changes in language. On the one hand, thousands of small ancestral languages disappear, as the social ecologies on which they were based are transformed by the processes of globalisation. Part of the sense of fragmentation is created by an increasingly spirited refusal to allow these languages to be lost, and resistance to linguistic imperialism. English is nevertheless becoming both a *lingua franca* and a *lingua mundi* (see Lo Bianco, Chapter 4 above). Seventy-five per cent of the world's mail and 80 per cent of the world's e-mail is now in English (Geary 1997), while the majority of the speakers of English now speak it as a second language. This changes what English is and what English does. Now, the spread of English is the result of a kind of pragmatics, of having to learn English in order to read the labels in the global products, to watch CNN, to read into areas of academic specialism, or to participate in global communities of experts. Yet, in another important sense, the spread of English does not have to mean reduction in language diversity. English itself becomes fragmented into hybrid and unstable forms that are less and less mutually intelligible; the creoles of postcolonial societies, the dialects of urban ghettos, the arcane vernaculars of divergent youth cultures, the specialist discourses of experts, and the technicalese of sports and hobbies. Where one spread of diversity is destroyed, another springs up.

At the same time, the relationship between the public and the personal is being dramatically transformed. Workplace and civic discourses are becoming highly personalised. At work, command structures, with their written memos and formal letters, are being replaced by the informality of management by workplace culture. This puts an increasing emphasis on vernacular orality; and even new forms of writing, such as e-mail, become less formal and more like speaking. A discourse of familiarity once kept to the realm of the private is introduced into the workplace and civic spaces.

One of the consequences of this highly personalised public discourse makes ever more stark the immediacy and proximity of differences. Personalised discourse plays up differences, even to the extent that differences become the source of narrative tension; a focus for the anxieties of fragmentation. Personalised public discourse is also the basis for fragmentation in the form of exclusion. It is easier for outsiders to enter the stratum of technological, managerial and political power when it is carried by the older discourse of formality than when it is drenched in the lifeworld vernacular of those who already hold power.

The new communications media, moreover, are more personalising in their very nature. They draw you in, as an active subject in the meaning-making process. Television broadcasts out, says Gilster, while the Internet draws people in (Gilster 1997, p. 38). Instead of being told things ('viewers' in the era of broadcast television), pointcasting allows Internet users to 'personalise their newsfeed'. With ever more channels, even television watchers become more like 'users' than old-style 'viewers'. Masters of the remote control, they sit swapping and changing in such a way that the meaning-product is more a viewer-made collage than a network-made programme. The effect once more is a sense of fragmentation, heightened still further by shorter grabs and the rapid juxtaposition of flicking and switching. Whole worlds of meaning are conjured up in a few moments of image plus music plus gesture plus tone of voice – the multimodality of these communications channels cramming huge amounts of cultural reference into a few seconds, at least compared to the ponderously slow newsprint or radio texts of the era of mass culture. As we conjure up the references and flash to the next image set, the insistence of mass culture which had once turned us all into homogenised individuals is replaced by the insistence of the meaning-maker-as-subject. Intrinsically, this is the stuff of variety.

In a bleak view of these differences, they remain as that; as fragmented and fragmenting. Cultures in the plural make for a voluntary form of apartheid between the isolationisms and separatisms of one kind or another; from the ethnonationalisms of the post-Cold-War world to drop-out communities and New Age alternatives; to defeated, defiant, and lawless ghettos. And in so far as persons invariably live in many, now deeply personalised, subcultures, personality heads in the direction of a metaphorical schizophrenia. Underlying all of this is an increasingly fractured and decentred consciousness. After the submitting to the authority of mass culture as an object, a person more spoken to than speaking, the revival of the subject is accompanied by cultural relativism, with all the chaos and amorality of 'anything goes' and 'live and let live'. In the world of high culture, this form of consciousness is often labelled by its aficionados 'postmodernism'.

So what do schools do in the face of this fragmented community? The easiest thing is to go with the flow of fragmentation: the 'shopping mall' curriculum of 'choice and diversity'; the community-run schools that do their own cultural things; the back-to-basics nostalgia for a time that has gone; the facile and tokenistic multiculturalism of food and festivals.

If diversity is a fundamental fact of our moment in modern times, an integrating pluralism is a necessary antidote to this fragmentation. Diversity must become the paradoxical basis for cohesion. In personal life, the place to start is with the person as a social being, and the integrating potential of Multilayered Identities. This is a strategically optimistic response to the end of mass culture and the increasing fragmentation of community.

In the area of consumption, Productive Diversity raises the possibility of customisation extended to the point where customers are integrated into the design of the product or service. This can happen at a number of points: either in the lead-up to production or in the development of products and services which are subjectivity-friendly, software-adjustable, customer-sensitive, open and flexible. This, however, requires an abandonment to a significant degree of the bottom line, price-equalising logic of the market and its replacement by a logic of cultural-quality differentials (Cope and Kalantzis 1997a).

In popular culture and the media, new technologies and economies of small scale allow local access and control of the most dynamic media of cultural creation. Community autonomy does not have to mean fragmentation, however. It can give people a voice they didn't have before, to become citizens interlinked by the integrating federalism of Civic Pluralism. It can give strength and vibrancy to the overlapping cultural networks that are the backbone of Productive Diversity.

In the area of language, we can take as a constructive starting point another of the paradoxes of globalisation, that its universal spread intensifies particularisation at least as much as it forces homogenisation. In the context of global and local linguistic diversity, for instance, systems for managing multilingualism may well prove cheaper and more effective than the nationalist project of getting everyone to speak the one language; with telephone interpreters working all over the world making any language-to-language combination possible, in any place at any time; with organisations working market niches by recruiting bilinguals and deliberately presenting themselves multilingually; and, maybe even in the near future, with the possibility of machine translation. Globalisation does not have to mean the dominance of English at the expense of other languages. However much English spreads as a *lingua mundi*, other languages may well go from strength to strength.

And it may well be that dialect and discourse divergence within English is something that should be celebrated and supported. Discourses vary because they do different things – technical things, things of history and identity, things of affiliation and affect. Dynamism and divergence are explorations of alternative ways of being human: different ways of using tools and different ways of living in and through culture. The critical challenge is to develop integrative inter-languages as an antidote to fragmentation, so the results of each subcultural experiment are made generally available. Customer-speak needs to make technical-speak intelligible to lay outsiders. Systems of interpreting, translation, and using a *lingua franca* need be developed that provide entrees from one subculture into another, and thus make the most of the mutual benefits that will flow from networking, collaboration, interchange and hybrid recreation.

The personalising of the public and the making public of the personal could present productive interrelational possibilities. It introduces sub-jectivity – desires, interests, affect – into realms previously dominated by the hidden agendas of instrumental rationality and abstract systems. Life becomes a matter of design, in the constructivist as well as the morpho-logical sense. You are designed as a cultural being, in language and consciousness; and you are designing, a maker of your personal life as you combine and recombine the range of resources in the layers of your identity. Productive Diversity, Civic Pluralism and Multilayered Identities put the onus on the activity of designing, of making and remaking cultural connections and on cross-cultural relationality. The focus on designing and subjectivity immediately introduces the complexity and variety of lifeworld experiences in the life of the person and the life of the world. It requires a new form of consciousness. Beck speaks of 'the self-critical society' (Beck 1994) and Lash of 'reflexivity' (Lash 1994). For pluralism, this means constantly reading the world critically to comprehend the divergent cultural interests that inform meanings and actions, their relationships and their consequences.

Education has reached a crisis point. On the one hand, the familiar territories of curriculum seem eerily irrelevant. The 'basics' appear to be vacuous now because the main ground has shifted from the old-fashioned, page-bound written texts and the dislocated 'standards'. What literacy teaching used to promise to do, we don't seem to need any more; and even if it is of some use, some of the time, it's certainly not enough. On the other hand, a trivialising multiculturalism or the fractured, 'shopping mall' curriculum doesn't provide equity measured in terms of access to work and public participation.

If identity is in its nature social and multilayered, and if the latest mutation of modern times is one in which divergences need to be made a productive and paradoxically cohesive force, then the essence of what education does needs to change. Rather than fall prey to the forces of fragmentation and destructive divergence, schools need to work with a new ethics and a new pragmatism: the ethics and pragmatism of pluralism, of divergences that complement each other and that in their diversity create new and productive interrelationships. This has become the new moral and practical civic mission of education.

Taking the domain of literacy pedagogy, the Multiliteracies framework is one suggestion as to how this new schooling might come about. Its starting point is the situated selves of learners, the starting point of a transformation that does not leave those selves behind in the fashion of assimilation, but which recognises and builds upon those selves, in their diversity and in the multilayered nature of each person's identity. The starting point is not the generic individual and learning as an identically replicated process. Rather, it is multiple languages and dialects, multiple community histories and life experiences, multiple intelligences, in sum, multiple ways of being human. In so far as the role of education is transformation, it is by way of extension of one's repertoire, boundary crossing and expanding horizons, rather than having to leave old selves behind (see Situated Practice, Chapter 11 below). A pedagogy of pluralism works on differences by reviewing their form in relation to their cultural location. For instance: where is this text from? what are its multiple sources? what is it doing? who is it doing it for? how does it do it? how do we get into it? what could it do for us? (see Overt Instruction and Critical Framing, Chapter 11 below). It also works on productive relationality: how can we use these meaning sources, extend our repertoire and relate to other lifeworlds – by entering them, by forming networks and alliances, by setting up complementary collaborations? (see Transformed Practice, Chapter 11 below).

It is in this spirit that Carmen Luke speaks of the potentials of cyber-schooling with its pedagogies of networking and collaboration, crossing boundaries of difference down the hall and across the world (see Luke, Chapter 3 above). Joseph Lo Bianco speaks of the necessity of multi-lingualism as an additive process, extending one's linguistic repertoire in the context of irreducible diversity (see Lo Bianco, Chapter 4 above). Martin Nakata speaks of the logistics of Torres Strait Islanders acquiring forms of English that will get more things done, not in order to leave their identities behind but in developing a cultural interface position (see Nakata, Chapter 5 above). And James Paul Gee speaks of negotiating distributed systems, of relating dispersed parts in systems where there is no privileged centre (see Gee, Chapter 2 above). These are just glimpses of some of the things an education for pluralism might do.

Changing times and strategic possibilities			
	From	*To*	*To*
Work	Fordism	PostFordism	Productive Diversity
Civics	Nationalism	Decline of the civic	Civic Pluralism
The personal	Mass culture	Fragmented community	Multilayered Identities
Corresponding forms of education	Exclusion or assimilation	Superficial multiculturalism	Pluralism

Part III

DESIGNS OF MEANING
The 'what' of multiliteracies

INTRODUCTION

The changes described by the various authors in Part II of this book are no less than enormous. They mean that, if we are to do justice to the dreams and aspirations of our students and the communities from which they come, what counts for literacy simply has to change. This part discusses the 'what' of Multiliteracies; the things literacy pedagogy needs to achieve in addition to, or different from, what it has traditionally achieved.

In Chapter 7, Gunther Kress explains why the language-based theories of communication that have dominated our understandings of meaning are no longer adequate. There are two main strands in his argument. First, the texts of the era of Multiliteracies are intrinsically multimodal as the visual, the audio and the gestural are becoming increasingly significant in the media, in computer-mediated information systems, and so on. The dominance of language in education, and Western society generally, has been at the expense of thinking about and teaching and learning about modes of meaning other than the linguistic-textual. One consequence of this has been the suppression of synaesthesia, or the human potential to represent meanings using multiple senses. The second major strand in Kress's argument is that language-based theories of meaning, including the theories about language traditionally taught as grammar in schools, have focused on static systems of elements and rules. The Design notion, however, focuses on the way in which every meaning-making utterance is intentional, taking the meaning-making resources available in the world and transforming them. Here the emphasis is on change rather than convention, active design rather than detached critique, and curriculum as an interested design for social futures rather than cultural reproduction.

Norman Fairclough goes on to explore some of these themes in Chapter 8. Beginning with the Design notion, he develops a dynamic theory of language in which identity, difference and change are at the centre. He conceives of language as action in contemporary life, analysing examples which illustrate the enormous changes associated with the 'marketisation' and globalisation of everyday life. To make his case, he introduces key concepts for a dynamic theory of language, such as intertextuality and hybridity.

In Chapter 9, Gunther Kress returns to the question of multimodality, with an extended analysis of the issues raised by Fairclough in the previous chapter, and in his own Chapter 7. The new information technologies and media landscapes of the communication revolution, he explains, lend themselves to the representation of visual, gestural and audio meanings. Indeed, changes in the contemporary communications environment lead us to a new understanding of language itself, in which we might uncover neglected aspects of linguistic meaning. Language is itself invariably multi-modal; writing is visually designed and spoken language has profoundly important audio qualities. As an instance of the kind of recovery required to counterbalance the language bias of our communications theories and school curricula alike, he suggests some dimensions of a grammar of the visual.

Bill Cope and Mary Kalantzis draw together in Chapter 10 a number of recurring themes to indicate the broad shape of the 'what' of Multi-literacies – the general subject matter, in other words, of an extended version of literacy pedagogy. They begin the chapter with an overview of the relationships of design and transformation to cultural differences and cultural change. The chapter then goes on to examine five possible dimensions to designs of meaning (representational, social, organisational, contextual and ideological), across linguistic, visual, gestural, spatial, audio and multimodal modes of meaning. These are presented in the form of a series of critical questions about meanings in context – not in order to draw conclusions about general rules of meaning, but questions through which learners might be able to investigate specific differences in meaning and the varied human interests that they represent. The chapter concludes by examining the restrictions and limitations of literacy teaching narrowly conceived, and contrasts this with the challenges presented by the new multimedia technologies. Here, the two central concerns of the Multi-literacies Project present themselves as acutely interconnected: the nature of the new communications environment, and the paradoxes of globally enmeshing communications technologies which at the same time highlight the significance of diversity.

7

DESIGN AND TRANSFORMATION

New theories of meaning

Gunther Kress

New theories of representation

The semiotic changes which characterise the present and which are likely to characterise the near future cannot be adequately described and understood with currently existing theories of meaning and communication. These are based on language, and so, quite obviously, if language is no longer the only or even the central semiotic mode, then theories of language can at best offer explanations for one part of the communicational landscape only. Theories of language will simply not serve to explain the other semiotic modes, unless one assumes, counterfactually, that they are in every significant way like language. Nor will theories of language explain and describe the interrelations between the different modes, language included, which are characteristically used in the landscape of Multiliteracies, of always multimodal semiotic objects – the 'texts' – of the contemporary period.

As a first requirement, the multimodal texts/messages of the era of Multiliteracies need a theory which deals adequately with the processes of integration/composition of the various modes in these texts: both in production/making and in consumption/reading. This in turn presupposes adequate understandings of the semiotic characteristics of the various modes which are brought together in multimodal compositions. At this level, a semiotic theory which is too much tied to and derived from one particular mode – for instance, our conventional language-based theories of communication and meaning – will permit neither an adequate nor an integrated description of multimodal textual objects, nor of multimedia production. In other words, an adequate theory for contemporary multimodal textual forms needs to be formulated so as to permit the description both of the specific characteristics of a particular mode *and* of its more general semiotic properties which allow it to be related plausibly to other semiotic modes. Take as an instance the need for any semiotic mode which is used in human communication to be able to express the meaning 'social distance'. This is done in specific ways in language, for instance through the use of the pronoun 'we' rather than the pronoun 'I' ('We regret to inform you . . .' rather than 'I regret to inform you . . .'), or through the use of the 'past tense' (as in 'I wanted to ask you for a loan of your car') rather than the 'present tense' (as in 'I want to ask you for a loan of your car'). This meaning is expressed in quite other ways, necessarily, in images: for instance by the distance of viewer from object – not close and friendly, but distant and formal; or by the vertical angle: '*looking up* to an object or person of power' or '*looking down* on a person or object of lesser power'. Both the relatedness of the means through which this is expressed (e.g. 'distance' in both cases: temporal distance in one case and spatial distance in the other), and the differences in forms of expression between two given modes need to be readily describable in an adequate theory of meaning.

A second and major issue is that contemporary, and in particular mainstream, theories of semiosis are implausible as theories of meaning and inappropriate to the needs of communication through Multiliteracies. Current theories describe the *use* of an existing stable system and of its elements rather than of remaking and transformation. That is, individuals are seen as users, more or less competently, of an existing, stable, static system of elements and rules. This view has diverse causes. Some are historical; others are to do with contemporary social and political-ideological factors. One foundational aspect with the most far-reaching consequences is the widely entrenched common sense about the arbitrary relation in the sign between signifier and signified, between form and meaning. That relation is regarded as both established and sustained by a motiveless social convention. Yet all and any of the examples of everyday communication speak of change: changes in forms of text; in uses of language; in the communicational and representational potentials of all elements of 'literacies'. Indeed change is one of the unchanging aspects of systems of communication. But change and conventionality are not easy bedfellows: the common understanding is that convention impedes change, that convention is a force for the maintenance of stability. When the theoretical element of the arbitrary relation of form and meaning is added to this, there seems neither reason for nor explanation of change. If change and convention are not to be treated as mutually exclusive terms, then the question still remains, forcefully, how we are to account for change.

The argument of the Multiliteracies Project is that the semiotic landscape is changing in fundamental ways, and that this change relates to other changes in social, cultural, economic and technological domains. While a semiotic theory which could not easily account for change was never adequate to the facts of semiosis, it may have been sustainable in periods where change was less intense than it is at the moment, and when the forces of control were stronger, and less open to challenge at every point. A semiotic theory which does not have an account of change at its core is both simply inadequate and implausible in the present period.

Dominant theories of semiosis – in linguistics by and large – are theories of use in which language is seen as a stable (and largely autonomous) system of elements, categories, and rules of combination. The facts of the communicational landscape are facts about changes in the use, extension, and function of both the categories *and* the rules of all and any system of representation. In other words, they show a quite different situation to that portrayed – implicitly – in current theory. The crucial point is to provide a theory which explains the changes in use, form and system. This requires turning current common sense on its head. Instead of regarding individuals as mere users of a system, who produce no change, we need to see that changes take place always, incessantly, and that they arise as a result of the interested actions of individuals. It is a need on the part of individual makers of texts/messages which leads them to stretch, change, adapt, and modify all of the elements used, all the time, and thereby change the whole set of representational resources with its internal relations.

An adequate theory of semiosis will be founded on a recognition of the 'interested action' of socially located, culturally and historically formed individuals, as the remakers, the transformers, and the re-shapers of the representational resources available to them.

Consider this example: a three-year-old is attempting to clamber up a very steep, grassy slope. He says, 'This is a heavy hill'. His interest here is to express/represent the great effort which it is taking him to climb this slope. He doesn't have the word 'steep' as an available lexical item, as an available resource. So he uses an element which he does have, and which most adequately expresses in its already existent (lexical/semiotic) form the meaning which he wishes to represent – something like: 'it is really hard; really heavy work for me to climb this hill'. In this process 'heavy' has been re-shaped, remade, transformed, in relation to its prior range of uses and potentials. We can of course decide – and that would be the usual path in contemporary theory – that the child's competence is inadequate, and we need to teach him the (proper use of the) word 'heavy'.

An alternative is to say that this is in fact an entirely usual process, though usually less visibly so, of all our uses of the resources of semiotic systems of all kinds. That is, our interests in representation and communication at a particular point are never readily matched by the existent semiotic resources, but rather that we choose the most apt forms, the forms already most suited by virtue of their existing potentials, for the representation of our meanings. As there is never a total 'fit', the resources are always transformed.

Notions of language use – that is, deployment of existing resources without changing them – will need to be replaced by notions of the constant remaking of the resources in the process of their use, in action and in interaction. The remaking of the resources is an effect both of the demands of particular occasions of interaction and of the social and cultural characteristics of the individual maker of signs. Both together account for the sign-maker's interest in representing a phenomenon in a particular way, and in communicating it in certain media. This interest is personal, cognitive, affective and social, and it shapes the 'direction' of the remaking of the resources. In this way the remaking on the one hand reflects individual interest and, on the other, owing to the social history and the present social location of the individual, also reflects broad socio-cultural trends. Semiotic change is thus shaped and guided by the characteristics of broad social factors, which are individually inflected and shaped by the action of the individual in interaction with social others.

The interested action of those engaged in semiosis is the crucial matter in attempts to get beyond a theory of *use*. It defines one central aspect of the process of semiosis: the sign is the expression of the maker's interest through the motivated expression in apt form of the meaning of the sign-maker. This action is transformative rather than totally creative: that is, it is action on and with existing semiotic (cultural) resources. The more the sign-maker is in the culture, the more he or she is 'socialised', the more the shapedness of the social and cultural resources will be in the foreground; but the transformative, re-shaping action is always seemingly present, however invisible.

With this approach, use is replaced by transformation and remaking. In present semiotic (-linguistic) theories the action of the individual is use, the implementation of the potentials of an existing system; in a semiotic (-linguistic) theory of transformation and remaking the action of the individual is that of the changing of the resources: using existing resources in the guiding frame of the maker's interest. If competence in the use of the possibilities of an existing stable system is the goal of present theories, the capacity of design through the (re-)shaping of the potentials of existing resources is the goal of the latter. The two approaches assume very different notions of individual action and of individual responsibility. Consequently the two approaches have deeply differing potentials and implications for applied areas – whether in language use and language learning or in education more generally.

Interest and design

From the outside, semiotic systems, language included, are seen as sets of resources available in a given culture, which are given their regularities by larger cultural values and social contingencies. They are deployed according to cultural histories and individual interest in particular social interactions with their distributions of power. They are used according to this communicational and representational potential as it has been developed in a particular culture. They are remade innovatively in the making of always novel signs by individuals in social interactions. Use is replaced by remaking, which is transformation; and the notion of the semiotic system is now replaced by that of a dynamic, constantly remade and re-organised set of semiotic resources.

The focus on language alone has meant a neglect, an overlooking, even a suppression of the potentials of all the representational and communicational modes in particular cultures; an often repressive and systematic neglect of human potentials in many of these areas; and a neglect equally, as a consequence, of the development of theoretical understandings of such modes. Semiotic modes have different potentials, so that they afford different kinds of possibilities of human expression and engagement with the world, and through this differential engagement with the world they facilitate differential possibilities of development: bodily, cognitively, affectively. Or, to put it provocatively: the single, exclusive and intensive focus on written language has dampened the full development of all kinds of human potentials, through all the sensorial possibilities of human bodies, in all kinds of respects, cognitively and affectively, in two- and three-dimensional representation.

Just at the point where 'literacy' – socially made forms of representing and communicating – is undergoing radical changes in the context of the deeply revolutionary effects of social, political and economic re-alignments, produced in part as effects of the 'Electronic Age', it is essential to ask this question about the adequacy of present theories of semiosis and their effects. The fast developing technologies of virtuality are promising and threatening a new and more intense distancing – a new alienation of ourselves from our bodies. This demands the most serious rethinking at this point. If we do not take this opportunity, we not only deny ourselves the possibility of actively participating in the shaping of this 'age' but we may unwittingly collude in a new diminution of the potentials of being human.

Here our focus is predominantly on the issue of design, and in particular, on a shift from a view of representation and communication as strictly bound by systems held firmly in place by arbitrary relations of form and meaning, held in place by the force of convention. If interest is, instead, seen as the motivating force of representation, then the shape of existing resources of representation can be explained entirely without any split between the agency of the individual, and the determinative power of cultural forms and social structures.

Interest works prospectively: that is, I want to represent something in order to communicate it, for someone (even if that someone is myself). To do so I use the representational modes which are most apt for my purposes;

and I also make a selection of which mode, in an ensemble, is to be central at a particular point in an interaction; and which modes are to carry which aspects of my message. This represents a complex act and process of Design. Design is thus both about the best, the most apt representation of my interest; and about the best means of deploying available resources in a complex ensemble.

This process involves constant transformation of the existing resources at every point. However, these resources are always the result of prior transformation by myself (in my prior reading/internalisation) and by countless others in the history of these resources in my culture. I am thus always working with the stuff which has been transformed in line with the prior (social/cultural and individual) interests of others in my culture. I am always working with the products of prior design. My own representational action is thus both an always new making in the implementation of my new designs; and it is always also the constant reshaping, the Redesign of the materials, which reflect the prior designs of others.

In this view, individual action and agency is brought together with the effect of social form and structure, without any incompatibility. From the point of view of the Multiliteracies Project this is essential, as the representational and communicational demands of the present period, and increasingly of the coming era, will demand the ability to act precisely in this fashion: an era of constant social dynamic, of change, and of difference of all kinds in all dimension requires exactly this facility.

This view may seem challengingly novel in the domain of communication. It is, however, no more than an expression of what is regarded as entirely commonsensical in other domains. Fashion design, for example, works in precisely this way. Using existing design, such as previous styles, existing fabric and colour schemes, it produces transformations of these out of the social and individual interest of designers, who are expressing larger social interests – ideas about shifts in forms of gender, and so on. Transformations, whether here or in communication, are always transformations of entities produced out of a prior interest which was social and individual.

Synaesthesia

This newer theory of representation may prove adequate to the demands of several urgent tasks posed by wide social and economic changes, including the electronic technologies: the need for dealing with constant change; the need to treat individuals as agentive in relation not only to the production of their textual objects but also in relation to their constant remaking of their community's representational resources; the interaction of many semiotic modes in a text; and to do so from both the maker's and the reader's point of view. The interaction of different modes and of different possibilities of expression in multimodal texts and multimedia production poses questions not only at the level of text but also at the level of cognitive processing: new demands are made cognitively and no doubt affectively by the new technologies and by their textual forms. A new theory of semiosis will need to acknowledge and account for the processes of synaesthesia, the transduction of meaning from one semiotic mode to another semiotic mode, an activity constantly performed by the brain. In other words, a theory of semiosis which incorporates the facts of multimodality also needs to be a theory in which synaesthesia is seen as an entirely usual and productive process, essential equally for the understanding of semiosis in a multimodal semiotic landscape as for the possibilities of real innovation, rather than, as too often now, seen as a pathology to be remedied.

In the most immediate past, as in our present, synaesthetic activity has been suppressed in institutionalised education, owing to the social and cultural dominance of language in the written mode in the public domain. Culture affects and even structures, through privileged and thereby habituated usages, which semiotic modes are available; which are made focal and valued; which are made usable; and which are ruled out of or into the public landscape of communication. Social and cultural forces thus determine which modes are 'there' for humans to use in particular domains; they affect the manner in which they are used. The school, in Western societies, says that writing is serious and most highly valued; music is for the aesthetic development of the individual, as is visual art. These structures, pressures, and actions have shaped not only the representational landscape but also the cognitive and affective potentials of individuals. A more developed understanding of these processes is essential to open up full and productive access to the multiplicity of representational and communicational potentials which will be essential for competent practice in the electronic age, in the socialities and economies of the near future. At the moment our theories of meaning (hence our dominant theories of cognition) are entirely shaped by and derived from theories founded on the assumption of the dominance of language. Meaning is in fact identified with 'meaning in language'. This constitutes a major impediment to an understanding of the semiotic potentials of, among other modes, the visual and its role in cognition, representation, and communication. In the project of Multiliteracies these relations have to be entirely rethought.

From critique to Design: the new curricula of communication

In a theory of use, the task of the individual is to understand and to have competent control of the representational system and its capacities. Although the potentials of the system make possible a vast – even infinite – range of textual forms, their scope remains relatively circumscribed by

159

convention: hence the valuation of 'creativity' as rare in such a theory. In that theory, change, other than as that rare event of creativity, is produced via critique: that is, existing forms, and the social relations of which they are manifestations, are subjected to a distanced, analytical scrutiny to reveal the rules of their constitution. It is now essential to offer a critique of critique, by showing it to be a response to particular circumstances in a particular period, showing it as a historical phenomenon and not as naturally there. In periods of relative social stability critique has the function of introducing a dynamic into the system. In a situation of intense social change, the rules of constitution both of texts and of social arrangements are in crisis: they are not settled, but in process of change. In the new theory of representation, in the context of the multimodal, multimedia modes of textual production in the era of electronic technologies, the task of text-makers is that of complex orchestration. Further, individuals are now seen as the remakers, transformers, of sets of representational resources – rather than as users of stable systems, in a situation where a multiplicity of representational modes are brought into textual compositions. All these circumstances call for a new goal in textual (and perhaps other) practice: not of critique but of Design. Design takes for granted full competence in the use of resources which includes a full understanding of the communicational (hence political, ideological) potentials of these resources. But beyond that it requires the orchestration and remaking of these resources in the service of frameworks and models expressive of the maker's intentions in shaping the social and cultural environment (see Buchanan and Margolin 1995). While critique looks at the present through the means of past production, Design shapes the future through deliberate deployment of representational resources in the designer's interest. Design is the essential textual principle and pedagogic/political goal for periods characterised by intense and far-reaching change.

Design rests on a chain of processes of which critique – as distanced analytic understanding – is one: it can, however, no longer be the focal one, or be the major goal of textual practices. Critique leaves the initial definition of the domain of analysis to the past, to the past production (and Design) of those whose processes are to be subjected to critique. It leaves the design and definition of the agenda to those whose purposes are to be the subject of critique, and are not mine. The task of the critic is to perform analysis on an agenda of someone else's Design. As a result, a considerable degree of inertia is built into this process. The idea of the intellectual as critic corresponds to social arrangements and distributions of power, rights and responsibilities of certain social arrangements and of certain historical periods: namely arrangements in which some individuals and groups set the agenda and others either follow or object. Design takes the results of past production as the resource for new shaping, and for remaking. Design sets aside past agendas, and treats them and their products as resources in setting an agenda of future aims, and in assembling means and resources for implementing that. The social and political task and effect of the designer is fundamentally different from that of the critic.

It is here that I wish to make two brief points about curriculum. Curriculum is a design for the future (see Kress 1995). The contents and processes put forward in curriculum and in its associated pedagogy constitute the design for future human dispositions. They provide one set of important means, and resources for the individual's transformative, shaping action in making herself or himself as social humans. That is one point. The other is that the sites of education are now also in question, as are their aims. The state's threatened withdrawal from institutionalised education, with its aim of producing citizens, in favour of the market, with its aim of producing consumers, is one strand in that. In that shift, new (and also very ancient) sites of education are coming back into the foreground: the workplace prominently (as in the ancient guild system), and now also the multiplicity of modes of mediated communication. These are not only or no longer just the 'mass media', but quite new media – media that, as yet, are only hazily knowable in their effects – with the Internet of course the dominant metaphor at the moment – and their educational aims and effects. All these pose entirely new questions for 'curriculum'. In all of these the category of Design is foundational.

Critique and Design imply deeply differing positions and possibilities for human social action; and deeply differing potentials for human subjectivities in social and economic life. The likely shape of the near future is such that the facilities of Design rather than those of critique, will be essential for equitable participation in social, economic and cultural life. It would be an unforgivable dereliction of the responsibilities of intellectuals if the potentials of representation and communication – of literacy in a very broad and metaphoric sense – offered by current developments were not fully explored, and a concerted attempt made to shape their direction to bring about at least some of the much talked-about utopian visions of communication in the electronic age.

8

MULTILITERACIES AND LANGUAGE

Orders of discourse and intertextuality

Norman Fairclough

My focus in this chapter is to develop the view of language which the Multiliteracies Project is built upon, and which it will hopefully continue to develop both here and in the future. Given that one of the core concerns of the Project is to address the increasingly multisemiotic nature of texts in contemporary society and how they draw upon and articulate together different semiotic modalities (e.g. language and visual images), the issue is not simply how one theorises language, but how one theorises semiosis more generally. However, it is important to address specifically the question of language within this broader perspective, because how language is conceptualised has a pervasive influence both on theories of semiosis and on views of literacy and literacy education. The relationship between language and other semiotic modalities has, of course, already been discussed by Gunther Kress.

The concept of Design being developed in the Multiliteracies Project (see Chapter 1 above) is, of course, just a starting point. In centring the concept of Design, we are suggesting that meaning-making is a creative application of existing resources for meaning (Designs of meaning) in negotiating the constantly shifting occasions and needs of communication. In this process of Designing, the resources for meaning are themselves transformed. This is not to deny the repetitiveness and predictability of mundane aspects of life and meaning-making, but to treat them as the limiting case rather than as the model for meaning-making in general; in contemporary life, instability and change are primary experiences, and our view of meaning-making needs to reflect that.

How we view meaning-making necessarily has implications for how we theorise language. What is implied here is a conception of language which centres difference, change and creativity. There is a tradition within linguistic thought which does this, though it has until recently been marginalised within the discipline of linguistics. In broad terms, this tradition stresses both the social diversity of language, the multiplicity of co-existing but socially differentiated forms of a language, its 'heteroglossia'; and the possibilities for creatively articulating together these diverse forms of a language in texts which are mixed, heterogeneous, in terms of, say, social dialect or genre. The tradition is particularly associated with the Bakhtin school (Bakhtin 1986), though it has been widely taken up in recent work, including work within critical discourse analysis (see, for instance, Fairclough 1995a; Thibault 1991).

My aim in this chapter will be briefly to describe and illustrate one version of this view of language. I shall be arguing in particular that such a view of language needs to bring together a theory of language structure and a theory of discourse – that is, a social theory of language use. I shall focus upon two central concepts of a theory of discourse which are I believe of fundamental importance to the view of language underlying the Multi-literacies Project: orders of discourse and intertextuality. Before doing so, however, I want to elaborate a little on the connection pointed to above between features of contemporary social life and views of meaning-making and of language.

Contemporary life and language

We are living through a period of intense social and cultural change which is pervasive and universal in its global, national and local effects, and which involves the breakdown and redrawing of boundaries and relationships of all sorts. I believe that this radical unsettling of social life is driven by economic change and the search for profit; and it gives rise to struggles to resist, try to reverse, or alter the direction of change. In part these fundamental changes are changes in language, involving the breakdown and redrawing of boundaries between different language practices understood in the broadest sense – between different languages, different dialects, different genres, different discourses. Let me illustrate with two examples of boundary change at different levels: marketisation and globalisation of discourse practices.

Marketisation

By marketisation I mean the extension of market modes of operation to new areas of social life – the terms commodification and consumerisation are also used to refer to the same processes (Featherstone, Lash, and Robertson 1995; Wernick 1991). For instance, there has been a radical marketisation of public services in some countries during the past couple of decades. This means that public services like hospitals, schools or universities are increasingly having to operate like private businesses.

Universities for instance are raising an increasing proportion of their funds from private sources, operating according to financial plans, cutting 'unprofitable' departments and areas of work (those which don't attract students or research funds), and 'investing' in those which have the capacity to yield higher profits, using approaches to staff training, appraisal, and so on taken from business management, putting a great deal of energy into marketing their 'products' to potential 'consumers'. Marketisation of public services is part of the spread of economic neo-liberalism, which entails the weakening of the welfare state, and widespread privatisation of public industries, utilities and services.

These processes of marketisation are in part linguistic in nature: they involve a marketisation of language, in the sense that the language of areas like public services is being colonised by the language of the market. The genre of advertising for example has been widely extended to new domains, leading to a multiplication of different types of advertising which are generically hybrid – they share some common features with ordinary commodity advertising, but these are combined with generic features which are specific to the particular domain in question. For instance, the university prospectus has undergone a shift from a densely written description of courses and the regulations governing them addressed to insiders, to a marketing document addressed to the outside world which combines features of the traditional prospectus with features of commodity advertising genre.

Let me just focus on one aspect of this shift: its implications for social relations and social identities. Compare Figures 8.1 and 8.2, which date from 1967 and 1993 respectively (see Fairclough 1993 for a fuller account). The earlier prospectus reflects the economic circumstances of British universities and power relations between institution and applicant in the 1960s: the institution is constructed in various ways as having authority over the applicant. The most obvious example is in the lower right-hand side of the text where the text refers to the university's requirements for degree schemes. Here there are a number of obligational modalities which make the authority of the institution over the potential student quite explicit. For example, 'second year undergraduates . . . are required to take'; 'Third year undergraduates must choose . . .'; 'Any one course . . . may be offered by an undergraduate'.

But marketisation entails a shift in social relations and social identities which results in ambivalent and contradictory authority relations. The essential point is that once an institution begins to treat the people it provides services for in a market way, as consumers or clients to whom they are trying to sell 'products', then they acquire some authority – the authority which comes from the power to choose, and to shop around. How then does the institution maintain control over its own processes and procedures when it is trying to sell them to consumers on a market? This problem is pervasive in contemporary marketised public services, and it is evident in the second prospectus, especially where it refers to its entry requirements and its requirements for degree schemes. It is noteworthy that at these points there is a shift from continuous text to a more diagrammatic layout. This allows summaries with phrases rather than full sentences – for instance, 'A/AS level grade: BCC or equivalent'. This avoids explicit obligational meanings, such as, for example, 'you must have BCC or equivalent'. It is a way round the dilemma in that it allows the institution to specify its requirements without overtly claiming authority over its 'consumers'. Even where requirements are more explicitly worded, obligational modalities are avoided – so for instance a requirement is turned into a description as in 'You take at least three of . . .'. These are attempts at textual resolutions of the contradictions between regulating and selling universities. The impact of selling is evident in the way the institution is constructed with a collective personal identity – identified as 'we' – whereas the potential applicant is addressed as an individual – 'you' – echoing the practices of commodity advertising.

In other words, there is a breakdown and redrawing of the boundary between higher education and the marketplace, which is in part a breakdown and redrawing of the boundary between the language of higher education and the language of the market. This is one example of a widespread marketisation of public language, which entails amongst other things a pervasive ambivalence in authority relations. I have referred to the 'dilemmas' which follow from this; in broader terms, we can say that these changes open up a new terrain of struggle in and over the discourse of public services.

Globalisation

By globalisation I mean the tendency for economic, social, political and cultural processes to take place on a global scale rather than within the confines of particular countries or regions (Featherstone, Lash, and Robertson 1995). Much of the debate on globalisation has focused upon economic changes, but cultural globalisation is also an important aspect of the more general phenomenon (Lash and Urry 1994). And cultural globalisation can be seen to include a globalisation of language practices. This obviously involves changing relationships between languages, and the increasingly important role that a few major international languages – and most obviously English – are taking on at the expense of the great majority of languages. But it also involves what we might call a globalisation of discursive practices (see below for this term), a globalisation of ways of using language which to a degree cuts across boundaries between languages. For instance, the marketisation of areas of life previously outside or on the edges of markets seems to be happening on a global scale, and so

English

The undergraduate courses treat English as a whole subject and not as two divergent specializations. Accordingly, when English is taken as a major subject for the degree of B.A., no specialization in either language or literature separately is permitted until the third year of study when a very limited concentration on either is allowed. For higher degrees, specialization in either language or literature may be complete or subjects may be offered which connect these two branches of study.

In the study of *language* for the B.A. degree, modern English is central and is combined with some general linguistics and phonetics, and in Part II with history of the language. Language specializations in the third year include optional courses on older forms of English, and also on various aspects of the modern language and of linguistics. The study of English language throughout the first degree course will include fieldwork, special studies of varieties of modern English and the use of language laboratory techniques. The Language course is so constructed as to be of value to those who wish to specialize in English as a second or as a foreign language. As much as possible of the material used for literary study is also used for the study of language.

In the study of *literature* the syllabus is divided into periods, each taught with emphasis on a different aspect of literary study. The first-year course, based mainly on modern literature, deals with problems of reading and with the forms and functions of literature in contemporary society. In Part II, various periods are studied, two in two-year courses and the remainder in one-year courses.

The special interests of the Department include the following:

1. Project work in the drama courses using the facilities which will be available in the Theatre Workshop, at present being designed.
2. Special studies of the relationship between language and literature, including work on literary structures from a linguistic point of view.
3. Poetry as a performed art and its links with song.
4. Relations between the study of literature and of philosophy.
5. Relations between literature and scientific thought.
6. Relations between literary and historical study.

Undergraduate studies

PART I (FIRST YEAR) COURSE

The course consists of three parts:

(a) Language: a general introduction, including some elementary phonetics and linguistics.

(b) Literature: a course on problems of reading, and the forms and functions of literature, based on modern English poetry and prose fiction and on texts from three different types of drama (Classical, Renaissance, Modern).

(c) Special courses: each undergraduate will choose one of the special courses referred to below, the choice being determined by his other first-year subjects:

III

Figure 8.1

166

(i) For those taking groups involving History or Economics or Politics or French Studies or Classical Background, a study of certain historical aspects of literature in the seventeenth century.

(ii) For those taking groups involving Economics or Politics or Philosophy, a study of some of the relationships of literature and philosophy, centred on the works of William Blake.

(iii) For those taking groups involving Environmental Studies, Mathematics or Philosophy, a study of certain scientific texts from a literary and linguistic point of view.

The Part I course, or selected parts of it, will also (timetable permitting) be available as a one-year minor course for certain second-year undergraduates majoring in Boards of Studies A, B and C who did not take English in their first year.

PART II (SECOND AND THIRD YEAR) COURSES

Major course

Second-year undergraduates majoring in English are required to take four lecture courses – two in literature and two in language, from the following:

(a) Literature 1780-1860
   Literature 1660-1780
   Elizabethan Drama, including some project work in the theatre

(b) Varieties of Modern English I (study of the varieties of modern English outside the United Kingdom)
   History of the English Language I
   Principles and Techniques of General Linguistics, with special reference to English

Third-year undergraduates must choose four courses: *either* three language and one literature, *or* three literature and one language, *or* two of each. Any *one* course in language or literature may be offered by an undergraduate as a special option to be examined as such in the Final Examination. Third-year courses listed for 1966-67 (subject to the availability of staff) are as follows:

(a) Literature 1850-1966, Literature 1550-1660, Mediaeval Literature, Jacobean Drama.

(b) Old English, Middle English, Old Norse, Writing Systems, Linguistic Study of Style, Varieties of Modern English II, History of the Language II, Principles and Techniques of General Linguistics II.

Combined major course in English and French Studies – see page 118

Combined major course in English and Philosophy – see page 118

Combined major course in Latin and English – see page 118

Figure 8.1 continued

LINGUISTICS AND HUMAN COMMUNICATION

SOCIAL SCIENCES | 133

Places available: 30
Admissions tutors: Jenny Thomas (Linguistics courses); Greg Myers (Human Communication)

A/AS-level grades: BCC or equivalent; AS-levels accepted
GCSE: Maths and normally a language for Linguistics courses
Scottish Highers: BBBBB
International Baccalaureate: 30 pts
BTEC: at least merits in BTEC National
Mature students: we are keen to recruit mature students

All accepted candidates are invited to open days; interviews in special cases.

The Department of Linguistics and Modern English Language is one of the largest in the UK with a teaching staff of fourteen. We offer a series of flexible degrees with a wide range of courses in 'core' areas like phonetics, grammar and discourse analysis, areas which connect strongly with other disciplines, like sociolinguistics and psycholinguistics, and more 'applied' areas like adult literacy, language teaching and the linguistic study of literature. We have strong links through collaborative degrees with English, Computer

Science, the social sciences (especially Psychology and Sociology) and Modern Languages.

We received a grade 4 (national excellence in most areas of Linguistics and international excellence in some) in the 1989 research ratings carried out by the Universities Funding Council. We are especially well known for our research work in Linguistics in relation to language teaching, for the study of language in social settings (e.g. school classrooms and interaction between cancer patients and their carers), for the automatic analysis of texts by computer, and for the linguistic study of literature.

We are a friendly and flexible group of teachers who like to have social contact with the people we teach. Every year, students are invited to join staff for a walking weekend in the nearby Lake District. There are also opportunities for students to spend part of their second year in Copenhagen as part of an ERASMUS student exchange arrangement. We are currently exploring similar links with universities in other European countries.

Assessment

For Linguistics and Human Communication courses: coursework (at least 60%) and exams

For courses run by the English Department: coursework (50% in the first year, usually 40% in later years) and exams.

What our graduates do

Linguistics and Human Communication offer useful training and expertise that are of special professional relevance to many working in education, language teaching, speech therapy, translation, industry and commerce, management, the mass media, creative arts, social work and counselling.

Recent graduates have gone to work or train as teachers of English overseas, teachers of English as a mother tongue, computer programmers and consultants, bankers, chartered accountants, O & M analysts, air traffic planners, managers in the retail industry, personnel managers, journalists, social workers, nurses, and so on. A sizeable proportion of our Linguistics graduates take up employment overseas.

A degree in Human Communication or Linguistics does not commit you to any one career, but can open many doors.

Figure 8.2

too no doubt is the marketisation of language. Certainly higher education in many countries is undergoing a process of marketisation similar to that illustrated above. But this is not simply a matter of practices becoming marketised in the same ways in different societies, it is a matter of global marketising tendencies which interact in highly complex ways with different linguistic traditions and practices in different societies giving many different outputs, many different ways of articulating the language of the market with other linguistic practices. Globalisation is best seen as a dialectic between the global and the local, or 'glocalisation' (Robertson 1995). I should add that globalisation is a process not only between societies but also within societies: many contemporary societies are characterised by considerable cultural and linguistic diversity, and the boundary shifts I have referred to as taking place between societies are also taking place within culturally complex societies.

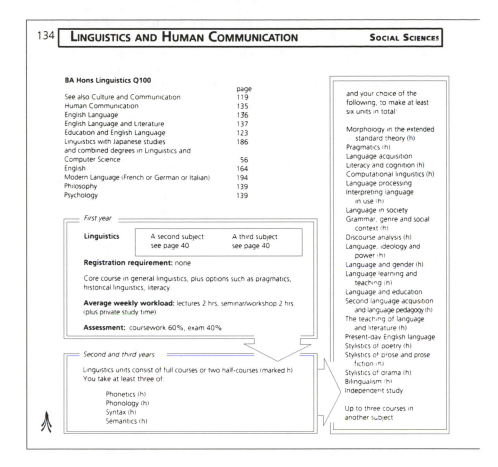

134 | **LINGUISTICS AND HUMAN COMMUNICATION** | **SOCIAL SCIENCES**

BA Hons Linguistics Q100

	page
See also Culture and Communication	119
Human Communication	135
English Language	136
English Language and Literature	137
Education and English Language	123
Linguistics with Japanese studies	186
and combined degrees in Linguistics and	
Computer Science	56
English	164
Modern Language (French or German or Italian)	194
Philosophy	139
Psychology	139

First year

Linguistics | A second subject: see page 40 | A third subject: see page 40

Registration requirement: none

Core course in general linguistics, plus options such as pragmatics, historical linguistics, literacy

Average weekly workload: lectures 2 hrs, seminar/workshop 2 hrs (plus private study time)

Assessment: coursework 60%, exam 40%

Second and third years

Linguistics units consist of full courses or two half-courses (marked h) You take at least three of:

Phonetics (h)
Phonology (h)
Syntax (h)
Semantics (h)

and your choice of the following, to make at least six units in total:

Morphology in the extended standard theory (h)
Pragmatics (h)
Language acquisition
Literacy and cognition (h)
Computational linguistics (h)
Language processing
Interpreting language in use (h)
Language in society
Grammar, genre and social context (h)
Discourse analysis (h)
Language, ideology and power (h)
Language and gender (h)
Language learning and teaching (h)
Language and education
Second language acquisition and language pedagogy (h)
The teaching of language and literature (h)
Present-day English language
Stylistics of poetry (h)
Stylistics of prose and prose fiction (h)
Stylistics of drama (h)
Bilingualism (h)
Independent study

Up to three courses in another subject

Figure 8.2 continued

Designing

What I have said so far is from the perspective of structure and system. I have been referring to the restructuring of the resources for meaning, the available Designs of Meaning – the systemic potential from which people select in Designing. But one can also look at language in contemporary life from the perspective of action, focusing upon the process of Designing itself, and in particular what is at stake for those who are engaged in the work of Designing – for the Designers. An important issue here is social identity. Accounts of social action which construct the heterogeneities of social identity in terms of differentiated complementary roles, and represent social subjects as enacting predesigned roles, seem hopelessly inadequate in the face of our experience of contemporary social life. Theories which centre the contradictoriness as well as the plurality of the

169

social subject, and see social action as ongoing and never-ending processes of negotiation of self as well as other identity, attempts so to speak to construct a coherent self out of the chaos, seem to have more purchase. Yet these processes are fundamentally linguistic in nature – they are a matter of articulating and rearticulating together diverse language practices, diverse 'language games'.

'Orders of discourse' and 'intertextuality'

These comments on language in contemporary life point to the need for the sort of dynamic theory of language I alluded to earlier. Let me now give a more detailed account of what such a theory of language might look like. What I want to suggest is that such a dynamic theory requires a theory of language in the conventional sense, a theory of language as system, to be combined with a theory of discourse, a socially conceived theory of language use. Both theories are concerned with the specification of resources – systems – from which choices are made in particular interactions and particular texts, but the theory of discourse is concerned also with how these resources are drawn upon in discursive practice. Critical discourse analysis (Fairclough 1995a, 1995c) is an attempt at such an integration.

I see the critical discourse analysis of any instance of discourse – be it a conversation, an interview, or a newspaper article – as involving a dual focus on the (spoken or written) text: as language, and as discourse. In analysing the language of a text one is referring the text to a grammar or grammars, and seeing it in terms of rules (for some) or systems networks (for others). In analysing the text as discourse one is referring the text to an order of discourse or orders of discourse, and seeing it in terms of practices. So 'order of discourse' has a roughly parallel status to grammar, but with respect to discourse and not language. We might say they are both types of convention to which text producers and consumers are oriented.

An order of discourse is the set of discursive practices associated with an institution or social domain, and the particular relationships and boundaries which obtain between these practices. For example, the order of discourse of contemporary British higher education (universities) includes such discursive practices as lecturing, holding seminars and supervisions, and having meetings; as well as writing memoranda and reports, writing research papers, giving conference presentations, and writing books. Practices may be in complementary or contrastive relationships to each other, and the boundaries between them may be relatively closed or relatively open, and – importantly – these relationships are shifting. For instance, it seems that the line between academic writing (research) and teaching is less clear-cut than it was as commercial pressures push academics into producing books which can serve as course texts. An order of discourse is shaped by its shifting relationships with other orders of discourse – as the earlier example of university prospectuses indicated, the order of discourse of British higher education has become marketised – that is, closer than it was to business orders of discourse. Orders of discourse are also contested – so for example marketisation of particular practices in the order of discourse of higher education may be accepted by some people but resisted by others, so that competing practices emerge (compare for instance Figures 8.3 and 8.4, two very different ways of advertising university posts which are respectively traditional and marketised). Summing up, orders of discourse are very much open systems, and their value analytically is in allowing a focus on the shifting nature of and boundaries between discursive practices.

The concept of Multiliteracies focuses two key developments in contemporary societies: first, cultural hybridity increasing interaction across cultural and linguistic boundaries within and between societies, and, second, multimodality: the increasing salience of multiple modes of meaning – linguistic, visual, auditory, and so on, and the increasing tendency for texts to be multimodal. The concept of 'order of discourse' is potentially useful for both of these. Cultural hybridity can be broadly conceived to include boundary crossing within cultures as well as boundary crossing

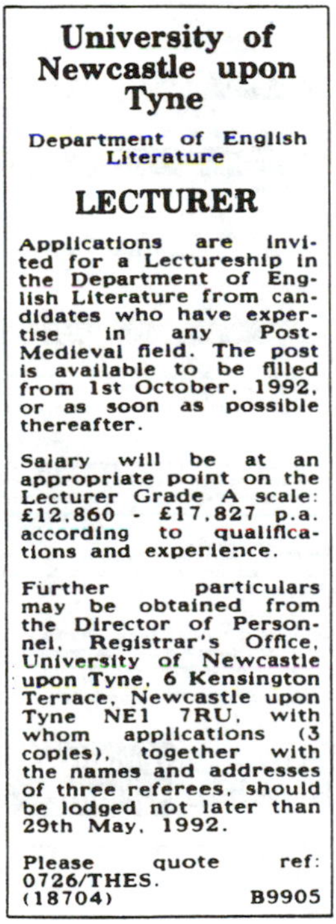

University of Newcastle upon Tyne

Department of English Literature

LECTURER

Applications are invited for a Lectureship in the Department of English Literature from candidates who have expertise in any Post-Medieval field. The post is available to be filled from 1st October, 1992, or as soon as possible thereafter.

Salary will be at an appropriate point on the Lecturer Grade A scale: £12,860 - £17,827 p.a. according to qualifications and experience.

Further particulars may be obtained from the Director of Personnel, Registrar's Office, University of Newcastle upon Tyne, 6 Kensington Terrace, Newcastle upon Tyne NE1 7RU, with whom applications (3 copies), together with the names and addresses of three referees, should be lodged not later than 29th May, 1992.

Please quote ref: 0726/THES. (18704) B9905

Figure 8.3

SCHOOL OF ENGINEERING

With our reputation as one of the UK's leading centres of teaching excellence and research innovation, we're making a lasting impact on the next generation of innovators and business leaders in the field of Engineering — and you can help.

With your ambition, energy and expertise, you will be committed to teaching at both undergraduate and post-graduate level, while enjoying the advantage of our close links with Industry and applied research initiatives to add to both your own reputation and ours.

SENIOR ACADEMIC POST
VEHICLE EMISSION TECHNOLOGY

Up to £31,500 p.a. plus substantial enhancement available by negotiation.

The School of Engineering is renowned for its innovative work in the area of Vehicle Emission Technology and is a leader in the field of Automotive Research. A team leader is now required to join this active team to help build on our success.

This leading post requires an outstanding Engineer who can bring expertise in at least one of the following:- Vehicle Pollution, Hybrid Vehicles, Air Quality Systems. You'll also need to be dedicated to progressing research and consultancy whilst lecturing to undergraduate and postgraduate students.

Along with appropriate qualifications, technological expertise and industrial experience, you will need to have energy, enthusiasm and communication skills to motivate your team.

We offer an excellent salary and benefits package, but more importantly the ideal environment and opportunity to really make a contribution to the future of automotive engineering.

You may be awarded the title of Professor if the relevant criteria are met.

For an informal discussion about the post please ring Professor David Tidmarsh, Director of School of Engineering on (0742) 533389.

Application forms and further details are available from the address below. Ref. 40/92.

LECTURERS/SENIOR LECTURERS/ PRINCIPAL LECTURERS

£10,949 — £28,851 p.a.

COMPUTER AIDED ENGINEERING

With expertise in one or more of the following: CAD, CAM, FEA, Expert Systems, AMT. Ref. 41/92.

QUALITY SYSTEMS

Applications to both Design and Manufacturing Engineering, offering expertise in one or more of the following areas; TQM, SPC, BS5750, BS7000, Taguchi Methods. A capability to contribute to the teaching of operations management will be an advantage. Ref. 42/92.

MANUFACTURING TECHNOLOGY

With expertise in one or more of the following: Metal and Polymer Forming, Non-conventional Manufacturing, AMT, Environmental Impact of Manufacturing. Ref. 43/92.

OPERATIONS MANAGEMENT

With expertise in one or more of the following: Expert Systems, Database Systems, Simulation, Manufacturing Planning and Control, CIM, CAPP, MRP. Ref. 44/92.

ENVIRONMENTAL ENGINEERING
(Two Posts)

Post 1: With expertise in one or more of the following: The chemistry of air water pollution, the impact of geology, hydrology and ecology on environmental issues, impact of transport on the environment. Ref. 45/92.

MAKE AN IMPACT ON THE NEXT GENERATION

Post 2: With expertise in Electro-hydraulic Control Systems, Automation, PLCs, Environmental Noise, Noise Control, Acoustics, Vibrations. Ref. 46/92.

MATERIALS ENGINEERING / MATERIALS RESEARCH INSTITUTE

An experienced graduate Materials Scientist or Metallurgist, ideally with an appropriate higher degree, to undertake research and development work in the Metals and Ceramics Research Group. The research work will involve the use of extensive SEM/STEM/XRD and surface analysis facilities applied to a range of metallurgical problems with a particular emphasis on surface engineering. Ref. 47/92.

For all the above posts you will ideally have industry-related experience to add to your degree and a record of achievement in research and/or consultancy activities. You will be committed to teaching excellence at both undergraduate and postgraduate levels and also have the enthusiasm and ability to be part of an active group and to initiate and supervise research, consultancy and short course programmes.

If you feel you have the ideas and expertise to make an impact in a dynamic, forward-looking environment, then please send for an application form and further details to the Personnel Department, Floor 3, 5 Storey Block, Pond Street, Sheffield S1 1WB. Telephone/0742 533950. Closing date 8th June 1992.

We are actively implementing equality of opportunity policies and seek people who share our commitment. Job share applicants welcome. Women are under represented in this area and applications from this group are particularly welcomed.

The University working in partnership with industry and the professions.

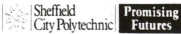

Sheffield City Polytechnic | Promising Futures

Figure 8.4

between cultures, so as to include marketisation and conversationalisation. Cultural hybridity can be conceptualised and analysed from a discourse perspective in terms of shifting boundaries and flows between orders of discourse. Moreover, it seems reasonable to extend the concept of order of discourse to modes of meaning other than language, so as to include combinations of modes of meaning and shifts across modes of meaning within the dynamic movements of orders of discourse.

The relationship between order of discourse and text is, typically, a complex relationship. A text may draw upon diverse discursive practices, cutting across boundaries within and between orders of discourse. It is in textual practice that the boundaries between orders of discourse are negotiated and redrawn. Texts that are hybrid, or mixed, in the discursive practices they draw upon, texts that are linguistically heterogeneous, are not exceptional and abnormal. Rather, they are quite normal, especially in a period of intensive change like the present. One area of such normal hybridity is marketisation of discourse.

The analysis of a text within this framework is a combination of a linguistic analysis and an intertextual analysis. The linguistic analysis maps the text on to a grammar or grammars, the intertextual analysis maps the text on to the social network of orders of discourse – it identifies genres and discourses that the text draws upon, and the ways they are articulated together. Orders of discourse mediate the relationship between society and culture on the one hand, and language on the other. With respect to particular texts, the intertextuality of a text mediates the relationship between the social context of the text and the language of the text. That is, properties of the social context of a text are realised in the nature of its intertextuality – whether it is relatively normative or relatively hybrid/ creative, which particular practices it draws upon and how it articulates them – and these intertextual properties are in turn realised in its language. A text which is intertextually relatively normative will be relatively homogeneous in forms and meanings. A text which is relatively hybrid or creative will be relatively heterogeneous in forms and meanings. For example, the second of the university prospectus extracts (Figure 8.2) is, as I argued earlier, relatively hybrid, and there are correspondingly hetero-geneities of form and meaning. I pointed out for instance that readers are directly and individually addressed as 'you', but this is not consistent throughout the text. Sometimes potential applicants are addressed as if they were actually students in this direct way, but elsewhere students are referred to in the third person. For example, 'Every year students are invited to join staff for a walking weekend . . .'. It would be quite possible to take direct address one step further here and say, 'Every year you will be invited to join staff for a walking weekend . . .' but that would alter somewhat the textual compromise which is arrived at here between the demands of marketing and of institutional regulation. As this example indicates, fine adjustments can be made to the ways in which dilemmas are negotiated by shifting the mix between genres or discourses.

In other words, the significance of centring the concepts of order of discourse and intertextuality for this approach to critical discourse is that it provides a means of systematically mapping properties of society and culture on to properties of texts by way of intertextual analysis. It highlights change and hybridity in discourse, or perhaps rather in Bakhtin's terms (Bakhtin 1981) the tension between 'centripetal' and 'centrifugal' pressures in texts: pressures towards convention and normativity, and pressures towards difference and change. And it provides a systematic way of relating changing discursive practices to wider processes of social and cultural change.

Difference and change

I shall now show how this view of language helps in the prioritisation of difference and change which is a characteristic of the Multiliteracies Project – change as the dynamic negotiation of cultural and linguistic difference.

It is useful here, however, to differentiate two different time frames within which we can think about change in discourse; two different lenses through which we can look at change itself, both in the orders of discourse (long-term change) and in texts (ongoing change).

In terms of the view of language sketched out above, marketisation of discourse is a shift in, or a relaxation of, boundaries between the order of discourse of the market, and various public and professional orders of discourse, and indeed the orders of discourse of ordinary life – the 'lifeworld' which I will discuss below – in so far as they too may be marketised. These shifts between orders of discourse lead to shifts within orders of discourse, in the nature of and relationships between discursive practices. Globalisation involves relationships between different languages but it can also be thought of in terms of shifting boundaries between orders of discourse – though the orders of discourse in this case may belong to different language communities – and consequential shifts in relationships within orders of discourse.

Let me briefly refer to another major contemporary change affecting orders of discourse: the conversationalisation of public discourse. By this I mean the tendency for public discourse to become increasingly like ordinary conversation. Conversationalisation involves a boundary shift between orders of discourse of public life and orders of discourse of ordinary life or the 'lifeworld'. For instance, practices of interaction between various categories of professionals – doctors, teachers, and so on – and the nonprofessionals they provide services for – patients, students, and the like – have tended in recent decades to become more like conversation than they were previously. So doctors, for example, seem to be increasingly careful to avoid traditional models of professional authority and language – such as the use of specialist medical terminology, or maintaining a formal and distant relationship with the patient – and to use increasingly a conversational language which both minimises the knowledge gap between doctor and patient and projects the doctor as having a lot in common with the patient, especially the culturally prized virtue of being 'ordinary'.

This example suggests a rather optimistic interpretation of conversationalisation as a facet of the democratisation of social life. Political democratisation in societies like Britain and the USA would seem to have led on to a more general social and cultural democratisation, including a general valorisation of informality (and therefore of the conversational) and a corresponding problematisation of more traditional practices in which professionals like doctors claim authority over the people they provide services for. However, conversationalisation often appears to be rather a strategically motivated simulation and appropriation of lifeworld practices linked to objectives such as winning political support (in political discourse) or selling goods (in advertising) so one consequence of the marketisation of public discourse referred to earlier is a conversationalisation of it. There is in fact a fundamental ambivalence about conversationalisation (Fairclough 1994).

Change in texts, or ongoing change, can be explored, as I have already suggested, in terms of the concepts of hybridity and heterogeneity change. This is constituted through the hybridisation or mixing of different discursive practices in a text, which is realised in the heterogeneity of its linguistic and other semiotic features. The critical discourse analysis of texts can be conceived of as linking together or mapping on to one another three different sorts of analysis: linguistic (semiotic) analysis of text, intertextual analysis of text, and sociocultural analysis of discursive event.

I now want to discuss a specific example, an extract from a late-night political television programme entitled *Midnight Special* which was broadcast during the April 1992 British General Election campaign (see Fairclough 1995b for a fuller analysis). The part of the programme I am focusing on involves a television journalist, Vincent Hanna, questioning a panel of MPs representing the three main political parties: Conservative, Labour and Liberal Democrat. The extract below comes at the beginning of this part of the programme immediately after a report on a Conservative Party election broadcast which was centred upon the personality of John Major, who was then the Prime Minister. The extract is a discussion of the report between Vincent Hanna and the former Conservative MP Jonathan Aitken.

> *VH:* /spendid piece there by Fiona Murch// the arts
> correspondent of Channel 4 news . now you struck me during
> that as if you weren't sure whether to laugh or throw up

JA: /well I'll give him an Oscar (*laughter*) . in a loyal way .
5   (laughs) it looked to me rather attractive I mean it is a
        good story you have to admit that
VH: yeah
JA: the boy from Brixton who's made it to Number 10 e: left
    school at 16 it's a good yarn a good script . um
10 VH: (unclear)
JA: should think John Schlesinger's probably e:m
VH: (but unclear)
JA: done a first class job I I'm looking forward
    to it . looking forward to seeing the real thing// =
15 VH: =backing nervously away from this question
        Jonathan (unclear)
JA: what is the question sorry (*laughter*)
    I said I'd give him an Oscar (*laughter*)
VH: do you find it (laughs) /do you// find it embarrassing that
20   the . party leaders descend to this kind of .
JA: /no I think it's showbusiness it's pol/ modern politics //
VH: thing . . . right . . . fine OK
JA: um . and e: I mean I I wonder how many votes are in it I
    mean. I think in the last election we just saw a s-soupçon of
25   it there. Neil Kinnock's broadcast with the Beethoven's
        9th. it was an outstanding
VH: right
JA: piece of
VH Brahms Brahms 1st
30 JA: /no it was Beethoven's 9th
VH: no
JA: anyway . let's not argue about the music // but it was the
    um the rather stunning um presentation of Kinnock
    /in a much better light than certainly I'd ever seen him
35   before// and . it didn't make a tupenny ha'penny worth of
        votes in the end. I mean the so I think it's part of the
        razzmatazz of electioneering but . /the British
        people are not fooled by . any . director's presentation I
        think in the end . uh it is the issues an and the substantive
40   things that count //
VH: well from one practising journalist to another. /Ro//
    Robin Corbett

I want to focus here on what I call the perspective of action, and
specifically the discoursal negotiation of social identity. However, it is
necessary first to say something about the perspective of structure to try
to specify the structural conditions which frame action and negotiation of

identity. Politics has been characterised in terms of the interaction of systems: the political system, the social system, and the economy (Held 1987). The nature of politics varies in different times and places depending on how these systems interact. This means that the boundaries of politics are constantly at issue – for instance in terms of whether issues in ordinary life, such as the family, are constructed as political. This view of politics can be interpreted in discoursal and linguistic terms as the shifting nature of politics and can be characterised in terms of shifting relationships between shifting articulations of orders of discourse of the political system, the social system, and the economy. For instance, political discourse in contemporary broadcasting articulates the orders of discourse of the political system, the lifeworld (the social system), and the media as a culture industry (the economy). The competitive economic conditions of the media as a culture industry mean that even in its workings as a public sphere, media outputs must be effective in winning audiences.

Broadcast politics, as in this example, is under pressure to work as entertainment. It becomes 'infotainment', constructing audiences as consumers and not (just) as citizens. Infotainment is a form of marketisation of discourse practices. One long-term aspect of audience attraction in broadcasting (Cardiff 1980; Scannell 1992) has been an accommodation to the conditions of reception within the home and the family, including an accommodation to the discursive practices of ordinary life – a conversationalisation of media discourse. The emergent television genre of 'chat' (Tolson 1991), which is evident in the extract above, condenses these marketising and conversationalising tendencies. Chat is conversation as a form of entertainment, a recontextualisation – adaptation, transformation (see Bernstein 1990b; Van Leeuwen 1993) – of the conversational discourse of the lifeworld within the media as culture industry. The order of discourse of the political system is only one external order of discourse which is recontextualised within, and articulated with, these practices of conversationalised entertainment – so too are for instance scientific and technological discourse, and various types of academic discourse.

Returning to the perspective of action, politicians are confronted in these structural conditions with complex problems of identity negotiation. They have to try to reconcile continuing to be politicians with pressures to pass both as ordinary people, co-members with their audiences of the lifeworld, and as entertainers who can attract audience-consumers. Media presenters are faced with analogous problems of identity negotiation and, in fact, negotiative processes are best seen as jointly engaged in by all participants in interactions. These negotiative processes involve the mixing 'hybridisation' of different genres and discourses, including, in this example, conventional political interview genre and political discourses, simulated conversation as well as entertainment performance – 'act' and even comedy routines. The second and third can, as I have suggested, be seen to be condensed as 'chat'. This mixture of discourse practices is realised in textual heterogeneity. One might see the aim of the analysis as showing how the contradictions of contemporary politics and the dilemmas facing contemporary politicians are manifest in the heterogeneities of texts.

Let me begin with elements of conventional politics. The most obvious presence of conventional political interview genre is in the control exercised by VH, the television presenter, over turn-taking and topic, and the compliance with this control in the politicians' responses to VH. Although VH does not always ask questions, his talk counts as elicitations which require, and receive, relevant responses. For instance, in lines 2–3, 'you struck me . . . as if you weren't sure whether to laugh or throw up'. The elicitation in lines 15–16, 'backing nervously away from this question Jonathan', might be taken as fulfilling the conventional interviewer's responsibility to sanction an interviewee who fails to answer the question. But it is heavily mitigated, by humour and by first-name address. There are also elements of a political discourse in lines 37–40, which consist of two hackneyed formulae of political speech making: 'the British people are not fooled by . . .', and 'in the end it is the issues . . . that count'. The shift into this discourse is marked by 'but' in line 37, and also marked by a shift to a more measured delivery and in a bodily way by a sober facial expression.

Turning to conversational elements in the generic mix, before VH speaks there is a snatch of talk and laughter presumably directed at the report and VH's first word, 'splendid', is audibly said 'smilingly', and in fact he is smirking through the first part of this contribution. Such features are normal in conversation but not in conventional political interview. The same is true of VH's elicitation, 'you struck me during that as if you weren't sure whether to laugh or throw up', in terms of its force, a comment on JA's apparent response to the report, its conversational idiom, and its style – note the lexical expression 'throw up' – as well as, perhaps, the absence of explicit nomination of JA to respond. And it elicits a personal response from JA as an individual rather than from his position as representative of a party. VH in making the comment and JA in answering it in a personal way jointly enact a conversational interchange. A feature of this exchange, and the extract generally, which helps constitute this conversational orientation to person rather than position, is the density of mental process clauses with verbs including 'struck' (2), 'weren't sure' (3), 'looked' (5), '(I) should think' (11), '[I]'m looking forward' (13), 'do [you] find' (19), '[I] think' (21), and '[I] wonder' (23). A number of these operate modally as what Halliday calls 'subjective' modality markers, highlighting the subjective basis of commitment to propositions. A further conversational feature is the responses from VH during JA's contributions – for instance, 'yeah' (7), 'right . . . fine OK' (22), and 'right' (27). Notice also how VH's elicitation in 15–16 'latches' on to the end of JA's contribution giving it the force of a rejoinder. In the disagreement about the music (29–30), both VH's interruption of JA to correct him, and JA's assertive and mock-outraged response, are again more typical of conversation than conventional political interview.

The most obvious feature of the extract as entertainment is its humour. As noted already, in VH's opening elicitation in 1–3 a major element of this section of the programme is systematically registered by participants in their smiles and laughter. The element of 'chat', referred to earlier, entails witty conversation as entertainment, and performance. In line 17, JA's response to VH's humorous elicitation, 'what is the question', has the split-second timing of a line in a comedy double-act. Even some of the apparently serious parts of the programme have an undercurrent of humour. For instance, there are elements of ironic humour, such as 'we just saw a soupçon of it' (in 24–5), in JA's serious answer in lines 23–40. The ground rules of the programme seem to require serious political talk not to be sustained for more than a few seconds without being 'lightened' by humour.

Another aspect of the presence of elements of conversation and entertainment is the way in which viewers are addressed and constructed in the programme. Apart from VH, at points of transition between report and the studio discussion, the audience is not addressed in this part of the programme, and indeed there is little surface evidence at all of orientation to audience or of contributions being designed for viewers rather than co-participants. The talk is designed ostensibly as if the studio were a private place and as if this were a private conversation – an intricate pretence, of course, for like all broadcast talk the programme is carefully designed for its audience. The programme is constructed as a spectacle for, rather than an interaction with, the viewer, and viewers are positioned as consumers of the spectacle, yet at the same time as 'knowing' with respect to the act and the pretence – as when Robin Corbett jokingly reveals a professional secret, 'just . . . inside this studio because I know it won't go anywhere else'.

Negotiating identities within such a complex configuration of discursive practices is not easy, and politicians are by no means always successful in doing so. Moreover, as they attempt to balance the conflicting demands of different discursive practices, it may be unclear to audience members how to take what they say – which generic interpretative principles are relevant to interpreting what they say where several different genres are in play. Let me illustrate these points with reference to JA's response to VH's first elicitation. I am not sure whether to take it 'at bottom' as a conventional political response, a defence of his leader mitigated in a way which accommodates it to the ground rules of the programme, or as a performance, an entertainment, where the audience is invited to share the joke of JA dutifully going through the motions of defending Prime Minister Major. As a politician in an election campaign, JA is bound to defend his leader against attack, yet in the cultivated intimacy of studio conversation he cannot solemnly defend what is commonsensically agreed to be indefensible – electoral 'razzmatazz'. Being positive about Major's perform-ance in the indirect, metaphorical and humorous way of 'well I'll give him an Oscar ... in a loyal way', allows him to reconcile these conflicting demands.

The rest of JA's contribution seems on the face of it a more serious defence of Major. It is very defensive. Notice the low-affinity modalities 'it looked to me', 'I should think', 'probably', and the hedges 'rather', 'I mean', and 'you have to admit'. There is also, as VH points out, a nervous quality to it, both in the repetitiveness and its rhythm of delivery. But the apparent shift to a more serious key is offset by the fact that JA continues to smile throughout, and by lexical markers of continuing humorousness such as 'the boys from Brixton' yarn. One could see the defensiveness and the nervousness and the continuing humorousness as indicators of the difficulty JA is having in performing the balancing act – aggravated perhaps by the potentially derailing interruptions which VH seems to embark upon at two points, in line 10, and the disaffiliation VH expresses in the way he says 'yeah' in line 7.

But an alternative reading is possible according to the interpretative principles of entertainment. JA's answer can be read as a joke which depends upon our recognition of JA going through the political motions of defending his leader, where the conspicuous defensiveness and nervousness are cues to help us 'see' the joke. I am left, as an interpreter, not being sure how to read the identity which JA is constructing in this answer. Although perhaps the ambivalence in this case might be taken as success on his part, in that it gets him through a difficult dilemma in a way that does not allow him to be pinned down or easily blamed.

What this example shows is how existing Designs for Meaning (designs in the domains of politics, media and ordinary life) are creatively articulated together in new ways within the process of Designing; how existing relations between and within orders of discourse are intertextually reworked in interaction. This process is structurally framed in the shifting relations between the economy, the political system, and the social system. It is a process which cumulatively produces 'new' Designs for Meaning – new ways of doing practices, new identities for practices. It shows change as the dynamic negotiation of difference.

Conclusion

In this chapter I have focused on the concepts of 'orders of discourse' and 'intertextuality' because I believe they are fundamental to the view of language which the Multiliteracies Project rests upon. I have illustrated how these concepts help to show in detail the process of Designing as depending upon but also transforming existing Designs of Meaning.

I would like to conclude with two cautions. First, although we need to theorise language in a way which is compatible with the dynamic, creative, and transformative properties of discursive practice which I have alluded to, this does not by any means entail that discursive practice inherently has these properties. Whether it does or does not depends upon sociohistorical circumstances. Some domains of discursive practice in some societies may have a substantial creative potential, others may have very little. Periods and points of rapid social and cultural change, where power relations are relatively unsettled and insecure, are in broad terms most favourable to creative discursive practices. We can specify the discoursal, as opposed to the more general sociocultural conditions for creativity in discursive practice, as a conjunction of a particular state of the order or orders of discourse, and a particular state of what Gunther Kress calls representational resources. To put the point in Bourdieu's terminology, creativity requires not only particular properties of openness in the 'field' (= order of discourse), it also requires a particular 'habitue' (= representational resources) on the part of agents operating within the field.

My second caution arises from the *Midnight Special* example, and it is that the creative and transformative mixing of discursive practices can be a difficult achievement which people quite commonly do badly. The complex communicative practices which are put in focus within the Multiliteracies Project constitute heavy demands on the communicative abilities of people. The communicatively dynamic and boundary-transcending utopia which the Project posits needs to be carefully thought through in terms of feasibility.

9

MULTIMODALITY

Gunther Kress

Why? and why now?

Over the last two or three decades a revolution has taken place in the area of communication which forces us to rethink the social and the semiotic landscape of Western 'developed' societies. The effect of this revolution has been to dislodge written language from the centrality which it has held, or which has been ascribed to it, in public communication. Perhaps the most obvious example is the increasing prominence – dominance even – of the visual in many areas of public communication as well. While this is obvious, the implications of that shift have not in any sense begun to be drawn out or assessed in any coherent, overt, fully conscious, and consistent fashion.

But the visual is just one example. Other modes of communication have become prominent; and increasingly significant in public communication. At times we tend to shield ourselves from these changes, not wishing them to be the case, treating them as peripheral, as explicable in the framework of existing language-based theories of communication. Yet these theories no longer work in relation to the new communicational situation. Other modes are increasingly pushing into the centre of public communication: music; and the body and its movements. The case of music allows us to make a distinction between the contemporary situation, and its trends and those of the more immediate past. Of course, it will be pointed out, music has been a constant feature of human societies. Yet over the last century or two, however, the actual elites of Western Europe decided to break the continuous chain between music in its everyday appearance and music as an aesthetic form, or music in its ritual aspects. A deep division has been produced, so that the latter two have remained the subject of attention for the elites: *not* now as everyday forms of representation and communication, but as forms which belong entirely in the domain of the aesthetic and of good manners. Music is now no longer seen as a form of communication but as a means of expression; the same has happened with the visual mode and others.

The general effect of this, and of the very similar movement in relation to the visual – with fine art separated from other forms of visual expression – has been to leave the two modes of the visual and of music outside a general theory of communication, to leave them untheorised, or at least under-theorised, and certainly to take them out of the school curricula, except as specialist activities. As a consequence we, in the 'West', find ourselves singularly ill-equipped in the new landscape of communication, whether that is generally speaking, or institutional and non-institutional education.

The revolution which we discern is likely to continue, and perhaps even to intensify, as the reasons for its inception are, if anything, increasing. These reasons range from changes of a social and cultural character to those more to do with technologies of information and of transport; to far-reaching economic changes in the post-industrial societies largely of the northern hemisphere. An instance of the first kind is pluri-culturalism, whether intranationally and regionally, or internationally and globally. It ensures that the most valued communicational modes of any one society are unsettled through the contestation by the valued forms of all the cultural groups. Perhaps predictably, this unsettling affects written language most intensely, and first of all. Technologies of information lend themselves to 'visualisation', the phenomenon in which information initially stored in written form is 'translated' into visual form, largely because the transport of information is seen as more efficient in the visual rather than in the verbal mode. Economic changes in the post-industrial world are in any case likely to be characteristically 'information-driven', or knowledge-based. And, as one other and fundamental reason, it may be the case that information of various kinds may be more aptly expressed in the visual rather than in the verbal mode.

In other words, there are the strongest possible reasons for taking a completely fresh look at this landscape, and for setting a quite new agenda of human semiosis in the domain of communication and representation. Such an agenda has, as some of its most urgent elements, the requirement for a theorisation and a description of the full range of semiotic modes in use in a particular society; a full understanding of the potentials and limi-tations of all these modes; of their present use in a society; of their poten-tials for their interaction and interrelation with each other; and an understanding of their place and function in our imaginings of the future. This agenda will be founded on an appropriate theory of semiosis. Present theories are inadequate both because they are founded on an understand-ing of one (multi)mode – language – alone, and because that understanding misconstrues the fundamental characteristics of human semiosis anywhere and at all times. The need for this agenda exists equally in industry and in education; in intranational as in international communication.

The appearance of modes other than language in the centre of the domain of public communication has several aspects: new, or newly prominent modes appear; texts, textual objects are more clearly seen to be multimodal, that is, to be constituted by a number of modes of representation. This is one major reason why theories of semiosis have to deal with objects which exist in modes other than language, as well as treating all text-like objects as multimodal. Importantly, the question arises whether modes such as 'written language' or 'spoken language' can, in any case, be regarded as 'monomodal': in fact, my view is that they cannot. This means that we have to rethink 'language' as a multimodal phenomenon. Our present conception of language is revealed as an artefact of theory and of common sense.

A large range of questions opens up. This chapter will deal with those which are central for the purposes of this book. First is the issue of the relation of 'mode' and of the 'material stuff' through which a mode is realised, which has to be related to the human body, its 'senses', and its engagement with the world. Second, there is the relation of semiotic mode to the medium of transmission or propagation.

The body's potential for engagement with the world: mode, materiality and medium

The issue of multimodality reminds us forcefully that human semiosis rests, first and foremost, on the facts of biology and physiology. Human bodies have a wide range of means of engagement with the world; a wide and highly varied range of means of perception. These we call our 'senses': sight, hearing, smell, taste, feel. Each is attuned in a quite specific way to the natural environment, providing us with highly differentiated information. Of course, none of the senses ever operates in isolation from the others – other than in severe pathologies. That, from the beginning, guarantees the multimodality of our semiotic world. How a culture selects from its range and chooses to develop these possibilities of engagement with the world is a quite different matter. In part the argument of this chapter is that so-called literate Western societies have for too long insisted on the priority of a particular form of engagement, through a combination of hearing and sight: with the sense of hearing specialised to the sounds of speech, and the sense of sight specialised to the graphic representation of sounds by 'letters', on flat surfaces. This combination, in which for some time now writing had come to have priority of value over speech, has been dominant at the expense of other uses of sight, as in relation to visual images for instance, and of course dominant at the expense of all the other senses and *their* mode of engagement with the world. This has gone so far that we have no means of representing whole areas of our sensory lives by either talking or writing. For instance, it is a common-sense notion that we cannot talk about tastes, not just because we have not developed an adequate set of words or an appropriate syntax for this in spoken or written language, but, so this common sense would have us believe, because tastes, smells, tactile sensations, and the like cannot be the subject of articulated semiosis.

To begin with the materiality of our semiotic (rather than our physical or physiological) world. Here the question is: what (physical) materials of representation has a society used and still uses; and to what degree has it developed that material into an articulated representational resource? By material(ity) I mean the 'stuff' which a culture uses as the means for the expression of (its) meanings. This can be physical stuff; (variation of) sound for instance; or marks on a surface, apprehended via the 'stuff' of light. At this level, materiality marks the interface of the natural world with the cultural world – facilitated by the fact that there are bodily means of apperception of these materials. Not only sight or sound but also the sense of touch could of course be used, as it is in a highly articulated form with braille; or in a less highly articulated form in the multitude of ways in which materials 'communicate' to us via our sense of touch – the texture of wooden surfaces, of concrete, of materials, and so on, used to varying degrees and often highly consciously and deliberately for purposes of representation and communication – for example, the lightness and smoothness of silk, as against the weight and roughness of the material of jeans.

But 'materiality' can also have a non-physical, appearance; the more a particular kind of material has been worked on culturally and semiotically, the more this 'secondary materiality' is available itself as 'material' for semiosis. For instance, languages have, usually, a highly developed lexicon, which is differentiated according to social and cultural factors, such as social categories of various kinds, or aesthetic categories. So certain areas of lexis will be regarded as 'lower-class', 'masculine', 'highbrow', etc. This social/semiotic organisation of signifier-material is itself usable as material from which to make meaning; for instance, selecting certain kinds of words systematically, when lexis of a different kind might be expected, and so on. In fact, most signs of social semiotic systems are of that kind, and work on and with that sort of material.

I use the mode to refer to the (full) semiotically articulated means of representation and communication. So for instance, graphology is a mode. It uses the materials of some physical surface (paper, metal, stone, cloth, canvas, and so on) which is physically marked in some fashion, whether by the application of a substance, such as ink, or by some other means such as incisions, scratching, or etching. There is, at the same time another 'material' involved, namely the more abstract organisation of the marks as a representational system. There is, then, further representation of that system existing in the interior of the brain in some form of neural organisation. On the basis of all these we can produce external representations. The example of graphology indicates that the transcriptional system of writing is a multimodal system. Graphology, as a mode, has a meaning-making potential which is quite separate from the meaning-making potentials of other aspects of the multimode of writing, quite different for instance from lexis, or from word-order (sequence on the page), or syntax (a more abstract level of representation). Language in the spoken mode is yet another multimodal system; it uses the whole plethora of devices available to speech – pace, pitch-variation, rhythmic variations, tone of voice. But it also makes use of the potentials of temporal, sequential ordering available to this time-based mode rather than the initially spatially displayed mode of writing.

The suggestion that language – either in the spoken or in the written mode – is a multimodal system may seem outrageous; we have been taught to think of language as a single and homogeneous system of representation, notwithstanding the fact that its definition is, to say the least, fuzzy round the edges. It is not clear, for instance, whether rhythmic features, or tone-of-voice, sex-specific or culture-specific aspects of sound, are in or out of the language system; it depends largely on who makes the definitions which of these features is considered. Intonation is very likely to be considered in the system, while rhythmic (rather than accentual) aspects may be 'out'. Tone-of-voice is very likely to be considered 'extra-linguistic', as will sex-specific and culture-specific aspects of the voice. The fact that these latter two are entirely systematic (there is an habituated muscular/gestural disposition associated with every language, and with every dialect) is likely to be disregarded. The very high degree and long history of theoretical investment in the description and theoretical articulation of language leading to concepts such as the grammar of a language have made it difficult to see this phenomenon freshly.

By looking at a different 'language' – sign language, for instance – we may be able to see the matter of multimodality more clearly. Sign language (the German term *Gebärdensprache* – gesture language – is actually preferable, as it avoids the commonsensical temptation to see sign language as simply a translation of verbal language) has, over the last decade or so emerged from under the previously skewing influence of linguistics (though, it has to be said, with the aid of some linguistics coming from traditional forms of linguists). Researchers now working on and with sign language are able to see it with fewer constraints, and freshly. This makes it possible to describe it as a multimodal system, using its own distinct 'material': facial expressions; disposition of the mouth and eyes; movements and dispositions of the arms; of the fingers; the general attitude and disposition of the upper part of the body. All of these are seen as independent meaning-making systems, which are however co-ordinated so as to produce a single, if complex, integrated and differentiated text-message.

Lastly, the issue of the medium, that is the issue of transmission and dissemination. Again, this is complex, but it is possible to start with some relatively straightforward instances. All those aspects have to do with the 'transport' of the (complex of) sign(s) – the text/message – as being an aspect of medium. In the case of speech, the medium is air. Other media – other means of transport – may interpose themselves, with specific effects. In the case of speech, for instance, variations of pressure in the medium of air can be transposed into variations in electric current, then into radio waves, and then re-converted into variations of pressure in the medium of air. Just as there are multiple modes involved in the production of any text, there often are multiple media. In the case of speech, for instance, I paid no attention to the medium of the (so-called) speech organs. The matter of media needs close investigation, and theorisation together with the question of multimodality. As far as speech and radio are concerned, obviously the shift from the medium of air, to the interposed electric/ electronic medium is one of the factors leading to the possibility of mass communication, with its quite enormous social, cultural, and individual consequences. From a usually one-to-one, face-to-face interaction, the mode of speech is moved to a one-to-many and impersonal interaction. This indicates the kind of meaning-effects of changes in media. If mode affects what can be said and how, media affects who can be and is addressed and how.

Mode and materiality, through their close relation with the body's means of taking in information, and its possibilities of engagement with the world more generally, have wide repercussions for the issue of subjectivity. The selection and concentration by a culture on one or several modes (and the non-selection of others) opens up and facilitates my bodily engagement with the world in these specific ways. At the same time it closes off, or makes more difficult, an engagement with the world in other ways. The focus on print engages my visual sense, and focuses all energy there. It ignores (and thereby effectively negates) all other senses. Two-dimensional interaction offers quite other possibilities than three-dimensional; the senses of touch and smell have different cognitive and affective potentials from the senses of hearing and sight. Assuming that we, as biological and physiological beings, are not all equally disposed to the forms most developed and valued by our cultures, some members of one culture will be less well served than others; some will be affectively and cognitively at an advantage over those others whose preferred sensory modes are not valued or are suppressed in their culture. There are very large and increasingly significant questions in this area, questions which need a resolution before too long.

Some key examples

The issues of multimodality can be thought about in at least three distinct and related ways. First, all texts are multimodal. It is my contention that no text can exist in a single mode, so that all texts are always multimodal although one modality among these can dominate. Second, there are texts and objects (of a semiotic kind) which exist predominantly in a mode or modes other than the (multi-) mode of language. And third, there are systems of communication and representation which are acknowledged in the culture to be multimodal, though, in fact, all such systems are multimodal.

The concept of multimodality forces a rethinking of the distinctions usually made between communication and *use*, and in particular between reading and use. For a theory of Multiliteracies this is obviously crucial. I will discuss this in more detail a little later in this chapter. Here I will focus on the issue by using two examples: one, a bottle of mineral water; and the other, an eighteenth-century Sèvres china spoon-tray. The former comes from the shelves of a supermarket, the latter is in a display case, with the rest of a dinner-set, at the Victoria and Albert Museum in London.

The mineral water bottle brings together the ambivalence of meaning and use in a particularly clear fashion. As we walk along the shelves of water in a supermarket, we 'read' the bottles. We respond to them as multimodal texts, which are meaningful in every aspect of their multimodality: we see the labels, and treat them, however fleetingly, as texts of language and image; we notice whether the bottles are glass or plastic – with some bottles emphasising their materiality and others disguising it; we notice their colour: green, or blue, or clear; and we notice their shape: squarish with moulded patterns (denoting foreignness or 'Frenchness'), elongated and without mouldings denoting 'localness' such as 'Britishness'); and so on. Our readings are of course cursory, in one sense: we do not often pause to read the details of the labels, either at the back or at the front – though these meanings influence our choice. In another sense the readings are already coloured by a former or an imagined use: how will this bottle look on the dinner table? how will it feel when I pour? how will it fit into my fridge?

The reading of the bottle as text points to one domain of use, the semiotics of 'taste' in the sense both of 'what we taste' and of lifestyle. Here the messages about and the discourses of health, heritage, environment are important. Here too the shape of the bottle is important: the clear-glass bottle of 'delightfully still' English water, with its square shoulders; its blue square label with gold printing and fake royal crest hints, intersemiotically, at gin bottles and at the social (semiotic) domains of 'social drinking', whether of the gin-and-tonic hour, or otherwise. The elongated green bottle of carbonated Scottish water, with its oval-shaped, coloured vignettes depicting an idyllic-mythic Scottish countryside, points intersemiotically to the meal-table and its practices. This is 'reading' as a semiotic cultural practice in which it is 'meanings' as much as water which are 'consumed'.

The other domain of use involves the body much more fully: not merely the engagement through sight and the multiplicity of meanings called up by that, but now also the tactile engagement of holding the bottle, the meaning of its touch, its weight, its temperature, the feeling of the embossing, and the taste and texture as I drink the water. This is consumption in the literal sense, it is use for physical, bodily physiological reasons: it is reading with the body. However, it would be entirely incorrect to assume either that this use is not fully semiotic: it is cultural; it is based on cultural training; and it is entirely connected with the multimodal semiotic of the first kind of use. The two are entirely connected with each other. The clear-glass bottle's 'delightfully still' already conjures up and disposes me towards a certain kind of taste. More, it expects me to behave in certain ways; namely to expect and savour 'stillness', even in anticipation; to have certain cultural, social and personal dispositions; to be a certain kind of person. And when the label on the back declares that its contents come 'from deep within the chalk of the Hampshire Downs, protected for millennia from the environment' it is registering an enormously complex reassessment of myself in relation to this newly re-classified environment, an entity until now to be protected, but now hostile: the environment from which both the water and I need to be protected.

The enormity of this ideological move, as of its political consequences (what you can now legitimately do to this environment!), are hard to overstate. But in this complex semiotic weave, older notions of 'reading' and newer ideas of 'use' are entirely indistinguishable. When I read the description I am positioned in certain ways; when I drink the water I am already prepared to be still in order to drink stillness. The feel and look of the clear-glass bottle; the coloured image of the English country house; the evocation of English landscape (the Hampshire hills – both Thomas Hardy and Edward Elgar are distantly brought to mind, as is the voice, for readers of my age, of John Arlott, the cricket commentator). All these form part of a reinforcing mesh of meaning. In a multimodal approach to human/social semiosis the metaphor of 'consumption' makes a new sense; and ideology becomes a bodily as much as a semiotic matter.

The concept of communication – as transport and transformation of meaning – is hugely extended in a multimodal approach to semiosis. The involvement and engagement of our bodies makes ideology (as systematic sets of meanings organised from a particular position) truly a lived experience. In this example there is the use of language, on the label on the front of the bottle, and also the label on the back. I have not, by any means, given a full description of the multiplicity of signs involved: the light blue colour of the label; the fake 'royal arms' suggesting the accolade of 'By Appointment'; the range of colours in the multicolour, realist watercolour representation of the country house on the label on the back of the bottle; and so on. But as there is language involved it may be felt that, 'in the last resort', it underpins the possibility of communication.

The Sèvres spoon-tray, on the other hand, is part of an eighteenth-century porcelain dinner-set, displayed in the porcelain room of the

Victoria and Albert Museum. It caught my attention because I had never come across such an object. That in itself is significant. It may well be that in certain cultural groups even now a spoon-tray is as usual an object as an ashtray is for others, in its setting. Both my interest and my ignorance point at once not only to the cultural and historical specificity of the object but to the fact that it is embedded in a web of cultural practices. These are practices performed by humans, so that humans have to be trained, educated, or socialised into performing them. That educational process means that the use of the spoon-tray becomes 'natural', and that the meanings of that use are also naturalised: just as are the meanings of the ashtray for the group for which it is a naturalised object – 'don't drop ash just anywhere!' The object – appearing without the support of any language – communicates as effectively as does the written text of a set of instructions. The appearance of the object on the dinner table is – for the individual who is socialised into its use – an instruction, a command, as potent as any spoken command. It is also a prop to the individual's subjectivity: a semiotic item in its proper place in the vast structure of meaning of social life.

But although the spoon-tray is unsupported by language, it is nevertheless multimodal. There are, first, the modes of the material itself – the preciousness and delicacy of porcelain and its meaning in eighteenth-century Europe (only a few decades after the re-invention of porcelain in Europe, at the court of the king of Saxony, breaking the monopoly of Chinese imports), and of the shape – a small square (about 10 cm square) with its raised edge (about 1.5 cm high), slightly undulating at the top; the colours painted on the surface and glazed into the object – light pinkish reds, a gold band along the top edge. The person setting the table, though not the people 'using' the spoon-tray, would have felt its weight and its texture, and heard the sound of spoon on spoon-tray. Just as the mineral water bottle exists in a meaningful system of shapes, each with particular local histories and meanings, so the spoon-tray once stood in a relation to other objects which functioned as receptacles for spoons on the dinner table; in relation also to the other elements of the dinner-set; as well, of course, as its relation to the unspoken and unspeakable possibility of the absence of such an object. I do not know the system of objects involved. The point here is simply to draw attention to the power of the 'object without language' to communicate, to mean; to its role and power in a vast semiotic structure, and in the support of individual subjectivity. The spoon-tray speaks of naturalised practices which reach deep into the psychic-cultural constitution of the people using it. It speaks of a human subjectivity built on refinement and exhibiting naturalised sensibilities and taste.

A particular kind of object gives insight into complex social practices, and into their individual ramification. The spoon-tray probably existed as one example of a multiplicity of such objects, so that discernment, refinement and discrimination – distinction in Bourdieu's use – could be shown by the choice of a particular example. In the case of the spoon-tray, its existence speaks of utility – perhaps saving the table or the tablecloth from getting stained; or perhaps – and more significantly – saving a diner from the painful experience of having to place a spoon directly on the table. These are culturally 'produced' effects (they are, after all, not absolutely essential to human survival); they have, nevertheless, an essential utility in the group which has come to use it ('you can't possibly set a dinner table without a spoon-tray').

The point is to insist on the semiotic, communicational, and meaningful aspect of objects. In the spoon-tray *use* is dominant over reading; though reading is not absent. Perhaps the most productive theoretical approach is not to insist on the distinction of reading and use at this level, but leave it as one means of articulating the differences due to specific modes of bodily engagement with the world: 'reading' as the term for engagement, through sight, with letters, predominantly; 'use' as the term for engagement, for instance, through touch with three-dimensional objects; while recognising that elements of each exist in both. The fact is that at the moment we tend to speak of having seen a film; of watching television; of using a CD-ROM; with video closer to watch than to use. However, in more theoretical debates it is entirely usual to speak of using video; less common to speak of using film; though in earlier debates in mass communication theories the notion of 'uses and gratification' was well established.

These examples show that the degree of elaboration and articulation of a semiotic mode is important. Is it systematic and highly elaborated? Is it weakly elaborated? And is its systematicity relatively local, focused on small groups? As an instance of what we mean by 'elaboration', take the mode of lexis. Halliday's (Halliday 1978) work on anti-languages (see also Hodge and Kress 1988) speaks of the lexicalisation of a particular domain (an idea widespread in linguistics, even if under different names, such as semantic field), and suggests that a domain may be overlexicalised – reflecting intense social-cultural concern and energy – or underlexicalised, reflecting relatively low levels of concern. So the various modes brought together in the multimodal system of language are generally speaking highly elaborated, in syntax, in lexis, in phonology, etc. The multimodal system of 'crockery' – that is, the system of objects integrally involved with social practices of domestic food consumption – is less elaborated, though differentially so for different social-cultural groups, as the example of the spoon-tray shows.

The issue of the materials through which the semiotic mode is realised is crucial for two reasons: because of their representational potentials, and because of their cultural valuations. Glass has different representational possibilities from porcelain, or from jade, or from clay – though there may be attempts on the part of the makers of objects to force one material in the direction of the potentials of the other: to make marble imitate the luxuriant folds of cloth for instance. The materials, apart from their inherent representational potentials and limitations also have culturally ascribed value. These no doubt derive in the first place from inherent (or semi-inherent) 'natural' qualities and characteristics, such as scarcity; hardness; malleability; colour; durability; ability to be inscribed, incised; and so on. So marble has inherent potentials as a representational medium due to its characteristics, and yet others due to its ascribed value in a particular culture. It is no surprise that it is a material favoured for monuments in European cultures. The early European explorers of the various parts of the globe made very good use of these factors – swapping glass beads and blankets for desirable bits of land.

The statement made somewhat casually earlier that language is itself a multimodal phenomenon may seem unnecessarily provocative, or outrageous. In sign languages such a statement describes what is now commonsensical. So in an introduction to this subject the modes out of which sign languages are fashioned are described in this way. The author of the next extract first lists the communicational media involved.

> *Communication-media of gesture language*
>   manual media:
>   hands and arms
>   non-manual media:
>   facial expression
>   looks
>   head
>   upper part of the torso
>   the configuration of the mouth [the 'mouth-image', [*mundbild*]

She then goes on to say:

> usually, when we think of gesture language, we tend to think of the use of the hands. Linguists began with the study of hand-signs, when they began their systematic study of gesture language. It became clear later that the non-manual channels of gesture language were used, not only for the expression of emotional or attitudinal states of the 'signer' – just as hearing people do with non-verbal means – but especially that these channels are of central importance for the communication of the grammar of the language. Because of this relatively late discovery we now know more about manual aspects of the structure of gesture language than we do about the non-manual.
>
> (Boyes Braem 1990)

There is no hesitation at all in this approach to describe the quite different modes of representation as part of the one communicational system, the 'gesture language'. Yet the regret expressed at the relatively lower level of knowledge about the function of the non-manual aspects of representation is telling. From my point of view it points precisely to the continuing after-effects of the central position of linguistics and its approach to language, exported to the description of another, fundamentally different semiotic system. Equally telling is this author's unquestioned acceptance of the common sense of linguistics about language: she is happy to continue to assert that the 'non-verbal means' of representation employed by hearing people have no central role in the grammatical core of language.

A multimodal approach to 'language' will require a factoring-out of communicational means similar to that indicated above for 'gesture language': pitch variation; pace; stress; phonological units (produced by a complex of organs); lexis; sequencing (as syntax); etc. The 'etc.' shows that it is as yet not possible to provide a full list of factors – nor to indicate at all clearly what would or should be included in the set of factors, and what should be excluded. Is it the case for language-as-speech that only those elements produced *inside* the head, the neck, and the chest cavity are to count as 'language' or as 'speech' (that is, only those features produced by the so-called speech organs) or does, for instance, the gestural disposition of the lips in speaking form part of language: non-hearing people can, after all, 'lip-read'? The point at this stage is to unsettle a settled common sense.

Potentials and limitations of semiotic modes

There is a general assumption that language is a communicational and representational medium which is fully adequate to the expression of anything that we might want to express: that anything that we think, feel, sense, can be said (or written) in language. The obverse of this assumption is that if something cannot be expressed in language (if there were such a thing) then that thing is in any case outside rational thought, outside articulate feeling, and therefore need not be said or should not be said. This assumption is anchored in popular as much as in theoretical common sense; countless theoretical assertions reproduce and re-entrench it constantly.

> Finally . . . many authors advocate a *principle of effability* according to which a natural language can express anything that can be thought. A natural language is supposedly capable of rendering the totality of our experience – mental or physical – and, consequently able to express all our sensations, perceptions, abstractions up to the question of why is there something instead of nothing. It is true that

no purely verbal language ever entirely achieves total effability: think of having to describe, in words alone, the smell of rosemary. We are always required to supplement language with ostensious, expressive gestures and so-called 'tonemic' features. Nevertheless, of all semiotic systems, nothing rivals language in its effability.

(Eco 1996)

While Eco's finely nuanced statement remains short of claiming 'total effability', it does claim an exceptionally privileged place for language. The assumption underlying a multimodal approach to communication and representation is that, on the contrary, humans use many means made available in their cultures for representation precisely because these offer differing potentials, both for representation and for communication. For instance, one oft-repeated account of the reason why sound became the favoured material for semiosis is that it enables the speaker and the hearer to continue with other, essential activities while they are communicating; similarly motivated reasons are given for the invention, development and continued use of writing. The issue is made more difficult because the (Western) accounts are by and large accounts which take Western forms of communication as unquestioned norms. Cultures other than 'Western' ones have, as we know, made use of different materials, and developed different modes: the cultures of communities of the totally speech-impaired, in relation to gesture languages, and Aboriginal Australian cultures in relation to visual representation being very good but by no means unusual cases in point (see, for example, Sacks 1996).

A further two assumptions, as implied earlier, are that the various modes have particular potentials and limitations; and that different modes have been developed, articulated, and specialised in particular ways by different cultures. There is a relatively high degree of articulation of the visual mode in the 'the West', though differentially in particular places: whether the specialisations of religious icons, and of religious iconography more generally, or the specialisations in particular art movements; or, yet again, the specialisations in particular scientific or technological domains in the use of diagrams and their components; and so on. Nevertheless it is also the case that the visual mode has not been developed into as highly articulated a state as spoken or written language are, for instance, or as they had been developed and conventionalised in other cultures – say, Egyptian hieroglyphics; Chinese pictograms; or Australian Aboriginal visual iconographies. In this section I wish to give one example to counter the notion that language is the one fully articulated mode of representation; and one example to suggest the idea of the potentials and limitations of modes, and of their specialisation. The first is a drawing by a six-year-old girl of an elephant; the second some pages from science textbooks of the late 1980s and early 1990s, produced in England, for, roughly, fourteen-year-olds.

Figure 9.1 (Redraw over a very faint original)

The drawing (Figure 9.1) is a precise representation of an elephant, from a particular point of view. If we attempt to 'translate' what it is into either speech or writing, we discover just how specialised this mode is. We can say little more than that it is drawn from in front and above the elephant at an angle of 45 degrees. But this 'translation' immediately points to the limits of 'translation': it gives no sense at all of what it is. This is simply not how we would articulate the topic 'elephant' in either speech or in writing; it would neither arise in that form nor be dealt with in this way. The two modes – language and the visual – simply start from different concerns, are embedded in distinct ways of conceptualising, thinking, and communicating.

The drawing of this elephant shows an astonishing degree of conceptual/ cognitive grasp, and an astonishing imagination – though perhaps our astonishment is a reflection also of the common sense about language mentioned earlier. Even if this child had invented a narrative in which she, Peter-Pan-like, had the ability to fly through the air, and she described how she approached an elephant, floating three metres above and in front of its head, in that narrative she would be unlikely then to focus her account on matters such as what proportion of the elephant's eyes she could see, that the tusks were invisible, and that the trunk seemed foreshortened. Any one semiotic mode positions us, from the very beginning, in relation to its systems of criteria of relevance: speech and narrative towards criteria to do with action, event, sequence; the visual, image and display towards criteria to do with focus-field structures, towards a representation of visually salient elements and of their spatial relation with each other.

The point here is to keep sight of the cognitive work performed; the complexity of thinking matches, in all ways, the complexity demanded by the production of a verbal account. It may even be more and greater, given that in a verbal account the elements of the narrative – words, characters, textual structures – are readily 'available' in a quite important sense. This is not to underestimate the work and the transformative action performed in the making of a narrative, but to emphasise that in the drawing of this elephant there is if anything a greater productive/creative effort needed. In the making of a 'story' the word elephant is 'to hand', as are the adjectives which I might employ for further qualification or to elaborate its description. In the making of the drawing, there is no equivalent 'stock' of images.

Frequently, even when the cognitive and conceptual achievement of visual representation is acknowledged, it is assumed that it is, nevertheless, a translation from or via language. But there is no pre-existing linguistic account of this elephant's head. What there is, or what there are, are 'intervisual' links – perhaps elephants from Walt Disney movies or cartoons, or toys. In other words, there exists a mode of representation and of communication *in the* visual medium, independent of the verbal. The visual functions at one level as an independent and relatively autonomous semiotic mode, in which meanings are transported, made, and remade (this elephant's head is, after all, not identical with a Walt Disney cartoon drawing). This mode does not depend on language for its transmission; language is not the guarantor of the efficacy of working of this mode.

That is the one issue. To develop the point about the functional specialisation of the modes I will first examine another drawing, also by a six-year-old, and compare it with written 'stories' of a similar event (Figure 9.2). This drawing was made on the prompting of the teacher after the class had visited the Toy Museum in London's Bethnal Green. The child's spoken account was 'Mouse, turtle, doll, Jack-in-the-box. Me looking at all the toys'. The varied experiences of a morning's visit are not represented as events, in sequence; rather, the child's representation transforms and condenses these experiences into a number of salient elements (the toys which she represents) shown in a particular relationship. They are shown on a shelf, evenly spaced, and arranged in size from small to large, with the drawer shown in front *not* 'looking at all the toys', but visually addressing us, the viewers.

Again there can be no doubt about the cognitive/transformative work done here: a whole morning's events are distilled into a representation consisting of two main elements: toys and observer, and the former is shown as a classificatory set – 'these are the kinds of toys you can see at the Toy Museum'.

Here by contrast is a story (which is entirely representative and characteristic): 'On Monday we went to the British Museum. First we went

Figure 9.2

to Goodge Street on the Tube. Then we walked to the museum. I liked the mummy best. Then we went home.'

Here the focus is on events; in a sequence. No doubt the children were as fascinated by the things they saw here as the other child had been. However, the demand for a *written* story focuses the child's attention towards actions, events; and they are organised through temporal sequence. It is possible to represent classifications in language – salient elements and their relations – as for instance in 'there was a mummy; and there was a mask; and there was a cat; etc.'. The 'normal' engagement with the world through speech seems to be that of action, and event, in sequence.

Figure 9.3 shows an example from the realm of science textbooks. This page is from a book first published in 1988. The language is about events: relatively simple sentences (one or two clauses), which are about actions – what had been done; what is to be done; what might happen if . . . The diagrams represent the core information of this bit of the curriculum: what a circuit consists of, and in what relation its components stand to each other.

This is an example of specialisation: one representational mode, language, is used for a pedagogic purpose, to direct, remind, organise the

197

12·9 Electronics

Circuits

In your first circuits you used torch bulbs joined with wires. Modern electrical equipment uses the same basic ideas. But if you look inside a computer there are not many wires or torch bulbs. The wires and bulbs have been replaced by electronic devices like transistors, chips and light-emitting diodes.

Transistors and chips are examples of *semi-conductors*. They are made from special crystals like silicon. Transistors work because they only conduct electricity in the right conditions. They are useful because they can turn on and off very fast, and they need very little electricity.

An electronic light

● You can make electronic circuits with wires like the circuits you made before. The difficulty is that the contacts are poor, and sometimes things do not work. It is far better to *solder* the components.

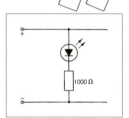

Here is a simple circuit to operate a light-emitting diode (LED).

This design shows the same circuit soldered on matrix board. The board is cheap and can be re-used.

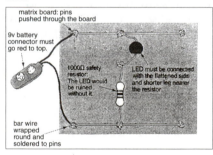

140

Figure 9.3

Transistors

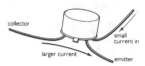

A transistor is a special semi-conductor. It has three connections: a base, a collector and an emitter. When a small current is put on the base, it lets a much larger current flow between the collector and the emitter. So a tiny current can control a much larger one.

● Try this water-detector circuit.

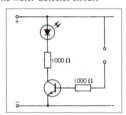

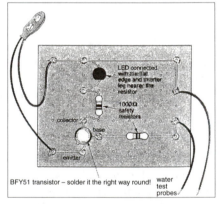

BFY51 transistor – solder it the right way round!

When the probes touch something wet, a very small current goes from the battery through the water to the base of the transistor. This current is big enough to make the transistor work, so the LED lights up.

students. Another representational mode, visual images, is used to convey the central information. The images show what significant elements this bit of the world consists of, and in what relation they stand. This is a fundamental change to earlier forms of textbook, in which language was the dominant medium, and images served to illustrate (to 'repeat visually') what had already been verbally communicated.

Just as there are variations in types of actions (mental action, physical action) and differences in temporal location in the language (past versus future), there are variations in the types of relations indicated, and particularly in the level of abstractness at which they are discussed. The first diagram is highly abstract; it is a topological account of the elements and of their relation. The second diagram, which in the original is in colour to indicate, among other means, its greater 'realism', is topographical. It shows what a circuit might actually look like, realisitically enough to serve as an instruction for producing a circuit. While the first diagram serves for theorisation, the second serves for application.

Grammar and Multiliteracies: the example of the visual

Implicit in the project of Multiliteracies is not merely the assumption that we communicate through and with a range of quite different modes, but also that each of these modes displays regularities which are akin to – though never the same as – those of spoken or written language. Cultures differ in this respect: some have developed the visual into a fully articulated system of communication – Chinese pictographic writing for instance, or certain forms of Australian Aboriginal representation. Others have developed bodily movement – as in the gesture language of the speech- and hearing-impaired.

In each case the meanings of the culture find expression in the relevant mode, or set of modes. In fact, textual objects – spoken, signed, written, drawn – always occur in a multiplicity of modes; and this realisation has to be given full recognition in a project of Multiliteracies. The deep logics of each mode are related to, or derived from, the materiality of the semiotic mode – sound, and temporality and sequence; visual images, and simultaneity and spatiality; gesture, and temporality, sequence, and (three-dimensional) spatiality; and so on. The syntax of speech (and by a more complex development in the visual form of writing) derives from the logic of sequence, and of its potentials. That is, firstness in time and lateness in a temporal sequence can be developed into a complex arrangement of (grammatical) meanings, such as, 'subject of an action', followed by 'the resultant action', followed by 'the participant affected by the action'; and so on.

In the visual semiotics, it is, among other means, the logic of the disposition of elements in a given space which leads to 'visual grammar'.

The 'other means' include what can be done with markings on a surface (and the resultant effects produced by *light*). We assume that any grammar, whatever the mode, must serve three communicational demands: to communicate about events and states of affairs in the world; to communicate about the social relations of the participants in a communicational interaction; and to have the ability to form internally coherent entities – messages.

The semiotics of the visual space

What follows is a brief account of how a grammar of the visual might function (for a fuller account see Kress and Van Leeuwen 1996), with which we will conclude the argument. With respect to the task of forming internally coherent and meaningful texts, we are here pointing to a use of the visual space (the page, a part of the ground, a wall, a rockface, a plaque, etc.) such that regular meanings attach to parts of that space. In relation to the 'page' in Western alphabetical cultures, with a left–right, top-to-bottom reading direction (and with the history of the visual/aesthetic culture of Western Europe), we posit a left–right, bottom–top distinction, such that four quadrants are formed (Figure 9.4).

To the bottom section of an image we assign the value 'real'; to the top section the value 'ideal'. Each of these may be given particular meanings in certain contexts, for instance 'ideal' may mean distant in time, whether 'of the past' or 'in the future'; 'an ideal form'; 'a wish'; etc. 'Real' may have the specific meanings 'here and now'; 'empirically so'; etc.

The left–right distinction has a different meaning: left, as the starting point (in reading across a line) tends to have meanings such as (what is taken as) given, 'taken for granted', 'assumed to be the case', etc. Right, as the finishing point, tends to have meanings such as 'what is new', 'what is an instance (of the taken for granted)' etc. In other words, the top–bottom distinction relates to ontological judgments; the left–right distinction to the social status of information.

The specific placement of the horizontal and vertical division between real and ideal, and given new, is relative to the interest of the maker of the image (or page). Similarly, what kinds of semiotic materials are placed there is both culturally shaped and determined by the interest of the maker of this structure. What is stable is the meaning of these divisions: material placed in the bottom left quadrant will be understood to be given and real, etc.

Other distributions of the space are possible and are in use in different cultures – for instance, a distribution of centre versus margin, where what is central has a different valuation to what is marginal. Different cultures have differential uses. Within a pluri-cultural society therefore quite different dispositions may be in use, though some may be dominant in relation to others.

'Ideal'

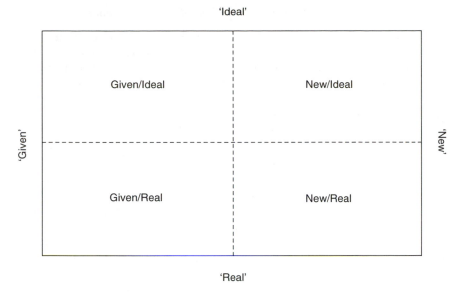

Figure 9.4

The semiotics of states of affairs in the represented world

With respect to the task of communicating about events (and their internal structures), objects, events, and states of affairs, we assume a use of visual elements which both indicates what are treated as major elements, and what the relations between them are. In a diagram, for instance, two elements may be connected by an arrow, so signalling one as the origin, originator, or cause, and the other as recipient, goal, effect. The famous communication model of S → M → R is one such instance (except that this has three elements). It might be read as: a message M originates with S; it passes to R, where it comes to rest. Images with realist or figurative elements – for instance, a person passing something to another or a person looking at another – fit easily into this scheme.

At the same time there are images which do not represent (inter)action, but rather represent states of affairs. A picture of an Antarctic explorer in a textbook shows in schematic form what he needs to wear: fur hood, heavy mittens, fur-lined coat, boots. This shows visual analysis: 'X has these parts'. Or there may be an image of a scientific instrument objectively represented. Images of this latter kind are quite as common as the former; usually there is some indication of a focal element, but not necessarily so. Pages in science textbooks often have entirely regular arrangements of small images 'in blocks': here the task, and the syntax, is that of classification.

The semiotics of the social relations of viewer and image

Lastly, with respect to the task of representing and communicating about the social relations of the viewer of the image to the image (a relation which parallels that of the maker of the image to the represented object), we assume a use of visual elements which indicate a set of social relations judged to be significant in that society. For instance, indications of social distance may be coded by the size of the element represented; or in its coded distance from the viewer: attitudinal relations may be coded by the viewer's lateral position in relation to an element (e.g. 'front on', 'to the side of', 'from the margin'). Relations of power are coded by the position of the viewer in vertical relation to the object; if the object is more powerful we look up to it; if we are more powerful, we look down on it, and so on. Forms of 'factuality' may be coded by kinds of realism, so that in relation to our main example we might say that the mode of representation is in a hyper-realist form (perhaps a surrealist form) of everyday realism. In Figure 9.2 the child-drawer looks straight out from the image, in a kind of 'visual statement'.

Interested readers should use the much fuller description available in Kress and Van Leeuwen (1996). Here we simply want to indicate that there are regularities of structure, and regularities of a 'grammatical' kind in different modes and to use this skeletal framework to indicate one of the urgent research tasks for a project of Multiliteracies.

10

DESIGNS FOR SOCIAL FUTURES

Bill Cope and Mary Kalantzis

Design, culture, transformation

Meaning-making, as Gunther Kress has observed, is prospective; it is interest-laden and future-oriented (see Kress, Chapter 7 above). Semiosis involves the representation of interest (a need to communicate); selection from the range of representational resources (drawing from Available Designs, be they, for instance, in various Linguistic, Gestural, Visual, Spatial or Multimodal forms); and representational action or the meaning-making process itself (Designing).

Thus, meaning-making involves Design in both its senses. 'Design' in the sense of morphology, that is, structure and function, such as the design that 'is' a motor car or a skeleton, for instance; and design in the sense of an active, willed, human process in which we make and remake the conditions of our existence, that is, what 'designers' do. Design, therefore, refers both to structure and to agency.

Design is a process in which the individual and culture are inseparable. The representational resources available to an individual are the stuff of culture; the ways of making meaning that an individual has learnt and used perennially over the course of their life; as well as those new ways of making meaning that they know are there and that they could pick up with more or less effort if and when they were needed. Others' interests have already been expressed though Designings that have resulted in the Redesigned, and these, in turn, become Available Designs for the individual in their own meaning-making. Culture is no more and no less than the accumulated and continuing expression of agency; of Designing.

These propositions seem obvious and, in a way, a kind of common sense. The notion of Design, however, entails a very different conception of meaning-making from that which traditionally underlies both theories of language and practices of literacy teaching. It also entails a very particular concept of culture.

Building upon the arguments developed by Kress in Chapter 7, there is a common view of language in particular, and patterns of meaning-making in general, as inherently stable systems of elements and rules. The focus here is on convention and use. Individuals are at worst passive recipients of these systems, at best they are agents in the reproduction of conventions. This view finds its expression in language and literacy curricula which focus on grammar and form, and which measure results against the official 'standard' of the national language. It also finds its expression in many 'immersion' models of language learning, in which students are expected to drift in the direction of a standard form of the language as a result of being immersed in texts of ostensible literary significance, or social power.

In either case, culture is implicitly or explicitly regarded as stable, and teaching and learning fundamentally a business of leading students in the direction of a singular norm – variously understood to be 'national culture', 'common culture', 'core culture'. This is a view of culture in which students come to be passive bearers of culture more than active and responsible cultural participants. It is also a view of culture that is not very good at explaining change.

These views of language and culture are very much a product of the era we have already described in Chapter 6, when the systems logic of Fordism, nationalism and mass culture attempted to force the cultural simplicities of homogeneity on a world that was inherently heterogeneous. Some of the more simplistic versions of multiculturalism try something which is, in essence, much the same. They neaten up the boundaries of cultures in an attempt to impose the stamp of 'identity' in its literal sense; they focus on maintenance as if they were curators in some kind of museum of human life forms; and they retreat into fragmented separatisms.

The Design notion, on the other hand, starts with a very different set of assumptions about meaning and ends with a very different notion of culture. Instead of a focus on stability and regularity, the focus is on change and transformation. Individuals have at their disposal a complex range of representational resources, never simply of one culture but of the many cultures in their lived experience; the many layers of their identity and the many dimensions of their being. The breadth, complexity and richness of the available meaning-making resources is such that representation is never simply a matter of reproduction. Rather, it is a matter of transformation; of reconstruing meaning in a way which always adds something to the range of available representational resources.

There are two elements to change or transformation. One aspect is 'voice'. The last few hundred words of this chapter have never been written this way before; there is something unique about them, even if there is nothing particularly startling about the words or what they are saying. And, no matter how everyday their context and content, the next few hundred words you say could not be said in precisely the same way, have the same

204

'feel' about them and embody the same expression of personhood, as anyone other than you at this particular moment in your life, with your own life history and exposure to a peculiar range of representational resources.

The second element of change or transformation is hybridity. The many layers of identity, the many aspects of experience, and the many discourses that represent the Available Designs of meaning, are ever being related, combined, and recombined in such a way that all utterances are poly-morphous reconstructions. The range and complexity of representational resources at a person's disposal are such that every representation is invariably unique and hybrid. There is just so much to draw from in the breadth and subtlety of Available Designs that every Designing re-creates the world afresh. Every Designing picks and chooses from all the bits in the world of Available Designs and puts it back together in a way it has never quite been before. In both of these aspects – voice and hybridity – agency is the critical factor. Available Designs are transformed in the act of Designing.

This view of meaning embodies an understanding of culture which fits well with that strategically optimistic analysis of our near futures already presented in Chapter 6: a future of Productive Diversity, of Civic Pluralism and of Multilayered Identities. Culture is hybrid; dynamic, open and for-ever undergoing transformation. This is also an understanding of culture capable of accounting for change, both retrospectively in the sense of how our history and our lives have changed, and prospectively in the sense of how we are designers of social futures and makers of our own futures. And finally, it is an account of culture which has implications for individual responsibility and the ethics of participation. As transformers of meaning and makers of culture, we are all deeply responsible for the immediate consequences of our Designing and, in a larger sense, our individual and collective futures.

Yet there is agency and agency; Designing and Designing. All meaning and Design is transformative in one sense: human agency constitutes mean-ing (Designing) and remakes the world in the process (the Redesigned). Yet in some moments, agency or Design is more transformative than in others – transformative in this sense being more a matter of creative change than sticking to existing Designs of meaning. Some Designs, or transformations, are more in the nature of cultural copies and are thus more predictable, more passively compliant and more neatly within conventional cultural boundaries. Others are more creative, more hybrid and complex in their cultural sources, and more reflexively conscious of their own replication of, or divergence from, their cultural and representational roots.

Then, there is also change in a positive and constructive sense, and there are changes in a myriad of miserable, exploitative, and humanity-denying senses. It is one thing to have a theory of meaning and culture that can account for change. It is quite another to have a theory that can evaluate different kinds of change and the comparative merits of various attempts at being human – cultures or moments within cultures. It is one thing to say there are cultural differences, and then to stand back, to live and let live; it is another to evaluate the import of these differences.

The concept of 'lifeworld' helps us differentiate between transformation in the sense of cultural reproduction and transformation in the sense of creative change. The lifeworld is the world of everyday lived experience; a world where transformation occurs in a less creative and self-conscious sense: richly organised, to be sure, and laden with linguistic and cultural tradition, but serving immediate or practical ends. The lifeworld is pre-given – already there – as the surroundings that shape every individual as they becoming human, as babies and then children are 'socialised', and in our simply assumed or 'commonsense' surroundings as adults.

In Husserl's terms, the lifeworld is 'the world valid as existing for us', the 'intuitive surrounding world of life', the 'realm of original self-evidences', 'habitually persisting validities', 'everyday practical situational truths', 'the world of straightforward intersubjective experiences' (Husserl 1970, pp. xl–xli, 109, 121, 127–8, 109, 132, 133). The lifeworld is just there; it is what we unreflexively expect to be there because we know it is always there; it is the world in which our everyday understandings and actions have some purchase. It is the ground of our everyday lives.

For the individual, the basis of the lifeworld is the functioning, kinaesthetic ego. 'Thus we are concretely in the field of perception, . . . and in the field of consciousness . . . through our living body.' The way of knowing within the lifeworld, of knowing its Designs if you like, is in the manner of 'naive experiential self-evidence, the certainty of coming to know, through seeing, touching, feeling, hearing etc., the same thing through its properties, through "repetition" of the experiences'. However, for all its pre-given, everyday, intuitive, self-evident character, the lifeworld is no less a site of subjectivity and agency than any other. Although it 'is always already there, existing in advance for us', we are nevertheless 'wakingly alive in it, . . . always somehow interested subjects' (Husserl 1970, pp. 108, 343, 142).

This lifeworld is the raw material of culture; a shared set of assumptions about what is both practically achievable or good in the world, as well as what is practically useless or bad in the world. It is 'all the built-up levels of validity acquired by [people] for the world of their common life'. This build-up Husserl calls 'sedimentation', a process soaked with culture in which 'all of us together, belong to the world . . . through . . . living together'. Language is one of the primary media in 'the unavoidable sedimentation of mental products'. Indeed, we fall under the spell of what Husserl calls 'the seduction of language', in which the apparently fixed 'validities of association' make things appear natural, permanent and universal by virtue of their having been named. They are none of these things, he warns, and we cannot but be 'disappointed by subsequent experience' (Husserl 1970, pp. 133, 361–2).

What Husserl doesn't say, however, is that the lifeworld is also inherently diverse; it is polymorphous, multilayered and capable of multiple combinations in all the senses elaborated upon in this book. There is not one lifeworld but an infinity of overlapping lifeworlds; always unique at any moment in time and space and yet, in the nature of sedimentation, always referenced elsewhere to established patterns of representation and culture.

Although fully a place of Design and transformation, therefore, the Designing of the lifeworld takes place within limited horizons – horizons, indeed, the limits of which will not necessarily be visible to the actors in their Designing and transforming. Though fully willed, transformation purely within the lifeworld involves a limited field of vision. It is no more than an unreflective appropriation of representational and cultural resources that are circumstantially available. Within the lifeworld, 'active consciousness . . . is surrounded by an atmosphere of mute, concealed, but cofunctioning validities'. What lies beyond the 'horizon of interest' or beneath the surface in the deep structures of culture and meaning 'does not disturb the course of normal practical life' (Husserl 1970, pp. 145, 379, 344).

So, the lifeworld is a place of Design and transformation within practically limited horizons. This, of course, is the datum point of Situated Practice in the Multiliteracies pedagogy outlined in the next section of this book. Overt Instruction and Critical Framing are both strategies to extend students' cultural and representational horizons beyond where they already are and take these broader practices back into the lifeworld in the form of Transformed Practice. This also means that the lifeworld is the datum point for the process of transformation that is the purpose of the education, which we have already described in Chapter 6.

Beyond the horizon of the lifeworld are more expansive and deeper forms of knowing and meaning, which Husserl calls 'the transcendental'. We will start here with Husserl's concept, and then extend it. Husserl's transcendental is rather like natural science; it is 'a method which is designed for progressively improving, through "scientific" predictions, those rough predictions which are the only ones that are possible within the sphere of what is actually experienced and experienceable in the lifeworld'. The transcendental looks at the world from various angles, seeking new ways in which the world might exhibit itself, such as the 'alteration of perspectives' and developing a theory-like synthesis. These are some of the ways in which 'we measure the lifeworld . . . for a well-fitting garb of ideas'; some of the ways in which we can know and mean in ways that have greater depth and broader horizons than what is possible within the lifeworld (Husserl 1970, pp. 51–2, 110, 158).

But the transcendental does much more than conventional natural science. Science often naively tends to name things as objective truths or facts, as if they stood in isolation from human interests. The transcendental, by contrast, always reflects back on the lifeworld, to reflect on which facts interest us, and why they are presented as if they were self-evident, objective truths (Husserl 1970, pp. 59, 159, 205). This means that we have to suspend belief and stand back from the world – a process Husserl calls 'bracketing' off the 'habitual one-sidedness' or 'naive objectivism' of the lifeworld (Husserl 1970, p. 152).

How do we do this bracketing? It is at this point that we extend and apply Husserl's notions of lifeworld and the transcendental into a critical theory of cultural pluralism.

For a start, there are the phenomena of cultural difference. Lifeworlds are evidently different, either in terms of the characteristics of groups 'living together' or in terms of the unique flows of influence that create multilayered identities, those uniquely hybrid designs of meaning in every utterance, and 'voice'. Lifeworlds immediately strike you as distinctive by way of contrast, for the differences that simply stare you in the face. Differences are the phenomena; the first impressions, the immediate appearance, of lifeworlds.

Beneath this, however, the hard work of the transcendental can uncover two more layers of cultural sedimentation. One is the most basic of the institutional structures of everyday life, fundamental ways of being, of thinking, of making meaning in the world and of imagining possible futures. In our modernity, for instance, it might be possible to uncover the motives and outcomes of the market, or liberal individualism. People live these things in various ways, but the fundamentals are not always immediately visible; nor are the ways in which these fundamentals affect the lives of recruits from other forms of life – immigrants from peasant farming communities, or indigenous societies, for instance.

And, digging yet another layer further, there comes a point at which we need to get completely out of the this-ness of any particular culture and ask the unfashionable question, what is our species being? From which follows the equally unfashionable questions, what are the universal elements of our human natures? what is the meaning and purpose of culture? and what does this imply for the way we do this bit of our culture or the way they do that bit of their culture? If there is one irreducible fact of human species being, it is the fact of culture. This is not just a fact, moreover; it is a moral imperative. As a species, we subsist through culture and culture gives us meaning by which to live. In some moments, our actual cultural experience is true to our natures, true to our species being. In others, it is a travesty. This is not to imply that there is a single or clear answer to the question of our human natures. Rather, it is to suggest that this is an important question that needs to be addressed to provide an ethical grounding for critical readings of meaning.

Starting with the cultural phenomena of differences in the lifeworld and always returning to those cultural phenomena, the transcendental

The lifeworld of everyday experience

The Designed

Designing

Types of transformation

- The world of everyday experience and 'commonsense' self-evidence. You 'know' what you do because certain expressions of meaning have purchase on the world, because they seem to work.

- Voice: making subtly variant meanings based on the unique mix that is individual life experience
- Hybridity: drawing from the enormous range of Available Designs, and recombining these meanings in a way never quite done before
- Change is semi-conscious and not always obvious: more like cultural reproduction – uncritical, relatively predictable, passively compliant

Larger processes of system and structure

The Designed

Designing

Types of transformation

- Expanded horizons for meaning-making and social action, such as working with underlying theories (discipline knowledge) or knowledge of other cultural practices.

- Analytical, reflective, systems thinking. Meaning-makers more reflexively conscious of their own meaning-making or Designing processes (in the fashion of an architect compared to the home renovator), as well as the extent of their replication of, or divergence from, the cultural and representational roots of their meanings in Available Designs.
- Depth dimensions: knowing and using larger, explanatory patterns of meaning, their social contexts, purposes and effects

<table>
<tr><td></td><td>• Breadth dimensions: cross-cultural comparison, seeing things from multiple cultural perspectives and using those perspectives</td></tr>
</table>

Our human natures

The Designed	*Designing*
	Types of transformation
• Human needs and their expression through meaning	• Ethical action, action on the basis of universal moral imperatives, such as human rights

adds perspectives along two dimensions: the dimensions of depth and breadth.

To take the depth dimension, we need to go beyond our reading of the phenomena of culture and differences and measure these phenomena against the deep structures of everyday life and meaning (digging down to the second layer of critical cultural analysis) and the moral facts of our species being (digging down to the third layer of critical cultural analysis). Suspension of belief or bracketing on a depth dimension involves critical thinking, systems thinking (Senge 1990), reflexivity (Beck 1994; Lash 1994), holistic thinking, working through interrelations between apparently separate phenomena, and figuring out paradox and contradiction. This depth dimension itself has space, time and structure dimensions within it, and this is what we attempted in our reading of the state and nationalism, and of postFordist work, in Chapter 6.

And, on a breadth dimension, we need to undertake the process of cross-cultural comparison; how does this particular lifeworld, our lifeworld (or, to be more precise, each of the layers of the multiplicity of overlapping lifeworld sources which constitute our daily experience) measure up against alternative ways of being human, of doing culture? Nationalism and racism, for instance, are prominent examples of knowing and meaning within the horizon of the lifeworld; and with them come practical orientations to the other lifeworlds one encounters, such as exclusion or assimilation. Measured up against a more expansive view than that which is possible from within the lifeworld in which racism and nationalism are generated, they are decidedly inadequate views of our pasts, our future and our species being (see Kalantzis and Cope, Chapter 6 above). Nor is this cross-cultural breadth simply the view of a disinterested observer, in the manner of a kind of anthropological curiosity. In an era of increasing local diversity and global interconnectedness, this breadth must be the stuff of practice; of learning by constantly crossing cultural boundaries, of shunting backwards and forwards between one lifeworld context and another.

Both depth and breadth dimensions are processes for 'denaturalising' the lifeworld, of making the everyday strange in order to cast new light on it and have a more informed basis upon which to design both imminent meanings and our larger social futures.

Designs of meaning

How, then do we describe meanings? Following is just one suggestion, examining five dimensions (representational, social, organisational, con-textual and ideological) across five modes of meaning (linguistic, visual, gestural, spatial and audio). It is simply indicative of the kinds of questions we might ask ourselves in order to add depth (systems and structure) and breadth (cross-cultural) dimensions to teaching and learning about the meaning of meanings.

Multimodal meaning is no more than the other modes of meaning working together, and much more as well.

The 'no more' is based on the fact that all meaning-making is in its nature multimodal. Multimodal meaning is no more than the other modes of meaning working together. And work together they always do. Linguistic meaning in the form of speaking, for instance, is achieved in combination with audio meaning (prosody) as well as gestural meaning, not to mention spatial meaning (the words of the lecturer compared to the conversation of two students sitting next to each other). And linguistic meaning in the form of writing is linked to visual, from the business of handwriting itself (graphology) all the way through to the heavily designed pages of desktop publishing in which fonts, point sizes, leading, kerning, bolding and italics are all integral to the grammar of the words – and the organisation of linguistic meaning around headings, subheadings, indents, bullet points, pictures, diagrams and open spaces.

Yet multimodal meaning is also much more than the sum of linguistic, visual, spatial, gestural and audio modes of meaning. It also involves processes of integration and moving the emphasis backwards and forwards between the various modes. At the heart of the processes of integration is the inherent 'multiness' of human expression and perception, or synaesthesia. Meanings come to us together: gesture with sight, with language, in audio form, in space. And, we can shift our meaning-making emphasis, through processes of transduction or transcoding. We can describe in words scenes that might otherwise be represented pictures, or represent three-dimensional spaces visually in two dimensions, or represent

Dimensions of meaning, with some examples

		Linguistic examples	Visual examples	Spatial examples	Gestural examples	Audio examples
Representational: What do the meanings refer to?	Participants: Who and what is participating in the meanings being represented?	Naming words, which make sense in terms with their relationships with nearby words and contextual pointers	Naturalistic and iconic representations, visibly distinguishable contrasts	Objects in relation to nearby objects, part/whole relationships, contrasts	Mimicry, gesture-shapes	Naturalistic representations in sound (e.g. recording of bird sounds); iconic representations (e.g. alarm sounds)
	Being and acting: What kinds of being and acting do the meanings represent?	Processes, attributes, and circumstances	Vectors, location, carriers	Placement, topography, scale, boundaries, location	Direction, location, size	Tempo, tonality, accompaniment
Social: How do the meanings connect the persons they involve?	The roles of the participants in the communication of meaning: How does the speaker/writer mean to draw the listener/reader into their meaning?	Participant relationships and vicarious observer relationships	Perspective, focal planes of attachment or involvement	More or less negotiable spaces: e.g. parks versus prisons	Visible sentiment, relationships of persons	Listening, overhearing
	Commitment: What kind of commitment does the producer have to the message?	The kind of affinity meaning-makers have to the propositions they are making, and the degrees of certainty they express – 'modality'	Contextualisation, depth, abstraction	Emphatic (fences, barriers), or less insistent spatial designs	Gesture as order; gesture as incidental expression of personality	Beethoven versus easy listening

	Linguistic examples	Visual examples	Spatial examples	Gestural examples	Audio examples
Social continued	**Interactivity:** Who starts the inter-change, and who determines its direction?	Agenda-setting, turn-taking, topic control	Eye contact, response	Spatially determined interchanges: audiences by a theatre, students by a classroom	Patterns of gesture response and interaction	Orchestra compared to cassette in car (start, volume, balance etc.)
	Relations between participants and processes: How are the participants connected to each other and with the actions and states of being that are represented?	Agency, or transitivity, 'nominalisation'	Agency as represented through vectors, eyelines, perspective	Principles of layout	Agency: e.g. sulking compared to assault	Mood
Organisational: How do the meanings hang together?	**Mode of Communication:** What is distinctive about the form of communication, and what conventions and practices are associated with this form of communication?	Spoken or written language; a part of what is going on or representing what is going on; monologic or dialogic	Still or moving images, two- or three-dimensional representation, representational versus interactive	Architecture topography geography	Gesture, demeanour, fashion	Natural sounds, prosody in voice, music

	Linguistic examples	Visual examples	Spatial examples	Gestural examples	Audio examples
Organisational continued					
Medium: What is the communication medium and how does this define the shape and the form of the representation?	Physical medium, such as recorded or ephemeral speech	Different media, such as oil painting versus photography	Natural environment, building, website	Hand gesture, facial looks, clothing	Sound waves in the air; recorded or ephemeral
Delivery: How is the medium used?	Intonation, stress, rhythm, hand-writing, typing	Brushstrokes, photographic film	Construction	Expression	Intonation, stress, rhythm, pitch, loudness
Cohesion: How do the smaller information units hold together?	Information structure, reference, omission, conjunction, wording	Left/right, top/bottom, centre/margins, framing, salience/gravitational pull	Structural, aesthetic	Rhythm, opening and closing gestures	Notes, bars and scales; repetition, parallelism, elaborations, contrasts
Composition: What are the overall organisational properties of the meaning-making event?	Genre, such as romance novel or doctor-patient conversation	Genre, such as landscape photography compared to photojournalism	Building or environment types	Demeanour, style	Genre, such as jazz or reggae
Contextual: How do the meanings fit into the larger world of meaning?					
Reference: How do meanings point to contexts and contexts point to meanings?	Frame of reference, pointers, metaphor	Frame of reference, foregrounding/backgrounding, resemblance/metaphor	Location, prominence, metaphor	Setting	Where the sounds are heard; resemblance and analogy

	Linguistic examples	Visual examples	Spatial examples	Gestural examples	Audio examples
Contextual continued					
Cross-reference: How do meanings refer to other meanings?	Intertextuality, hybridity	Pastiche, collage, icon	Motifs	Expressive traditions	Motifs, riffs
Discourse: How does the whole of what I communicate say something about who I am in a particular context?	Primary and secondary discourses, dialects, register, orders of discourse	Imagery	Topography, architectonics	Persona	Repertoire
Ideological: Whose interests are the meanings skewed to serve?					
Indication of interests: How does the meaning-maker declare their interests?	Authorship, context and purpose of meaning	Naturalistic or stylised images	Façades, signs	Demeanour and clothing pointing to role	Where and why the sounds are produced
Attributions of truth value and affinity: What status does the meaning-maker attribute to their message?	Assertions as to the extent of the truth of a message, declaring one's own interest, representing agency	Realistic (e.g. scientific diagrams), versus heavily authored (e.g. artistic) images	Spatial arrangements, such as of a courtroom compared to a park	Acting/mimicry compared to expressions of authenticity, inner feelings	Intensity
Space for readership: What is the role of the reader?	Open and closed or directive texts, anticipated and unanticipated readings	Highly detailed panoramas versus propaganda	Alternative ways of using a space, directive or allowing alternatives	Directness versus ambiguity of expression	Capacity to turn sound on/off, volume, balance, sampling

		Linguistic examples	*Visual examples*	*Spatial examples*	*Gestural examples*	*Audio examples*
Ideological continued	**Deception by omission if not commission**: What's not said and what's actively one-sided or deceptive – deliberately or unconsciously?	Selectiveness in foregrounding and backgrounding, non-declaration or obscuring of interests	Foregrounding and backgrounding, distortion, perspective	'Front' and 'back' spaces, public and private	Using the covering of larger motions to blur small motions; social front, decorum	Aura, such as mood music when a plane is taking off
	Types of transformation: How is a new design of meaning created out of available designs of meaning?	Extent of creativity, degree of self-consciousness of representational resources and their sources	Extent of creativity, degree of self-consciousness of representational resources and their sources	New or hybrid forms of spatiality: e.g. websites, food courts	Conscious versus unconscious behaviours	New and hybrid forms of music, or faithfulness to received traditions of the repertoire

through the gesture language of signing what might otherwise have been said in spoken words. We visualise a thought before the words come. Or we hear a word and a whole lot of visual and audio senses seem to fill our minds. It is revealing how naturally metaphors from one mode of meaning slip over to describe meaning processes in another: 'imagery' in written text, or 'perspective' in oral argument, or 'visualisation' of alternative word-centred 'points of view'.

Synaesthesia and transduction are the stuff of our human nature. However, as Kress argues, in our recent modernity we have privileged linguistic meanings, and particularly written or literate linguistic meanings, over other modes of meaning (see Kress, Chapter 7 above). Not only does this represent a reduction expressive possibility. It is also increasingly anachronistic given recent social as well as technological trends in our communications environment which extend the range and technical integration of multimodal communication – from the highly designed audio-linguistics of radio, for instance, through to the digitalisation of words and images which allows the unprecedented integration of visual and linguistic design. The culture of literacy, the future of our communications environment, and the changing role of education are the subjects of the remainder of this chapter.

Designs for social futures: the case of literacy

Literacy is just one aspect of linguistic meaning. Yet it has been highly privileged in modern education at the expense of other modes of meaning and even orality as another aspect of linguistic meaning. This privileging of literacy is accompanied by all sorts of claims about what literacy does for people and their futures; claims that it is inherently superior as a represen-tational tool to oral language and visual or gestural meanings; that it will bring about progress in the sense of an improvement in material well-being; that it is an instrument of cultural and scientific progress; or that it enhances cognitive development. Such claims range from the exaggerated to the just plain false (Olsen 1994, pp. 3–19). They are, nevertheless, claims about written language which promise personal and cultural transformation.

And, indeed, the historical transformation that has accompanied the spread of literacy in the modern world has been enormous. Phillipson documents the process of linguistic imperialism in which the teaching of literate forms of imperial and national languages does enormous damage to most of the ancestral and primarily oral languages of the world, as well as their cultures (Phillipson 1992). Mühlhäusler traces the destruction of language ecologies – not just languages but the conditions that make these languages viable – by what he calls 'killer languages' (Mühlhäusler 1996). The result is that, of the estimated two hundred and fifty languages existing in Australia in the late eighteenth century, two centuries later there are only seventy left possessing more than fifty speakers; perhaps only a dozen languages will survive another generation; and even those that survive will become more and more influenced by English and interconnected with Creole (Dixon 1980).

Language change of this order is what the pundits of English literacy education and national development might have predicted and even recommended. But it's more than languages that have changed; more than the ostensibly arbitrary relationships of signs to signifiers. Whole ways of being have been transformed as well. The transition from oral to literate culture, Ong says, transforms our very ways of relating to the world. Oral as compared to literate cultures, he claims, are additive, rather than subordinative; aggregative, rather than analytic. They are redundant and copious in contrast to linear, in which each thing needs to be uttered only once. They are conservative in the sense of relying on repetition to ensure that people remember what has been learnt over generations, rather than intellectually experimentative because things forgotten can be retrieved from written text. They are situational, rather than abstract; empathetic and participatory, rather than objectively distanced. Moreover, they are close to human lifeworld rather than operating through a distancing and denaturalising neutrality in the fashion of science (Ong 1982, pp. 37–49). Olsen says that writing performs a new epistemological function; it is the basis of an understanding of the conditions of knowledge, theoretical thinking and critical and reflexive consciousness (Olsen 1994, pp. xv, 21, 258–82). Vygotsky says that writing is 'more abstract, more intellectualised, further removed from immediate needs' than oral language and requires a 'deliberate semantics', explicit about context and self-conscious of the conditions of its creation as meaning (Vygotsky 1962, pp. 98–101). Luria contrasts the situational, analogical thinking of adults who had grown up speaking only the oral languages of Soviet Central Asia with the abstract and conceptual language of literate adults (Luria 1976).

Whatever the truth of each of the particulars of these claims, literacy and its modern accoutrements affect the depths of people's being: how we think, how we see the world, what we do in the world. The transformative project that is literacy teaching is always chancing upon differences, and handles these differences in several ways: through exclusion ('literacy measures you as an irretrievable loss to civilisation, certainly in its higher forms'); through assimilation ('we can teach you to be literate, and you will pick up at least some of the benefits of becoming like us'); or through the marginalisation inherent in a simplistic version of multiculturalism ('we will recognise your differences as interesting and colourful extras in the human museum of folk life, but that recognition will not extend so far as to shift the fundamental course of literate culture or our developmental designs on your life').

The shapes of the first two of these approaches to differences are clear cut. 'We leave you off the literacy agenda', or 'we teach you the standard, written form of national languages'. The third approach is more subtle as it appears to be sensitive to difference, but is not really about difference at all.

An Anglican mission was established at Angurugu on Groote Eylandt in Australia's Gulf of Carpentaria in 1921. This was the first sustained contact with Europeans for the several thousand speakers of the various dialects of Anindilyakwa, then living across the several thousand square kilometres of the island. For decades, the relentless project of the mission was assimilation: the word of God in English and the words of English taught in the mission school. Now, the missionary tells us in a literacy research project that took us to Groote in the mid-1990s, people want to keep their culture strong, and this is why she is translating the Bible into Anindilyakwa. Meanwhile in the schools, which are now run by the Northern Territory government, there has been an uneven attempt to introduce what is variously called 'two-way' or 'both ways' education and bilingual education, which are, needless to say, culturally sensitive education initiatives (Cope 1998).

One of the missionary's linguist offsiders tells us that Anindilyakwa is the world's hardest language – the number of pronouns, the number of cases, the number of tenses, the amount of inflection which makes translating the Bible difficult. 'Aboriginal languages break things down into their component parts', the offsider tells us. 'There is lots of redundancy. For example, both pronouns and verbs indicate person. In writing the Bible down, a lot of the redundancy is removed, edited out.' This is the business of completely transforming Anindilyakwa by writing it down, of making it simple after the style of the culture of writing.

In school, the old Dick and Jane readers have been thrown away, and now it's apparently empowering and relevant reading and writing which have taken their place. The Aboriginal Schools Curriculum Materials Project starts with students' own cultural experience and then applies a particular notion of genre: as 'staged, goal oriented social process'. In the box is an ostensibly relevant example of narrative genre in the materials from another part of northern Australia.

'Narrative genre is goal-oriented because it has a purpose', the materials tell us. And 'the purpose is: to entertain [and] to help people think about the meaning of life and experiences in life. Narratives open the door to the world of literature.' Little Red Riding Hood, the materials explain, works in the same way (Northern Territory Department of Education 1993).

Narrative in this form, however, is just as deeply a product of the cultural orientation of the English written word as the structures it replaces. Making the curriculum culturally relevant in these terms means reconstructing things Aboriginal as stories and myths – a variation on the epistemological

Orientation

Long, long ago, a giant serpent called Inganarr lived in Arnhem Land. He ate people wherever he went. He moved from west to east, eating people as he went.

Complication

Inganarr went to North Goulburn Island and ate all the people there. He returned to the mainland and rested. Two boys, out hunting, were surprised when their spears came back to them when they threw them in a certain direction.

Crisis

Inganarr slowly made his way to eastern Arnhem Land. He had eaten too many people. He felt sick. Suddenly, he opened his mouth and threw up.

Resolution

Out came all the people, still holding their hunting weapons. They settled down in eastern Arnhem Land and never returned to the west. And that is why, to this day, there are no people living on North Goulburn Island, and there are more people in eastern Arnhem Land than in the west.

theme of Little Red Riding Hood, from entertainment all the way through to the literary canon.

But it is when linguistic and educational relevance translates into literacy in indigenous languages that the full complexity of 'cultural sensitivity' comes into play. As the linguists and educators develop their word lists and dictionaries, they have to overcome the difficulties inherent in these languages of abstraction, of metaphor, of overlaid references so complex that their meaning required dedicated lifetimes. What becomes a word was once a person, a place, a god in a cosmological narrative, or an object in the natural world. It was, perhaps, once a clan, an iconically represented image in body painting and art, or a motif in sacred song and sacred dance. In fact, this overlay is not even metaphorical or abstract; it is like nothing previously existing in the culture of literacy. If anything it is more like a relationship of identity rather than metaphor. Here also the visual, the spatial, the gestural, the audio and the linguistic are located together in inseparably multimodal forms of representation.

Nor was this world of representation in any way fixed. As a person died, his or her name could no longer be mentioned. So the whole world had to be renamed, and all the layers of reference in their name. As a person progressed through life, the world was represented in progressively more complex and arcane oral, visual and danced languages of age. Women represented their world in ways different from men. Clans represented their lands and other people's lands in dialects of affected differentiation. Your relationship with everything was evident in how you named it differently, pictured it differently or danced it differently, by tribe, moiety, age, or gender. And everything was always up for renegotiation, for reappropriation through renaming, for singing again, for telling again, for redrawing, for creating the world anew by remembering and refashioning its manifold meanings. The songs, dances and images of ceremony and law were sung and resung, danced and danced again, drawn and redrawn, but never twice the same way. Ceremonies were points of negotiation; of living with constant change by constantly taking control of the change; of always throwing sovereignty into question by reopening the discussion about words and people and places and history. This was a society of continual re-creation; of people actively negotiating their identities and remaking their history all the time. And the fundamental cultural logic was one of differentiation, of meaning-in-divergence, making it clear who you peculiarly were in the cosmos by the way you named and drew and danced that cosmos (Christie 1993; Cope 1998; Dixon 1980).

In contrast, the words of English, the language of the world of supposed progress and even 'future shock', are fixed in dictionaries, signifier representing signified in a seemingly static and nearly non-negotiable relationship. We might like to claim as a virtue that English has 150,000 words – more than any other language – even though most of them are practically useless to almost all of us almost all the time. The evidence is that the reading vocabulary of an average literate adult is about the same as the vocabulary of most Australian languages (Dixon 1980). But the grammar, the pronouns, the relating of ourselves in the world are far simpler. You can count English pronouns on a little more than one hand versus the hundreds of pronouns in Anindilyakwa; and there are just a few English tenses compared to the manifold complexity of Anindilyakwa pasts in relation to presents in relation to futures. Fundamentally this means that today's culture of English literacy, which has designed us and with which we design our futures, is very much reduced to the world of the concrete, the predictable and the repetitive; units forced by the process of abstraction to be sufficiently identical that they can be counted, which is quite obviously a peculiarly mechanical and repetitive version of abstraction. There is very little scope here to renegotiate meanings and very little scope for change, let alone scope for participating in change.

The reductions and simplifications of the culture of literacy continue to the level of genre, with the reports that remove voice ('always use the third person'), and which exude authority by pretending naturalistic truth, as if the natural or social world were speaking for itself – and the narratives which play the game of fiction, as if entertainment were innocent fun and the message in the medium the product of the author's own creative whimsy rather than the communal voice of culture and politics.

There are two issues here. One is the nature of the cultural sensitivity of a naive multiculturalism. When languages like Anindilyakwa are put into the straight lines of lists in a dictionary, meaning and reference are frozen in the same way that written English is based on frozen meaning; on frozen referents. Only then, however, can they be taught in schools. Only then can they be read in bibles. Only after the epistemological scaffolds have been set in place, with Anindilyakwa reconstructed as a written language which forces these texts from another lifeworld into the genre of myth-narrative with its invisible cultural frame internalised, can the scaffolds be allowed to fall away. Then, it would appear, language and culture have been preserved.

At this point, of course, liberal sensitivity to difference has become a white lie. The linguists and educators have really listened to the language of difference only so they can write it down and then teach it on their own terms. Such sensitivities to difference are the niceties of a kinder, gentler racism but they are racism nevertheless.

The second issue concerns our contemporary crisis of meaning and futures. Clearly, we in the modern world do not have the conceptual and cultural resources to be able to face the future in such a way that we can be confident that there will even be a future. There is great relevance, then, in alternative ways in being human; in alternative designs of meaning and meanings for social futures. There is even relevance in knowing that such alternatives are possible. It's not that there are any immediate answers to the peculiar problems of modernity in these different attempts at being human, nor that there is any point in trying to preserve cultures in a kind of anthropological museum, nor that there is any possibility of nostalgic regret holding back change. Rather, it's a question of the possibilities inherent in hybrid experimentation and re-creation as we tackle the problems of culture, economy and environment which sometimes seem nearly intractable to us now. It is also a question of who's in control of the change in communities such as Groote Eylandt. Is it those with enduring roots outside of the modern world or the modernisers who have come from the outside, even if they perform the conceit of sensitivity to difference? For the results will invariably be very different from what is intended.

Our times are making unusually difficult demands upon us. What, for instance, might we be able to recover from the social logic and grammar of productive divergence inherent in indigenous languages? The paradox is that our conditions, such as globalisation and the nature of local diversity, are such that the conceptual tools of the era of national languages and standardised literacy are no longer serving us well. Instead an epistemology of productive divergence may be what we need, albeit of course a very different one from the epistemology inherent in indigenous languages. As we face a crisis of the environment, what might we be able to recover from the deeply personalised science inherent in indigenous languages and their epistemologies? As we face a multimedia revolution, what forms of cross-modal synaesthesia might we recover from worlds where words and landscapes and iconic religious visual imagery were overlaid in a way comparable to, but perhaps very different from, our own notions of metaphor, mimesis and abstraction? Just as the visual-symbol languages and gesture languages of indigenous cultures were *lingua francas* developed in the face of a close proximity to language diversity, so globalisation and local diversity force similar developments in media and multimedia. The paradox here is that the world of our recent modern past, dominated as it was by a word-centred rationality both straightforward and descriptive with stable signs fixed to stable signifiers, is fast disappearing. To address the fundamental problems of contemporary existence, we simply have to go looking for other ways of being human.

Thus we make the move from addressing the large questions of our futures and the measure of our human natures back to the more mundane stuff of literacy pedagogy. Let's consider a couple of examples in which a kind of contrastive linguistics and critical pedagogy might make us creatures of modernity truer to our natures as humans. Kress has argued that multimodality and synaesthesia are in our natures because our senses never operate independently of each other. Yet the culture of literacy suppresses our human potential by favouring one, restricted form of meaning-making, that is the written word (see Kress, Chapter 7 above). Investigating the subtleties of synaesthesia in oral cultures and exploring the multimodality of the new, globalised communications media can both be part of the process of recovering wasted human possibility. And, to take another example, it is simply knowing that other cultures have resources for scientific and personal meaning very different to the genres of report and narrative in their classical modern forms that allows us the possibility of a science that makes human interest and the sources of the self visible, and narratives that acknowledge their political interests more readily than 'entertainment' and the 'literary canon' can do (Christie 1990).

Designs for social futures: the case of multimedia

The newly emerging communications environment seems at first to involve a mere technological jump which primarily raises issues of medium and delivery. In fact, we will argue that the changing communications environment involves, more profoundly, a cultural jump; a jump in which the issue of cultural divergence is crucial. Possibly even, the jump will be as radical as was the contrast between the intrinsic cultural pluralism of 'first nation' Australia and the standardising, nationalistic and monocultural culture of literacy.

It is incontestable that computers and multimedia are changing the world we live in. But precisely what do we mean by 'multimedia'? This is, it becomes evident on analysis, a very slippery word which can in general usage possess four different meanings.

Definition 1: Multimedia is a technical thing, a description of the characteristics of the focal machines themselves. In this definition, multimedia is conceived in terms of the mechanics of the information medium.

Definition 2: Multimedia describes the way in which different forms of information are stored and managed, in which there is a convergence of media based on a common, digital medium of recording and representation. Convergence now means that the same machine – the multimedia computer – can do many things, from music and text to still and moving pictures. Convergence also means that even those machines still dedicated to one form of representation are developing increasingly computer-like qualities.

Definition 3: Multimedia is manifest primarily in multimodal representation; it is in this definition the form or content which defines it. In a practical sense, the development of multimedia has led to the conflation, or at least closer integration, of many formerly arcane and separate craft forms into one all-embracing multimedia.

Definition 4: Multimedia is to be defined in terms of its inner logic, its narrative structure, and the peculiar orientation of the viewer, reader, or user. In this definition, two characteristic features of multimedia are brought into the foreground: interactivity and the logic of hypertext.

Unfortunately, these four definitions of multimedia do not simply and comfortably overlay each other. Multimedia machinery (definition 1) and digital media (2) are not intrinsically interactive or hypertextual (4), even though that possibility is clearly immanent. As a consequence, the machines (1) and the digital medium (2) can be used for long-established forms of representation without impacting in any significant way on either form or content (3 and 4) – such as newspapers. The transition in these cases might simply be a matter of increasing productivity and reducing costs. Multimodal representation, moreover, (3) does not have to be entirely digital, or even digital at all. And the relationships of readers, viewers or audiences to representations of meaning can be transformed in ways analogous to multimedia (4) without any of the technology (1 and 2).

Nevertheless, computers are, undoubtedly, changing the world and multimedia represents the cutting edge of computer-based communication and information technology. This is what a whole raft of literature – old-fashioned academic and popular writing, as well as new types of writing published on the Internet – is telling us today. In one sense, this is a statement of the obvious. Yet the tone of much of this writing, wending its way through the well-trodden territories of science fiction triumphalism and apocalyptic techno-enthusiasm, gives us immediate cause to be sceptical.

The new information and communication technologies, we are told, portend the end of space as we know it. Once we lived in a civic world where you had to go to particular places to do particular things. The infobahn, by contrast is antispatial. It puts an end to geographical and institutional separations. And, with the demise of spatiality, so the social distinctions of space also wither away. Now, for instance, you can live and work anywhere and the distinction between home and work becomes blurred. This spells the end of social distinctions and 'civic legibility'. The bank's façade, the boss's suit and the fancy letterhead are all reduced to the level playing field of Web pages and e-mail messages, a kind of vernacular republic. The new information/communication environment is also asynchronous, unlike the necessary coincidences of time as well as space in the pre-information city. It is, moreover, a place of disembodiment; of messages detachable from bodies and times and places. Without the reference points of the pre-information world, this environment is also a place of easy concealment and multiple identities. Perhaps the cyborg is a key metaphor to capture the physiology of computer connectivity. Perhaps even, the mechanics of the virtual might mean the collapse of the self–other distinction. Or perhaps, the technological trend to miniaturisation that is at the heart of the computer revolution might eventually mean dematerialisation, and a focus on trade in cultural symbols rather than a trade in things. These are some of the current philosophical-technological speculations in the literature on computers, information systems and multimedia (Gilster 1997; Mitchell 1995).

As a consequence, it is argued, forms of representation are also transformed in the new multimedia environment. The form of the message is transformed by the nature of the medium; or perhaps the scope and technological possibilities of the medium create a space for the creation of new forms of message, new ways of seeing and speaking and thinking the world. Gilster refers to a new, digital literacy which, contrary to the sequential reading of the printed word, is non-linear and discontinuous. We become browsers instead of readers. Information is packaged into screen-size fragments, linked by the user's hypertextual choices. So whereas the stuff of book-length arguments and narratives demands sustained attention, hypertext is the stuff of reader-constructed pastiche. Gilster also speaks of new relationships of cultural creators and their audiences. Whereas television is exclusive, he says, the Internet is inclusive; whereas television broadcasts out, the Internet draws users in (Gilster 1997).

As a consequence, established forms of meaning-making, such as the work of literature, will be transformed. Take, for instance, the relationships between the work of art and its audience. According to Sal Humphries, we are now witnessing a transition from the 'simple branching structure of CD ROMs with a point and click interface' to 'an immersive 3D virtual environment where a user and other people and artificially intelligent

creatures co-author a narrative of undecided outcome'. The rise of
'interactive narrative' means a shift in the framework of literary production
and reception in which the 'audience moves from being actively engaged
on an interpretative level to actively intervening in the representation'.
This means a 'convergence of creator with the spectator' (Humphries
1997).

Andy Cameron foretells the end of the world as we know it, in which
narrative itself comes under challenge. History, politics, memories, and
even our subjectivity, our sense of identity, he says, are all representations
in narrative form – signifiers chained together in temporal, spatial and
causal sequence. But, in its very nature, the new regime of interactivity
is on a collision course with the old world of narrative. We are in the midst
of 'a general transformation from a culture of stories to a culture which
expresses its truths through an immersive, interactive medium'. He takes
the computer game 'Hellcats' to be paradigmatic. Narrative closure is not
inevitable, and has to be fought for; and whereas traditional narrative is
of the past, the simulator places the player firmly in the present; and the
player is just that – in a position more closely resembling an actor rather
than an audience, though without the script. 'Digital computers and digital
communications will provide a unified site for first world culture in the
near future', he concludes, somewhat enigmatically (Cameron n.d.).

For every multimedia utopia, however, there is a dystopian alternative.
For every techno-enthusiast, there is a technophobe, somebody who
expresses at least some reasonable cause for anxiety.

Some of the dystopian forewarning comes even from the enthusiasts,
recognising that access to the benefits of the new communications environment will invariably be uneven. Clearly the world of the information
superhighway will be more accessible to some than to others. Such is the
way of commerce, and capitalism. So Lash writes of the geography of 'wild
zones' that are 'communication-dead' – from urban ghettos to Third World
regions. The new information and communication technologies may well
be the basis of a new reflexivity – a central concept in Lash's sociopolitical
analysis of our late modernity (Lash 1994). But, in every moment during
which new relationships of civic communication and participation are
created, a new machinery of exclusion leaves out those who were previously
left out in other ways. This is not just a question of access to the Internet
for poor whites, or women at home, or immigrant minorities. It's also
a domestic question of who's holding the remote or the Sega controller. Or
who can afford only the copper-wire telephone connections to the 'world
wide wait', versus those who can afford the fast, fibre-optic connections.
Here, Mitchell speaks of a new 'bandwidth disadvantaged' (Mitchell 1995).

Paul Virilio provides a more systematically dystopian version of our
imminent multimedia communications future. The new technologies, in
his view, are forms of 'electronic dazzlement: optical, acoustic and tactile',

in which the able-bodied person is modelled on the disabled person. These technologies make us 'telepresent'; a state of being virtually anywhere and everywhere without ever having to leave. The person comes to be like a terminal, computer-like, 'sedentary man'. This leads to a phenomenon he calls dromospheric pollution, which comes from the Greek word *dromos*, meaning running or racing. Telepresence creates forms of contamination in which the space between the object and the subject (the trajective, or journeying) is abolished. It also leads to the creation of a 'civilisation of forgetting' epitomised in the paradoxical immediate memory in the all-powerful nature of the image, which actually spells the end of a traveller's tale and a loss of memory. This world of 'telepresence', or 'trans-appearance', or 'tele-existence', creates an environment in which we are deprived of both horizon and optical density; it is an environment lacking in depth of field. There is no longer a clear distinction between the here and the there, the inside and the outside, the virtual and the real. In the end, we will be living in a 'grey ecology' devoid of regional distinctions, where local cultures are collapsed into the cultural grey of the global dromosphere, and where the exotic has disappeared. As relationships of immediate proximity give way to remote relationships, we make strangers of those close to hand, and we come to experience a 'generalised insecurity of territorial hold' (Virilio 1997).

Virilio's is a relentlessly totalising technological dystopia. It is a dystopia not just where distance and difference are destroyed. It is also one capable of forms of centralisation of knowledge and power, coupled with systematic surveillance barely imaginable even in Orwell's *Nineteen Eighty-Four* dystopia.

There is also, however, a chaotic-fragmentary version of technology-induced dystopia. When every culture or language or subculture and dialect can have its global channel of communication – on cable television or on the Web – what common culture will we conceivably share, locally let alone nationally? Not to mention every subcultural group with every conceivable interest, and style, and sense of affiliation. Does the technology lead us into a kind of babel; a world of cultural fragmentation where we share less and less with those who are closest to us? Does not the technology promote a fragmenting cultural divergence, quite the opposite of Virilio's oppressive, 'greying', global convergence?

Add the utopias to the dystopias and they come out to something like zero. But zero is not the answer; things really are changing. The answer seems to be more like a paradox, and, as we will argue later, a paradox in which the logic of cultural pluralism is central.

Before addressing the nature of this change, there are important respects in which in the technological changes (multimedia definitions 1 and 2) need not make any great cultural or representational difference. In other words, there is no necessary flow-on from the technologies into the multi-modal, interactive and hypertextual aspects of multimedia highlighted in definitions 3 and 4, even though the technology seems to beg such applications. On the other hand, the cultural effects achieved in multimedia definitions 3 and 4 do not require multimedia technology. This means that there is nothing so very new about the representational forms of multimedia in its multimodal, intertextual and hypertextual aspects.

For a start, probably in the bulk of its uses, multimedia technology is simply a tool for increased productivity. There is less interactivity in computerised banking transactions than there is in relating to a teller; and multimodal representations are of the simplest iconic variety and there is nothing hypertextual of any note. And, after all, most of the zeros and ones zooming along the information superhighway add up to numbers so dreary as to justify automation. Multimedia does boring things in a way that adds nothing other than efficiency to older paperwork systems. Or it does inspiring or deliberately aesthetic things in ways directly analogous to other representational media. When Jukurrpa artists <http://www.ozemail. com.au/~jukurrpa> or Yothu Yindi <http://www.Yothu.Yindi.com> put themselves on the Web, they do nothing more than they would in a printed mail order catalogue. They might reach people in a different way, reach them more quickly, and possibly reach different people. But the Web has not affected the way they do art; they are not doing art on the medium and they are not adopting any of its multimodal, interactive, or hypertextual resources as a representational tool. At most, the Web is an advertising medium. The art and the representational innovation happen elsewhere. In other words, for much of their life, the new communications technologies do nothing new, or nothing new at least in terms of the revolutionary cultural potentials suggested by utopians and dystopians alike.

And when the new technologies are recruited to do things that are new – genuinely multimodal, or interactive, or hypertextual, for instance – one is always left with a nagging sense of *déjà vu*. The methodology of hypermedia, Hilf points out, evolved from the conventions of cinema, with stages directly analogous to cinema's processes of pre-production, storyboarding, script development, production, post-production or editing (Hilf 1996). The first of the Web browsers, Mosaic, was modelled on television; and the hypertext language Java makes the Internet even more television-like, argues Gilster (Gilster 1997). Certainly there are new things about multimedia, but they draw on existing traditions of production and have more than a ring of familiarity in their reception.

The argument about the novelty of interactivity in multimedia is also dubious. Communication is, in its very nature, interactive. This was precisely Umberto Eco's point about 'the role of the reader' (Eco 1981). Readers, after all, have never been mere receivers of texts for they choose what they read; they read as much of a text as interests them; and they read into texts what they will. The meaning in literature is as much in its reception as in its production. There is always interaction between the world of artists and the world of audiences, whether as applause, or ticket sales, or reviews. Indeed, interacting with audiences becomes a prime focus in most moments of art, from theatrical engagements which necessessarily incorporate audiences to the shock value of modern art. These are all interactive media.

Nor are the precise techniques of multimedia new. For example, the film by the Argentinians Fernando Solanas and Octavio Gettino, *La hora de los hornos* (*The Hour of the Furnaces*, 1976), was presented at the time as a 'film act', designed in such a way that the audience might interact with the controversial political and cultural issues it raised. The projectionist stopped running the film on cues which raised critical questions. The film was 'branched' to suit audience response, much in the fashion of interactive multimedia. The film was also left open-ended so the audience could construct its own narrative resolution (Hilf 1996). And, to give another example, in the late 1980s there developed a genre of adolescent novels that provides stories with multiple paths and multiple endings. The text was divided up into many small parts, with cross-links at the end of each part akin to those of hypertext – if you want the story to go such and such a way, turn to page *x*, or this other way, turn to page *y*. The whole book, therefore, is scrambled, in the sense that, apart from the introductory framing, text fragments are placed in arbitrary order. The path of the story, and its ending, are constructed by the interests and inclinations of the reader. The most interesting thing about these examples is that they are at best obtuse and obscure, or at worst junk. The key representational resources of multimedia interactivity have always been available, if rarely used.

There are, of course, domains of interactive multimedia in which the reader is made author in a way far more radical than the traditional artist–audience relationship. These, however, are rarely considered to be art. Arcade, television and computer games are perhaps the best examples of cutting-edge multimedia interactivity to date. But their lineage is not from the world of art; it derives from the world of board games and sport. Here the player becomes like an actor in a narrative that is partly open (choices in the range of possible moves) and partly constrained (the rules and the aim of the game). The closure of the narrative is the triumph or failure of the will or skill of the player. And much of the fun of the engagement is the framework of restraint, the restrictions on the scope of player interactivity, and the pitting of will against closures which relentlessly restrict that will. In one sense, however, this is only an extension of the anxieties, and hopes and expectations of the interested 'reader' as they relate to the restraint on their will that is traditional, authored narrative.

Similar generalisations might be made about hypertext. Not only have conventional texts always had their own hypertextual devices, such as contents pages, indexes, footnotes and explicit cross-references, to facilitate non-linear readings. Hypermedia technology, in fact, uses terms such as such as 'browsing', 'bookmarking', 'home pages' and 'searching', taken directly from the world of the printed text to describe the reading process. More broadly, however, art is in its nature hypertextual, the stuff of cross-references in the form of allusions, iconic representations and metaphor, for instance. And the fragmentary, non-linear, anti-narrative feel of hypertextual readings is very much like the effect deliberately created by modernism, by Joyce or Kafka in literature for instance.

Then there is the phenomenon of 'the virtual', the ostensible verisimilitude created by multimodal representation. And, once more, there is a remarkable ring of familiarity to this discussion. It feels like something we have been talking about for a long time, even though we are supposed to think that 'virtual reality' is something special or new. In their time, the photograph, the telegraph, the newspaper, the book-novel, the telephone, the radio, the television were all credited for their remarkable virtualness – remarkable for the 'real' being so far away, yet here so easily, so fast, and so seemingly true to life. In their time, each of these new virtual presences became a new kind of reality; a new 'telepresence' in our lives. We virtually lived through wars, through the medium of newspapers; and we virtually made ourself party to the lives of other people in other places in other times through the medium of the novel. Multimedia is just another small step in the huge journey that is the cultural logic of modernity. For art, multimedia simply reopens the fundamental questions of aura, authenticity and location raised by Walter Benjamin in the 1930s in his discussion of 'the work of art in the age of mechanical reproduction' (Benjamin 1970).

Furthermore, there's an even bigger question here, as representation is, to a greater or lesser degree, an exercise in virtualness, bringing the distant, the other, into close proximity with the reader or the audience. Yet there are defined limits, and this is the point of the medium. The great thing about novels and paintings is that you can be there to the extent that you want to, without the burden of actually being there. The implied objective of virtual reality is verisimilitude. But the allure of most communication media is systematic lack of verisimilitude – why, for instance, a telephone call is a better and not just a quicker way to communicate than going there, or why 'chat rooms' on the Internet work precisely because they are in some important respects quite unlike chatting in rooms, so identities can be constructed around particular forms of unreality. So it is with art. The art is in the less-than-virtualness, the nature of the representation in the context of the constraints of the medium – a meaning expressed in two dimensions and paint on canvas, the evocation of physical location in words alone.

We might weave our way between enthusiastic utopias and bleak dystopias, yet still be left with the sense that nothing is really changing, and this despite the aura of cultural transformation that surrounds multimedia technologies. Yet there is a one important thing that is without a doubt happening, and this is centred on the paradox that is cultural pluralism.

The factual socioeconomic-technological variant of the pluralism paradox is that the more the world becomes interconnected by the global cultural web of communication and information technologies and integrated into a single accessible market, the more significant these differences become. For every moment of the global convergence of cultures and peoples, there is another moment of divergence. And here is the in-principle political and cultural variant of the paradox of pluralism. In the face of the inexorable reality of difference, the most powerfully integrating political and cultural forces are those most comfortably able to negotiate differences, and those that are able to operate pragmatically on the basis of the devolutionary principles of subsidiarity and federalism (see Kalantzis and Cope, Chapter 6 above).

Let's spell out the socioeconomic-technological facts, first, and illustrate the argument by way of the example of the news media. Information and communication technologies of our recent past operated in a fashion that came to be characterised as 'mass media'. The three or four major newspapers, and later the half a dozen or so radio stations and four or five television channels, together created the 'we' of the modern nation-state. This was the basis for the illusion of common experience upon which the nation state imagined its citizenry into existence. The presumption was cultural and linguistic homogeneity; the process of negotiating difference was cultural assimilation to the imagined community of nation through the creation of a 'mass culture'.

Recent developments in information and communication technologies might soon provide us with hundreds of television channels. They already provide us with millions of websites. In a way, this makes us even more strongly interconnected, and seems to put our lives on progressively more convergent cultural paths. However, while all this is true, it is also quite untrue. As soon as there are dedicated Croatian, or gay, or biker television channels and websites, we are moving away from a media regime that forces us in the direction of common cultural experience. Our interest and aspirations at once become more expansive than the nation-state, and more narrowly refined. By way of direct counterpoint to the era of 'broadcasting' and the mass media, the new media regime is often called 'narrowcasting'. These developments are not just the result of technical possibility, even though the main lesson of consumerism must be that supply is the parent of demand. The same is happening in areas where there have been no significant technological developments in the com-munication medium, such as in the proliferation of subculturally defined specialist magazines, each with their own progressively more divergent and arcane discourses and imagery.

Overlaying this is the next aspect of the socioeconomic-technological paradox of pluralism. For all the domination of the new media by the likes of Murdoch and Gates, and for all its domination by the language of an ethnic group who just a few centuries ago lived only around London, the new media are more open than ever to forms of expression other than these domineering voices. Digital media are cheaper than their analogue equivalents, and less demanding of technical-craft skills. And on the Web, distance costs nothing. Short-run production costs no more than long-run, and the marginal cost of reproduction is zero. The Web's general accessibility can be accounted for in part in terms of its origins in environments quarantined from commercial imperatives – the US military and higher education – and it has proved notoriously hard to turn into marketable product. The consequence is that more powerfully interconnected global diasporas have become possible and affordable, and there are no economies of cultural scale. Every culture, every subculture and every subtle variation on every subculture can have its say. And whereas non-alphabetic scripts produced enormously expensive difficulties for analogue text reproduction, digitisation is the great leveller.

Even the character of English is changing. Ken Wark talks of 'netlish', a strange *lingua franca* or interlanguage in which an increasing proportion of the communicators are not speakers of English and the conventions of 'standard English' don't seem to matter (Wark n.d.). On the other hand, divergence is a phenomenon already existing within English itself, in part a result of its peculiar character as a world language, a *lingua mundi*. English has different national forms different dialects from Creole to 'wog English', and an increasingly mutually unintelligible number of register variations from professional to hobbyist. The name of the communicative game is not so much learning an international standard as negotiating language differences within English on a global scale.

The possibility also arises for machine translation, now available in as yet fairly crude forms, and no doubt destined always to be limited. This is further evidence that the new communication technologies might not be an homogenising force. In fact, they could be quite the reverse as they could conceivably obviate the practical need to be proficient in the standardised form of the language of global power.

The paradoxes of pluralism extend still further than this. The forces of globalisation engender, as their obverse assertions of difference, a kind of resistance to the possibility of cultural homogenisation. Indeed, it is doubtful whether there is even any longer much cultural sense in homogenisation. The differences are the reasons why the newfound proximity is of interest. There is no point in having the exotic closer to home if the process of bringing it closer makes it more like home. Such is the case with tourism, and film, and, for that matter, websites. You take each of these journeys only because they take you somewhere else. This means that people visit only for that 'somewhere-elseness', more or less preserved, or celebrated, or exaggerated in order to encourage the visiting. The paradox here is that the technologies of connection and communication, technologies that glory in global reach and local exoticism, intensify the significance and poignancy of differences.

Then there's the increasingly important role of the reader and of more active audiences – of 'churn rates', 'site visits', and the interactive relationships of multimedia. Once again, the broader the audience that is drawn into the communication-information system, and the more scope it allows for their subjectivities, the more important differences become in the making of cultural meaning. In the era of mass media and supposed mass culture, culture makers could almost afford to be blasé about differences, with more than a little moral backing from public ideologies such as assimilation and the melting pot. Now the key ideas are 'customising your information feed' on the Net and, more generally, niche marketing of culture and information.

These are the socioeconomic-technological paradoxes of pluralism. They fit within a larger frame of reference in which multiculturalism and pluralism become central factors within a new kind of social contract. Charles Taylor points out that the modern nation-state and liberal-democratic political philosophy were founded on the universal individual, with the interests and needs of all citizens conceived of as identical (Taylor 1994). This vision of the state has reached a crisis point, particularly since the end of the Cold War. This crisis is most clearly manifest in the politics of difference, from the crazy ethno-nationalisms that have replaced Cold War frontiers as the primary reason for wars to the rise of forms of identity politics that do not fit comfortably on to the old left–right political spectrum (Kalantzis 1997).

The solution can be only in new forms of overlapping sovereignty, cultural as well as political, where it is possible to live and work across self-governing communities, shunting backwards and forwards between them. Being, for example, a member of an Aboriginal people, to being part of the self-governing Aboriginal and Torres Strait Islander Commission, to being Australian, and gay, and part of the global movement of indigenous peoples. The stronger states of the post-Cold-War world will be strong only because they are federal as a matter of cultural principle, taking strength from their ability to delegate cultural control, to negotiate differences, and to take their cue as subsidiary groups delegate cultural responsibilities to groups whose responsibility is more broader and integratory.

Differences are an inexorable cultural reality. They are more critical than ever, and the new communications and information environment is just one of the things that makes them more critical. Cultural pluralism, paradoxically, makes for stronger integration than forced homogeneity.

Literacy education as a design for social futures

Literacy is perhaps the pivotal element in the project of modern education. In this chapter we have mounted three major arguments about how we as educators might change the 'what' of literacy pedagogy. Through these arguments, we have attempted to challenge the place accorded to literacy understood narrowly as reading and writing the standard form of a national language. And so we have argued for a redefinition of the project of literacy education in which literacy might be understood more broadly – as 'Multiliteracies'.

First, literacy is a matter of design or transformation; drawing on available designs of meaning, to be sure, but always adding something of yourself and thus changing the world in your designing. Thus, we add agency, or the dynamics of designing, to earlier 'transmission' notions of literacy teaching. We also recognise diverse resources for meaning, as well as hybrid redesigned meanings.

Second, literacy is in its nature multimodal – a matter of visual as well as linguistic design. And multimodality itself is becoming more significant in today's communications environment where, from multimedia desktops to shopping malls, written text is represented in a dynamic relation to sound, visuals, spaces and gesture. Globalisation and local diversity also progressively transfer the balance of meaning away from language. As a consequence, literacy teaching and learning need to be an increasingly interdisciplinary endeavour, in which the boundaries of literacy with art, drama and music are no longer so clearly defined.

Third, there are no rules of correct usage. The metalanguage of design that we presented in this chapter is more in the nature of a series of critical questions with which to locate variations in meaning-form in relation to variations in meaning-function. This is not the kind of 'grammar' that you can get right and wrong. Rather, it is a grammar that contrasts and accounts for different usages, not only between languages but within what might otherwise be regarded as the one language – differences in meaning-making according to age, or gender, or regional origins, or ethnic background, or social class, or occupation, or fashion, or fetish . . . or whatever.

These three changes of emphasis, we have been arguing, will lead us in the direction of a pedagogy of Multiliteracies. Certainly such a pedagogy represents a more relevant and useful educational design for the social futures of our students.

Part IV

PEDAGOGY
The 'how' of Multiliteracies

INTRODUCTION

If the 'what' of literacy teaching and learning needs to be extended in the ways outlined in Part III, then the 'how' will invariably need to be extended as well. Part IV examines the 'how', or the pedagogy, of Multiliteracies. Mary Kalantzis and Bill Cope introduce the section in Chapter 11 with a brief overview of the four aspects of pedagogy suggested in the Multiliteracies framework. Each of these aspects builds on the different kinds of teaching tradition or approach. Situated Practice builds on pedagogies of process, immersion and experiential learning; Overt Instruction builds on pedagogies which explicitly teach rules and conventions; Critical Framing builds on pedagogies of critique and contextualisation; and Transformed Practice builds on pedagogies which relate theory to practice and focus on the transfer of understandings from one context to another. The Multiliteracies argument is that each of these teaching traditions is valid and useful, but limited if used entirely by itself. Relating the four more closely adds considerable depth to each tradition. This chapter shows how this might happen, and illustrates the argument with some classroom examples.

In Chapter 12, Courtney Cazden addresses the challenge of taking cultural differences into account. She discusses a programme for Mexican-American students in California, the 'Puente' or 'bridging' English Course, and New Zealand's Reading Recovery programme. She explains the process of Situated Practice, in which the teacher needs to be like an ethnographer, finding out what students know as a starting point, as well as embedding Overt Instruction, or scaffolded assistance, into the teaching and learning process. This takes teaching and learning beyond the limitations of 'process' or 'immersion' models. She also discusses the ways in which Critical Framing links closely with Transformed Practice, so that the critical becomes more than critique – something which, alone, can produce cynicism and further alienation. Transformed Practice engages students in the real world, the world of social action in which they live and have to communicate in the contact zone of cultural differences.

Sarah Michaels and Richard Sohmer provide, in Chapter 13, a detailed classroom illustration of the language demands of school learning. They trace the dynamics of a classroom discussion in which a group of nine-year-olds are reasoning about seasonal change and its causes. Here they illustrate how one student sounds like they are doing science, and another sounds like they are speaking in everyday terms. The one student's scientific-sounding language is further from the mark, however, than the other students' non-scientific explanations that use narrative and personal experience. This detailed analysis highlights one of the fundamental challenges for Multiliteracies pedagogy – to recognise the truth of students' understandings in Situated Practice, and the processes by which some learners will find themselves either excluded or privileged.

11

A MULTILTERACIES PEDAGOGY

A pedagogical supplement

Mary Kalantzis and Bill Cope

Four elements are proposed in the 'pedagogy of Multiliteracies' schema: Situated Practice, Overt Instruction, Critical Framing and Transformed Practice. These are not intended to be a rigid learning sequence. Nor are they intended to displace existing practices of literacy teaching, or to imply that what teachers have already been doing is somehow wrong or ill-conceived. Rather, they aim to provide ideas and angles with which to supplement what teachers do.

Parts I and II of this book discussed the multimodal and multicultural or multilingual aspects of our changing communications environment, and suggested ways in which teaching based on the written word of national languages might be supplemented – extended rather than replaced. In this chapter, we will take a number of angles on the Multiliteracies pedagogy to show the ways in which it might supplement – as opposed to negate or supersede – current teaching practices. In the next section of the chapter we will give some examples of how this supplementing happens in classroom practice.

To take an historical and methodological perspective on the four aspects of the Multiliteracies pedagogy, it is important to stress that there is nothing radically new in any of these four aspects. Each, in fact, represents a tradition in pedagogy in general and literacy teaching in particular, some of which sit in direct opposition to each other and were developed to replace prevailing orthodoxies. So Situated Practice sits squarely in the tradition of many of the various educational 'progressivisms', from Dewey to whole-language and process writing (Cope and Kalantzis 1998). Overt Instruction, on the other hand, sits in the tradition of many teacher-centred transmission pedagogies, from traditional grammar to direct instruction (Kalantzis and Cope 1993a) and Critical Framing is a development of the more recent tradition of critical literacy (Luke 1992). Transformed Practice, however, is somewhat harder to place, but its antecedents can be seen in the various strategies for the transfer of learning from one context to another; turning theory into practice, and so on (Lohrey 1995).

Each of these orientations to learning has often been the subject of consistent criticism and it would be easy, in fact, to mount a substantial critique of each one here. However, our fundamental argument is that all four aspects are necessary to good teaching, albeit not in a rigid or sequential way. For when all four aspects are put together in various combinations each is, at least, softened and, at best, enhanced and transformed by the others. Situated Practice when linked to Overt Instruction is no longer simply situated, with all the limitations that come from being no more than that. Singlemindedly progressivist literacy teaching often suffers from its blindness to cultural context; its blindness about how some students seem to succeed in immersion environments because they just seem to know the hidden rules of the game as a kind of second nature, while 'outsiders' to the cultures of literacy and power do not. It's rather too simple to take the view that learning to read and write in school can somehow be like learning oral language at home and in communities (Kalantzis and Cope 1993a). However, when Situated Practice, which works from a base of students' own interests and lifeworld experience, is supplemented with Overt Instruction, which explicitly uncovers and contrasts the hidden rules of meaning in various cultural contexts, the Situated Practice itself becomes something broader, more analytical, and more reflective.

So it is with the other aspects of the pedagogy. Overt Instruction when linked to Situated Practice becomes more like teacher scaffolding than teacher-centred transmission pedagogy of rule-bound traditional grammar. Instead, Overt Instruction involves comparing and contrasting different patterns and conventions of meaning in different cultural contexts – the lifeworld of the local community, compared to the professional discourse of the doctor, for instance. And Critical Framing when linked to the others becomes more grounded in everyday human purposes, and less airy-ideological and impossible to achieve in practice. When closely linked to Transformed Practice, Critical Framing also gets over some of the inherent difficulties of critique isolated from practical action (see Kress, Chapter 7 above), which tends to foster cynicism and reinforce alienation.

In this way, the four aspects of the pedagogy do relate back directly to the main traditions in literacy teaching, problematic as each of these may be in their more doctrinaire and isolated forms. This is what we mean when we say that our aim is to supplement what teachers already do. One of our guiding principles in the Multiliteracies Project is to attempt to find ways to extend existing traditions and practices of literacy pedagogy, rather than to pretend to be introducing yet another grand new literacy schema as people so often have done in the past.

There is also an epistemological aspect to the four aspects of Multi-literacies pedagogy. In the worlds of public life, work and formal learning, knowledge is made through immersion in 'hands-on' experience (Situated Practice); coupled with explicit concepts and theories which explain underlying processes (Overt Instruction); through locating knowledge in its relevant context and reflection on its purposes (Critical Framing); and through transferring knowledge gained in one context to another context, which will be inevitably similar and different in certain respects (Transformed Practice). The four aspects of the pedagogy represent epistemological orientations, four ways of knowing, four 'takes' on the meaning of meanings that will provide students with multifaceted ways of reading the world.

We can also view the four aspects of the Multiliteracies pedagogy through a cultural perspective. All learning and knowing needs to be firmly grounded in everyday experience, be that the familiar experiences of students' lifeworlds or immersion in less familiar practical experiences which are nevertheless intelligible because they relate sufficiently to the student's everyday cultural experience or acquired knowledge. A certain kind of multicultural education, however, goes no further than this. Its aim, quite properly, is to honour students' cultures and experience. But that is all it does. Education, however, is a process of transformation (see Kalantzis and Cope, Chapter 6 above). Overt Instruction and Critical Framing represent two kinds of journey away from the experience of the lifeworld, a process of expanding one's cultural horizons. You may (or may not) come back to the lifeworld newly committed to its values. But you never come back the same person.

Overt Instruction examines underlying system and structure; how meaning is organised, how meaning works. It involves processes of concept formation, generalisation, and theory-making quite unlike the meaning-making processes of pragmatic, everyday life. As a consequence, you see everyday life in a new light. Its meanings have a new depth. Critical Framing interrogates contexts and purposes, adding breadth to one's perspective on the lifeworld. What cultural alternatives might there be in approaching this or that particular challenge in everyday experience? Which approach is taken in which context? Why? Whose purposes and interests does this approach best serve? Transformed Practice, finally, is the result of having taken the kinds of cultural journeys away from the lifeworld represented by Overt Instruction and Critical Framing. It is just as situated or grounded in real-life experience as Situated Practice, but represents one of two possible journeys: transfer of acquired knowledge and experience to an unfamiliar cultural context (the lifeworld of another local or ethnic community, or a new workplace or professional culture, for instance); or return to the lifeworld of one's original experience with fresh perspectives and newly relevant knowledge of underlying processes (the depth perspectives of Overt Instruction) or other worlds (the breadth perspectives of Critical Framing).

Once we are talking of journeys like this, the four aspects of the Multiliteracies schema seem to have become neatly linear, as if they are a kind of lock-step learning progression. However, these kinds of cultural journeys, or ways of seeing meaning, are never neatly linear. Often they happen simultaneously, or with one aspect in greater focus in the foreground but with the others still in the background. And the shift in focus can happen in all kinds of order, shifting focus frequently or slowly or irregularly from one aspect to another. So the challenge of Transformed Practice (doing something in an unfamiliar context) might lead one into the explicitness of Overt Instruction (what do the rules of the game seem to be?). Or Overt Instruction (this is how meanings work in this particular context) might lead into Critical Framing (why do they seem to work this way?) which relates comparatively back to the Situated Practice of students' lifeworld experiences (how do similar or different meanings work for you?).

From theory to practice

From these large and abstract generalisations, let's consider how a pedagogy of Multiliteracies could work in practice. To do this we will look at brief case studies from four school and curriculum experiences already undertaken in Australia. The first is at Bamaga near the tip of Australia's Cape York Peninsula. Bamaga High School is the northernmost high school on the Australian mainland. Some of its students come from local Aboriginal communities; some are Torres Strait Islanders who set up a new community on Cape York fifty years ago after fleeing an outbreak of malaria on the islands; some are Aboriginal people who had been moved many hundreds of kilometres from Mapoon when mining operations commenced there thirty years ago. Here we have been working on the Multiliteracies pedagogy with a teacher of art and English.

The second classroom and curriculum experience is at William Ross High School in Townsville, North Queensland. Here an English teacher is working on video clips with her Year 9 English class. The third school is also in Townsville, but this time crossing what you would expect to be an enormous disciplinary distance from the school subject 'English' to 'Science'. Here a science teacher is working on an electricity unit with her Year 9 Science Class at Ryan Catholic Community School. The fourth curriculum experience is with the Foundation Studies Division of the New South Wales Technical and Further Education Commission, in Sydney. Here we are working with Foundation Studies to produce a module entitled 'Finding Out About Business' as a part of an 'English for Business' course for adult migrants who do not speak English as a first language but who wish to move on to do the business courses offered by TAFE.

Situated Practice

The art and English teacher at Bamaga is working with the students on visual design, transforming natural form through successive stages of simplification and modification to create an abstract design. Situated Practice: the students examine traditional Torres Strait and New Guinean art which represents the natural world; they examine naturalists' scientific photographs of animals; they talk through the traditional stories that link the animals of the natural world to the cultural meanings represented in the traditional art.

The English teacher at William Ross High School in Townsville has got her students to bring in CDs of some of their favourite songs. They play some of their songs, relating the music to their own interests and life experience – rap, or heavy metal, or techno. The students also fill out a music survey: their personal top five songs, the style of each song, their favourite style of music and what is typical of the lyrics, the music and the video clips of that style. They also go out to find reviews of their latest favourite records in music magazines.

The students at Ryan Catholic Community School turn their classroom into a cyclone shelter – Townsville is in a tropical cyclone region. The classroom is darkened, and set up with a battery radio, candles and basic canned food supply. This leads on to the question, how are we going to survive when there is no electricity?

There are seven units in the 'Finding out about Business' module under-taken by the adult immigrants in their Foundation Studies English for Business course. Amongst the Situated Practice foci in this work, students are asked whether, when, and what they have found out about how business works in Australia or starting a business. To do this they have had to talk to people who already have businesses; or get government information booklets; or go to a business information seminar; or watch a business pro-gramme on television; or look up a business textbook; or search the World Wide Web; or look up advertisements and make telephone enquiries. What do they already know about business and how have they found it out?

Overt Instruction

The students at Bamaga discuss the process of stylisation. They compare the photographic representation of animals in a science textbook with the ways in which these animals are represented in New Guinean and Torres Strait Islander art. They examine the ways in which traditional art concentrates salient features of the world and the artistic processes of abstraction. Then they examine the links between traditional story (Linguistic Meaning) and the artistic images (Visual Meaning). As a result, they develop a metalanguage to describe meaning that meshes both of these with the core concepts of the art syllabus, as well as the concepts of narrative relevant to

243

Situated Practice

Immersion in experience and the utilisation of Available Designs of meaning.

Designs of meaning are drawn from the students' own lifeworlds and from simulations of 'real-world' relationships to be found in the existential world of Designs, such as workplaces and public spaces.

Immersion in Designs of meaning that make 'intuitive' sense, common sense, or at least something more than half-sense.

In a learning context this might include either or both:

- the Designs in the students' lives, the students' own lifeworld experiences
- throwing students in at the 'deep end' with Designs that are different in some respects as well as similar in other respects to those of their lifeworld experience. These Designs will make, perhaps, only half-sense at first, but with lots of contextual clues provided – for example, cultural scaffolds or bridges to other worlds of meaning.

Assessment: What works, for instance, a problem solved, albeit intuitively, with an expert's help, by looking up answers, with scaffolded assistance.

the English syllabus. They also develop the multidisciplinary, multimodal approach to meaning which is one of the key interests of the Multiliteracies Project.

At William Ross High School, the teacher presents the students with the written lyrics of a Toni Childs song. Her discussion with the class leads them to notice and identify the devices and conventions of poetry such as verses, rhetorical repetitions and alliteration, as well as the specific conventions of song lyrics such as the repeated chorus. These are more immediately visible on the printed page than they are in the listening. She asks them to predict the style of music.

Then she plays the song on CD. She asks what the music adds to the lyrics and how it does it, with the students examining beat, timbre of voice and its relation to the lyrics, changing volume, and genre or style. She asks the students to predict the kind of imagery that might be in the accompanying video clip. Then she plays the video clip. She asks how the imagery of the clip (predominant colours, pace of editing, imagery of setting, and so on) and the facial expressions and gestures of the singer add to the meaning of the song.

The students have now completed an analysis of the multimodal grammar of the song. When they come to examine the music reviews they have found in magazines regarding their favourite songs (and this at a different time for we are not presenting these classroom/curriculum experiences in the order of their teaching), she asks the students to work out how reviews are organised. This not only includes an analysis of the kinds of concepts the reviews use to describe how linguistic (lyrics), audio (musical) and visual, spatial and gestural meanings are made (the video clip) but also includes an analysis of the Linguistic and Visual Design of the review itself. Students talk about how reviews are laid out on the page of the magazine, including headings and accompanying illustrations, and how the various information elements are arranged, such as (in one example) the name of the band, the name of the album, comparison with previous work of the band, the reviewer's assessment of the overall quality of the band, a description of the sound, the reviewer's assessment of this particular record and individual tracks, and an overall star-score rating.

In the science class at Ryan College, the students examine the electricity chapter of their textbook. Here they find three main kinds of scientific meaning about electricity represented: naturalistic photographs of electricity in the real world (of a street lit up at night, and a photograph of wires linking a battery to a light globe and a switch in a laboratory context); a scientific explanation of electricity in words; and a circuit diagram. The students compare the purposes and layout of two of the photographs, the one designed to show lighting at work and the other showing how lighting works, and contrast the accompanying words. One presents an historical narrative on the discovery of electricity; the other presents a few paragraphs of scientific explanation with several technical terms highlighted in bold-face. The students discuss the relationships between the technical terms that have been highlighted. This they then compare with diagrams, including one of the structure of an atom drawn as if it could be seen; and circuit diagrams which use particular conventions for the abstract representation of wires, lights and switches.

In the Foundation Studies course, the students listen to a taped conversation in which one person asks another about how they started their business. They also read a local newspaper story centred on a personal profile of the proprietors of a small family business. They examine the kinds of questions needed to get information on the personal experience of starting a business, and how the newspaper story turns a personal story into lessons about business. They examine the format and information content of government information booklets, including signs such as logos that give the information an unbiased and official character; contents; headings and subheadings; dot-point lists; and boxed or shaded sections. They examine the way a video or television programme presents practical information about business. They then proceed to work out the steps involved in accessing business information services on the World Wide Web.

Overt Instruction

Systematic, analytic, and conscious understanding.

This requires the introduction of explicit metalanguages, which describe and interpret the Design elements of different modes of meaning. For example, this might involve giving greater depth to the meanings in a particular situation by asking the following kinds of questions (see Cope and Kalantzis, Chapter 10 above):

- Representational – What do the meanings refer to?
- Social – How do the meanings connect the persons they involve?
- Organisational – How do the meanings hang together? (Design as morphology)

It may also involve developing a language to describe the processes of how we make meaning, such as:

- the patterns in Available Designs of meaning, that is, the resources we can find and use to make meaning
- how we do Designing
- how meaning becomes Redesigned. How much does new text express personal voice, experience and so on (Design as agency).

Assessment: The student now has a way to describe the patterns in Available Designs of meaning and the processes of Designing meaning.

Critical Framing

At Bamaga, the students compare and contrast the different cultural contexts and purposes behind representations of the natural world in photographs of animals in the science textbook, in the stylised images of animals in the traditional art and in the stories of oral tradition. Different forms of meaning-making they then see can achieve different ends in different places in different ways.

At William Ross, the students bring in their favourite songs. Analysing the music survey, they work out which students like which styles – who likes rap, techno, house, reggae, grunge, heavy metal, 'easy listening', or whatever. What do their preferences say about who they are, about their identity? What are the main kinds of message in each style? They also compare different types of review in different kinds of magazine. For example, how is heavy metal reviewed in a middle-of-the-road rock magazine compared to a heavy metal magazine or a black music magazine? How does the Visual Design of the page, as well as the Linguistic Design of the text, vary between one kind of magazine and the next? What does this say about the kinds of people who read each kind of magazine?

At Ryan, the students consider the different social uses of different kinds of meanings about electricity: the kinds of domestic meanings appropriate to the cyclone shelter discussion; the written text of a scientific explanation of electricity; and the circuit diagrams that electricians use. Each way of making meaning has its own setting, its own 'feeling', its own culture, its own way of representing the world, its own purposes – everyday life as compared to science as compared to working as an electrician.

In the Foundation Studies course, students compare the perspectives and truth value of commercial promotional material, government information, and personal business stories as told in conversations or on television business programmes.

Critical Framing

Interpreting the social and cultural contexts of particular Designs of meaning.

This involves the students standing back from what they are studying and viewing it critically in relation to its context. For example, this might involve giving greater breadth of perspective to the meanings in a particular situation by asking the following kinds of questions (see Cope and Kalantzis, Chapter 10 above):

- contextual: how do the meanings fit into the larger world of meaning?
- ideological: whose interests are the meanings skewed to serve?

This may involve asking how Design fits in with local meanings and more global meanings.

- what is the immediate function of the Design? (what's it doing: to whom? for whom? by whom? why?)
- what's the structure and immediate context of the Design? (situation, connections, systems, relationships, effects)
- what's the larger social and cultural context of the Design? (culture, history, society, politics, values)

Assessment: The students show that they know what the Design is for; what it does, why it does it and whose interests it serves.

Transformed Practice

At Bamaga High School, the students plan their own designs. They write stories that give their designs meaning and depth; they make printed sarongs; and they create designs for sports shoes (an obsession with these adolescent students) which take their design ideas still one step further in the direction of stylisation and abstraction. Here we see two of the focal elements of Multiliteracies: the multimodal connections being made between Linguistic and Visual Design, and the cross-cultural aspects of meaning-making.

At William Ross High School, the students go on to write a song, perform it and make a video clip. They also write their own music reviews and mock them up into a class music magazine.

At Ryan College, the students create an electrical circuit for an alarm. They write an interpretation of this circuit in commonsense language, in order to explain to their parents what the alarm does, or to sell their product. They explain how the alarm works in scientific language and they draw a circuit diagram so that an electrician can install their design.

In the Foundation Studies English for Business course, the students interview a person who has successfully started a business and draw lessons from this; they decide on the area of business in which they are interested and access relevant government assistance services by phone and by reading government information; and they search the Web in the area of their interest.

Transformed Practice

Making transferred meanings and putting these to work in other contexts or cultural sites, for example applying the Design in a different context, or making a new Design.

- transfer: taking a meaning to another, real-world context and making it work
- voice: addressing one's own particular interests, adding something of myself/ourselves
- intertextuality and hybridity: making the connections, recognising influences and cross-references of history, culture and experience – including different degrees and types of transformation of meaning, from close reproduction to significantly creative change
- meaning-making: Designing that changes the designer. This means learning as transformation, with the student becoming a new person by being able to do new things.

Assessment: Good reproduction (if that's the game); or the extent and value of creativity in the transformation; aptness of the transformation or transfer to another context (does it work)?

12

TAKING CULTURAL
DIFFERENCES INTO ACCOUNT

Courtney B. Cazden

One issue raised as part of the initial discussion for the Muliliteracies Project involved how we can ensure that differences of culture are not barriers to educational success. More positively, we must ask ourselves how we can take cultural differences into account in designing programmes and pedagogies, or, in the terms of one of Bernstein's recommendations, 'weaken the relation between social class and educational achievement'. How should we 'weaken the framing regulating the flow of communication between the school classroom and the community(ies) the school draws upon' (Bernstein 1990a, p. 79)? In suggesting solutions to these issues, I will refer to observations from my research during the 1995–6 academic year as well as to published literature.

I worked as a participant observer in a California community college programme called Puente, Spanish for 'bridge', designed for Mexican-American students, who are part of what is now the fastest-growing and poorest ethnic group in the United States (Goldberg 1997), and who are significantly underrepresented in higher education, especially in California. Although transfer to four-year colleges and universities is one of the missions of two-year community colleges, the transfer rate for Mexican-Americans has been extremely low. Puente, now fifteen years old and in thirty-two colleges across California, has been dramatically successful in raising the transfer rate from 2 per cent to over 40 per cent. Griffith and Connor give a comprehensive vision of community colleges as 'democracy's open door' (Griffith and Connor 1994). Their mention of Puente's history (Griffith and Connor 1994, pp. 30–4, 63, 701) is one of the few published references to it. Thus I need to give some programme details here.

Puente is a two-semester English (not ESL) course co-taught by an English teacher of any ethnicity and a Mexican-American counsellor. In the English classes, the Puente teachers create a textual bridge through literature – fiction, poetry, essays – in the first semester, all by Mexican-American authors. The Puente counsellors create a human bridge through themselves: emphasising the importance of managing time for study, giving explicit guidance for how to use the college as a resource for learning and transfer; and often commenting on classroom topics from the experience they share with the students as fellow Mexican-Americans. They also build another human bridge by connecting each student with a community mentor of the same ethnicity and often related occupational interest, who is a college graduate and community leader.

While Puente has been designed specifically for Mexican-American students, the classes may be more mixed. Depending on the demography of each college community, there will be more 'Latino' students from other Latin American countries in some Puente classes than in others. Moreover, although the mission and course design focused on one ethnic group can be clearly stated, legally all classes must be open to all who wish to take them.

If it seems surprising to present a single-ethnicity programme in a discussion of Multiliteracies, remember that for any cohort of Puente students this homogeneity is only partial and temporary: two semesters of English out of a total programme. In the words of Mary Louise Pratt quoted at the end of this chapter, Puente is somewhat of a 'safe house' in which to gather strength – but also, in Puente's case, skills – for the more diverse world outside. Puente also exists in a smaller number of California high schools. Mehan *et al.* (Mehan *et al.* 1996) report their study of the AVID high school programme, also in California, which has many of the same purposes as Puente but with an ethnically heterogeneous group of students.

Academically, Puente's two semesters emphasise writing. In the first semester, students write about their own lives, the literature they read, and their first experience with their mentors. In the second semester, authors are drawn from other cultural groups, and writing assignments expand beyond narrative to the more analytical texts expected in college. A major aim of teacher, counsellor, and mentor alike is continuously validating the students' cultural identity; and both teachers and counsellors believe that the intensive writing programme is critical for developing not only skills but also a growing sense of personal power. I was a daily participant in the Puente class in two community colleges in different San Francisco Bay communities, and I will merge material from both here.

The discussion that follows separates three arguments for taking cultural differences into account: to adapt instruction more successfully to the needs of individual literacy learners, to recognise collective as well as individual identities, and to support in learners and future citizens positive intercultural attitudes and skills. The chapter ends with three issues in Multiliteracies pedagogy.

Individualising instruction

In the language of the Multiliteracies framework, in any literacy practice in the classroom there are potentially two sources of available Designs. One source is the repertoire of discourses and representational resources that are the learners' personal accumulation from previous Design experiences. The second source is made up of the discourses and representational resources now conventionalised in mainstream society that the teacher introduces into the Designing activity. It has become almost an instructional cliché that learning is enhanced if the learner makes some connection, finds some continuity, between the two, especially in literacy learning.

For twenty years I have argued that teachers need to learn about the cultural background of their students in order to build that continuity (for example, see Cazden, John and Hymes 1972; and some of the essays reprinted in Cazden 1983). Recently (Cazden and Mehan 1989) I have worried that such information, when transmitted in readings and lectures about 'others', may do more harm than good. With the best of intentions, we may reinforce, even create, stereotypes and lower expectations, and the information may make teachers less observant of their students rather than more.

Consider as an alternative what happens in the Reading Recovery programme, a short-term (approximately fifteen-week) daily individual tutoring programme for the lowest-achieving six-year-old children who have not caught on to reading and writing after one year in school. Originally designed and implemented in New Zealand, it has been imported into Australia, the United States, Canada and Britain, with careful evaluation studies (e.g. School Curriculum and Assessment Authority 1995) documenting its success with all but 2–3 per cent of the children. Like Puente, it is an accelerated programme in which students, with temporary help, are able to 'catch up' and then continue to learn at least at an average rate in regular programmes.

Because the lowest-achieving six-year-olds in each of these countries will include disproportionate numbers of children from non-dominant culture and language groups, one might expect that such differences among children would be discussed in the guidebook that is the basis of the intensive one-year teacher education course and periodic subsequent in-service workshops (Clay 1993). Surprisingly, that is not so. There is accommodation in two countries to language differences: Reading Recovery in Spanish in the United States and in Maori in New Zealand. But there is no mention of accommodating to cultural differences among English-speaking children.

Questions come to mind. Are such differences less important in the literacy education of younger children? Does the unusually high degree of individualisation in the sequence and pacing of instruction take into account whatever aspects of cultural background are relevant to beginning literacy? Are Reading Recovery teachers trained in ways that make unnecessary the provision of specific cultural information?

The first two weeks of Reading Recovery lessons with each child (ten daily half-hours) is called 'Roaming around the known'. During this time, the teacher's task is not to introduce any new teaching, but rather is to get to know as completely as possible the individual child's strengths – not weaknesses but strengths. Of special importance among these strengths, important in any literacy programme, is the child's oral language.

At least in the USA, special emphasis has been given in Reading Recovery teacher education to the importance of understanding each child's language as a resource for the literacy learning to come, no matter how 'non-standard' in vocabulary or syntax that language may seem to the teacher (Gay Su Pinnell, personal communication, October 1995). In the early weeks, a child's non-standard-language readings of standard-language texts are accepted. Then, as the child progresses, the teacher continues to appreciate the child's oral language while increasing the challenge: '"That would make sense, but look at this – " as she points to the text, asking the child to cross-check familiar oral language with the less familiar information system in the visual text on the page.'

The teacher is thus learning to be an ethnographer, so to speak, learning about what the child knows and can do through her own careful observations. And she is learning how to build on the child's knowledge and strategies as an indispensable beginning, whether or not that knowledge fits what would have been her own pre-professional conceptions about relevance. (Shaughnessy's now classic analysis (Shaughnessy 1977) of the writing of underprepared college students in the first years of open enrolment at the City College of New York has an analogous focus on understanding and building on student strengths.)

More informal ways of inventorying student knowledge can be devised. Herbert Kohl (Kohl 1973) took his first graders on neighbourhood walks, or invited them to contribute empty food cans and boxes for a play store, in part so that he could take stock of their knowledge of, and strategies for, reading environmental non-book print. Older students can themselves engage in a contrastive analysis of their indigenous knowledge – for example, Vygotsky's spontaneous concepts (Vygotsky 1962) and knowledge structures in the curriculum in Vygotsky's scientific concepts. Heath (Heath 1983) describes how fifth grade students investigated with their teacher the differences between the language of foods and farming in their communities and their school texts. As anthropologist Catherine Bateson sums up her experiences living and working in several countries, 'Participant observation is more than a research methodology. It is a way of being, especially suited to a world of change' (Bateson 1994, pp. 7–8).

I don't want to portray being a teacher ethnographer as a simple matter. Michaels and Sohmer (Chapter 13 below) show how hard it can be for even the best-intentioned questioner to ask in a way that will elicit what a student knows. And Carol Lee's (Lee 1993) analysis of how an African-American teacher helped her African-American students transfer their cultural knowledge of the oral language practice of 'signifying' to the understanding of figurative language in literature suggests that for teachers who are outsiders to students' culture it may not be obvious where to look for transferable design resources. But adopting the initial assumption that all students have such resources, and that it is part of teachers' responsibility to try to understand them, are indispensable first steps.

Recognising collective identities

Heath's curriculum suggestion and Lee's teaching strategy both go beyond the knowledge of individuals to the knowledge of groups: culturally shared ways of talking about foods and farming, and culturally shared conversational forms. By making such shared knowledge part of the official curriculum, the teacher simultaneously learns about her students and places public value on their culture(s).

In a recent book, *Multiculturalism: Examining the Politics of Recognition* (Gutman 1994), an international group of philosophers and political theorists explore controversies over multicultural principles and practices in public life. In her Introduction, editor Gutman distinguishes between two kinds of recognition:

> Full public recognition as equal citizens may require two forms of respect: respect for the unique identities of each individual regardless of gender, race, or ethnicity, and . . . respect for those activities, practices, and ways of viewing the world that are particularly valued by, or associated with, members of disadvantaged groups.
>
> (Gutman 1994, p. 8)

Although these authors focus on recognition of citizens, their discussions apply as well to recognition of learners. In the same volume, Canadian Charles Taylor addresses their needs:

> Enlarging and changing the curriculum is therefore essential not so much in the name of a broader culture for everyone [part of my third argument, below] as in order to give due recognition to the hitherto excluded. The background premise of these demands is that recognition forges identity, particularly in its [Frantz] Fanon application: dominant groups tend to entrench their hegemony by

inculcating an image of inferiority in the subjugated. The struggle for freedom and equality must therefore pass through a revision of these images. Multicultural curricula are meant to help in this process of revision.

(Taylor 1994, pp. 65–6)

Whereas thinking in terms of cultural differences may focus our attention only on 'activities, practices and ways of viewing the world' of students' home cultures in their more traditional forms, thinking instead in terms of collective identities helps to call our attention also to those characteristics, such as the internalised images of inferiority mentioned by Taylor, that are the result of contact with 'the activities, practices and ways of viewing the world' of the dominant group.

Ogbu and Matute-Bianchi (Ogbu and Matute-Bianchi 1986) discuss this same contrast as primary versus secondary cultural characteristics:

Primary cultural differences are those different cultural features that existed *before* two populations came in contact, such as those brought by immigrant minorities from their countries of origin to the United States. *Secondary cultural differences* are, on the other hand, those different cultural features that came into existence *after* two populations have come into contact, especially in contact involving the subordination of one group to another.

(Ogbu and Matute-Bianchi 1986, pp. 96, 97)

Ogbu and Matute-Bianchi analyse secondary cultural characteristics in 'caste-like minorities', such as Native Americans, Mexican-Americans and African-Americans in the USA and indigenous groups in other countries.

Recently a discussion developed among Reading Recovery teachers about whether it is sufficient to fine-tune instruction to the unique constellation of what each child, as an individual, knows and can probably learn next, effective as that practice has been. Specifically, what about the criteria for selecting books for the child to read: shouldn't aspects of the child's collective identity figure here?

In selecting a new book for each child to read each day, the Reading Recovery teacher's criterion has been the optimum degree of challenge at each point in the child's progress as a reader, an aspect of that child's unique, albeit constantly changing, identity. But, argues the Reading Recovery coordinator in St Paul, Minnesota, ethnicity of characters and setting should also be considered, in order to make sure that all children see themselves in their texts (Garrett 1994).

As students get older, this argument increases in importance, simply because teachers have to counteract more negative images that 'the hitherto excluded' will have internalised from their experiences in and out

254

of school. For many children, the first awareness of being members of a group with second-class status will come in school, hard as that may be for teachers to acknowledge. And, as Puente co-director and former English teacher Patricia McGrath points out, for students who grow up in another language culture, *English* classes can be perceived from past experience as a 'special invitation to failure' (Griffith and Connor 1994, p. 70).

The first essay read at the beginning of the school year in one Puente class was 'On being a Mexican-American', Joe Mendoza narrates his gradual awareness of 'who I was' growing up in a barrio neighbourhood in East Los Angeles:

> In the beginning I learned to be a Mexican from my relatives. We all ate the same food, and we all ate it the same way. As I grew, I shared other Mexican experiences with my friends, who, I might add, also looked like me. We dressed alike [and] we spoke the same language, a certain form of Spanish. But by junior high school, I suddenly awakened to the fact that Mexicans were considered different from and even inferior to others. For the first time, I experienced segregation.

One day a teacher found Mendoza on the wrong side of a line on the playground on his way to a rest room during a soccer game:

> Her parting remark was a stern admonition not to cross the line and to stay with all the other Mexicans. Then I looked at the building, which was divided in half, one wing for whites and the other for Mexicans. I was overwhelmed with emotions that I could not understand. I was hurt, disappointed, and frustrated. But more than anything else, I was profoundly angry.

It is because experiences more subtle than Mendoza's but carrying the same message are still common for non-dominant groups that collective identities have to be recognised in school.

A case study of an extended incident at the University of Alaska reminds us how easily that recognition can be withdrawn. Through analysis of public documents and student narratives, two white faculty and a Native Alaskan graduate student (Gilmore, Smith and Kairaiuak 1997) document the results of a remark by another faculty member reportedly questioning the academic credentials of Native Alaskan students. The remark and the ensuing controversy over it reverberated through the university and public press for months, deeply hurting all Native Alaskan students.

Recognition of students' collective identity is one reason for the design of the Puente programme. The purpose of reading and writing assignments about identity is not to reinforce victimisation. On the contrary, it is to validate whatever similar experiences the Puente students may have had; show them that other Mexican-Americans have gone beyond similar personal histories, like the author who is now a university graduate; and give the students skills, social support, and the growing confidence that they can do the same.

Because the Puente counsellor and student group share a Mexican-American background, that shared background can be validated without being objectified in explicit discussion. In another Puente class, the first reading of the year was 'My Name', an essay by Sandra Cisneros (Cisneros 1989), short enough to read aloud and discuss in a single class period. As they listened, students were asked to mark what Puente teachers have learned from their professional writing workshops to call 'strong lines', especially memorable phrases or sentences, and be prepared to read them aloud at the end.

The narrator of 'My Name' is a young girl growing up in a Chicano barrio whose name is Esperanza, 'hope', after her great-grandmother,

> a wild horse of a woman, so wild she wouldn't marry. Until my great-grandfather threw a sack over her head and carried her off. Just like that, as if she were a fancy chandelier. That's the way he did it. And the story goes she never forgave him. She looked out the window her whole life, the way so many women sit their sadness on their elbow. Esperanza. I have inherited her name, but I don't want to inherit her place by the window.
>
> (Cisneros 1989, p. 11)

As we went around the circle reading our chosen strong lines, the most repeated sentence, especially but not only by the women students, was 'I have inherited her name, but I don't want to inherit her place by the window'.

In working with individual women students, Puente counsellors support their efforts to explain to parents the importance of home study time, or later of leaving home to attend a university. But in that class, neither teacher nor counsellor used 'My name' for any generalised, objectified discussion of the place of women in Mexican or Mexican-American culture.

As with learning about individual strengths, I do not want to oversimplify the task of validating collective identities. The identities felt to be important by students will be of many kinds (gender, religion, and sexual orientation being three obvious ones, in addition to ethnicity/colour); and there will be variability and hybridity even within a group seemingly and intentionally as homogeneous as Puente students might seem to be.

I received permission from sixteen students in one Puente class to make copies of their assigned writings during the first semester, including an 'identity essay'. It was written after the students had read and discussed a history of Mexico in fictionalised narrative form, *El Indio*, which emphasises the Indian roots of Mexican people and culture (Lopez y Fuentes 1937/1992), with illustrations by muralist Diego Rivera, and two identity essays by published authors – one by a 'Chicano' and one by a 'Hispanic'.

Here are the self-identifications expressed in the students' essays: ten 'Mexican', of whom three were born in Mexico, five were first-generation born in the United States, and two second-generation; two 'Mexican-American'; one 'Mexican-Aztec American'; one 'Mexican-American and Hispanic'; one 'Puerto Rican, Mexican and Aztec Indian'; 1 'Xicano' (Chicano in Spanish spelling). Both individual hybridity and variability within the group are evident in this list, and both should be expected in any close look at collective identities. In the Puente programme, there is no attempt to decrease or control this variability. On the contrary, assigned readings deliberately represent a range of identifications (from 'Chicano' with more radical connotations to 'Hispanic' used by the US government as an umbrella label for people originally from any Spanish-speaking country). And there is an assumption that identifications self-selected now may well change as students' lives change in college and beyond. The only firm programme expectations are that they succeed in college, and that they become responsible for 'giving back' to their communities the support they are now receiving from others.

In the Multiliteracies schema, hybridity refers to a relationship between different designs of meaning, 'highlighting the mechanisms of creativity and of culture-as-process particularly salient in contemporary society'. In his Foreword to an analysis of *Hybrid Cultures* in Latin America, anthropologist Reynato Rosaldo differentiates two meanings of the term:

> On the one hand, hybridity can imply a space betwixt and between two zones of purity in a manner that follows biological usage that distinguishes two discrete species and the hybrid pseudospecies that results from their combination. On the other hand, hybridity can be understood as the ongoing condition of all human cultures, which contain no zones of purity because they undergo continuous processes of transculturation (two-way borrowing and lending between cultures). Instead of hybridity versus purity, this view suggests, it is hybridity all the way down.
>
> (Rosaldo 1995, p. xv)

Both meanings are used widely in referring to Mexican and Mexican-American culture and identity by the Spanish adjective *mestizo*, hybrid, and noun *mestizaje*, hybridity. Fitting the first more pure and static meaning, the Plaza of Three Cultures in Mexico City refers separately to indigenous Indian culture, European Spanish culture, and the mestizo mix of the two. Fitting the second meaning of continuing processes of transculturation is the analysis of all Mexican culture as inherently mestizo, and Mexican-American as doubly so, adding 'American' to the Indian/Spanish mix.

Rosaldo's second meaning of 'hybridity all the way down' fits the Multi-literacies discussion and also several of the Puente readings. For example, in *Borderlands/La Frontera: The New Mestiza*, author Gloria Anzaldua identifies herself as a 'border woman' who grew up on the border between Texas and Mexico. In the preface she discusses psychological, sexual, and spiritual borderlands; and expresses her exhilaration in participating in a border mestiza identity that she sees as 'the further evolution of humankind' (Anzaldua 1987).

Many white Americans also identify themselves in hybrid terms. Waters (Waters 1990) analyses the 'symbolic ethnicity' of later generations of white immigrant groups that she calls voluntary; however, for her informants 'Ethnicity is not something that influences their lives unless they *want* it to' (Waters 1990, p. 7). At the end, she provocatively suggests:

> A potential social cost of this symbolic ethnicity is in its subtle reinforcement of racism . . . The celebration of the fact that we all have heritages implies an equality among those heritages. This would obscure the fact that the experiences of non-whites have been qualitatively and quantitatively different from those of whites.
>
> (Waters 1990, p. 164)

Inculcating positive intergroup attitudes

Bateson (Bateson 1994) differentiates between 'identity multiculturalism' and 'adaptive multiculturalism':

> The term *multiculturalism* is used to refer to at least two different but complementary strategies: one that supports individuals in their own ethnic or racial identities [identity multiculturalism] and one that enhances everyone's capacity to adapt by offering exposure to a variety of other traditions [adaptive multicultural-ism]. [The first] makes good sense as a place to start. Adaptive multiculturalism has more to say about learning through a lifetime, in a continuing process of encountering difference. Traditional liberal education was identity-based for the privileged and identity-threatening for others.
>
> (Bateson 1994, pp. 167–71)

If Reading Recovery book selections become more inclusive, children in the programme will experience images of themselves and children from other groups as well. In the Puente programme, the first semester focuses on identity multiculturalism in ways I have exemplified, and the second semester extends the curriculum to adaptive multiculturalism. In one Puente class, a second-semester unit of readings on the theme of education included short pieces by Mexican-American poet Jimmy Baca and African-American leader Malcolm X, both on their language and literacy self-education while in prison; by working-class Italian-American now university professor Mike Rose; and by Brazilian Paulo Freire.

The importance of reaching beyond one's own group was highlighted at the annual two-day California Chicano/Latino Intersegmental Convocation attended by some 1800 administrators, faculty and students from all three tiers of the state educational system – community colleges, state universities, and (research) universities – at which Puente received an award. Topics of the seventy-two workshops included academic services, alternatives to gangs, Chicana/Latina identities, facing HIV/AIDS, and the history of the Chicano/Latino struggle. Like the Puente reading lists for the two semesters, speakers at the two conference banquets expressed both identity and adaptive multiculturalism. The luncheon banquet was addressed by leaders of the United Farm Workers, who stressed the continuity of struggle between students today and their parents and grandparents in the field; the dinner banquet was addressed by African-American the Reverend Jesse Jackson, who called for coalitions of minority groups, women, and labour to take up again the struggle for a more democratic society.

More generally, former 1960s activist Todd Gitlin, now professor of communications, journalism, and sociology, in his 'The Twilight of Common Dreams' (Gitlin 1995) critiques what has come to be called 'identity politics' because it has fragmented the very coalition that Jackson calls for. Bateson may be right, as I think she is, that identity multiculturalism is a good, even necessary, place to start. But she's also right that we can't stop there, not only for the sake of coalition politics but because to do so would leave the attitudes of the dominant group unchallenged and unchanged.

The first two articles in the autumn 1995 issue of the *American Educational Research Journal*, both by tenured professors at major research universities, illustrate Bateson's two multicultural strategies. The first, by African-American Billings Ladson (Ladson 1995), describes 'the culturally relevant teaching' of eight California elementary school teachers (five African-American and three white) who had been nominated as outstanding by African-American parents. It is a success story of identity multiculturalism in which African-American students succeed academically while retaining their cultural identities and becoming aware of the 'political underpinnings of [their] community and social world' (Ladson 1995, p. 477).

The second, by white M. Cochran-Smith (Cochran-Smith 1995), is a rarer analysis of the difficulties she has encountered in 'confronting the dilemmas of race, culture and language diversity' in her own teacher education programme. It is a story of less clear success in adaptive multi-culturalism as student teachers 'struggle with the idea that racism includes – the privileges and disadvantages that both shape and are embedded in the institutions we live by, especially our educational institutions' (Cochran-Smith 1995, p. 503). And, I would add, struggle with their own responsibility, as future teachers, regarding how the pattern of 'privileges and disadvantages' can be changed.

That pattern of privileges and disadvantages should be included as part of the 'activities, practices, and ways of viewing the world' of the dominant culture. Whereas Ogbu and Matute-Bianchi (Ogbu and Matute-Bianchi 1986) point out secondary cultural characteristics only among caste-like minorities, I want to extend their construct to the dominant group as well. Just as non-dominant groups adopt certain behaviours and internalise certain self-attitudes in response to perceived oppression, so members of the dominant group analogously adopt certain behaviours and internalise certain self-attitudes in response to perceived dominance and resulting entitlement.

To emphasise the school's responsibility for changing dominant attitudes, the term 'anti-racist' education is often used, rather than 'multi-cultural'. 'Anti-racism' was the label adopted by one independent primary school in the Boston area for its ongoing work. (See Greeley and Mizell (1993) and Mizell et al. (1993) for articles by staff members, and Cazden (Cazden 1994) for an outsider's brief summary.)

In ways common to other intentionally multicultural schools, these teachers attend carefully to their instructional materials: having 'multi-cultural crayons' with eight skin cultures, so all children can portray accurately how they and their peers actually look (and even note changes after a vacation in the sun!); and choosing books that in pictures and texts give a more inclusive and therefore more accurate understanding of both history and the contemporary world.

Less common is these teachers' attention to more subtle ways of acting and talking. For example, in the kindergarten one year, the teachers noticed that, in dramatic play during recess, the white boys not only directed the action but sent the African-American boys out on raids. Nobody got physi-cally hurt, but the pattern of dominance relationships mirrored too closely the dominance relationships in the larger society. The teachers worked with the children, in both single-ethnicity and mixed groups, so that every-body could learn to take on different roles. In another situation in the combined first and second grade, during a discussion of what Native American author Michael Dorris might look like, a white child said, 'They [Native Americans] look just like us'. After the teacher gently asked three times, 'Who is "us"?', the child paused and said, 'Oh, I think I meant white people. And we're not all white' (personal communication, 1995).

In Bernstein's terms with which I began, the boundary between school and the cultures the children come from has to be strengthened in some ways and weakened in others. Teachers should affirm aspects of children's primary home cultures, especially for non-dominant students – whether in single-ethnicity programmes like Puente or mixed-ethnicity programmes like Cambridge Friends School. But they should act just as firmly to interrupt and counter aspects of prior home socialisation that Ogbu and Matute-Bianchi (Ogbu and Matute-Bianchi 1986) call secondary cultural characteristics: those that arise from their collective identities as members of non-dominant or dominant groups in the larger society.

Issues of pedagogy

The Multiliteracies framework stresses the importance of opportunities for learning new discourse skills, oral and written, through a lifetime of changing social and employment contexts. As Jesse Jackson said at the Chicano/Latino convocation, 'We have to go beyond pride; we can be proud and still poor'. Of course education alone cannot create a supply of jobs at above poverty-level wages. But even if the analysis of relationships between education and the economy projected in this book (and in a similar analysis by two economists, Murname and Levy (Murname and Levy 1996) turns out to be wrong, the vision of education is still worth working for, as long as it is truly available to all students (Mehan 1996). Students so educated should be better prepared not only for jobs but for citizenship and social action.

We argue that learning opportunities for all need to include a four-part pedagogy of Situated Practice, Overt Instruction, Critical Framing, and Transformed Practice. But I want to acknowledge the tension that can exist among these four components, even as we argue that all are essential. That tension can be seen in the ways that the influential ideas of Soviet psychologist Lev Vygotsky have been incorporated in literacy programmes, and indeed in Vygotsky's ideas themselves. It is involved in the combining of Situated Practice and Overt Instruction, in the addition of Critical Framing and its related component of Transformed Practice, and in the challenges of teaching 'the arts of the contact zone'.

Situated Practice and Overt Instruction

In the United States at the present time, the two components of Situated Practice and Overt Instruction are often seen as representing opposing philosophies: in teaching beginning reading, we read arguments for 'whole-language' versus 'phonics'; in teaching writing at any age, we read arguments for 'process writing' versus 'genre pedagogy'. It turns out that proponents of these supposedly contrasting pedagogies cite different sections of Vygotsky's writings in their support. Cazden (Cazden 1996b) lays out the contrasting citations. Here I can only briefly exemplify the contrast.

One group of educators, centring on Briton James Britton and Americans Kenneth and Yetta Goodman, are leaders in what has come to be called 'whole-language', 'process writing', or 'progressive pedagogy'. Britton (e.g. Britton 1987) emphasises the importance of inner speech and tacit knowledge; the Goodmans (e.g. Goodman and Goodman 1990) argue for immersion (a term from second language acquisition that is similar in import to the more recent 'Situated Practice'), and against any explicit teaching.

The second group consists of many educators who advocate literacy programmes that can be described as 'scaffolded assistance' in the learners' zone of proximal development. Clay and Cazden (Clay 1992) analyse Reading Recovery in these terms. Another visible and well-documented model in the US school reform landscape is the elementary school programme called 'community of learners' developed by psychologist Ann Brown (e.g. Brown and Campione 1994), which uses a science curriculum of semester-long themes such as 'endangered species' to teach learning-to-learn strategies of inquiry and both comprehension and composition strategies for expository texts.

Programmes in this second category embed Overt Instruction in some kind of Situated Practice but, in contrast to the first group, the teacher plays a more active role in making sure that all students attain the programme goals. In the four-category analysis of literacy programmes by University of Bristol researchers (Reed, Webster and Beveridge 1996), programmes in both my categories would be described as 'high learner initiative', but only the second would have 'high teacher involvement' as well.

Both groups cite Vygotsky (Vygotsky 1962), but there is a striking disjunction in their citations.

Consider here references only to sections of *Thought and Language*: while Britton relies on the final chapter 7, 'Thought and Word', the second group relies on the penultimate chapter 6, 'Development of Scientific Concepts in Childhood'. According to recent articles by Vygotskian scholar James Wertsch (Wertsch 1996a, 1996b), such disjunction is not surprising; it is inherent in Vygotsky's own thinking: in his 'two minds on the nature of meaning' and his 'ambivalence' as an 'Enlightenment rationalist'.

Chapter 7 of *Thought and Language*, 'Thought and Word', focuses on the child's internal, private, psychological world of idiosyncratic 'sense' and the tension between this and the public social world of conventional meanings; in sharp contrast not acknowledged by Vygotsky, chapter 6, 'Development of Scientific Concepts in Childhood', focuses on the essential contribution of school instruction in the child's development towards that external, public social world in the context of school instruction, with its strong homogenising force of systemic ('scientific') concepts. In Wertsch's analysis, drawing on Toulmin (Toulmin 1992), chapter 7 expresses Vygotsky's legacy from Renaissance humanism, with its emphasis on the oral, the particular, the local, and the transitory, while chapter 6 expresses his legacy from Enlightenment rationality, with its emphasis on the written, the general, the universal, and the timeless. Chapter 7 probably comes from Vygotsky's life-long interest in literature (e.g. his thesis on *Hamlet*) and drama (e.g. Stanislavsky's construct of 'subtext' in chapter 7), chapter 6 from the task he took on in the late 1920s and early 1930s (until his death in 1934) of creating a theory of human development that could contribute to education of the new 'Soviet man' in the world's first planned (to-be-classless) society.

Our world and our task today are very different. Not included anywhere in *Thought and Language* is any mention of differences of language or culture, though they certainly existed in the Soviet Union. Thus Britton's London colleague Tony Burgess (Britton 1987) argues for a third interpretation of Vygotsky's ideas with additional citations from his contemporary Mikhail Bakhtin. In Burgess's view, Britton's reading of Vygotsky over-emphasises the individual and considers the 'social' only as interaction while ignoring issues of power and conflict that must be included in considerations of the 'cultural' in development and education. Perhaps if we keep Britton's view of inner speech as the source of creativity but enlarge our understanding of its content, as Burgess suggests, beyond the idiosyncratically individual to the collectively cultural, we can see it as a source of not only creativity but critique. Vygotsky's 'spontaneous concepts' (in chapter 6) and 'sense' (in chapter 7) then become not just something to be transformed but a source of transformational power as well.

Critical Framing and Transformed Practice

One aspect of Critical Framing that bears a special relationship to cultural differences is the way in which persons, especially in their collective identities, are referred to or portrayed in images and words. Students of all ages should become sensitised to, and continuously critical of, how people are represented in whatever they hear, see and read, or which people are not presented at all. Remember how that primary school teacher questioned, and prompted a reconsideration of one child's referent for the pronoun 'us'. Critical literacy in this meaning of 'critical' is a more prominent part of education in Australia and England than in the USA. I can give only a few suggestive examples.

One day in a Puente classroom, we read aloud and discussed a signed 'Editorial notebook' article from the *New York Times* of May 1992, a month after the verdict in the Rodney King trial and its aftermath of rioting and demonstrating in Los Angeles, where police officers were cleared of assaulting a black man. Topically, the essay titled 'The War Against Street Gangs' (Staples 1992) was related to an autobiographical book, *Always Running* (Rodriguez 1993), that the class would soon be reading. Formally, as the Puente teacher pointed out, the editorial was a problem/solution essay. What we did not discuss, but could have done, was the way the author, or one of his informants, described a 'visionary' anti-gang programme being tried at that time by the Los Angeles Police Department: 'Called Jeopardy, its task is to prevent high-risk youngsters from falling into gangs in the first place. This sometimes means hauling kids to school in handcuffs to make sure they attend' (Rodriguez 1993).

In *Always Running*, Rodriguez shows from his own experience how one reason those whom the columnist calls 'high-risk youngsters' join gangs is a lack of dignity accorded them in school and community. When African-American Staples talks about 'hauling kids to school in handcuffs', either he or a programme spokesperson whom he quotes too unthinkingly is denying them that very dignity – not only by the handcuffs in the police programme but in the choice of verb in the editorial. 'Hauling' is how one transports a load of wood, or manure, not people, and such connotations dehumanise any persons who are its object. Such language should make the reader at least question the attitudes behind the recommended solution.

Critique alone may engender only cynicism or further alienation. That's why the best programmes combine critique with Transformed Practice. In one Australian classroom, teacher Jennifer O'Brien found ways to incorporate both in her programme for children aged five to eight. When seven-year-old Christie commented that in books she'd noticed that aunts were often portrayed as mean, O'Brien interrupted her plans and asked the children to draw on knowledge of their own worlds to resist and challenge the stereotypes frequently found in children's fiction. Then for Mother's Day, O'Brien created a set of activities around junk mail Mother's Day catalogues. The children compared how the mothers in the catalogues were like and unlike their own mothers, and then together created a new catalogue in which 'mothers would be constructed differently' (Comber and O'Brien 1993, pp. 5–6).

Critical framing is especially important when using computer programmes, whose authorship is frequently more hidden than in books (see 'Information and Education: The Need for Critical Understanding' in Cazden 1992). As an example, consider one highly rated historical simulation of US history, the CD-ROM *Oregon Trail*. Bigelow (Bigelow 1997) gives a detailed analysis of the programme. It teaches a lot of US history in an engaging way, but there are problems. The power, and the danger, of interactive CD-ROMs is that 'students don't merely identify with a particular character, they actually adopt his or her frame of reference and act as if they were that character. In Oregon Trail, a player quickly bonds with the "pioneer" maneuvering through the wilderness' (Bigelow 1997,

p. 85). And while women, black people, and Native Americans are present, the dominant perspective is of white males. At the end, Bigelow has excellent suggestions for Transformed Practice, including student research on the lives and words of the underrepresented groups, and student improvisations of interactions that could have been included.

Text forms as well as contents should be subjected to critical discussion. Cazden (Cazden 1996c) explores the dilemma of combining socialisation and critique in the case of the canonical school 'report' genre, and questions its hidden curriculum of truth as universal and timeless 'facts' that may make openness to changing knowledge and shifting perspectives harder to achieve.

Teaching 'the arts of the contact zone'

One of the central ideas of the Multiliteracies argument is that negotiating across differences is now a life-and-death matter, and literacy pedagogy has to play its part in developing the discourse skills that such negotiation requires.

Mary Louis Pratt, Professor of Spanish and Comparative Literature at Stanford University, has described what happened when that university changed a required Western culture course into a course 'that centered on the Americas and the multiple cultural histories (including European ones) that have intersected here' (Pratt 1991, p. 39). Because her important article is not easily accessible, I end with an extended excerpt about the teaching that the course change required:

> As you can imagine, the course attracted a very diverse student body. The classroom functioned not like a homogeneous community or a horizontal alliance but like a contact zone . . .
>
> It was the most exciting teaching we had ever done, and also the hardest. We were struck, for example, at how anomalous the formal lecture became in a contact zone. The lecturer's traditional (imagined) task – unifying the world in the class's eyes. This task became not only impossible but anomalous and unimaginable. Instead, one had to work in the knowledge that whatever one said was going to be systematically received in radically heterogeneous ways that we were neither able nor entitled to prescribe.
>
> The very nature of the course put ideas and identities on the line. All the students in the class had the experience, for example, of hearing their culture discussed and objectified in ways that horrified them. Virtually every student was having the experience of seeing the world described with him or her in it. The sufferings and revelations were, at different moments to be sure, experienced by every student. No one was excluded, and no one was safe.

The fact that no one was safe made all of us involved in the course appreciate the important of what we came to call 'safe houses.' We use the term to refer to social and intellectual spaces where groups can constitute themselves as horizontal, homogeneous, sovereign communities with high degrees of trust, shared understandings, temporary protection from legacies of oppression. Where there are legacies of subordination, groups need places for healing and mutual recognition, safe houses in which to construct shared understandings, knowledges, claims on the world that they can then bring into the contact zone.

Meanwhile, our job in the Americas course remains to figure out how to make that crossroads the best site for learning that it can be. We are looking for the pedagogical arts of the contact zone. These will include, we are sure, exercises in storytelling and in identifying with the ideas, interests, histories, and attitudes of others; experiments in transculturation and collaborative work and in the arts of critique, parody and comparison (including unseemly comparisons between elite and vernacular forms); the redemption of the oral; ways for people to engage with suppressed aspects of history (including their own histories), ways to move into and out of rhetorics of authenticity; ground rules for communication across lines of difference and hierarchy that go beyond politeness but maintain mutual respect; a systematic approach to the all-important concept of cultural mediation.

(Pratt 1991, pp. 39–40)

In some places, the Multiliteracies argument seems to suggest that it is government's role to negotiate differences. While that role may exist formally, as in laws and court decisions, we cannot rely on it, if for no other reason than that government action too often favours dominant interests. We all live in the contact zone and have to take responsibility for negotiating within it. In her brief description of education at 'the crossroads', Pratt includes all four of our literacy components: Situated Practice in the larger class; Overt Instruction in 'exercises' and 'ground rules'; Critical Framing in 'critique, parody and comparison'; Transformed Practice in 'experiments in transculturation and collaborative work'.

13

NARRATIVES AND INSCRIPTIONS

Cultural tools, power and powerful sense-making

Sarah Michaels and Richard Sohmer

Introduction

This chapter, like Courtney Cazden's, elaborates that aspect of the Mutliliteracies framework which challenges us to take cultural differences seriously and, by so doing, create educational practices and environments that will lead to 'productive diversity'. In discussing the 'what' and 'how' of a pedagogy for Multiliteracies, the New London Group has proposed a set of tools, a metalanguage, for talking about and working with language, texts, and meaning-making interactions. In this chapter, we suggest that the tools themselves – the tools we as teachers or researchers trade in – are rarely examined critically. Through a re-analysis of interviews with fourth-grade children reasoning about seasonal change, we take a close look at the use of narratives and inscriptions, at the ways these discursive tools enable and constrain us – teachers, students, and researchers alike – and at the implications of this for those of us who take the notion of Multiliteracies seriously.

First, however, we would like to make a brief note about the authorship and stylistics of this text. This is a co-authored paper involving a re-analysis of data collected by Sarah Michaels in 1988. Thus the co-authors have different histories and relationships to the data being analysed. Rather than mask our differing experiences with respect to data collection and analysis, we have segmented the text into distinct sections and made the primary authorship clear (using 'I' to stand for the primary author of a given segment and 'we' to stand for text that was developed jointly). Throughout the text we will juxtapose the findings from the original study with our re-analysis.

In accepting the Nobel Prize in Literature in Stockholm in 1993, Toni Morrison (Morrison 1994) presented an oral address – first published, interestingly enough, as an audiotape. In her presentation, she argued for narrative as a powerful tool for generating knowledge, 'one of the principal ways in which we absorb knowledge' (Morrison 1994, p. 7), and a primary way in which we make sense in and of the world. Others before her have argued this case. What was particularly striking about Morrison's text is that she used narrative itself to bring off her argument – instantiating while at the same time characterising narrative's distinctive powers to inform, transform, and create new meanings.

Morrison told a story – in two parts – about an old, wise, black woman, completely blind, but regarded in her rural community as having special powers to see and heal. She is approached by some young teenagers from the city, who want to show her up as the fool and fraud they believe her to be. The youngsters, knowing she's blind, demand that the old woman tell them whether the bird one of them is holding is alive or dead. The old woman's response is soft but stern. 'I don't know. I don't know whether the bird you are holding is dead or alive, but what I do know is that it is in your hands. It's in your hands' (Morrison 1994, p. 11). The second uttering is not a repetition for emphasis. The shift in stress (apparent in oral version but not in the written) from 'in' to 'your' – signals the children's responsibility for the bird – its life or death.

Morrison then developed, from the old woman's reprimand, an analysis of the bird as language – as either alive (generating meaning) or dead or dying (destroying or denying meaning).

> if the bird in the hands of her visitors is dead, the custodians are responsible for the corpse. For [the old woman] a dead language is not only one no longer spoken or written, it is unyielding language content to admire its own paralysis . . . Ruthless in its policing duties, it . . . actively thwarts the intellect, stalls conscience, suppresses human potential. Unreceptive to interrogation, it cannot form or tolerate new ideas, shape other thoughts, tell another story, fill baffling silences.
>
> (Morrison 1994, pp. 13–14)

The contrast Morrison put forth is 'word-work':

> Word-work is sublime . . . because it is generative; it makes meaning that secures our difference, our human difference – the way in which we are like no other life.
>
> We die. That may be the meaning of life. But we do language. That may be the measure of our lives.
>
> (Morrison 1994, p. 22)

The story comes to a point of neat closure, a point where the old woman's words – extended by Morrison's analysis – could be taken as profoundly wise and generative. As a listener, one expects the story to end there. But the close is a half-cadence only, and the story shifts into part two. Returning to the voices of the seemingly cruel and misguided youth, Morrison gave them reason, sense, and sensibility – showing the inadequacies and limitations of the old, wise woman's perspective. The old woman's words, which seemed at first like a great example of 'word-work' (pithy and full of potential for teaching and transforming the youth), were then shown to have been a way of ignoring and closing down meaning, completely shutting the teenagers out of her story. It turns out they never had a bird in their hands in the first place. But they refuse to be boxed out by the old one's words and respond:

> Your answer is artful, but its artfulness embarrasses us and ought to embarrass you. Your answer is indecent in its self-congratulation . . . Why didn't you reach out, touch us with your soft fingers, delay the sound bite, the lesson, until you knew who we were? . . . You trivialise us and trivialise the bird that is not in our hands.
>
> (Morrison 1994, pp. 25–26)

The children are resilient. They demand she give them authentic language, the true and rich particularities of her own life, and in turn tell her a haunting story of their own, as an example of what they are looking for from her.

In being given access to their story, the old woman comes to know and trust them. As the two parts of the story come together and interpenetrate, the old woman and her young interlocutors (and the listeners to Morrison's speech as well) are transformed by the living bird of language. In the old woman's parting words: 'I trust you now. I trust you with the bird that is not in your hands because you have truly caught it. Look. How lovely it is, this thing we have done – together' (Morrison 1994, p. 30).

Morrison was arguing for more than the power of narrative per se. The first partial narrative is itself shown by the second to be something of an analogue to dead language. Rather, she is arguing for the power of narratives or divergent perspectives in contact – provided that each is unfrozen enough that it can be penetrated, challenged, and transformed in contact with others.

The alternative – set forth in no uncertain terms in Morrison's angry though ultimately hopeful text – is domination:

> the language of surveillance disguised as research; of politics and history calculated to render the suffering of millions mute; language glamorised to thrill the dissatisfied and bereft into

assaulting their neighbours; arrogant pseudo-empirical language crafted to lock creative people into cages of inferiority and hope-lessness . . . lethal discourses of exclusion blocking access to cognition for both the excluder and the excluded.

(Morrison 1994, pp. 18–19)

Thinking with inscriptions

In his compelling 1986 work *Visualisation and Cognition: Thinking with Eyes and Hands*, Bruno Latour writes from a different perspective, place, and tradition, but, like Toni Morrison, focuses on the relationship among individuals, tools for thinking, and domination. In characterising and explaining what is 'specific to our modern scientific culture' (Latour 1986, p. 1) Latour rejects grandiose dichotomies and 'grand causes' – for example, shifts in contents or structures of individuals' minds, or large-scale shifts in social relations or modes of production.

In Latour's view, the genesis of modern scientific culture can be traced instead to the invention and dispersal of writing and imaging craftman-ship. The rise of the technologies of *inscription* – the use of paper, signs, prints and diagrams as weapons, allies, forces – is a simple but powerful explanatory link among individual minds, social practices, and power in the world. These practices – so material and mundane, so practical, so modest, so pervasive, so close to the hands and the eyes that they escape our attention – are, from an historical perspective, radical modifications of the fundamental way in which people strive with one another for power.

Latour develops his argument through historical anecdotes, and by synthesising ethnographic and historical literature about shifts in tech-nologies for simplifying, abstracting, *deflating* the world so that it can be brought together in new places, and assembled in increasingly complex and abstract ways – ultimately allowing the few to dominate the many.

In the process of deflating, via techniques and technologies of inscrip-tion, we reduce the world and its infinite and polymorphous complexities into a finite number of relevant aspects. These aspects, these simplifications – or, more accurately, the charts, diagrams, formulas, statistics, tables, models which are their representations – come to be taken as more relevant than 'mere' experience itself. Inscriptions transform, simplify, and trans-port aspects of the world in forms that are at once mobile (easily and widely circulated), immutable (held constant across time and space), presentable, and combinable. In modern, bureaucratic settings, it is these inscriptions which are the primary means by which one recruits allies and amasses power and influence.

Thus, Latour argues, both the tools of inscription and the ways these tools help to gain and sustain allegiances in the world must be considered together if one is to understand modern, scientific culture.

A man is never much more powerful than any other – even from a throne; but a man whose eye dominates records through which some sort of connections are established with millions of others may be said to dominate . . . In other words, the *scale* of an actor is not an absolute term but a relative one that varies with the ability to peruse, capture, sum up and interpret information about other places and times.

(Callon and Latour 1981)

The great man is a little man looking at a good map. Such tools and techniques of deflation are:

a requirement that European culture demands of its analysts: phenomena must be rendered as representational versions of themselves that are then amenable to rational manipulation . . . Within this praxis the worldly phenomena themselves are lost and their objective representations stand in their stead.

(Liberman 1990, p. 187)

Using this cultural tool, 'some serious analytical victories may be won' – every tool empowers; on the other hand, however, 'detailed explications of embedded conversational detail is usually foregone' (Liberman 1990, p. 187) – every tool constrains. And in the glow of empowerment, the constraints often go unnoticed.

Consider a map – an ordinary street map. We can plan our strategies, calculate our investments, arrange our logistical networks – all from above, as it were, all without having to consider who it is that lives in even one house. This is power! But – how if it is discovered, as the order of battle begins on schedule, that it is *your* sister or *your* child who is lost somewhere in the city under the falling bombs. The very information with which you might find her – names, nicknames, peculiarities, habits, desires, emotional ties, in short, all that is thoroughly irrelevant to the making of maps – has of course been left out of the map.

The map encodes (reduces) inhabitants, neighbourhood – on to a flat surface that can be held in one's hands, passed around from person to person or transported from place to place with no change in information content, combined with other documents, enlarged or shrunk. It brings an entire city into focus, into one's hands and mind. But does it? The potholes are gone. Your house is gone. The smells and sounds and trail of stories are gone. What's left are abstractions that 'stand for' the real (and, at that, only some aspects of the real).

Hence, while there is tremendous power in the immutability, abstraction, mobility, and combinability of inscriptions, there are also inherent limitations and powerful disadvantages. At each level in the rise above the

271

particular, the process of abstraction which the process of inscription entails results in greater generality and scope. As each increase in abstraction is accompanied by an irretrievable loss of information, higher and higher levels of abstraction become reified. The explanation is mistaken for that which it was to explain. The map is mistaken for the territory, and the menu for the meal.

Here Latour and Morrison – each concerned with power in the world, and the power of semiotic tools to dominate others – can be brought into constructive dialogue. Two very different sorts of verbal armamentaria are under consideration: (on the one hand) the deflating, simplifying, monologising tools and techniques of inscription, which in modern life are as unproblematic (hence invisible) as they are effective at weeding out the 'irrelevant'; and (on the other hand) the generative, complexifying, multi-voiced particularities of stories, of narratives like those in Morrison's text. What is the relationship between these two different cultural tools (or, more aptly, tool kits)? What are their effects on world, self, and others? How do these different cultural tools both enable and constrain us?

In what follows, we present some data that bear on these questions – beginning with a group of fourth graders reasoning about seasonal change and its causes, a topic they encountered in school science. We will see in their performances – in concert with those of the interviewers who elicited their reasoning – both types of cultural tools. In addition, we carry out a re-analysis – setting up a juxtaposition between two stories of our own – using the original analysis of the fourth graders as data – so that we can examine both what the kids were doing (what discursive resources and tools they used as they talked and reasoned) and what the original researchers were doing (how their ways of seeing and interpreting made it easy to see some kinds of meaning-making and difficult to see others).

In the end, we argue that we 'mainstream' researchers and the kids we think of as 'mainstream' kids are all too often doing what Toni Morrison warns us about – blindly using a kind of inscription-based language that is closed to interrogation. In the process of mistaking the map for the territory, we omit engaging in one very necessary kind of critical intellectual practice. We are ourselves failing to interrogate the inscriptions we trade in. We are well able to appreciate the clarity of our vision as it is enabled by our inscriptions – but how aware are we of the ways in which our inscriptions constrain our vision? Inasmuch as we are scarcely able to apprehend the bare existence of what is obscured or obviated by our inscriptions, we seldom name or notice our own blindness.

This opens up the unfortunate possibility – for those of us who are actively concerned with social justice, with understanding and intervening in the lives of 'non-mainstream' kids – that we can unwittingly do real harm. Here we are critiquing ourselves, our own work – not others. And it is, indeed, an uncomfortable story.

272

Story 1

In 1988, Sarah Michaels (henceforth 'I'), collaborating with Chip (Bertram) Bruce, who was a co-interviewer in the 1988 project and a co-author of the original papers, conducted open-ended interviews with fourth graders in an ethnically and socioeconomically diverse public school in Cambridge, Massachusetts. The fourth grade class had quite recently completed a curricular unit of study on seasonal change, reading a textbook, discussing it, seeing a demonstration with kids posing as earth and sun. The following is a quote from 'Discourses on the Seasons', reporting on this work (Michaels and Bruce 1988):

> In our attempt to understand more deeply what these fourth-graders had learned about seasonal change from the textbook, we engaged each of them individually in an extended, very informal interview probing various aspects of their knowledge related to seasons. [We sat together outside their classroom, on the floor of a carpeted landing. The conversation was informal and relaxed.] The kids had known us for months by now as friendly, frequent visitors, Chip and Sarah. However, the framework of the interview was always the same. We began with the intention of asking some version of these questions:
>
> What makes the days longer in the summer than in the winter?
> What makes it hotter in the summer and colder in the winter?
> If you went south from Cambridge (and then farther and farther), what would happen to the temperature?
> When it's summer in Cambridge, is it summer everywhere in the world?
> What makes night and day happen?
> Where did you learn all this?
>
> (pp. 13–14)

We talked at length with each student (at least fifteen minutes per interview), asking as many as fifteen or twenty follow-up questions about a given topic. As a result, each interview is unique; each is a product of the student's and our sense-making in concert.

Ultimately we were interested in knowing 'why some students succeed in mastering science, while so many others find it impossibly difficult and frustrating? What attitudes and values (and ways of knowing) are transmitted in the science classroom along with the science that is learned?' (Lemke 1990, p. ix).

Quoting again from the 1988 report:

> In the jointly produced discourse, we can look at the facts that

get elicited, juxtaposed, and embedded in explanations, at the students' underlying causal theories in light of our analysis of the school text these students read and discussed, and at the way the students' discourse is organised and accomplished. In short, we get a glimpse of how these students talk science in a particular content domain, and indirectly, what their assumptions are about scientific discourse and what counts as appropriate scientific explanation.

(Michaels and Bruce 1988, p. 14)

Out of this work came a series of papers and conference presentations which focused on the interviews with four focal students, Christopher, Jennifer, Nathaniel, and Teresa – all of whom were talkative, articulate, and fully engaged in reasoning through the problems posed. In these write-ups, we reported that even though none of the students' explanations was correct, and that both the textbook representation and the teacher's understanding of the underlying phenomena were factually incorrect and rhetorically problematic, none the less one of the four students appeared markedly more 'scientific' than the other three, indicating a differential appropriation of the speech genre of scientific explanation.

For a start, none of the students' explanations was correct. In this class-room, after reading the text and having a lengthy discussion and demonstration by the teacher, not a single student learned the correct explanation of what causes the seasons to change. Transcripts of the interviews make clear that the students brought (to the interview and to the initial reading of the text) different facts and vocabulary knowledge in the domains of astronomy and geography. However, in spite of their differences in factual knowledge, nearly all the children were working with the same underlying understanding (the 'proximity theory') of heat. Applying this model of heat to seasonal change, all explained the fact that the days are hotter in the summer by stating that, in some way or another, the earth gets closer to the sun at that time of year. (In fact, we in the northern hemisphere are, owing to the eliptical orbit of the earth around the sun, actually slighter closer to the sun in the cold months of winter than in the summer. It is the tilt of the earth, the earth's revolution about the sun, and the resultant changes in the angle and dispersal of solar radiation – and hence, heat – that causes seasonal variation.)

The textbook which the students read was critically flawed by multiple errors of both fact and rhetoric. In addition, the teacher's own understanding of the causes of seasonal change (which the school curriculum required her, willy-nilly, to teach) was inadequate. She supplemented the text with relatively little in the way of discussion and demonstrations (to which the text made cursory and, on occasion, inaccurate appeal) of the physical principles involved. Sharing the same 'proximity' theory as the kids – that is, that the closer you are to mother's skin, the campfire, the oven, or the steam radiator the warmer it is – the teacher was neither able to teach the theory to the children in her own words nor to register (much less identify and correct) the presence of specific inadequacies and errors in the text.

Finally, only one of the four students appeared markedly more 'scientific' than the other three, indicating a differential appropriation of the speech genre of scientific explanation.

Despite the fact that the four focal students advanced the same (in this domain, incorrect) 'proximity' theory, Nathaniel appeared significantly more 'scientific' than Christopher, Jennifer, and Teresa. Observations (by the original researchers and all subsequent readers of the interview transcripts) about the interviewees fall into two categories: first, positive remarks upon Nathaniel's abilities as a budding scientist, and second, characterisations of the other interviewees as mistaken, illogical, non-scientific, confused, and/or hard to understand. The net effect – keeping in mind the fact that all four students relied upon the same (incorrect) explanation – is to confirm the observation by Michaels and Bruce that the two groups differ in what we might call (following Goffman) 'presentation'. To readers conversant with school-based science, Nathaniel appears to be 'doing science'. Christopher, Jennifer, and Teresa – evaluated only on this presentational dimension – suffer by comparison with Nathaniel. They appear (regardless of their actual competences) to be 'doing science' markedly less well than Nathaniel.

The 1988 study concluded that, with reference to the two groups (Nathaniel on the one hand, and Christopher, Jennifer, and Teresa on the other):

> they had different ways of 'talking science,' that is different ways of integrating facts into explanations, using models in the service of explanation, and deciding how to signal a causal explanation of a particular phenomenon. These differences have implications both for how students learn and for how they are perceived.
>
> (Michaels and Bruce 1988, p. 1)

In what follows, we present a set of transcripts from the interviews. The notations used to indicate intonation and prosody were developed by John Gumperz and his collaborators, based on the work of John Trim. Speech is first chunked into tone group units (that is, segments with a continuous intonational contour). These units are then designated as minor tone groups signalling 'more to come' (akin to a comma and indicated as /), or as major tone groups ending with some indication of utterance closure (akin to a full stop in writing and indicated as //). Pausing is indicated either by '. .', which indicates a break in timing, '. . .', which indicates a measurable pause, and '/', which indicates overlapping speech.

In addition we provide quoted summaries from the 1988 analysis – in order to illustrate the researchers' (Michaels and Bruce 1988) thinking at that time. The goal of keeping two separate kinds of data in focus at once is to look at the co-construction of the interviews (and what discursive resources the children deployed), and the researchers' differential construction of the children as scientists.

At the outset of the interview, we elicited from Nathaniel his theory about the fact that the days are longer in the summer than in the winter:

1 *Chip*:   Uh / what makes it sometimes / what makes the day be
              longer in the summer / and shorter in the winter? //
   Nathaniel: In the summer the sun can stay out longer / because how
              the earth is pointed / the sun can stay out longer //
5 *C*:   What do you mean by pointed? //
   N: Like the earth spins / and sometimes we are like real close
              to the sun / and sometimes we're far away //

We then ask seven follow-up probes, getting Nathaniel to clarify for us his sense of how the earth moves (in order to account for it getting closer and farther away at different times of year). During the dialogue Nathaniel constructs and employs a physical model using his hands as the earth and sun. He shows and tells how the earth spins on its axis once every twenty-four hours as well as revolves around the sun:

1 *Sarah*: What – what does having / what does being / close to the sun /
             have to do with / how lo:ng the day is? //
   N: Because like if I'm / wicked like / this close to the sun / [yeah]
             the day is going to happen all day // . . . if I always have my –
             like my face to it [uh huh] / but if I'm like / this far away from
5   – the sun it won't / reach me / . . . oh yeah / you're right //
   S: What do you mean I'm right? //
   N: B-being far way or close doesn't make a difference / it's the
             spinning around part that counts //
10 *S*:   Say more about that //
   N: Like / you know how the earth spins around [uh huh] like this
             / [uh huh] / and goes around the sun [uh huh] it spins around
             um:/ when it spins around / it makes the – um night and day /
             [uh huh] but when it goes around it makes the differing /
15   temperatures //
   S: OK / how – explain how that works //
   N: Sorta like when the / when it goes around / sometimes it
             gets closer and sometimes it's – gets further / from the sun? //
             [uh huh]

Quoting from the 1988 report:

Nathaniel used 'because' as a causal connector rather than evidentially, as in 'It rained last night because there are puddles on the ground.' Many of the kids use 'because' in both ways, but Nathaniel uses 'because' as a causal connector 6/6 times. Each time he uses it to explain the underlying cause of a particular phenomenon, invoking as evidence non-experiential knowledge (facts that came from adults or books, such as that the world revolves around the sun) ... Nathaniel reasoned with models – verbal and physical ones constructed with his hands. In example 2, line 3, he creates a model of the earth and the sun, saying 'because, like if I am wicked/ like / this close to the sun / the day is going to happen all day / if I always have my like my face to it.' He mentally runs the model, using if/then constructions, and halts midway, saying 'Oh yeah / you're right.'

(Michaels and Bruce 1988, pp. 16–17)

Note that Nathaniel treated Michael's question 'What does being close to the sun have to do with how long the day is?' as an implicit (teacher-like) cue that his earlier answer was wrong, something the interviewer hadn't intended – as if the interview had been for Nathaniel an *Initiation-Response-Evaluation* recitation (with right answers which we knew and were guiding him to get), a language game at which he was masterful in the classroom. The 1988 report continues:

Nathaniel's discourse, punctuated by the causal use of 'because' and the discourse marker 'like' used to build models to explain the mechanisms underlying seasonal change, tends to be both theory-explicit and mechanism-explicit. His facts are often wrong. (He says there is a 24 hour time difference between the U.S. and Russia.) His underlying causal theory is incorrect. He assumes ... that distance from the sun is the primary explanatory principle at work. In spite of all this, his discourse sounds scientific.

(Michaels and Bruce 1988, pp. 17–18)

In each of the various reports that were written, we characterised the other interviewees in contrast to Nathaniel: his was the unmarked case. Thus we characterised the other kids as reasoning via narratives of personal experience, blending discourse worlds (the lifeworld with the school-based world), as magical, teleological, confused, and/or hard to understand.

Now we turn to Christopher, whom we characterised in one paper as using 'personal, narrativised discourse' – at the same spot in the interview as we were with Nathaniel.

1   *Chip*:   Are – are the day and the night the same length/ the same number of hours? //

  Christopher: No/ because in the summer the days are longer and in the winter the days are shorter//

5   *Chip*:   Okay// Why – why is that?//

  Chris: Because you have to set your clock one hour back//

  Chip: But what/ what makes it happen?// I mean why/ why does it –

  Chris: 'Cause it's more colder and the sun goes down// earlier

10   than / it stays / than it goes down in the summer//

  Chip: Uh huh// So w – so why – why does it go down earlier?//

  Chris: 'Cause they/ – um/ they put the/ they um made the clock go back/ one hour//

  Chip: So then – / does setting the clock make it go down

15   earlier?// Or is – or is

  Chris: No! No / you'd think it's / like one time but it's later than it is//

  Chip: Uh huh//

  Sarah: Are you talking about daylight savings time sort of? //

20   *Chris*:   Yeah and you have to make the clock go back one hour // [uh huh]

  Chip: Is there something about the way / I mean / do-does the sun shine longer in the summer? (nod) // what's making it shine longer? //

25   *Chris*:   Because it's more hotter//

  S: Do you think it has to do with the heat? // how does that work do you know?//

  Chip: Do you know what makes it hotter? // It just happens? //

  Chris: No / cause the sun / the um the earth turns over to the sun/

From the 1988 report:

In this example, Christopher uses 'because' six times, three times with evidential rather than causal force. This is characteristic of Christopher's explanatory discourse throughout the interview. He uses 'because' in an evidential sense 6/16 times, and in 9/16 cases where he uses 'because,' the facts he embeds in his because clauses are derived from personal experiential knowledge, about setting back the clocks, when the sun goes down, etc. He rarely creates a model to explain his theories and then only when prompted by us to show us what he means by 'the earth turns over to the sun.' He uses discourse level 'like' only twice in the entire transcript, and only once in a what might be called a modeling context. Every occurrence except one of 'when' or 'then' is a real time marker:

'when it's winter'; 'when it's summer'; 'when you get around South Carolina'; 'when it's hot'; indexing elements in an explanatory framework, but not running a mental model.

(Michaels and Bruce 1988, pp. 19–20)

In addition to Christopher's recurring strategy of interpreting why questions as requests for evidence for a belief, he also justifies his reasoning using personal, experientially based evidence. For example:

1 *Chip*:   When would it start getting colder? //

    Chris: When you get around, like (pause) South Carolina/ I been / I never been there but I think it's cold there // [uh huh] 'Cause I always go to North Carolina // I never been to South // So I

5   don't know //

    Sarah: So you think it would get warmer if you went South? //

    Chris: No north // North is hot //

    S: North is hot? //

10 *Chris*: Yeah // N – [interruption] North Carolina is hot //

    Chip: So if you uh –

    Chris: Well / in the summer / I have never been in the winter //

As explained in the 1988 report:

> Christopher articulates many facts, and exactly the same distance theory that Nathaniel uses . . . His explanatory discourse, however, tends to be theory- and mechanism-implicit, so that if we had not probed repeatedly for mechanisms and relationships between facts, his active theorising might not have been apparent. But what was easily apparent to us as listeners was the narrative, evidential quality of his discourse, most noticeable when his personal experience actually led him astray as in the South Carolina example. Christopher, in short, does not sound scientific.
>
> (Michaels and Bruce 1988, p. 21)

Note that we were careful not to claim that Nathaniel is, while Christopher, Jennifer, and Teresa are not, 'doing science'. It is rather that *to readers conversant with school-based science* Nathaniel appears to be 'doing science'. The inevitable result, however, is that Christopher, Jennifer, and Teresa – evaluated only on this presentational dimension – suffer by comparison with Nathaniel. They appear (regardless of their actual competences) to be 'doing science' markedly less well than Nathaniel.

This was not written about overtly as a lack (or deficit) in the non-mainstream students. Mindful as we were in 1988 of Bernstein's work on social class, linguistic codes, and pedagogic discourse (Bernstein 1971,

1986), the work of the genre theorists in Australia (Christie 1987; Martin 1984), and Lisa Delpit's influential call (Delpit 1986) to teach minority students the 'discourses of power', the articles located the genesis of group differences not in the children's reasoning abilities per se, but rather in their control of specific discursive resources privileged in school. One of the papers concludes with a series of educational implications, pedagogical 'suggestions' for a different (more deliberate) mix of 'invisible' and 'visible' pedagogies citing various sources (Bernstein 1971; Cope and Kalantzis 1993; Delpit 1986) with the explicit purpose of honouring divergent ways of speaking while creating greater access for those students who don't already control the discourse of school science.

But the story did not end there. In spite of several polished texts to trade in, I was left with a nagging feeling that I had really not quite understood. I sensed that there was more to the story than Chip and I, in 1988, could articulate and give voice to. The analysis led to an undeniable conclusion – which I found distasteful and resisted – that Nathaniel, the scientific-sounding kid (and not the others) had a set of discursive/cultural tools and the wherewithal to deploy them in ways that more closely approximated the standard tools/practices of science. While explicitly professing a commitment to 'honouring divergent ways of speaking', I had implicitly promoted a cognitive-deficit model in characterising the differences across the children.

And interestingly, this version of a 'deficit' theory is all the more pernicious because it was in the guise of an analysis celebrating 'difference', in the stated service of equity and a pedagogy of access. What was never examined was the fact that the discursive tools (of comparison, quantification and categorisation) that we – Chip and I – were using to give voice, ostensibly, to these 'non-mainstream' students, to explore their logic and cogency as thinkers, were, in the end, not particularly helpful. But they worked very well in establishing what Nathaniel was doing. The danger, in both Nathaniel's and Chip's and my case, is that these tools, when naturalised, seem transparent, innocent, and disinterested – just doing their jobs – in the service of social science, that is, 'truth'.

In the autumn of 1994, working with a colleague, Richard Sohmer, I started looking at this data from a fresh perspective. We began noticing recurring instances in the interviews in which Christopher, Jennifer, and Teresa, our 'non-scientific' or 'non-mainstream' kids, mentioned everyday experience that seemed to be contradicted by the textbook theory. Interestingly, in each case, Chip and I had, as interviewers, on the spot, responded badly, seemed to miss the point, and had then (later) characterised them as deviant (with respect to Nathaniel) for confounding 'personal data' and 'science'.

So here we begin a second, different story – just as Morrison does – by re-introducing (and giving new reasonableness to) the voices of the kids.

Story 2

We (now Sohmer and Michaels) found ourselves asking what is it about what Nathaniel (the mainstream kid) does that is so compelling, that seems so 'smart', so well reasoned, so scientific, even when we know he's completely missed the mark with respect to the actual scientific facts? What's scientific or 'mainstream' about it?

That Nathaniel 'sounds' scientific we aren't challenging. Moreover, he sounds as if he is genuinely attempting to explain (and understand) a complex phenomenon. This is immediately recognised by any reader of his transcripts who is adept in the ways of schools. What is not so obvious is that he has absolutely no basis in the material world for any of his claims, for any of the facts he musters. His causal claims are all extraordinarily counter-intuitive, contrary to everything he sees, feels, does in his daily life, and he is not the least bit bothered by it. He doesn't even notice this fact – and neither did Chip and I as interviewers or discourse analysts, and neither did any of the readers of the transcripts over all these years. This is all the more interesting because Christopher, Jennifer, and Teresa – the non-scientific-sounding ones – noticed and were bothered by it. They struggled with it, seriously, even doggedly. They noticed that a lot of what they were taught as explanations of this phenomenon just did not square with reality, and refused to ignore it – and in this sense were far more engaged with what we might think of scientific explanation (if it doesn't make sense, square with evidence, don't ignore it). Ironically, this sincere effort to make sense out of their phenomenal experience, the evidence in front of their eyes, so to speak, was, in each and every case in the interview, held against them as an instance of 'off the mark' or magical reasoning. A few examples:

Teresa talks fluently about what she has gleaned from the textbook. (At times, it almost sounds as if she is reading from the textbook.) When asked about the way the earth turns, she says in a teacherly tone of voice, 'Well, we know that it has an imaginary line in the middle called the equator and a line through the middle that spins around called an axis. And it spins about every 24 hours, but we can't feel it. (pause) I guess it's because of gravity.' She then talks about the earth's axis – which she defines as a pole that helps the earth turn around on it saying, 'it's imaginary just like the equator line. You can't see them but they're there.' In answer to a follow-up question about the tilt, she says, 'The axis is tilting, it's tilting this way, and – I think it's this way – and the earth turns. (pause) No it's this way, [she motions with her hands in the opposite direction] I think I saw it in a book this way. It turns around on its axis, but it's tilted.' Then Teresa pauses, and with an impish, just-between-you-and-me kind of grin says, 'But the earth isn't tilted, because if it was tilted, we would all be sitting like this [tilts her torso over] or something, so it's not really tilted.' And then in utter seriousness, she says, 'The earth isn't tilted, but the pole is and you can't see it.' Here

281

science and the real world are reconciled – scientific facts assume the status of real but 'imaginary'. (This is consistent with the textbook's stress on the imaginary status of the axis, poles and equator.) Interestingly, this excerpt of Teresa's reasoning was written about in a 1988 paper as evidence of her 'non-scientific' mode, of her ability to move between discourse worlds – the scientific and the folksy. But in paying attention to her reality, the fact that she was upright and not tilted over, Teresa was aligning herself (with misplaced faith) in an enterprise that values rigorous sense-making that accommodates and accords with material evidence.

Jennifer, too, struggles to make sense out of counter-intuitive evidence and school-based facts. At some point in the interview Chip asks Jennifer, 'Is the sun moving or the earth moving?' She says, 'The sun's moving.' Chip prompts her for a model, saying, 'Is it – how does it do? Does it just go – can you show me what . . .' Jennifer says:

1 *J:* No // The earth is moving // [the earth's moving?] Because when
   you look up / the / clouds are moving / but the / globe isn't moving
   // But – but – / (pause) but the earth is moving / but we can't – /
   but we're not moving with the earth //
5 *S:* We can't feel it? //
   J: But it's just up there that's moving but we're not / we're not (. .)
   moving //
   S: So the earth's not moving but – but stuff is moving around it?//
   J: Uh huh / like when you / when you get like / when you / when
10 you're / like – playin' somethin' / and you / always spins yourselves
   around / try and run / like / it's like / it's like / like / you're – you're
   goin' around / it seems like / you're goin around / like in a circle//

Jennifer here is grappling with the difficult question of whether the earth or the sun moves. While we're not totally confident that we fully understand her reasoning here, we think she is making the connection of seeming, but non-actual, movement of the earth (earth moves – that's what we've been told, but it really doesn't, we don't actually move, it just seems to because the clouds 'up there' move). The analogy (in lines 9–12), relates the experience we've all had of spinning around and then stopping and feeling like everything around you is spinning – when it's actually not. Here the analogy serves not to model the phenomenon in question (the movement of the earth) but to call up a familiar everyday experience that mirrors, evokes (or perhaps one could say models) seeming but non-actual movement. The analogy is not in the service of an explanation of how the earth moves, but in the service of calling to mind a familiar sensation of knowing or feeling something that is counter intuitive.

Analogical processes – A:B as C:D – are considered a rich source of factual and conceptual information for learning about scientific phenomena

(Gentner 1983; Vosniadou and Ortony 1989). Here our initial impression was that this poor kid was reasoning magically, was off the topic, or simply illogical and incoherent. In fact, this transcript was initially set aside as 'unusable' because Michaels couldn't make head or tail of her discourse and couldn't see the point of displaying unanalysed or possibly un-analysable reasoning. Now we view it as an inability (deficit) on the part of Michaels and Chip Bruce as interviewers, and later as analysts, to see and collaboratively clarify and extend her quite cogent attempts to grapple with a complex phenomenon – how you can say something moves when you have no sensation of it. Only after a shift in our framing of what counts as valid, respectable intellectual work in these transcripts, does it become clear that there is logic in the use of analogy by this child, that the issue she was dealing with was legitimately 'scientific' – we want to argue she was engaged in the intellectual practice of making her deflated, globe-like representation of the world spinning and her phenomenal experience square with one another.

At an earlier part of the interview with Jennifer, she's asked:

```
 1   C:  Tell me, do you know why the sun rises and sets?//
     J:  (softly) No.//
     S:  Do you know what's happening?// What makes it / happen?//
         Show us with your hands what you think happens with the – with the
 5       earth and the sun //
     J:  Well I know something about the equator // [uh huh] When-when
         – like / when you see it on the globe / you can just pick the globe
         up / it doesn't mean that you're gonna pick the whole world up //
         [uh huh] Not like I'm flying //
10   S:  Not like the what? //
     J:  It's not like I'm flying //
     C:  Not like she's flying //
     J:  Like when / someone picks you up you're not flying // [uh huh]
         So-so when someone picks the globe up / the other side of the
15       globe's not flying // So when you're out the globe / you're not
         flying / 'cause someone picks the globe up //
     S:  (pause) Uh huh (pause) Now show – show me again // I want – I
         still want to know more about what makes the sun / what you think
         is happening when the sun / rises and sets? // Pretend one (. . .)
20   C:  What's – what's moving? // Is the sun moving? / or the earth
         moving or? –
```

The striking thing here is that Jennifer's talk about the globe is in the service of explaining or demonstrating to us how to understand the equator – a term she feels she really knows something about. Again the issue is how to understand the realness of something imaginary, something that is representational of something real, but not the thing itself. And so the globe is used as an analogy to the line on the globe – it's there (and real as a representational tool) but not itself the real thing. The other notable feature of this exchange is that Michaels and Bruce simply don't know how to respond. They hem and haw and as quickly as they can get their bearings, redirect her back to their original question. Her story has not in any way penetrated, challenged, or intermingled with theirs.

Later, Chip asks Jennifer about terms like axis, and again, the equator comes up.

1   C: How about the equator?
      J: Yeah // Equator // I know all about the equator // Equator is
            a-a- line / around the globe / um but / it's not / it's an ordinary
            line but it's around the globe and it's a dotted line / um – when it
            / like it's only on a globe / but when it's on earth then you can't
            see it / 'cause it's / it's like it's splitted up//

What we see in the transcript is the struggle to differentiate and reconcile the representation with the thing represented, and, again, Michaels and Bruce fail to recognise (on the spot, or later in their offices) the intellectual work it evidences.

Discussion

So how do we understand – from a new vantage point – what it is that 'mainstream' kids like Nathaniel are doing when they ignore or make no sense out of evidence and yet *sound* so appropriately scientific? And how do we reframe our understanding of Christopher, Jennifer, and Teresa – 'non-mainstream' kids who, though far more seriously engaged in the fundamental scientific enterprise of making sense of the phenomena, are so easily perceived as impoverished or lacking in their reasoning or in their discourse?

Simple dichotomies for characterising so-called 'scientific' and 'non-scientific' moves will not likely hold up. The practice of science is not simply a matter of excluding yourself, your experience, or your body from the explanation. Nor is science sufficiently differentiated from other coherent human activities (theology, plumbing, or stamp collecting, for example) – as some analysts engaged in thinking about gender or ethnicity in science education would have it – by the use of a bounded (as opposed to unbounded) domain and a restricted tool kit for reasoning.

Furthermore, the simple distinction between 'mainstream' and 'non-mainstream' students as disembodied or embodied reasoners will not hold up. Nathaniel uses his face as the earth in answering the interviewers' question about the relationship between proximity to the sun and length of day. Moreover, our attribution to the 'non-mainstream' students of being caught up in the use of narrative or personal evidence as opposed to inscription-like terms that deflate our experience and sensation will also not stand up to scrutiny. The so-called 'mainstream' reasoners in this group use personal experience (of days being longer in the summer and daylight savings time) as facets of their explanations. And all of the kids use scientific, deflating terms like the earth's rotation, the equator, direct and indirect rays, the earth's axis.

What is striking here is the struggle on the part of the 'non-mainstream' kids to reconcile these inscriptions with their understanding and experience in the world that these inscriptions represent. We now see these examples as intances of real-world evidence brought into contact with their inscription-like representations, rather than as 'reasoning with narratives' of personal experience. The stuff that the school delivers – in books, teacher demonstrations, and general discussion – is brought into dialogue (sometimes productive, sometimes unproductive) with their own 'on the ground' experience. With 'mainstream' reasoners on the other hand, the dialogue of science – the striving for connection between phenomena and inscription, seems largely non-existent. It is as if they merely abandon or ignore their own experience in the world in favour of others' inscriptions of it. The map is mistaken for the territory.

And this willingness or ability not to see and take seriously what's in front of you, in favour of the inscriptions, is evident as well in Michaels and Bruce's performances, both as interviewers and as analysts. They could not grasp Christopher's (or Teresa's or Jennifer's) struggle to integrate inscriptions with experiences as coherent, legitimate reasoning. In consequence, as mentioned above, they characterised these 'non-mainstream' kids' efforts as folksy, teleological, magical, or non-scientific-sounding.

We are now able to see that the struggle to square school-based inscriptions (scientific concepts) with our bodies and our experiences represents a crucial intellectual practice that mainstream reasoners – young students and academics alike – instantiate all too rarely. Notice that, in spite of our own heightened awareness of the perils of inscription-based reasoning, we have used the terms 'mainstream' and 'non-mainstream' (typically with scare quotes, or qualified by the hedge 'so-called') throughout this analysis. These terms, too, are abstractions, an attempt to capture patterns and similarities while masking (and therefore ignoring) a wide range of differentiating particulars. Hence, treating Teresa and Christopher as equivalent members of the same class may well obscure as much as it reveals. Though they are strikingly similar in the way they differ from Nathaniel, they differ from one another in important ways that play no role in this analysis. Teresa, for example, is highly school-affiliated (perhaps accounting for her willingness to 'quote' from the textbook) while

Christopher, in and out of trouble at school, has already, in fourth grade, failed and been held back twice. In a study that treated school-affiliation as an overarching category, Teresa and Nathaniel might conceivably be grouped together and their 'data' aggregated. Here one sees the importance of sustained, ethnographic study. This particular study – carried out over an entire school year – resulted in data from a variety of sources (audiotapes, videotapes, field notes, interviews). The particulars, their richness and complexity, are still available, enabling us to recover and interrogate the sources of our inscriptions.

Conclusion

What general points can we draw from this particular case, this re-analysis of children's reasoning in science? We are not claiming that inscription-based reasoning is wrong or dangerous, in and of itself. It clearly is a powerful tool for subsuming, deflating, generalising – reducing the unwieldy complexity of particular experiences into capturable, useful, and compelling abstractions. The danger is in the reification of inscriptions, forgetting how we (or others) got from the particulars to the inscriptions, and therefore no longer having access to the particulars they subsume. This danger is clear and pressing in the case of children learning science in school: Nathaniel was considered a brilliant student but he never understood how the inscriptions he spouted related to his phenomenal experience; Jennifer, in contrast, struggled to do just that and was never once recognised as a thoughtful, capable learner.

For children to learn science, not merely 'do' it well in school, they must understand how inscriptions relate to the world they represent. They must know when it makes sense to generalise, to abstract away from particulars, and when it makes sense to stay close to the specific case. But 'knowing how' and 'knowing when' cannot be conveyed or learned by explicit rule. In Polanyi's framing, it is fundamentally tacit knowledge (Polanyi 1962), and can be learned only by acquiring the practice, being immersed and guided in situations where powerful sense-making occurs. This, of course, requires that teachers themselves understand the deflating practices and the histories of the inscriptions in a given domain; in short, it requires teachers who are themselves enculturated members of the practice – powerful sense-makers, and credible guides to sense-making in the domain. This means we have to rethink a great deal about how we organise science teaching in school and how we prepare teachers to do it well.

But what about the power of narrative as a tool for sense-making in science? We see its strength in grounding Teresa, Jennifer, and Christopher in their everyday world, in helping them use their own experience as evidence to generate theory from. We also see the way it limits Christopher when he says he hasn't been to South Carolina and therefore has no basis to think about the temperature there. Morrison's analysis of the bird as language – dead or alive – highlights the potential of frozen language to silence, mislead, or destroy meaning. She emphasises the simplifying potential of language, the potential to freeze or limit meaning-making. But, as we see with Christopher, narrative too can be frozen and act as a barrier to real understanding. It is as if in Morrison's story, the old woman's reprimand – wise sounding, widely encompassing, but pat – serves as an analogue to unexamined inscription-based reasoning.

As sociologists, psychologists, linguists, and ethnographers of schooling, we need better ways of characterising the very different potentials inherent in inscriptions and narratives to represent – in general and powerful ways – the complexities of situations. Moreover, we need to focus more explicitly on the enculturation processes and practices by which students come to speak with and through deflating representational tools, data points on graphs or runnable mental models like Nathaniel generates. At the same time we need to understand better the enculturation processes by which some students – like Christopher, Jennifer, and Teresa – learn to resist them, struggle with them. How is it that some kids come to school so ready and willing to ingest and then spit back wholly unanalysed inscriptions or representations that (at least at times) completely violate their phenomenal experience, while others aren't so easily convinced to ignore their world? To address these questions, of course, we need far better ways of characterising the intellectual practices of critiquing and unpacking the relationships between inscriptions and aspects of the world they represent. We need better ways of characterising what Christopher, Jennifer and Teresa are doing.

In spite of the unanswered questions raised, this re-analysis leads us to a tentative set of practical suggestions. In both the practices of schooling and in research on children in schools, we ought to explore more fully the power of situated exemplars, telling cases, what Bruner and other curriculum theorists describe as 'post-holing', sustained investigations of a complex domain where one has access to both particulars and the generalisations that grow out of them. This notion fits well with current work on category formation and mental models, suggesting we learn best when material is neither too diffuse with particulars nor too abstract. In Shore's recent book *Culture in Mind* (Shore 1996), he notes the shift, initiated by Eleanor Rosch's work in the 1970s, from the classical model of concept formation to the role of 'prototype effects' as manifested in exemplars, best cases, metonymy, typicality, and basic-level categories. Basic-level categories tend to be at a level of specificity intermediate between global inclusiveness and perceptual particularity. Basic-level categorisation employs part-to-whole associations (synecdoche). They serve as exemplar models for the identification of related objects, both more general and more specific (Shore 1996, p. 64).

This is in line with the call for a pedagogy of Multiliteracies that emphasises Situated Practice (rich immersion in the particulars of a practice), supplemented by Overt Instruction, focusing, and in particular Critical Framing on the part of the teacher – in guiding students to make sense out of the particulars as instances of more general phenomena. While there is a great deal of research and discussion about Situated Practice and Overt Instruction, we have few specific examples of Critical Framing as a pedagogical strategy. This is an area that warrants systematic investigation and the development of some 'telling cases' – as demonstrations and sites for analysis. It may well be that the explicit focusing and Critical Framing of Situated Practice is precisely what will make it possible for students – mainstream and non-mainstream alike – to hold in view the relationship between the particular and the general in a single, embodied case, and hence to see the situated interplay of narrative and inscription-based tools.

Part V

MULTILITERACIES IN PRACTICE

INTRODUCTION

Part V describes a number of initial engagements with the Multiliteracies ideas in curriculum practice.

Chapters 14 and 15 describe two very different higher education examples from South Africa. In Chapter 14, Denise Newfield and Pippa Stein describe a year-long engagement with the Multiliteracies framework involving twenty-four Masters in English Education students at the University of the Witwatersrand. These students are, in effect, writing back from a location in the developing world about a series of half-realised ideas and aspirations ignited by the notion of Multiliteracies.

David Bond discusses the engagement of his Associate in Management students at the University of Cape Town in Chapter 15. The students consist of people in workplaces who have not had formal management qualifications. They have entered the course because they have been historically disadvantaged, and missed out on formal management education and training. He describes a module on negotiation: Situated Practice includes role plays of real-life negotiations; Overt Instruction involves the discussion of various negotiation models or frameworks; Critical Framing allows students to examine the military and confrontational metaphors used in negotiation; and Transformed Practice takes the students back to the real-life negotiations in their own work experience.

Courtney Cazden closes the book in Chapter 16 by describing four curriculum experiments, all of which involve negotiating cultural differences: sharing time in two Boston classrooms; a revisiting of the Puente project which she first described in Chapter 12; the Tempe Languages High School in Sydney; and the Concentrated Language Encounters programme at Traeger Park School in Alice Springs. For her, these are all excellent cases in attempting to address the same objectives as the Multiliteracies pedagogy – to recruit previous experience, and to work in shared spaces in a way that produces productive cultural mixing. She uses the ganma metaphor from Yirrkala in north-east Arnhemland to capture the kinds of connections between Situated Practice, Overt Instruction, Critical Framing and Transformed Practice suggested in the Multiliteracies pedagogy.

14

THE MULTILITERACIES PROJECT: SOUTH AFRICAN TEACHERS RESPOND

Denise Newfield and Pippa Stein

Introduction

The present moment in South Africa is marked by profound and far-reaching change as South Africans struggle to redefine their histories and identities in the wake of the social transformations which have occurred since the first democratic elections in April 1994. The tertiary institution in which we work, the University of the Witwatersrand, is itself engaged in transformation as it strives to become more representative of South Africa's diverse communities. It is within this landscape of change that we, two English teacher-educators, first read the New London Group's article (New London Group 1996), 'A Pedagogy of Multiliteracies: Designing Social Futures' in the *Harvard Educational Review* (see also New London Group, Chapter 1 above) and decided to engage with the International Multi-literacies Project at a number of levels. First, as a pedagogic practice in our own classrooms; second, as a curriculum document for critical scrutiny and evaluation by our students, most of whom are practising teachers; and, third, as an international political project seeking divergent and multiple collaborations to make it work.

We have found the International Multiliteracies Project in many ways inspirational. We did, initially, have reservations about its top-down nature and whom it claimed to be representing. For while it had ambitiously established itself as a global project it then comprised only academics from Australia, the USA and Britain; all post-industrial societies with massive resources. However, simply to dismiss the Project as another form of neo-colonialism which we, in the developing world, were in danger of being sucked into, would have been too negative a response to a very positive initiative. Instead we have accepted the invitation to enter the public debate through this chapter, and take the opportunity to 'write back' and enlarge the potential scope of the project. In so doing, we hope to contribute to the consultative process which we believe is fundamental to democratic education, and make the project the truly international forum it has aimed to become from the outset.

This chapter is a highly contextualised account of 'local diversity' and describes how we and our twenty-four Masters in English Education students at the University of the Witwatersrand have appropriated aspects of the Project for our own uses. A major feature of it will therefore be a compilation of our students' individual responses to the relevance and applicability of the Project for their specific educational contexts, which range from under-resourced schools in remote rural villages to slick, Internet-linked suburban schools in the northern suburbs of Johannesburg.

South Africa is engaged at present in major processes of transformation from the macro levels of government and policy-making to micro levels affecting the daily lives of ordinary citizens. While it has always been a multicultural and multilingual society, new forms of multiculturalism and multilingualism are only now emerging to replace the systematic division the apartheid laws had drawn across race and language lines. In the area of education, for example, the previously seventeen education departments, which were split along the lines of race and language, have been trans-formed into one national department of education. There used to be two official languages which all children had to learn at school – English and Afrikaans. Now there are eleven official languages and an official multi-lingual language policy for schools in the Gauteng region in which we work. In terms of curriculum design and innovation, a new pedagogy aiming at equity, access and looking towards future employment and empowerment is official policy.

South Africa's media policy has likewise shifted, allowing for the diversification of television channels. From one channel only alternating English and Afrikaans at the inception of television in the 1970s, there are now three public channels and attempts to represent as many South African languages and cultures as possible. These channels broadcast home-grown and imported programmes, the latter mainly American, but becoming increasingly British. Satellite television is now available – at a price – and the airwaves are being deregulated.

In spite of a sense that South Africa has joined the global media community, acknowledgement of the role of the media in society and of different modes of communication has not been made in most of our schools. The verbal modes retain primacy and exclusivity; some would argue rightly so, since ours is a country with far from universal adult literacy. For the majority of South Africans, the Internet and even com-puters are a technology reserved only for the elite. South Africa is ranked fourteenth in the world when it comes to Internet usage, but 97 per cent of those who use it are from the affluent middle classes. Particular problems related to computer installation and usage are the absence of electricity or even phone lines in many areas.

The institutional context in which we work and had the opportunity to implement aspects of the Multiliteracies Project is the University of the Witwatersrand (Wits), Johannesburg, an historically white university with a history of liberalism and opposition to the apartheid government. Universities in South Africa are currently undergoing radical restructuring or 'transformation' in order to become more representative of South Africa's diverse communities and, in this regard, Wits is no exception. It is currently perceived by some academics and students as conservative, lagging behind other universities in affirmative action policies and representivity.

The Masters by Coursework in English Education was set up in 1996 as a joint initiative of three departments in order to address the changing needs of professionals working in the area of English education in a post-apartheid South Africa. This includes primary, secondary, and tertiary teachers, adult educators, English subject advisers, curriulum designers, ELT materials developers and educational publishers. In keeping with a complex view of the subject 'English', this course is interdisciplinary, drawing on teaching staff from the Departments of African Literature, Applied English Language Studies, English, Linguistics, and Education.

The course consists of a single mandatory core module within an otherwise optional modular structure. The aim of the core module is to explore 'cutting-edge' conceptual, political and pedagogical issues relating to the teaching of English as literature, language, and media from a local and global perspective. In contrast with existing postgraduate courses in southern African universities, the course experiments with different pedagogical models, modes of assessment and content.

This, then, is the sociohistorical and institutional context in which we read 'A Pedagogy of Multiliteracies: Designing Social Futures' (see New London Group, Chapter 1 above). What immediately attracted our interest was the highly contemporary, proactive nature of the document. The focus on 'designing social futures' converged with our own personal and political aims as English teacher-educators in South Africa. The pedagogical framework of Situated Practice, Overt Instruction, Critical Framing and Transformed Practice appeared to theorise some of our own pedagogic practices and beliefs. The emphasis on diversity, difference and change as a natural condition of living in the postmodern world mirrored our own experiences of social transformation. The concept of 'Multiliteracies' appealed to us as well as it is highly political in its challenge to the mono-lithic, autonomous model of literacy which currently dominates in schools and development agencies in South Africa. 'Multiliteracies' captures and validates the diversity of people's literacies in specific sites and has a flexibility which seeks to include rather than marginalise. In our teaching we have interpreted Multiliteracies in a broad sense to include techno-logical forms of communication as well as the literacies, mainly orally based, of communities in South Africa who have not had access to print-based or screen-based technologies. For us, the value of the document lies in its dual acknowledgement of Multiliteracies as the paradigm for social and cultural understandings and knowledges, and for multimodal and technologically based forms of communication available today.

We implemented the Multiliteracies Project in two ways; both as a pedagogic practice within sections of the Masters course and as a curriculum document for critical evaluation by our students on the Masters course. So although the focus of this chapter is on how we used the Multiliteracies Project as a curriculum document for critical evaluation by our students, we also want to describe briefly some of the ways in which we interpreted the pedagogical framework and basic principles of Design in our own teaching practices in order to provide an idea of other forms of our implementation of the Project.

Using the proposition that curriculum is 'a design for social futures' (see Cope and Kalantzis, Chapter 10 above), we implemented aspects of the Project within sections of the Masters course, where it usefully furnished key conceptual principles for both structure and pedagogic practice. In the module *Theory, Evaluation and Development of Teaching Materials*, the concept of exposing learners to multiple discourses and multiple Englishes through classroom-based materials which draw on their diverse representational resources (the visual, the performative, the written, the oral, the behavioural, the gestural) is an explicit course aim. One student began work on a multi-media CD-ROM aimed at developing children's environmental awareness in under-resourced rural communities. Another student devised a workbook on oral storytelling practices for Tsonga-speaking children, where students had to compare and contrast different English translations of a well-known Tsonga oral narrative.

The module *Visual Literacy and the Role of Media in English Education* aimed at exploring aspects of multimodality and media education especially in relation to the visual mode. The 'production assignment' required students to produce media materials or programmes with a prominent visual component, for the purposes of English education. Two students used video as an investigative medium in relation to 'rave' culture, while a group of three devised a slide-tape programme with authentic music to introduce South African students to the novel *The African Child* by Camara Laye of Guinea. A secondary school teacher got his class to portray Shakespeare's *A Midsummer Night's Dream* as a photostory in which they were actors and photographers.

In both modules, we paid particular attention to the concepts of Situated Practice and Critical Framing, constantly encouraging students to engage with their own classroom contexts and practices in a critically reflective way, taking into account the sociohistorical and ideological context in which they were working.

As the New London Group's 1996 article was one of the recommended readings for the core module section on language education, a small group of students summarised the article for oral presentation in class, and one student demonstrated how she was using the pedagogical framework to teach engineering students report-writing. Our own interest in investigating students' responses to the Project in a more systematic way developed only towards the end of the course.

The research process was qualitative in design and evolved over one year. It involved three forms of data collection: written responses from twenty-four students; videotaped interviews with six of the twenty-four students; and audiotaped oral interviews with two students. As will be evident in the following account, the dialogic and organic nature of the research process was central to capturing a range of diverse, complex and sometimes contradictory positions on the Project.

For the written responses, students were given the NLG article to read one week prior to the examination. In the examination they had one and a half hours in which to answer the following question:

> This article represents a statement of general principle. It is highly provisional, and something we offer as a basis for public debate . . . We want to stress that this is an open-ended process – tentative, exploratory, and welcoming of multiple and divergent collaborations. And, above all, our aim is to make some sort of difference for real children in real classrooms (New London Group 1996, p. 96)

> Provide a critical response to the International Multiliteracies Project in which you evaluate the relevance and applicability of the Project to English Education in the South/Southern African context (or to a particular educational site or sites within southern Africa).

> NB: (i) Your response should be located within an educational site or sites that you are familar with.

> (ii) Focus on one or a few ideas that are important to you and evaluate them carefully. It is imposssible to respond to more in the time available.

Before the students answered this question, they were aware of the very real possibility that their answers would be submitted to the New London Group. This crossing of the line between the genre of examination script, which is usually a discrete and confidential textual form, written for one reader, and locked away from the author for ever, and a written submission to a real audience in response to an invitation gave the written task an authenticity and immediacy which was reflected in the carefully considered nature of their responses. All twenty-four students took seriously the opportunity to engage in a critical dialogue with the New London Group about the relevance of the Project to their specific contexts, and this exercise was, we believe, a good example of Critical Framing in relation to Situated Practice.

The second phase of our implementation involved a modal and generic shift from a formal, written critical evaluation to a one-and-a-half minute video interview. We wanted to situate our students visually in their institutional contexts: 'Multiliteracies' implied giving our students more than one mode in which to respond, as well as challenging us to present the research through a range of media. We considered, for example, using photographic slides, as an inexpensive means of documenting the sites where our students worked, and which could be used as data to contextualise visually their written responses. However, we chose the medium of video on account of its capacity to capture both background and speech, contextualised and communicatively complex in its presentation of the place, manner, and author of the utterance, visually and verbally. The video would give voice literally to members of the student group in their places of work.

We edited in camera to reduce our own inevitable mediation and to aim for a documentary quality. In shooting at each site, we followed the conventional filmic structure of wide to mid to close shot, that is from the general to the specific. We wanted an establishing shot to capture the locales, for example, Soweto seen from the Teacher Training College, what the Farm School looked like; then a bridging shot, for example, of the teacher in her or his classroom, or arriving at the school, followed by a close-up shot of the person talking about the context and responding to the Multiliteracies Project. In terms of our generic choice, voice-over narration would have been counter-productive, so narrative linkage had to be achieved visually. As our interviewees worked in places geographically distant, culturally dissimilar, and disparate in terms of resources, although all within the Gauteng region, we tried to convey visually a sense of the literal and metaphoric journey we were undertaking. For example, we 'shot' Wilhelm Van Rensburg entering his office which was decorated with a large poster of Mandela next to a poster of Elizabeth I; we 'shot' a stream of smart cars driving up the road outside Micheal Goodman's school in Parktown, an upmarket business centre of Johannesburg, to contrast with Sean O'Connor arriving for work in his bakkie (a four-wheel-drive open truck) at the farm school. At Werner Paetzold's school in the once right-wing Afrikaner stronghold of Boksburg, we 'shot' a semiotically rich bridging sequence of a young blond boy raising South Africa's new flag.

As only a selection of the twenty-four members of the class were filmed, we held a viewing of the ten-minute video for the class as a whole, in which students were invited to respond to the video text. This was followed by further oral discussion on the video text, in a smaller group, which was recorded on audiotape. All in all, over a period of one year, these inter-textual dialogues gained their own momentum and cumulatively provided a rich, heteroglossic response to issues within the Multiliteracies Project from a highly specific context.

The video was shown and our students' responses presented to the Domains of Literacy Conference at the Institute of Education, London in September 1996. A copy of the video has been used in Australia, where the South African responses have themselves engendered further responses.

The data

Analysis of trends: general overview

What follows is an overview of the recurrent themes and ideas that emerged from the three sets of data collected: the written texts, the videotape interviews, and the conversations recorded on audiotape. Convergences and disagreements from the written data were recorded manually, and tested against the video interviews and audio recording of the oral conver-sations. The general overview of trends is followed by a selection of individual student's responses in order to provide a more in-depth record and to let their voices be heard.

In analysing the general trends in the data, we are fully aware of the problems revolving around the status of the written texts as examination scripts and our multiple roles as teachers, assessors and researchers. This may have impacted on the students' responses in certain ways. Similarly, because of the implicit power relations between institutions, students and teachers, our students were not in a position to refuse to answer the examination question or ignore the call to enter the dialogue on the Multiliteracies Project.

This being said, the overall response to the Multiliteracies Project in all three forms of data was highly positive and a clear sense of engagement with the document emerged in every case. Not one respondent rejected the document's relevance and applicability to southern Africa at the present time. On the contrary, in spite of serious misgivings about aspects of the document, every student responded positively to the Project's explicit call for curricular change, and to the document's positioning of itself as a vehicle of change. The document seemed to speak directly to the students' sense of urgency regarding 'transformation' within the tertiary institution where they were registered as students and within the institutions in which they were working or had worked. The need for change came through loud and clear – with regard to the changed and changing classrooms, especially in relation to racial and cultural difference; or, to the necessity for curricular and pedagogic change; or, to the importance of broadening the existing notion of literacy to enable children and adults to be educated in such a way as to prepare them for the present and the future. Hyreath Lodge sums this up by saying that the document is 'appropriate to the historical moment'. Magauta Mphahalele's and Desiree Raichlin's written responses serve as typical examples of what most respondees found laudable in the Project:

> The Multiliteracies Project is innovative and dynamic and tries to deal with issues that face English teachers all over the world.
>
> (Magauta Mphahlele: written text)

> I am a lecturer at Boston City Campus in the fields of English Education and Business Communication and the Multiliteracies Project article really spoke volumes to me. First of all, when it stated that its intention was 'to spark ideas for possible new research areas,' and that it might help 'frame curriculum experimentation that attempts to come to grips with our changing educational environment,' it reinforced my belief that external curriculum is a highly indeterminate animal and that the issue for curriculum theory in South Africa becomes one of providing an orderly, coherent set of experiences, each of which is flexible enough to provide the appropriate challenge and support to students whose knowledges, skills, socio-economic and political 'lifeworlds' may differ widely from one another.
>
> (Desiree Raichlin: written text)

Students found the Project 'exciting' (Magauta Mphahlele), 'a great project' (Pia Lamberti), and as expressive of a 'necessary utopianism' (Sean O'Connor). They felt it encouraged both experimentation and critical reflection; validated Howard Gardner's concept of multiple intelligences (Werner Paetzold); and was a fundamentally democratic, antiracist and socially responsible document (Anthony Johnson). A number of pedagogic strategies and aims in the document were found to be useful, such as Overt Instruction and 'scaffolding' (Wilhelm van Rensburg and Arlene Archer), and the offer of a variety of literacies and technologies within the English curriculum. Also positively viewed were the potential for introducing a broader and more inclusive canon that would incorporate popular culture, and the impetus given to Redesigning and Transformed Practice.

However, the data as a whole did not reveal an easy and uncritical acceptance of ideas in the document. Situated critique was a strong feature of the responses. A number of respondees found the document to be utopian, in its negative sense, for a range of reasons. Foremost among these were reservations about implementation, particularly in terms of human and material resources. Thandiwe Mkhabela and David Duma were concerned about the feasibility of retraining teachers that a Multiliteracies pedagogy would necessitate, especially in relation to knowledge about and skills in non-verbal modes. Sean O'Connor believed that unless social and economic problems are sorted out first in areas such as the peri-urban/semi-rural one in which his school is situated, implementing a Multiliteracies pedagogy would be futile. Others point to the difficulties in attempting to implement change through a democratic process in schools:

> It's very banal . . . There are a lot of committees going on in the country at the moment stressing openness, transparency and including all the stakeholders. What happens when they try to transform the syllabus or learning programs and the way in which subjects are divided up is that it becomes a slow and bureaucratic process which can be a bit disillusioning.
>
> (Ruth Nicola: oral interview)

A number of students express concern about the tensions between access to power through the dominant language/s and discourse/s and validation of marginalised cultures and languages (Catherine Beaton, Barbara Baloyi, Magauta Mphahlele). Sean O'Connor took issue with the document's tendency to universalise economic paradigms and workplace relations in post-industrial, complex societies:

> The South African workplace is the site of furious dialectical struggle between management and labour, which in one sense disqualifies the formation of 'flattened hierarchies' which are allegedly a feature of 'fast capitalism'. Indeed, our non-unionised workplace contexts are characterised by neo-feudal relations, made possible largely by the value of labour and the legacy of apartheid. There are elements of post-Fordist organisation in our economy but they are few and difficult to target.
>
> (Sean O'Connor: written text)

Some students were concerned about the thin dividing line between Overt Instruction and 'prescriptive authoritarianism'. Others were concerned about representivity and issues of power in relation to the Project, asking whether the project can truly be deemed international, and whether the Project, in spite of itself, does not serve further to privilege English and reinforce European conceptions of knowledge and culture. Anthony Johnson was amongst those who pointed to a possible conflict between the 'flattened hierarchies' of the document and the hierarchical demarcations, say, between father and son or teacher and pupil that are a common feature of African communities.

I'm interested in how this Project integrates into all sorts of cultures. If you read it carefully, the teacher is almost powerless in the classroom situation. Some quarters respect this type of division between the teachers and the students but it is not going to fit in properly into some cultures where there are demarcations – father and son, a teacher and a pupil . . . once you collapse the boundaries it's going to affect some aspects of the cultures – now pupils are no more respecting teachers . . .

(Anthony Johnson: oral interview)

A few students are particularly concerned with accepting a simplistic view of multiculturalism:

We cannot rely on the multiculturalists to protect and further the interest of black South Africans in particular. Teachers should challenge the English versions of democracy. Education produces not only knowledge but political subjects. The failure by educators to critically examine the implicit acceptance of middle class and white values has served to perpetuate the status quo in South Africa.

(Barbara Baloyi, written response)

A number of students point to the omission in the document of adequate discussion on the place of literature and on the role of assessment, and to a seemingly exclusive focus on education for children when education for adults is a huge concern for developing countries (Deborah Hunt).

The way in which the students responded to the document and the range of comments it elicited indicate a level of engagement with issues that interested them. It is clear that they did not respond to all sections of the document. They have indicated areas of consonance and estrangement between themselves and the document, and issued challenges to the Project for it to take up and consider.

Individual voices: the students respond

We have already indicated the multimodal levels at which students were engaged in responding to the Multiliteracies Project. In this section, we quote the students' written, audio and video texts in a more extended way, without commentary from us. The constraints placed on us by having only the written medium to work with in order to convey the vividness, complexity and essentially dialogic nature of the videotaped and audiotaped interviews are enormous. What we have decided upon, then, is to try to give you some sense of these intertextual dialogues by juxtaposing extracts from the videotext with sections of the audiotext. We have transcribed these texts verbatim, as we also wish to highlight the generic and modality differences in the textual forms which students produced. These are followed by the students' written responses, some of which are quoted at length to give a fuller sense of the structure of their critiques.

Extract from video text. Interviewee: Wilhelm Janse van Rensburg. Wilhelm says about himself, 'I am a detribalised, white Afrikaner who grew up on a farm but changed all of that for the big city. I switched from studying at a conservative Afrikaans-medium university to do all my post-graduate studies at English-medium, liberal and revisionist universities. I am an English teacher-educator.'
    Extract from Wilhelm's interview:

> I teach at the Soweto College of Education, a pre-service teacher-training institution . . . our students are mainly second or third language speakers of English and I think Overt Instruction is important for them . . . the idea of scaffolding activities so that they get acquainted with the language and can use the language fluently . . . I think it's also important that they are being increasingly called upon to teach in previously white schools in South Africa and we need to prepare them to teach in new cultural settings . . . I think there are two problems with the Multiliteracies Project . . . the first one is literature . . . the project itself mentions the fact that one should steer clear of the English canon but nothing more . . . and I think if one does want to give access to the dominant discourse it is important to give them a sense of the English canon . . . second the project itself mentions evaluation should be done in a developmental way but nothing more than that and I think more attention could be given to that.

Extract from video text. Interviewee: Magauta Mphahlele. Magauta says about herself, 'I'm a black woman from a so-called disadvantaged home, teaching in a predominantly white university. Perceptions are that I am privileged to be in that position. For me the word "privileged" is problematic – it means I am one of a few elites, but for me, my languages, my meanings and my voice are just that – mine.'

> One of the things that I think alienates black students from so-called white universities is the issue of language because they are torn between the need to acquire English and at the same time the need to feel that their languages, their cultures, are being acknowledged and the problem is although in a multicultural classroom other languages will be included I think that will always be tokenistic because at the end the students have to be assessed in the dominant language and within the dominant discourse.

Extract from audiotape. Setting: Seminar Room, Wits University. Context: Two students, Anthony Johnson (AJ) and Ruth Nicola (RN) have just watched the videotape and are being interviewed by Pippa Stein (PS) on their response to the tape.

Anthony Johnson is a secondary school teacher from Ghana, has lived in Swaziland and is a currently studying in South Africa. He is a published writer and oral poet. He says of himself, 'I love to teach in multilingual and multicultural classrooms where the English language is spoken from many tongues and in different tones but with one meaning – communication!'

Ruth Nicola has taught English in Israel and now teaches in a media centre in a primary school in Johannesburg. She says, 'I have taught English at various levels to second language speakers. I am interested in the way young children from diverse backgrounds use language/s with their peers.'

PS: Anthony, do you want to respond to any points that were made on the video . . .

AJ: Ya, the first point made about the canon –

PS: Talk about the canon . . .

AJ: Ya, the canon has been sort of contested so much . . . it's a sort of very paradoxical issue in the sense that if you are learning a language there must be some particular set of works which in fact you draw on, in every language not necessarily in English . . . it should be there as a beacon or a guidance . . . but at the same time I use the word paradoxical in the sense that at the same time we should also give recognition to emerging sort of writings . . .

PS: Do you think . . . do you accept the idea that there are some works of literature that are better than others?

AJ: I wouldn't say . . . use . . . the word better –

PS: What word would you use?

AJ: (laughs) I would use the word . . . that they are older . . . and something like examples . . . they have set a pace – they are pace-setters . . . because what I am saying is that for a language or a literature it must have some sort of history . . . we must start from a point and starting from that point we normally draw on those canons . . . the only thing we don't have to say is that they are better . . . we just have to say, 'They came first. This is how they did it and this is how we are doing it now . . . Are we different from them or the same?' . . . if you are acquiring knowledge you must have some sort of a map so drawing on the canon is like drawing a map . . .

PS: Well I suppose questions of value are implicit in that . . . Ruth do you want to respond to something from the video which struck you?

RN: Yes well let's talk about Wilhelm's point . . . I think he was referring both to the literary canon and to the use of language itself . . . standard language . . . and I think both aspects apply here . . . that we do have to give students access to the dominant discourse . . . in terms of questions of value I think a work of art may be better than another but not on the basis of being colonial or not from mother England . . .

PS: It seems to me one of the central questions – in relation to Multi-literacies and multiculturalism is around providing access . . . it goes to the heart of what Magauta is saying on the video about tokenism . . . how do you manage to get a balance or redefine the relationship between the dominant or so-called marginalised which you are trying to make emergent or dominant . . . are there just inherent contradictions?

AJ: I think that what is going to happen is that there's going to be some kind of osmosis . . . English drawing on other South African languages and other languages drawing on English . . . in some years to come a sort of emergent language will come out . . . from my experience with some of the West Afrcian languages there are some words in English you cannot avoid . . . it has become part of the language what's called Ghanaian English . . . it's a matter of languages being very flexible and absorbing from each other . . .

RN: English is a natural *lingua franca* and we should exploit it for that . . . I personally get enjoyment out of so called colonial literature which is really English literature from other countries . . . I get pleasure out of the fact that those writers learnt beautiful English and have a wider audience as a result . . . So I agree we need to keep that access, finding a balance is difficult . . .

PS: The Multiliteracies Project is written up in English . . . for an English-speaking audience . . . it seems to privilege English as a language . . . I wonder about the cultural politics of this, surely the Project is a project for all languages . . .

AJ: If people from developing countries had been brought in from the beginning, this might have been sorted out . . . but these questions can still be addressed . . .

Written text. Author: Barbara Baloyi. Barbara Baloyi speaks five African languages and works in English teacher development in rural schools where children speak English as a second or third language. Barbara is particularly keen to bring media education to these remote, under-resourced and marginalised schools.

So far, the education system in South Africa has managed to privilege English and speakers of English . . . even worse, it has privileged European conceptions of knowledge and cultures at the expense of indigenous cultures in the country. The experience of the European child has been validated in the school classroom and curriculum. This view of English learning as natural, neutral and beneficial seems to prevail amongst English teachers. There is even among black pupils, parents and academics in South Africa a self-satisfied assumption that English is good and can serve as a unifying tool to the diversity and multicultural nature of this country. English teachers have on their hands an enormous task of contesting the ways in which the English language is directly and indirectly imposed onto the lives of the many people who do not share this language as their first language and whose future is determined by the ability to understand or not understand English.

Extract 2 from video text. Interviewee: Micheal Goodman. Micheal Goodman is a deputy principal of Grantley College, a private, independent secondary school in Johannesburg which caters for children with learning difficulties. He says of himself, 'I am an openly gay teacher. I find therefore the Multiliteracies Project's need for an explicit pedagogy compatible with my world view. This allows me to hold with the Project despite my criticisms of it.'

I thought the Multiliteracies Project offered a great deal to our school in terms of offering our students access to a variety of literacies that they wouldn't have been exposed to previously . . . my reservations came however in terms of teachers' needs for such a project . . . the context I work in the teachers tend to be quite conservative and it concerns me that they would need to be re-educated and re-trained in those areas . . . of more concern was the idea that some of the designs require really specific knowledge or skills, for example, visual design. I have absolutely no competence in this, whereas the art teacher does, so a way around that would perhaps be to go towards a language across the curriculum option but that means restructuring our schools, reconsidering policy changes and issues in those sorts of areas.

Written response. Author: David Kaplan. David Kaplan is a secondary school teacher of English and Afrikaans at a Jewish community school in Johannesburg. He is extremely interested in the theoretical and practical ways in which English teaching is changing.

I teach at King David High School in Linksfield and many parents and pupils share the belief that there is no hope (for South Africa). I do not. I feel that we are facing challenges which are exciting and worthwhile. We have to move away from old established beliefs to create a country where all have equal opportunity and access.

English and the teaching of English can play a very important and vital role in this change.

We have a sister school, Eastbank, in Alexandra township which comes to King David once a week for lessons in various subjects. They have a debating team which compared to the King David team, is very weak. We decided to form a debating society. This theoretically was all very sound – we would impart our knowledge to the less fortunate. This led to many problems.

I discovered that the two worlds were completely different. They had nothing in common. It was useless to discuss a point because it meant completely different things to the sets of pupils. We had to come to some common ground. We knew nothing of their world and they knew nothing of our world. We decided to use the media, for I discovered that every one of the children whether from King David or Eastbank had a TV. Some of the more wealthy Eastbank children had video cameras. So I asked them to make a video of a typical day in their lives and next week we would discuss it. They did, and we found that we did have a great deal in common, their parents complained about the same things, their parents had similar aspirations for their children. The children had similar dreams and ambitions and fears.

What we had done, I think, is take an established design and re-design it. We had established a common identity from two previously thought of different identities. My experience in my classroom and with the Eastbank children has given me courage to test sacred cows, not to feel inferior, to encourage my pupils to constantly question established norms and designs. That re-designing does not necessarily mean disregarding what we have but reshaping it and allowing it to become accessible to a new generation.

Written extract. Author: Pat Hill. Pat Hill teaches language and communication on bridging courses for under-prepared engineering students at Wits University. She says, 'I find a tension between my responsibility to give access to a fairly rigid discourse and my aim to build confidence in my students.'

Engineering discourse is expressive of a discipline which regards itself as scientific, elitist and a strange mixture of the academic and practical. It is expressed in language which is concise, precise, and structured in a linear and tightly sequenced manner. It is especially frustrating for students from other cultures for whom being concise may be rude, who think in different temporal and spatial modes and who, as non-native speakers of English, may find it difficult to find the precise word. The genre of report writing is a peculiar convention with a rigid sequence and framework, minimal expression and voiceless objectivity. The students wish to master this as it is the gatekeeper to the profession.

For the first time, this year, I have explored with the students other modes of reporting in their own cultures. In their own language groups, students discussed and then reported back on such features as what was reported, who reported, how and why. They were excited and fascinated by the responses from other groups. It was found, inter alia, that events are reported through a hierarchy to the chief, mainly orally, and that community events are often reported non-verbally, for example, by flags. In one situation, when a delegate to a youth orientation is killed, his parents are told symbolically, by the pouring out of porridge. Differences were noted between rural and urban traditions, which brought in conventions of writing, so that as well as denaturalisng the very Western genre of Engineering report writing, this activity also built a bridge between it and reporting in other cultures. This was useful as a form of critical practice.

In terms of Transformed Practice ... and the practice across contexts, I find this difficult to imagine. I would hope that the variety of reports and other writing practised in the course would be capable of transfer to different branches and the confidence acquired would allow students to write for their own purposes.

Written extract. Author: Sean O'Connor. Sean is the principal of a small farm school outside Johannesburg which caters for the children of farm workers. He is interested in alternative schools and pedagogies.

I would argue that in the NLG's and other theorists' considerations of 'what students need' and hence 'what teachers must do', teachers are actually constructed or understood as capable. This is not always the case. It is all very well to encourage teachers to become 'transformative intellectuals' (Giroux's term) and urge them to locate and inhabit sufficient material conditions in order to operate efficiently, but the 'how' of this remains vague, even confusing. The terminology of 'design' related by the NLG typifies an obfuscating discourse, despite its pretensions to be helpful, especially in this context. South Africa in many contexts, (especially in township and rural schools) lacks a meaningful 'culture of learning' and by this I refer to typical problems encountered in the type of school I work in, where an average of 30 per cent of teaching staff are professionally unqualified. Attendance is sporadic, amongst staff and students. Child and alcohol abuse is common. Many of the pressing problems in our schools like gangsterism, may be alleviated, challenged or even eradicated by excellent teaching and learning, but it is unlikely. The 'professional' discourse of the NLG cannot take the other factors which bear upon this context into consideration. A shift in curricular content (accessing context) is imperative, yet such a shift should be couched in language that is itself accessible and not pungent with the discourse of power.

Written text. Author: Magauta Mphahlele (see previous biography on page 302).

South Africa needs an approach like the Multiliteracies Project but we need to question whether we have not only the resources but the teachers and students who have the capacity to implement such an ambitious project. This does not mean that South African teachers and students cannot or lack the mental capacity to deal with issues affecting their classrooms but the experience is that in schools teachers are battling with issues of coping with large student numbers and basic things like furniture. The issue of unqualified teachers and teachers' professionalism are still problems. There are still struggles and conflicts around the transformation of both schools and universities and one wonders how and where to start implementing such a project especially when sections of our community are obsessed with maintaining so called standards . . .

It is difficult to see how teachers can easily replace the old with the new especially when the new is primarily focused on challenging or changing the new status quo – which they are rapidly becoming part of. Teachers themselves are not sure of how to deal with these issues especially as most see themselves as transmitters of neutral knowledge that will serve their students well in the future.

The question of diversity is also crucial in our new democracy where because of its fragility, people are still tentative in their demands for change, or where those demands are expressed, a lot of compromises (often at the disadvantage of those advocating for change) have to be made.

Teachers in South Africa are unsure about their futures as talk about retrenchments and restructuring abound. Colleges are being closed down and resources directed elsewhere. Teachers have to make certain adjustments, for example, most have never taught in racially mixed and multilingual classrooms, some do not even speak the languages spoken by most pupils in their classrooms. Others, because of the previous government's influence on teacher education, especially black teacher education, and the top-down approach to curriculum development, cannot be said to be expert enough in their fields to be able to deal with and adequately implement the Multiliteracies project. We also live in a country where some teachers of English are not proficient enough in the language to be able to deal with the complex language involved in teaching, for example, metalanguage.

Violent eruptions in certain schools recently demonstrate that teachers are still not experienced in handling conflict that arises when students of different language and racial backgrounds come together. Teachers also carry loads from the past and need to rethink their positions when it comes to racial tolerance and acceptance. Teachers also need to redefine their roles both as teachers and citizens because some teachers have been known to resist teaching critical views of language saying that they are not politicians.

I have focused my critique on the problems within the teaching profession but this by no means implies that South Africa has no teachers who can face the challenges facing teachers here and all over the world. We have teachers in South Africa who have worked under the most taxing conditions but who have been able to do wonderful work.

Conclusion

Our year-long engagement with the Multiliteracies Project has been immensely rewarding. There was a kind of chemistry in the process that ignited half-realised ideas and aspirations, gave them form and meaning, and resulted in different modes of participation in public debate. The process of our engagement is, we believe, testimony to the Project's flexibility and potentiality which allows multiple entry points, interpretations and forms of implementation.

We would like to claim that our research process has indeed been a project in appropriating and redesigning an available design. 'Every act of meaning both appropriates Available Designs and re-creates in the Designing, thus producing new meaning as The Redesigned' (see New London Group, Chapter 1 above). This process of redesigning has paradoxically brought our own context into sharp focus, revealing clearly to us the complex and challenging space we inhabit in the transition between an apartheid past and a reconstructed future, where a relevant and useful curriculum is in the process of being invented. We believe that the Multiliteracies Project has a valuable contribution to make to that reconstruction.

We hope that the ideas generated through the research process we have described can contribute to the Project's ongoing theoretical and pedagogical development. We also hope that this act of 'writing back' from a location in the developing world assists in the diversification of the Multiliteracies Project by expanding its membership and enlarging the ambit of its debate.

15

NEGOTIATING A PEDAGOGY OF MULTILITERACIES

The communication curriculum in a
South African management
development programme

David Bond

Introduction

The main purpose of this chapter is to examine a South African course in
Management Communication through the lens of the Multiliteracies
framework. In doing this, I will be using emerging theory to review teaching
practice in a way which, I hope, will have benefit both for curriculum and
theory development.

South Africa has been experiencing dramatic developments in the past
five years, as the country seeks to establish a new economic democracy. The
backlog of apartheid, however, is immense and a national survey of the
formal education sector in 1994 found that approximately five million
people over five years of age had no education, four million had matriculation only, and 1.7 million had some form of post-matriculation education.
(The remainder had some education but did not reach matriculation.)
Furthermore, 80 per cent of Africans and 40 per cent of Whites could not
read or compute at the basic level of literacy. The total South African
population is estimated to be around forty million.

There are considerable economic and human resource consequences of
such educational failures. A University of Cape Town study of affirmative
action in the workplace found that, in 1994, among the companies it was
researching only 4.5 per cent of managers were Black and only 7 per cent
were women (Bowmaker-Falconer and Searl 1995). Interestingly, a more
recent update of the same research found that there has been a shift within
these companies towards 16 per cent of Black top managers (against a
10 per cent national average); while the percentage of women had risen by
only 1 per cent (Bowmaker-Falconer 1996).

What these examples tell us is that South Africa faces an immense challenge to make up for educational and economic backlogs and, at the same time, there are some fundamental shifts taking place in the workplace (see also Ludski 1996). The new South African government of national unity has introduced a number of measures to tackle both democratisation and redress in the workplace, whilst striving to become increasingly competitive in the global economy. Examples of this can be found in the establishment of the National Economic Development and Labour Council (NEDLAC) and the new Labour Relations Act (1995).

The Associate in Management (AIM) Program, which was used in this study, was established in 1991. Targeted at mature adults with good work experience and potential for advancement but who may previously have been 'overlooked' owing to lack of educational qualifications, or because of discrimination based on race or gender, the AIM admission criteria are stated as follows:

> Applicants must be at least 25 years old with a minimum of 5 years of work experience. AIM has no minimum educational barrier and thereby creates access to students who would usually be disadvantaged by their lack of formal tertiary education. Students are nominated on the basis of their demonstrated potential for development, and their demonstrated self-motivation.
>
> (Coombe 1996, p. 3)

The AIM curriculum is designed to deliberately exploit group work and cross-disciplinary courses to promote integrated learning and the ability to work effectively within diverse groups. AIM seeks to develop the functional skills, integrated knowledge, personal awareness and self-confidence needed to manage effectively in an environment of diversity, uncertainty and change. The ten-month intensive programme seeks to establish a very sound basis in a range of standard business and management subject areas, including financial literacy (Coombe 1996, p. 2). The courses include Business Process and Environment, Computer Skills, Economics, Financial and Management Accounting, Industrial Relations, Management Communication and Research Methods, Management and Leadership, Management of Information Systems, Management of Organisations and Human Resources, Management of Technology, Quantitative Methods, and a Workplace Research Project.

The class is characterised by very real diversity. Of the thirty-six students in 1996, there were thirteen women and twenty-three men. In terms of the old South African ethnic categories, there were twenty-one Africans, six Coloureds, three Asians and six Whites. Educational background ranges from Standard 7 (that is, nine years of formal education) to those with undergraduate degrees. Work experience is also diverse; students may have come from a range of functional areas (for example, operations or human resources); levels (for example, technicians, supervisors, junior managers); and industries (for example, mining, banking, transport, automobile manufacturing).

The nature of the AIM programme poses particular teaching challenges. The diversity of educational background makes it necessary to cater for an academic bimodality along with the unique complexity of each individual student. Drawing adults from the workplace into an intense formal educational programme requires mediation between academic and work-based learning. The formal university setting of the programme raises fundamental issues of appropriate evaluation, which is flexible enough to meet the needs of academic certification, student learning, and valuable workplace pertinence. In an AIM curriculum development workshop, some of the comments from lecturers regarding these issues included:

> At the start of the programme, there's a lack of understanding of both ordinary and discipline-specific language.

> Planning for lectures becomes difficult – not only from year to year but also from day to day.

> I've never had to negotiate my course before.

> The academic diversity creates new challenges and represents the real world.

> It forces co-operative learning at different layers of complexity.

The Multiliteracies framework has been designed to focus on the pedagogical demands of just such a situation of local diversity and global connectedness. There is, therefore, much in the challenges facing the AIM programme which matches the agenda for a pedagogy of Multiliteracies. It is this framework which I will use to focus on our teaching practice within the Management Communication course.

As it is part of the purpose of the Multiliteracies framework to develop a metalanguage (New London Group 1996, p. 77), I have borrowed freely from this language to describe the design and pedagogy of this course. In brief, its objective is to develop a critical management literacy by accessing academic literacy; developing the Multiliteracies of business and management; developing the ability to negotiate differences; and developing a metalanguage of Critical Framing.

In structure, the course consists of three main parts. The first part is concerned with access, and includes the principles of communication and learning; the fundamentals of reading and writing in academic and business contexts; and analysis and development of argument. The second part expands access to include critical engagement – negotiation; critical language awareness; recruitment and selection; as well as equity in the workplace. The third part develops the theme of productive diversity and is concerned with management and leadership in the South African context and involves a workplace research project. For the purpose of this chapter, I will focus mainly on one module of the second part; on 'negotiation', as an illustrative example of teaching design and practice related to the Multiliteracies framework.

Access and critical engagement: the negotiation module

It is possible to describe this module in terms of the pedagogical components suggested in the Multiliteracies framework, as an example of the broad teaching and learning process embedded in the design of the Management Communication course. As such, it highlights our attempts to synthesise real-world experience with new, abstract conceptualisation and Critical Framing, in ways which are relevant to Transformed Practice. It does this in the following ways:

Situated Practice
Exercises and role plays
Review of group dynamics within AIM

Overt Instruction
Definitions of 'negotiation' (metalanguage)
A model

Critical Framing
Identifying metaphors in framing

Transformed Practice
Assignment: applying a model and metalanguage to a real-life
    negotiation

Development: feedback, review, discussion, possibly more Overt
    Instruction and rewrite, learning points for next modules

---

The Situated Practice component is about the actual practice of negotiation. This brings to the surface some of the life experiences of students. Very fresh examples are available from the interpersonal negotiations which will have been taking place within the AIM learning groups. Course-specific role-play exercises (e.g. sellers and buyers of second-hand cars; writers and publishers; disputes with neighbours) help to focus on different roles in negotiation, differing types of negotiation and on the negotiation processes themselves.

The Overt Instruction component is where the facilitator has to draw out and offer the concepts and metalanguage to help interpret the designs of real-life practice. In the negotiation module, Overt Instruction is about moving from 'negotiating' to developing a metalanguage for 'talking and thinking abut negotiating'. It is here that the facilitator calls on students to step back from their experience and common-sense-level understandings in order to look at negotiation processes with more analytical eyes. Part of the Overt Instruction in this module includes close attention to the 'face-to-face behaviour' in negotiation, including the type of language used. This analytical process is fostered by the introduction and discussion of definitions of negotiation, by identifying and labelling different stages and roles and by introducing concepts which help to develop deeper understanding of negotiation processes. For example, a student's intuitive grasp of the dynamics of negotiation may be more clearly articulated, and hence expanded, with a fuller understanding of notions of power, alliances, positions, interests and alternatives within negotiation contexts (see Bond 1996). Introducing theoretical readings is an integral part of the Overt Instruction component. This process leads to the development of a model of negotiation which students then employ and test in subsequent Situated Practice exercises.

The Critical Framing section in this module is used to develop the use of metaphor as a tool for application in a number of contexts. For example, we discussed the use of metaphor in the National Economic Development and Labour Council (NEDLAC) negotiations of the new Labour Relations Act (1995). NEDLAC was established by the South African Government of National Unity to facilitate consensus-seeking discussions between representatives of government, business and organised labour. It was a forum intended to move away from the bitter conflicts of the past. Nevertheless, an analysis of the use of metaphor in the media (Bond 1996) indicated that one of the dominant metaphors was 'negotiations as war'. (Once the Rugby World Cup began, the dominant metaphor shifted to 'negotiations as rugby game'!) In other words a consensus-seeking forum was being seen by almost all participants as an adversarial conflict.

Spotlighting this use of metaphor provides a fascinating example of how participants were framing negotiation. It shows how analysis of metaphorical language can bring to the surface ideological assumptions which conflict with public policy statements. Furthermore, it provides examples of how efforts to establish new democratic structures, such as workplace forums, can be hampered by longstanding ideological positions and assumptions. By highlighting the ways in which metaphor can reveal underlying assumptions, students develop a critical analytical tool which they can use in diverse contexts. Highlighting the ways in which metaphors 'frame' the way we 'see' things also opens up conversations about the use of metaphor to identify, create and contrast multiple perspectives of organisations, workplace activities and the AIM programme itself (Morgan 1986; MachLachlan and Reid 1994).

The 1996 students evaluated this module highly, commenting on various aspects which relate to pedagogical elements of the Multiliteracies framework. For example, one singled out the Situated Practice, saying, 'I really enjoyed the practical side of learning negotiation and feel I benefited much more than a straightforward lecture'. Another spoke of Transformed Practice, saying, 'I particularly enjoyed the negotiation course as I found it to be work-relevant and relevant to everyday activities'. Whereas a third implicitly drew on Critical Framing to comment on ideological features in the negotiation discourse by saying, 'Thanks for exposure to the "macho" world of negotiation; now I am ready to take on the world!'

In the 1997 class, I asked the students to transfer the discussion of metaphors of negotiation to images of their current AIM working groups and the AIM programme as a whole. The results were interesting:

Images of working groups
Group 1: slowly but surely – one small step for each of us will lead to
   one giant step for AIM
Group 2: 'Simunye' – we are one
Group 3: Time is money
Group 4: A journey of a hundred miles begins with one step . . .
Group 5: Hawkeye Group 5 – looking for opportunities
Group 6: The sky's the limit – in thy light, 6 shall see the light.

Images of AIM
AIM: Standing on an abyss;

- There is light at the end of the tunnel (chosen by two groups)
- AIM is one of the doors to paradise
- Never taking things lying down
- Success awaits the AIM highway.

The images from this brief, simple exercise open up a range of possibilities for discussing differing and critical perspectives. For example, there are overlapping focuses on unity in groups and being on a journey of transition or access. This raises crucial issues of creating unity with diversity and the chance to critique differing notions of access. There are also starkly differing emphases on the daily demands of the present learning process and the foreseen, long-term benefits. In addition, there are interesting examples of intertextual and multicultural overlaps between, for example, biblical discourse, the 'American dream', Aesop's fables and indigenous South African culture. Not all of these issues had been taken up in classroom discussion at the time of writing, but they have provided a resource and basis for follow-on discussion later in the course, particularly in the Critical Language Awareness modules and the Career Development Workshops.

Nevertheless, the classroom discussion did expose a number of other images which groups had considered before singling out one for presentation. One novel image was: AIM is a desert where the students are flowers. This led on to a useful discussion in which students were able to highlight that many were struggling to blossom when workloads resulted in lack of sleep. The image also entailed that lecturers were cacti. In defence of lecturers, I pointed out that, although cacti have nasty thorns, they are also essential sources of moisture in arid conditions. I am not sure that all the students were convinced by my attempts to transform their metaphorical image.

Deliberate attempts to foster and test Transformed Practice are an essential component of a critical pedagogical framework. In the negotiation module of the Management Communication course this component of pedagogy takes three forms. First, there is an ongoing reincorporation of the concepts and metalanguage of Overt Instruction and Critical Framing in preparing and discussing subsequent exercises. Second, the main module assessment exercise requires students to use the new concepts and metalanguage to analyse a real-life negotiation in which they have played a significant role, or which they know about in detail. Third, the developmental nature of the programme allows us to incorporate an additional loop of teaching, learning and the writing process. Students who have considerable difficulty in applying and articulating clearly in writing a meta-conceptual analysis of negotiation have the opportunity to have personal consultations and feedback. They may then resubmit their assignment.

The assessment and feedback for these assignments does, however, pinpoint a dilemma facing this type of programme. It is partly the conventional requirements of assessment in a formal academic context which make us set this type of exercise of Transformed Practice assessment. It is also because we have confidence in the contribution of the writing process to learning (see, for example, Flower 1990). Certainly, weak assignments often indicated poor conceptual grasp of the module. This evidence led to further teaching and learning in consultations, which often (but not always) resulted in improved assignments, which we understood to mean also improved understanding.

Nevertheless, there were individuals who could articulate a reasonably clear conceptual grasp of the module in discussion, but who had battled more with articulating their understanding within the parameters of the writing task. Presumably, the real test of any management development pedagogy must be evidence of the transfer of learning to practice in the workplace. It seems unlikely that proof of transformed negotiation practice in the workplace will be in the form of a written essay! This is why the course has to build on the metalanguage and Critical Framing developed in the negotiation module in diverse ways later in the course – moving from access and critical engagement to critical language awareness, recruitment and selection, equity in the workplace.

What I have described as the 'access and critical engagement' part of the Management Communication course proceeds to focus on developing a critical language awareness (Fairclough 1995a). The materials are drawn or adapted from Janks's work (Janks 1996a, 1996b) in the South African context. The Situated Practice involves discussing a range of South African advertisements in terms of some of the marketing concepts which are introduced in another AIM course, Business Process and Environment. A close analysis of South African advertisements helps to develop further the metalanguage and Critical Framing established in previous MC modules. Hence, students are required to transfer some of their learning from the negotiation module to the marketing context. At the same time, they need to adopt a contrasting and critical perspective to their study of marketing. Again, this module explores the use of images (literal and metaphorical) to develop analytical and critical perspectives towards reading and language use.

Following the critical language awareness module (and after a two-week mid-year break), the MC course concentrates on recruitment and selection processes alongside issues of equity in the workplace. The ways in which this module relates to the NLG pedagogical framework can be summarised as shown opposite.

Conclusion: critical issues

The purpose of this chapter has been to demonstrate how the pedagogical framework designed by the Multiliteracies Project has been trialled in our Management Communication course of the AIM programme. The process of doing this has highlighted three issues in particular.

First, the review process emphasised the extent to which negotiation has emerged as a recurring theme within the course. In the first part of the course, students are introduced to a definition of communication as an interactive process of negotiated meaning. In the second part, negotiation as a formal process is studied to develop the students' ability to manage negotiations and to develop generic skills in Critical Framing. Thereafter, the metalanguage of negotiation becomes evident in all discussions. Not surprisingly, students increasingly use their sharp new instruments of Critical Framing to question some of the academic and conceptual

---

Recruitment and selection and equity in the workplace modules

Situated Practice
- Simulation and role play
- three-day workshop focus groups, self-exploration, exercises

Overt Instruction
- Analysis of process metalanguage of categorisation and criteria
- Developing a model
- Defining concepts

Critical Framing
- Reviewing simulation
- Focus on language and framing of justification, critique and exclusion
- Make explicit links with issues raised in equity workshop
- Focus on the role of ideology

Transferred Practice
- Joint assignment with the Industrial Relations course: consider the implications, in your workplace, of the new Labour Relations Act (1996) regarding residual unfair labour practices – recruitment, selection, and appraisal
- Developing principles for good practice
- The overall objective of this integrated module is to develop the language, tools and confidence to critique workplace practice in ways which will add critical new value to organisations.

---

assumptions underlying the programme itself. At another level the curriculum as a whole becomes subject to ongoing negotiation between all of the interested parties: students, lecturers, sponsoring companies, and the Graduate School of Business. This core concept of negotiation coincides with the Multiliteracies Project's call for language pedagogy 'to include negotiating a multiplicity of discourses' (see New London Group Chapter 1, above).

Second, the nature and form of academic assessment is raised for scrutiny. It is not self-evident that an academic-type written assignment will necessarily ensure the kind of Transformed Practice being advocated by the framework. In the era of postFordism or fast-capitalism, which is characterised by rapid technological change, there are no more national standards. This aggravates the difficulty of establishing appropriate assessment criteria in a programme which is constantly transforming and developing to keep abreast of changes in the workplace. The increasing awareness of the limitations of set academic standards has to be seen in the context of a nation seeking to establish a National Qualification Framework as a means of increasing equitable access to educational provision (Human Sciences Research Council 1995).

Third, the review of the course helped to reinforce both the crucial and difficult nature of setting up a Critical Framing approach. However, it also served as a valuable reminder of the potential of metaphor in attempting to develop Critical Framing. I would like to argue that metaphor is a particularly fruitful means of highlighting the metalanguage and approaches necessary to develop critical distance for identifying ideology in context.

Although the pedagogical components identified by the Multiliteracies Project are not necessarily new for those familiar with the work, for example, of Entwhistle and Ramsden (1983), or for those who have worked within traditions of critical pedagogy or new literacy studies, nevertheless the Multiliteracies framework forces practitioners to stand back and critically review their pedagogy by providing a succinct and coherent means of designing, developing, articulating, and assessing the teaching of language and communication. Indeed, the reflective process generated by writing this chapter has suggested features which deserve further study and which may well become substantive contributions to the International Multiliteracies Project – in particular, the need to expand the notion of 'negotiation' as a fundamental concept within a pedagogy of Multiliteracies; to develop a greater understanding of the exploitation of metaphor as a tool in Critical Framing and in the linguistic dimension of meaning design; and to develop more substantive and helpful responses to the problem of national academic assessment in a context of rapidly transforming global 'standards'.

16

FOUR INNOVATIVE
PROGRAMMES

A postscript from Alice Springs

Courtney B. Cazden

While in Alice Springs, Australia, in October 1997 for a conference co-sponsored by the Literacy Education Research Network and the Institute for Aboriginal Development, I realised the significance of two Aboriginal metaphors for the issues raised in my chapter on taking cultural differences into account (see Chapter 12 above).

One metaphor I had learned previously during earlier visits to Yirrkala Community School in east Arnhem Land, on the coast of the north-east corner of the Northern Territory. Yirrkala has organised its curriculum and teaching around a metaphor of the contact zone where rivers meet the sea, named *ganma* in one of the local Aboriginal languages. Literally, ganma is where fresh and salt water meet. Metaphorically, ganma is where cultures meet: fresh water is indigenous Yolngu knowledge and practices; salt water is the white Balanda knowledge and practices; and one place where they meet is in school.

Flying in a small plane from Yirrkala west to Darwin after a visit in 1993, I could see clearly the swirls of different colours in the ganma waters: bluer from the sea, browner from the land. Manduwuy Yunupingu, who was principal of Yirrkala when I first visited in 1991, has also described the role of Yothu Yindi, his internationally known rock group, in the meeting place of popular culture in these same ganma terms (Shoemaker 1994).

At first thought, this ganma metaphor may seem to ignore the important power differential between dominant and nondominant cultures in institutions like schools. But if you think again about literal relationships between fresh water and salt, the potential threat of unequal power is there: salt water tides and typhoons can flood the land, while fresh water cannot seriously harm the ocean. But if the two can be kept in balance in the *ganma* space, then the rich nutrients that come together from the mix of different waters nourishes richly diverse forms of life – biologically in the literal situation, culturally and intellectually in the metaphorical

Using this *ganma* metaphor, I will describe four educational programmes – three new here plus further observations from Puente included in Chapter 12 that have worked hard to create and sustain that balance. In doing so, they all reject the second Australian metaphor: '*terra nullius* education'. *Terra nullius* was the legal doctrine of 'empty land' that served to justify the invasion and appropriation of Australia by Europeans until overturned by the 1992 ruling of the Australian High Court in the case of Mabo *v.* Queensland. In their abstract for the Alice Springs conference, two staff members at the Yipirinia Aboriginal school in Alice Springs, Valerie Dobson and Rosalie Riley, adopted 'terra nullius' for the view of students, especially indigenous students, as being 'empty minds' until 'invaded' by teachers and texts. Rejecting the educational analogue of this doctrine, the four programmes find ways to validate and strengthen the fresh water knowledge all students bring with them to school.

The programmes vary in several ways. In terms of level, two are from primary schools, one secondary, and one tertiary. In terms of origin, the first two are from the USA and the last two from Australia. Finally, in terms of scope, the first takes place during Sharing Time in two self-contained classrooms; Puente has been replicated in more than thirty community colleges; while Tempe Language High School and Traeger Park Elementary School each involve an entire school. In describing them, I draw both on readings and on my observations of all except Sharing Time, with extended participant observations in Puente, and brief visits in the last two.

Sharing Time in two US classrooms

Karen Gallas and Steve Griffin teach first and second grades in Brookline, Massachusetts, a residential suburb of Boston. Brookline deserves its reputation as a community that cares about good schools, but its reality is more mixed in social class and ethnicity than its middle-class image would suggest. Among its schoolchildren, the mix is increased by the presence of African-American children from inner-city Boston who have been participating in a voluntary programme of busing out to the suburbs for several decades. In a community that sees itself as progressive both politically and educationally, the too frequent underachievement of the African American children has been a serious concern.

Gallas (Gallas 1994) reports on the language and discourse development of Jiana, an African-American six-year-old, during Sharing Time (ST), which is the US name for what is called in some other countries Morning News – a positive development, as it turned out, although the teacher took risks in departing from the usual primary school ST routines. Jiana moved into a homeless shelter near the school after some traumatic home life and only a few months of kindergarten. Academically she was on a pre-K level, and even had a hard time talking. 'Her speech was filled with stops and starts, long hesitations, and incredible difficulty at finding words for simple objects and ideas', Gallas reports. However, rather than referring her out of the classroom, Gallas decided to wait and see.

For reasons that had nothing to do with Jiana, Gallas had already decided to organise ST differently during this year, to let children take more control, so that she could follow Basil Bernstein's oft-quoted advice that, 'If the culture of the teacher is to become part of the consciousness of the child, then the culture of the child must first be in the consciousness of the teacher', and also so that she could 'expand the idea to include the notion of building a culture and community of the classroom where all the members participate in the community of each child'. Early in the school year, Gallas set the new ST structure. Each child had a designated day of the week when he or she could share. Each sharer sat in the teacher's chair, first narrating and then fielding questions and comments from peers. Gallas herself sat in the back of the room, participating as little as possible. What ensued, and was captured in Gallas's notes, was a series of transformations in 'the way the children talked and listened to each other'.

The development of Jiana's voice, and that of some of her peers as well, can be seen through a series of four of her stories over the school year. In the beginning, Jiana's narratives were hardly intelligible; but she persevered, and Gallas's attentive listening seemed to keep the rest of the class listening as well. Here is an early story about a half-finished bookmark, in which 'Karen' is the teacher and LEDP is an after-school programme:

Jiana:	I made this at LEDP
T:	I don't think they can hear you, honey.
Jiana:	I got this in LEDP, and . . . and I made it . . . and I didn't want it so . . . I'm going to give it to Karen.
T:	Do you want to tell more before you take questions?
Jiana:	Questions or comments? . . . Fanny.
Fanny:	What are you going to make it out of? What are you going to make it out of?
Jiana:	I'm not gonna make it.
Fanny:	But it's not finished . . . Well, you're going to have to show Karen how to do it because she doesn't know how to do it. And also, I think you need a needle for that.
Jiana:	I know.
Fanny:	Oh, do you have a needle?
Jiana:	No.
Fanny:	A fat one.

As Gallas sat and watched, 'other children like Fanny began to teach Jiana how to fill in her narratives' by their questions.

Three months later, Jiana was taking the sharing chair with a more upright posture and a stronger voice. Here is her recount of a trip to the Boston Aquarium taken with her after-school group:

Jiana: Oh. Um, and we saw the rainforest, we saw um, um, there was a um, thing on a, . . . like a say, tree, and there was a . . . a fake snake, and everybody, and, and some it was a fake snake but it was long and somebody was moving it in back of the thing, and and everybody thought it was a snake and everybody screamed.

Donald: Did you scream?

Jiana: No! Because . . . 'cause, a a snake couldn't be . . . yellow.

Several: Sure it could. It can.

Jiana: . . . And we saw, . . . and we saw um, little kinds of shells and we went to the pickup thing, where we pick up um, um, um, this big crab We get to pit it, pit it, we get to pit it up, and we pitted, picked it up, with some little things and they have a lot of legs.

Several: Starfish! Starfish!

Jiana: Yeah. Starfish.

About this time, Jiana also began commenting more after other children's stories, telling how, for example, she had cats too. Although Gallas didn't believe all Jiana's 'me too' extensions, she kept quiet.

Another month later, Jiana told the class about details of her personal life:

Jiana: My father was on stage talking to his friends, and he did it, he was in this programme. My father doing it . . . did something bad, and he's in a programme, and I can't tell you why . . . It's something white . . . It starts with a c, but I don't want to tell. And it's called . . . cocaine And that's why he's in the programme, and he'll never come out.

Robin: What do you mean by what you said, your father's doing it? I don't understand.

Jiana: It's like something bad, like mommy goes in a closet . . . and I say, 'what are you doing?' She says, 'You don't need to know', and she's sneaking a cigarette. And I say, 'That's not good for you.' My father sometimes . . . Sometimes if he says he's coming to pick you up . . . and he doesn't come . . . don't say he's a liar, say he's a fibber.

Gallas describes the scene:

The children listened carefully to her explanations, and there was a feeling of extreme seriousness in the group. They wanted to understand and questioned her closely about the meanings of words. They empathised, and they gave support; and as the discussion expanded, I was not uncomfortable because Jiana was very composed. She wasn't ashamed. She was just telling her story, and a look at her language shows how well-constructed and coherent her story is.

In the middle of the school year, Jiana started telling stories that were clearly fantasy – for example, about a trip to the zoo when the zookeeper took gorillas out for her mother to pet. Gallas's immediate response was to blurt out a reminder, which she later regretted, that ST was for 'true' stories. But Jiana persisted, and on subsequent days a few children tried to tell similar stories, while others followed Gallas's example in criticising their peers. Gallas finally asked herself why she had defined the sharing narrative to mean only true stories; she apologised to Jiana and announced that, during the next month, children could tell stories that were either true or 'fake', which was the children's word for fantasy.

Again, Jiana led the way into a new ST transformation. As her fluency and responsiveness to and from her peers increased, she told a fantasy story that included as characters the teacher and every child in the class: Here's the beginning of a fifteen-minute set of episodes:

> *Jiana:* When I went to Mars, um, Karen and Karen K, um, they had little pieces of hair sticking up [laughter] and, um, and Karen, uh, Karen [whispers to me, pointing to the rosebud necklace I am wearing, 'What are those?' I answer, 'Roses . . . rosebuds, rosebuds'] and when Karen had the rosebuds on, she had her little kid with her . .
> *Others:* She doesn't have one!
> *Jiana:* And it was Robin . . .
> *Others.* Ahhhhhh . . .

These fictional and inclusive narratives flourished, much to the enjoyment of most of the class. Most but not all. Gallas noticed that some of the Caucasian children, especially the boys, were uncomfortable with this new type of story. They muttered 'This isn't funny', became openly inattentive, and refused to try to tell fictional stories themselves. Jiana kept trying to include those boys, carefully and courteously; and Gallas increased the pressure on 'some very competent mainstream speakers' to try:

> William, for example, . . . absolutely would not make any attempt at the fantasy format. I literally had to force him to try it by refusing to let him share some X-rays of his brother's broken arm until he told us a fake story. After I realised how different and challenging

the fictional narratives were, I asked every child to try at least one fake story before they returned to a showing format.

By the end of the year, when Jiana herself had vanished, it was clear that all the children had expanded their narrative discourses, 'and continued to work on these skills long after Jiana had left us'.

In her conclusions, Gallas emphasises the relationship between story-telling and the development of classroom culture, especially when the tellers, starting with Jiana, grounded their stories not in a private egocentric world but in the very social reality of the classroom. Citing both US kindergarten teacher Vivian Paley and Russian literary theorist Mikhail Bakhtin, she argues that it was the inclusive classroom community, which the stories both came from and built, that enabled the children to learn from each other. 'Hence,' she concludes, 'to understand the transformation in Jiana's language, [and, I would add, the discourse of some of her peers] we begin and end with her place in the community of the classroom.'

Gallas and Griffin are both long-term members of a teacher research group that has focused attention on classroom discourse since its inception (Gallas *et al.* 1996), so it is not surprising that Griffin's report (Griffin 1993) on Sharing Time is similar in some respects to Gallas's. He focuses on the development of an African-American boy, David.

To summarise briefly, David started the year telling lengthy and elaborate fictions that became especially popular with his peers when he started making his classmates into his heroes and heroines. Griffin was initially uncomfortable: the length created time pressure for getting through the prescribed curriculum, and David's stories, while full of imaginative imagery, were only loosely constructed. But, with support from his teacher researcher colleagues, he let David continue.

About four months into the school year, David initiated a new genre when he announced from the sharing seat, 'For this story I need people. Who wants to be in my story?' As he told the story, his willing collaborators acted it out, as Paley routinely has her younger children act out their dictated stories. Needless to say, 'This served to accentuate the issues of anger, humor and other emotions expressed in the story, and elevated the audience response and their level of engagement'. For a while 'I need people' stories were a genre unique to David, while his peers recounted personal experiences in more typical monologue style.

Curious about the possible development of this or other genres by other children, Griffin announced that Sharing Time would now be for telling any kind of story, true or made up. Immediately, other children started telling 'I need people' stories. David remained the master, but his peers started incorporating more of his special devices – imaginative similes and echoes of other curriculum content. For example, after a unit on Martin

Luther King, he told a story about a David who fights a dragon not with a sword but with words.

Griffin also tracked David's growth in the tighter form of narrative more generally expected in school discourse. Elsewhere in the curriculum, Griffin gave David more explicit instruction during individual writing conferences. David was also hearing the stories of his classmates that had a more central organisation, and was acting in them as well. Especially through this ST experience, Griffin believes, David was 'guided into learning a more mainstream, school-based way of narration that had been difficult to acquire in the context of the typical school curriculum'.

Before the school year was ended, David not only told more coherent stories but even found his way – comparable to Jiana's in effect – to use stories to influence peer relationships, here between boys and girls. In one lengthy and very popular tale, told on a day after a torrential rain, he subverted stereotypical gender roles by having the boys go to the girls' house to play with Barbie dolls, while the girls were in the boys' house playing a computer game!

In considering these teacher reports, note the work that Gallas and Griffin had to do – work of listening and work of intervening – to keep the mix of ST discourse styles in balance. The children – whatever their discourse background – speak in the same discourse arena, the ganma space of Sharing Time. But just immersing children from different discourse communities in the central, shared, ganma waters is not enough. The teacher has to make those waters welcoming and respectful for all the children. Then, with their equal status within the group carefully sustained by the teacher, and the availability of alternative models actively encouraged, even scheduled, the children can and do reciprocally appropriate discourse models from their peers, and in the process transform relationship aspects of their own identities as well.

Puente in California community colleges

In the Puente programme, described above, the ganma space is centred in the English classroom but extends beyond it, into the counsellors' offices and the mentors' worksites. The fresh waters enter through the participation of the Mexican-American counsellors in the English class, the Mexican and Mexican-American texts read during the first semester, and the Mexican-American community mentors. The salt waters of academic knowledge expected in US colleges are embodied in the English teacher, and modelled in other texts read during the year. In Puente, as in Sharing Time, narratives become a powerful means of bicultural identity transformation. One required writing assignment in all Puente classes is a composition about students' experiences with their mentors. Here are excerpts from the beginning of the mentor paper of one student, whom I'll call Juan, which he read aloud on the day first drafts were due. It describes the breakfast gathering organized by the Puente counsellor in a local Mexican restaurant early in the school year, where students and their mentors first met. Ramon is the counsellor.

> As I walked through the door of the little restaurant on Main and Mission I could hear my heart beat. My hands were sweaty and I was nervous. What will my mentor look like, what will he say, what will we talk about, will he be intimidating, will I say something stupid, all of these things ran through my mind as I walked around the restaurant . . . Ramon invited us to get something to eat and sit down and he would get us if our mentor showed up. I got a plate, sat down, and began to eat my breakfast which consisted of huevos, arroz, papas, frijoles, and tortillas. I began to eat and when I was about half way done I heard Ramon call my name. It came to me as if he had said it in slow motion. 1 got up and walked over to Ramon and he introduced me to my mentor, Dr Calderon. We met and he asked me to get my plate and join him at his table. I said OK, went to get my plate and sat down with him in the corner of the restaurant. It was the moment of truth.

My field notes from that day include Juan's memorable opening and closing phrases – from his 'sweaty hands' to 'the moment of truth' – and that paragraph remained as the first paragraph of his final version in his writing portfolio. The full text recounts the hour-long talk in the restaurant and his subsequent visit to Dr Calderon's office as a college dean of students. It reports his biography, starting with 'picking' with the farm workers, his education, details of his present job and his advice: 'to learn the system, give myself chances, get to know myself as far as strengths and weaknesses and finally to keep moving and never give up'. The paper ends with an explanation of its title, *Giving Back*. La Raza is one name for the whole Mexican and Mexican-American community:

> After sitting down and talking with Dr Calderon for an hour and a half I was very confident and I felt good and proud not so much because he has made it and is successful but because he has taken time for me and is giving me hope, courage and support so that I can one day make it and be successful and give back to La Raza.

In Puente, autobiographical narratives serve two functions. First, writing, reading aloud, and discussing narratives about students' past serve to validate that past. Instead of being at best ignored, and at worst actively silenced in their earlier education, probably especially in English classrooms, here in the ganma space of the whole Puente programme, the students' past experiences and continuing identity as Mexican-Americans are validated, even celebrated. Second, narratives can look forward as well as back, envisioning a future and reconceiving one's own identity in the process.

Team teaching between English teachers and Mexican-American counsellors is a significant part of Puente's success. Few community college English teachers know enough about their students' culture and community to function so successfully alone.

Where teachers do work alone, as do Gallas and Griffin, they have to work very hard to be open to listening and learning from their students.

Where teachers from different backgrounds are working together in the shared ganma space, relations among the adults can be as significant and as problematic as among the students. One marvellous, and in my experience unique, resource for such teams is the booklet *Team Teaching in Aboriginal Schools*, published by the Northern Territory Department of Education (Northern Territory Department of Education 1986). Here the single *ganma* lagoon discourse space are team meetings for which both groups need to learn new ways of interacting. The Balanda teachers learn to give up dominating and to listen and learn instead; the Aboriginal teachers learn to give up silently resisting and speak up and talk back instead. The booklet could be a useful resource internationally, in situations where adult members of groups of unequal status in the larger society need to work together as equals within the schools.

Despite Puente's success, the programme is threatened by external forces in a shifting political climate, specifically two state-wide California referenda that have cut resources for immigrants and made illegal any state programmes that can be termed 'affirmative action'. So far, Puente has been saved by its strong political support in the Mexican-American community, and by the desire of colleges and universities to find some ways to maintain their diverse student bodies in a state that will soon be more than 50 per cent people of colour.

Tempe Languages High School in Sydney

Tempe Languages High School, like Puente, has been designed for immigrant students, in this instance from the many ethnic backgrounds which make up this multiethnic neighbourhood of Sydney. During my visits in 1993 and 1995, Tempe principal Peter James, himself a former chemistry teacher, explained the school's language history. Before 1986, the school had become what James now describes as a 'factory fodder curriculum' for its poor and immigrant students. It was producing 'students illiterate in two languages. Willing to take a chance on the international evidence that a second language is learned best if students are both fluent and literate in their first language', staff at Tempe embarked on what must have seemed a high-risk experiment.

The largest language groups in the school community are Macedonian, Vietnamese, Arabic, Greek and Chinese. All these language and literacies can be studied for at least four years. In addition, Japanese, Korean or French are taken by students not studying one of the community languages.

Because only 17 per cent of Tempe students are native English speakers, the importance of English is emphasised. To make room in student schedules for community and foreign languages, the time allotted to English has been cut back by almost 15 per cent. During this same period, the orientation of the entire curriculum has also been changed from outmoded 'vocational' to a future-oriented focus on social, political, organisational, technological, and economic skills. With these combined changes, student bilingualism and biliteracy have flourished, and scores on English proficiency tests have significantly increased.

As part of the professional development that made these changes possible, all Tempe teachers – mathematics and technology as well as languages and English – have had departmental in-service work with language consultants. The goal is to help all teachers, and thereby all students, attend to forms of language, from grammatical features to text genres, that are important in particular curriculum areas and may vary across languages and cultures (for example, see Cazden 1996a). The head of the languages faculty has even planned a special course for the oldest students that would accompany work placements in which bilingualism is a career advantage. In all these ways, Tempe is an entire ganma school.

Even though Tempe was showcased at a 1995 international Global Cultural Diversity Conference in Sydney hosted by the Australian government and opened by the UN Secretary General, it now is threatened, like Puente, by a changing political climate, specifically the election of a more right-wing federal government and more vocal anti-immigrant rhetoric. The school will of course continue, but its community language programme – the heart of its success – will suffer if high school certification for language study is cut back to languages considered of national economic importance such as Japanese, Chinese and Indonesian.

Traeger Park School in Alice Springs

Traeger Park Elementary School existed in Alice Springs until it was closed by the Northern Territory Department of Education in 1991. I can speak knowledgeably about only one part of the school's life and success – the Concentrated Language Encounters (CLE) developed by Brian Gray with the Traeger Park primary teachers in the 1980s. At that time, the students were about 75 per cent Aborigines; later the percentage was close to 100. My account draws on Gray's writings (Gray 1985, 1990; Gray and Cazden

1992), talks with him and two Traeger Park teachers, Sue O'Callaghan and Fiona McLaughlin, and observations in their classrooms in 1991, at the height of the tragically failed campaign to save the school. One indication of the school's success was the remarkable student attendance, reputedly a chronic problem in other Aboriginal schools. Even in its final term, on the day I happened to visit, attendance in the two classrooms was 22 out of 25 and 19 out of 22.

CLE was designed to create activity and discourse structures in which the children could come to understand not only how language is used to structure and organise what counts as knowledge in schools but also how language is used to negotiate school learning in schools. The activity structures were designed as condensed forms of significant interactional and discourse structures, focused by teacher direction, and often involving role playing in small groups so participation of each child is maximised, with the teacher as often the only 'native speaker' of the focal discourse participating in role.

So, for example, in a curriculum focused on health, the primary grade children took trips to the Aboriginal Health Centre, Hospital, and Ambulance Brigade in Alice Springs; and the Visiting Nurse visited the class. Transactional texts such as patient records and receptionist memos were practised in role plays; narratives of accidents or treatments were negotiated by teacher and children after the role playing, to emphasise event sequence; factual genres such as reports were similarly negotiated to summarise important substantive information that had been learned. Although the CLE programme was developed in detail only through the third grade, teachers of older students created their own extensions. In 1991, Fiona McLaughlin was teaching a CLE unit on the law to her Year 6 and 7 classes. They had sat in on court sessions; a local Aboriginal woman lawyer had visited the class; and they had role played aspects of legal discourse.

Two CLE features go beyond what is more typical in language experience and role-playing activities. One feature is the repeated experiences that children have, both first hand through field trips and classroom visitors and second hand through pictures and texts, with curriculum content knowledge. In those ways, they not only learn the content but also develop a foundation for speaking and writing with authority. A second feature is the active role of the teacher – both within the role playing and separately by scaffolding, modelling and giving explicit instruction in the oral and written discourse structures in which that knowledge is conventionally expressed.

CLE activities are designed for only one part of the ganma metaphor: to give the students access to Balanda English. There was also a powerful complementary Aboriginal presence in the school programmes and the whole school's life, which unfortunately has not been documented in published writings. Both must be somehow present in a ganma programme.

Conclusion

I would argue that all four programmes – Sharing Time in Gallas's and Griffin's classrooms, Puente, Tempe Languages High School and Traeger Park – have found ways to do what the original Multiliteracies document (New London Group 1996) calls for. They 'recruit learners' previous and current experiences', 'consider learners' affective and sociocultural identities' and 'constitute discourse arenas for risk and trust'. In fact, those common qualities may be one source of their educational power, despite their very different forms of educational enactment.

All four are vulnerable. True to the literal meaning of the ganma metaphor, the shared ganma space can be obliterated by the salt water of dominant group action. Subtly, in the absence of constant teacher vigilance to sustain equal status interactions in Sharing Time, through external legislative action and resource reallocations for Puente and Tempe; violently in the closing of Traeger Park. Successful Multiliteracies education programmes have to be not only created but fought for. And when we lose, as we sometimes will, we should try to retain documentary records of past successes, so we can build even stronger programmes in the ganma space when we have to start again.

REFERENCES

Alvarado, M. and B. Boyd-Barrett. 1992. *Media Education*. London: British Film Institute/Open University Press.

Anderson, Benedict. 1983. *Imagined Communities: Reflections on the Origin and Spread of Nationalism*. London: Verso.

Anzaldua, G. 1987. *Borderlands/La Frontera: The New Mestiza*. San Francisco: Aunt Lute Books.

Aronson, E. 1978. *The Jigsaw Classroom*. Beverly Hills: Sage.

Bachelard, Gaston. 1969. *The Poetics of Space*. Boston: Beacon Press.

Bakhtin, M. 1981. *The Dialogical Imagination*. Austin: University of Texas Press.

Bakhtin, M. M. 1986. *Speech Genres and Other Late Essays*. Austin: University of Texas Press.

Balsmao, A. 1994. 'Feminism for the Incurably Informed', pp. 126–34 in *Flame Wars: The Discourse of Cyberculture*, edited by M. Dery. Durham: Duke University Press.

Barrett, C. 1946. 'Torres Strait Islanders', *Walkabout*, 12:4, 7–11.

Barsalou, L. W. 1992. *Cognitive Psychology: An Overview for Cognitive Scientists*. Hillsdale: Lawrence Erlbaum.

Bateson, C. 1994. *Peripheral Visions: Learning Along the Way*. New York: HarperCollins.

Baym, N. 1995. 'The Emergence of Community in Computer Mediated Communication', pp. 138–63 in *CyberSociety*, edited by S. Jones. Thousand Oaks: Sage.

Beck, Ulrich. 1994. 'The Reinvention of Politics: Towards a Theory of Reflexive Modernization', pp. 1–55 in *Reflexive Modernization: Politics, Tradition and Aesthetics in the Modern Social Order*, by Ulrich Beck, Anthony Giddens, and Scott Lash. Cambridge: Polity Press.

Beck, Ulrich, Anthony Giddens and Scott Lash. 1994. *Reflexive Modernization: Politics, Tradition and Aesthetics in the Modern Social Order*. Cambridge: Polity Press.

Becker, H. 1992. 'A Model for Improving the Performance of Integrated Learning Systems: Mixed Individualized/Group/Whole Class Lessons, Cooperative Learning, and Organizing Time for Teacher-led Remediation of Small Groups', *Educational Technology* 32, 6–15.

Beckett, J. 1964. *Politics in the Torres Strait Islands*. Canberra: Australian National University.

Beckett, J. 1987. *Torres Strait Islanders: Custom and Colonialism*. Cambridge: Cambridge University Press.

Benedikt, M. 1991. 'Cyberspace: Some Proposals', pp. 119–224 in *Cyberspace: First Steps*, edited by M. Benedikt. Cambridge, MA: MIT Press.

Benjamin, Walter. 1970. 'The Work of Art in the Age of Mechanical Reproduction', pp. 219–54 in *Illuminations,* edited by Hannah Arendt. London: Fontana.

Bereiter, C. 1994. 'Constructivism, Socioculturalism, and Popper's World', *Educational Researcher* 23, 21–3.

Bereiter, C., and M. Scardamalia. 1993. *Surpassing Ourselves: An Inquiry into the Nature and Implications of Expertise.* Chicago: Open Court.

Bernstein, B. 1971. *Class, Codes and Control.* London: Routledge and Kegan Paul.

Bernstein, B. 1986. 'On Pedagogic Discourse', in *Handbook for Theory and Research in the Sociology of Education,* edited by J. G. Richardson. New York: Greenwood Press.

Bernstein, B. 1990. *Class, Codes and Control, Volume 4: The Structuring of Pedagogical Discourse.* London: Routledge and Kegan Paul.

Berston, R., and S. Moont. 1996. 'School Ain't What It Used to Be', *Internet.au,* 40–5.

Betsky, Aaron. 1995. *Building Sex: Men, Women, Architecture and the Construction of Sexuality.* New York: William Morrow.

Bigelow, B. 1997. 'On the Road to Cultural Bias: A Critique "The Oregon Trail" CD-ROM', *Language Arts,* 84–93.

Bigum, C., and B. Green. 1993. 'Curriculum and Technology: Australian Perspectives and Debates', in *Australian Curriculum Reform: Action and Reaction.* Belconen: Association/Social Science Press.

Bogard, W. 1996. *The Simulation of Surveillance: Hypercontrol in Telematic Societies.* Cambridge: Cambridge University Press.

Bond, D. 1996. 'New South Africa, Old Language? The Role of Metaphor in Reporting the Negotiation of the South African Labour Relations Bill' (locally published paper).

Borsook, P. 1996. 'The Memoirs of a Token: An Aging Berkeley Feminist Examines Wired', pp. 24–41 in *Wired Women,* edited by L. Cherny and E. Weise. Seattle: Seal Press.

Bowmaker-Falconer, A. 1996. *The Breakwater Monitor Research Report September 1996.* Cape Town: Graduate School of Business, University of Cape Town.

Bowmaker-Falconer, A., and P. Searl. 1995. *The Breakwater Monitor Research Report March 1995.* Cape Town: Graduate School of Business, University of Cape Town.

Boyes Braem, P. 1990. *Einführung in die Gabärdensprache und ihre Erforschung.*

Boyett, J. H., and H. P. Conn. 1992. *Workplace 2000: The Revolution Reshaping American Business.* New York: Plume/Penguin.

Britton, J. 1987. 'Vygotsky's Contribution to Pedagogical Theory', *English in Education,* 22–6.

Brooks, R. A. 1991. 'New Approaches to Robotics', *Science,* 253.

Brown, A. L. 1994. 'The Advancement of Learning', *Educational Reseacher,* 4–12.

Brown, A. L., D. Ash, M. Rutherford, K. Nakagawa, A. Gordon, and J. C. Campione. 1993. 'Distributed Expertise in the Classroom', pp. 188–228 in *Distributed Cognitions: Psychological and Educational Considerations,* edited by G. Salomon. New York: Cambridge University Press.

Brown, A. L., and J. C. Campione. 1994. 'Guided Discovery in a Community of Learners', pp. 229–70 in *Classroom Lessons: Integrating Cognitive Theory and Classroom Practice,* edited by K. McGilly. Cambridge, MA: MIT Press.

Brown, A. L., and A. S Palinscar. 1989. 'Guided, Cooperative Learning and Individual Knowledge Acquisition', pp. 393–451 in *Knowing, Learning, and Instruction: Essays in Honor of Robert Glaser,* edited by L. B. Resnick. Hillsdale: Lawrence Erlbaum.

Bruer, J. T. 1993. *Schools for Thought: A Science of Learning in the Classroom*. Cambridge, MA: MIT Press.

Buchanan, R., and V. Margolin. 1995. 'Discovering Design – Explorations in Design Studies', Chicago: University of Chicago Press.

Buck-Morss, Susan. 1989. *The Dialectics of Seeing: Walter Benjamin and the Arcades Project*. Cambridge, MA: MIT Press.

Buckingham, D. 1990. *Watching Media Learning*. Basingstoke: Falmer.

Buckingham, D. 1993. *Children Talking Television: The Making of Television Literacy*. Basingstoke: Falmer Press.

Callon, M., and B. Latour. 1981. 'Unscrewing the Big Leviathan', pp. 51–80 in *Toward an Integration of Micro and Macro Sociologies*, edited by K. Knorr and A. Cicourel. London: Routlege & Kegan Paul.

Cameron, Andy. n.d. 'Illusions of Interactivity', in *Dissimulations*. <http://www.wmin.ac.uk/media/VD/Dissimulations.html>.

Cameron, D. 1996. *Verbal Hygiene*. London: Routledge.

Campbell, A. H., L. Cameron, J. A. Keats, M. W. Poulter, and B. Poulter. 1958. *The Aborigines and Torres Islanders of Queensland*. Brisbane: Western Suburbs Branch United Nations Association.

Caplan, N., M. Choy, and J. Whitmore. 1992. 'Indochinese Refugee Families and Academic Achievement', *Scientific American* 266, 36–42.

Cardiff, D. 1980. 'The Serious and the Popular: Aspects of the Evolution of Style in Radio Talk 1928–39', *Media Culture & Society* 2 (1), 29–47.

Castells, M. 1996. *The Information Age: A Science of Learning in the Classroom*. Oxford: Blackwell.

Casti, J. L. 1994. *Complexification: Explaining a Paradoxical World Through the Science of Surprise*. New York: Harper Collins.

Cazden, C. B. 1983. *Whole Language Plus*. New York: Teachers College Press.

Cazden, C. B. 1988. *Classroom Discourse: The Language of Teaching and Learning*. Portsmouth, NH: Heinemann.

Cazden, C. B. 1992. *Whole Language Plus: Essays on Literacy in the United States and New Zealand*. New York: Teachers College Press.

Cazden, C. B. 1994. 'Visible and Invisible Pedagogies in Literacy Education', pp. 161–74 in *Discourse and Reproduction*, edited by P. Atkinson, S. Delamont, and B. Davies. Cresskill: Hampton Press.

Cazden, C. B. 1996a. 'One Australian High School's Version of "Language Teaching Across the Curriculum"', *TESOL Matters* 6.

Cazden, C. B. 1996b. 'Readings of Vygotsky in Writing Pedagogy', in *Child Discourse and Social Learning: An Interdisciplinary Perspective*, edited by D. Hicks. New York: Cambridge University Press.

Cazden, C. B. 1996c. 'A Report on Reports: Two Dilemmas of Genre Teaching', pp. 248–65 in *Some Contemporary Themes in Literacy Research*, edited by F. Christie and J. Foley. New York: Waxmann Munster.

Cazden, C. B., V. John, and D. Hymes. 1972. *Functions of Language in the Classroom*. New York: Teachers College Press.

Cazden, C. B., and H. Mehan. 1989. 'Principles from Sociology and Anthropology: Context, Code, Classroom and Culture', pp. 47–57 in *Knowledge Base for the Beginning Teacher*, edited by M. Reynolds. Oxford and New York: Pergamon Press.

REFERENCES

Cherney, L., and E. Weise. 1996. *Wired Women: Gender and New Realities in Cyberspace.* Seattle: Seal Press.

Christie, F. 1987. *Language and Literacy: Making Explicit What's Involved.* Sydney.

Christie, F., B. Delvin, P. Freebody, A. Luke, J. R. Martin, T. Threadgold, and C. Walton. 1991. *Teaching English Literacy: A Project of National Significance on the Preservice Preparation of Teachers to Teach English Literacy.* Darwin: Centre for Studies of Language in Education, Northern Territory University.

Christie, Michael J. 1990. 'Aboriginal Science for an Ecologically Sustainable Future', *Ngoonjook: Batchelor Journal of Aboriginal Education.*

Christie, Michael J. 1993. 'Yolgnu Linguistics', *Ngoonjook: A Journal of Australian Indigenous Issues,* 58–77.

Cisneros, S. 1989. *The House on Mango Street.* New York: Vintage/Random House.

Clark, A. 1993. *Associative Engines: Connections, Concepts, and Representional Change.* Cambridge: Cambridge University Press.

Clay, M. M. 1992. 'A Vygotskian Interpretation of Reading Recovery', pp. 114–35 in *Whole Language Plus: Essays on Literacy in the United States and New Zealand,* edited by C. B. Cazden. New York: Teachers College Press.

Clay, M. M. 1993. *Reading Recovery: A Guidebook for Teachers in Training.* Portsmouth, NH: Heinemann.

Cludski, H. 1996. 'Distinct Shifts Taking Place in the Workplace', *Cape Times,* South Africa.

Cochran-Smith, M. 1995. 'Color Blindness and Basket Making Are Not the Answers: Confronting the Dilemmas of Race, Culture and Language Diversity in Teacher Education', *American Educational Research Journal,* 493–522.

Cohen, E. G., and R. Lotan. 1997. *Working for Equity in Heterogeneous Classrooms: Sociological Theory in Practice.* New York: Teachers College Press.

Collins, J. 1995. *Architectures of Excess: Cultural Life in the Information Age.* New York: Routledge.

Comber, B., and J. O'Brien. 1993. 'Critical Literacy: Classroom Explorations', *Critical Pedagogy Networker.* Adelaide: The Flinders University, Education.

Coombe, N. 1996. *Associate in Management (AIM) Academic Review Report 1991–1996.* University of Cape Town Academic Planning Committee.

Cope, Bill. 1998. 'The Language of Forgetting: A Short History of the Word', pp. 192–223 in *Seams of Light: Best Antipodean Essays,* edited by Morag Fraser. Sydney: Allen & Unwin.

Cope, B., and M. Kalantzis. 1993. *The Powers of Literacy: Genre Approaches to Teaching Literacy.* Philadelphia: Falmer Press.

Cope, B., and M. Kalantzis. 1997a. *Productive Diversity: A New Australian Approach to Work and Management.* Sydney: Pluto.

Cope, Bill, and Mary Kalantzis. 1997b. 'White Noise: The Attack on Political Correctness and the Struggle for the Western Canon', *Interchange* 28, 283–329.

Cope, Bill, and Mary Kalantzis. 1998. 'Multicultural Education: Transforming the Mainstream', in *Critical Multiculturalism,* edited by Stephen May. London: Falmer Press.

Coyle, K. 1996. 'How Hard Can It Be?', pp. 42–55 in *Wired Women,* edited by L. Cherney and E. Weise. Seattle: Seal Press.

Crosby, P. B. 1994. *Completeness: Quality for the 21st Century.* New York: Plume.

Cross, K. F., J. J. Feather, and R. L. Lynch. 1994. *Corporate Renaissance: The Art of Reengineering*. Oxford: Basil Blackwell.

Crystal, David, and Randolph Quirk. 1964. *Systems of Prosodic and Paralinguistic Features in English*. London: Mouton.

Curtiss, P., and K. Curtiss. 1995. 'What 2nd Graders Taught College Students and Vice Versa', *Educational Leadership* 53, 28–33.

Darling, S. (1992). *Family literacy: The Need and the Promise*. Louisville: National Center for Family Literacy.

Davidow, W. H., and M. S. Malone. 1992. *The Virtual Corporation: Structuring and Revitalizing the Corporation for the 21st Century*. New York: Harper Collins.

Deal, Terrence E., and William A. Jenkins. 1994. *Managing the Hidden Organization*. New York: Warner.

Delgado-Gaiton, C. 1991. 'Involving Parents in the Schools: A Process of Empowerment', *American Journal of Education* 100, 20–46.

Delpit, L. 1986. 'Skills and Dilemmas of a Progressive Black Educator', *Harvard Educational Review* 56: 3, 379–85.

Dewey, J. 1916/1966. *Democracy and Education*. New York: Free Press.

Dixon, R. M. W. 1980. *The Languages of Australia*. Cambridge: Cambridge University Press.

Dobyns, Lloyd, and Clare Crawford-Mason. 1991. *Quality or Else: The Revolution in World Business*. Boston: Houghton Mifflin.

Doczi, Gyorgy. 1981. *The Power of Limits: Proportional Harmonies in Nature, Art and Architecture*. Boulder: Shambhala Publications.

Douglas, J. 1899–1900. 'The Islands and Inhabitants of Torres Strait', *Queensland Geographical Society* 15, 25–40.

Drucker, P. F. 1993. *Post-capitalist Society*. New York: Harper.

Eco, Umberto. 1981. *The Role of the Reader: Explorations in the Semiotics of Texts*. London: Hutchinson.

Eco, Umberto. 1996. *The Search for the Perfect Language*. London: Secker & Warburg.

Edwards, J. 1994. *Multilingualism*. London and New York: Routledge.

Eiser, J. R. 1994. *Attitudes, Chaos, and the Connectionist Mind*. Oxford: Basil Blackwell.

Enloe, C. H. 1981. 'The Growth of the State and Ethnic Mobilisation: The American Experience', *Ethnic and Racial Studies* 4, 123–36.

Entwhistle, N., and P. Ramsden. 1983. *Understanding Student Learning*. London: Croom Helm.

Faigley, L. 1992. *Fragments of Rationality: Postmodernity and the Subject of Composition*. Pittsburgh: University of Pittsburgh Press.

Fairclough, N. 1989. *Language and Power*. London: Longmans.

Fairclough, N. 1992a. *Discourse and Social Change*. Cambridge: Polity Press.

Fairclough, N. 1992b. 'Discourse and Text: Linguistic and Intertextual Analysis Within Discourse Analysis', *Discourse and Society* 3 (2), 193–217.

Fairclough, N. 1993. 'Critical Discourse Analysis and the Marketisation of Public Discourse: The Universities', *Discourse and Society* 4 (2), 133–68.

Fairclough, N. 1994. 'Conversationalization of Discourse and the Authority of the Consumer', in *The Authority of the Consumer*, edited by R. Keat, N. Whitley, and N. Abercrombie. London: Routledge.

Fairclough, N. 1995a. *Critical Discourse Analysis*. London: Longmans.

337

Fairclough, N. 1995b. 'Ideology and Identity in Political Television', edited by N. Fairclough.

Fairclough, N. 1995c. *Media Discourse*. London: Edward Arnold.

Featherstone, M., S. Lash, and R. Robertson. 1995. *Global Postmodernism*. Beverly Hills: Sage.

Felix, U., and D. Askew. 1996. 'Languages and Multimedia: Dream or Nightmare?', *Australian Universities' Review* 39, 16–21.

Flower, L. 1990. 'Negotiating Academic Discourse', in *Reading-to-write: Exploring a Cognitive Social Process*, edited by L. Flower. New York: Oxford University Press.

Ford, Henry. 1923. *My Life and Work*. Sydney: Angus & Robertson.

Fowler, R., R. Hodge, G. Kress, and T. Trent. 1979. *Language and Control*. London: Routledge.

Freire, P. 1968. *Pedagogy of the Oppressed*. New York: Seabury Press.

Freire, P. 1973. *Education for Critical Consciousness*. New York: Seabury Press.

Freire, P., and D. Macedo. 1987. *Literacy: Reading the Word and the World*. South Hadley: Bergin & Garvey.

Fukuyama, F. 1992. *The End of History and the Last Man*. London: Penguin.

Gadsden, V. 1995. 'Representations of Literacy: Parents' Images in Two Cultural Communities', pp. 287–303 in *Family Literacy: Connections in Schools and Communities*, edited by L. Morrow. Newark: IRA.

Gallas, K. 1994. *The Languages of Learning: How Children Talk, Write, Dance, Draw, and Sing their Understanding of the World*. New York: Teachers College Press.

Gallas, K., and S. Griffin 1996. 'Talking the Talk and Walking the Walk', *Language Arts* 73, 608–617.

Gardner, H. 1991. *The Unschooled Mind: How Children Think and how Schools Should Teach*. New York: Basic Books.

Garrett, L. 1994. 'Responding to Changing Demographics: Selecting Reading Recovery Books', *The Running Record*, 4–5. Columbus, Ohio State University, Reading Recovery Council of North America, Winter, pp. 4–5.

Geary, James. 1997. 'Speaking in Tongues,' pp. 50–6 in *Time*.

Gee, J. P. 1992. *The Social Mind: Language, Ideology, and Social Practice*. New York: Bergin & Garvey.

Gee, J. P. 1993. 'Postmodernism, Discourses, and Linguistics', pp. 271–95 in *Critical Literacy: Radical and Postmodernist Perspectives*, edited by C. Lankshear and McLaren. Albany: State University of New York Press.

Gee, J. P. 1994a. 'New Alignments and Old Literacies: From Fast Capitalism to the Canon', pp. 1–35 in *1994 Australian Reading Association Twentieth National Conference*, edited by B. Shortland-Jones, B. Bosich, and J. Rivalland: Australian Reading Association.

Gee, J. P. 1994b. *Quality, Science, and the Lifeworld: The Alignment of Business and Education*. Leichhardt: Adult Literacy and Basic Skills Action Coalition.

Gee, J. P. 1996a. *Social Linguistics and Literacies: Ideology in Discourses*. London: Falmer Press.

Gee, James Paul. 1996b. *Social Linguistics and Literacies: Ideology in Discourses*. London: Taylor & Francis.

Gee, James Paul. 1996c. *Two Kinds of Teenagers: Language, Identity, and Social Class*. Worcester, MA: Clark University.

Gee, J. P. 1996d. 'Vygotsky and Current Debates in Education', in *Discourse*,

Learning, and Schooling, edited by D. Hicks. Cambridge: Cambridge University Press.

Gee, J. P., G. Hull, and C. Lankshear. 1996. *The New Work Order*. Sydney: Unwin; Boulder: Westview.

Gellner, E. 1983. *Nations and Nationalism*. London: Basil Blackwell.

Gellner, Ernest. 1994. *Conditions of Liberty: Civil Society and Its Rivals*. London: Hamish Hamilton.

Gentner, D. 1983. 'Structure-mapping: A Theoretic Framework for Analogy', *Cognitive Science*, 155–70.

Gilbert, P. 1989. *Writing, Schooling and Deconstruction: From Voice to Text in the Classroom*. London: Routledge.

Gilmore, P., D. M. Smith, and L. Kairaiuak. 1997. 'Resistance, Resilience and Hegemony: An Alaskan Case of Institutional Struggle with Diversity', in *Off-white: Readings on Society, Race, and Culture*, edited by M. Fine, L. Weis, J. C. Powell and L. M. Wang, New York: Routledge, pp. 90–9.

Gilster, Paul. 1997. *Digital Literacy*. New York: John Wiley & Sons.

Gingrich, N. 1995. *To Renew America*. New York: Harper Collins.

Giroux, H. 1988. *Schooling and the Struggle for Pedagogies: Critical and Feminist Discourses as Regimes of Truth*. New York: Routledge.

Gitlin, T. 1995. 'The Twilight of Common Dreams: Why American is Wracked by Culture Wars'. New York: *Metropolitan Books*.

Goffman, Erving. 1959. *The Presentation of Self in Everyday Life*. New York: Doubleday Anchor.

Goldberg, C. 1997. 'Hispanic Households Struggle as Poorest of the Poor in the U.S.', *New York Times*, A1, A12, January 30.

Goldsworthy, A. 1992. *Critical Theory of Technology*. New York: Oxford University Press.

Goodman, Y. M., and K. S. Goodman. 1990. 'Vygotsky in a Whole Language Perspective', in *Vygotsky and Education: Implications and Applications of Socio-historical Psychology*, edited by L. C. Moll. New York: Cambridge University Press.

Gordon, D. 1991. *We Are All Family: A Multicultural Basic Education Manual for Family Learning*. Philadelphia: Lutheran Settlement House.

Gray, B. 1985. 'Helping Children to Become Language Learners in the Classroom', in *Aboriginal Perspectives on Experience and Learning: The Role of Language in Aboriginal Education*, edited by M. Christie. Geelong: Deakin University Press.

Gray, B. 1990. 'Natural Language Learning in Aboriginal Classrooms: Reflections on Teaching and Learning Styles for Empowerment in English', pp. 105–39 in *Language, Power and Education in Australian Aboriginal Contexts*, edited by C. Walton and W. Eggington. Darwin: Northern Territory University Press.

Gray, B., and C. B. Cazden. 1992. 'Concentrated Language Encounters: The International Biography of a Curriculum Concept', *TESOL* (Vancouver).

Greeley, K., and L Mizell. 1993. 'One Step Among Many: Affirming Identity in Anti-racist Schools', pp. 215–29 in *Freedom's Plow: Teaching in the Multicultural Classroom*, edited by T. Perry and J. W. Fraser. New York and London: Routledge.

Greenhill, A., and G. Fletcher. 1996. 'The Possibilities for Electronic Publishing on the Internet', *Australian Universities' Review* 39, 22–5.

Griffin, S. 1993. 'I Need People: Storytelling in a Second-grade Classroom', The Literacies Institute Technical Report, Newton, MA: Educational Development Center.

Griffith, M., and A. Connor. 1994. *Democracy's Open Door: The Community College in America's Future*. Portsmouth, NH: Boynton/Cook.

Gruber, S., J. K. Peyton, and B. Bruce. 1995. 'Collaborative Writing in Multiple Discourse Contexts', *Computer Supported Cooperative Work* 3, 247–69.

Gutman, A. 1994. *Multiculturalism: Examining the Politics of Recognition*. Princeton: Princeton University Press.

Haddon, A. C. 1904. 'Trade', pp. 293–297 in *Reports of the Cambridge Anthropological Expedition to Torres Straits*. Cambridge: Cambridge University Press.

Halliday, M. A. K. 1978. *Language as Social Semiotic*. London: Edward Arnold.

Halliday, M. A. K. 1994. *An Introduction to Functional Grammar*. London: Edward Arnold.

Hammer, M. 1996. *Beyond Reengineering: How the Process-centered Organization is Changing our Work and our Lives*. New York: Harper Business.

Hammer, M., and J. Champy. 1993. *Reengineering the Corporation: A Manifesto for Business Revolution*. New York: Harper Business.

Handy, C. 1989. *The Age of Unreason*. London: Business Books.

Handy, C. 1994. *The Age of Paradox*. Boston: Harvard Business School Press.

Harre, R., and G. Gillett. 1994. *The Discursive Mind*. Beverly Hills: Sage.

Hart, D. 1991. *Understanding the Media: A Practical Guide*. London: Routledge.

Harvey, D. 1989. *The Conditions of Postmodernity*. Oxford: Blackwell.

Harvey, D. 1993. 'From Space to Place and Back Again: Reflections on the Condition of Postmodernity', pp. 3–29 in *Mapping the Futures: Local Cultures, Global Change*, edited by J. Bird, T. Curtis, G. Putnam, G. Robertson, and L. Tickner. New York: Routledge.

Harvey, David. 1996. *Justice, Nature and the Geography of Difference*. Cambridge, MA: Blackwell.

Hayles, N. K. 1993. 'The Seductions of Cyberspace', pp. 173–90 in *Rethinking Technologies*, edited by V. Andermatt Conley. Minneapolis: University of Minnesota Press.

Heath, S. B. 1983. *Ways With Words: Language, Life, and Work in Communities and Classrooms*. Cambridge: Cambridge University Press.

Held, D. 1987. *Models of Democracy*. Cambridge: Polity Press.

Herz, J. C. 1995. *Surfing on the Internet: A Nethead's Adventures On-line*. Boston: Little, Brown & Company.

Hilf, William Homer. 1996. 'Beginning, Middle and End – Not Necessarily in That Order'. : http://www.cybertown.com/hilf.html.

Hobsbawm, E. J. 1993. *Nations and Nationalism Since 1780*. Cambridge: Cambridge University Press.

Hodge, Bob, and Gunther Kress. 1988. *Social Semiotics*. London: Polity Press.

Holderness, M. 1993. 'Down and Out in the Global Village', *New Scientist*, 25–9.

Holland, J. H., K. J. Holyoak, R. E. Nisbett, and P. R. Thagard. 1986. *Processes of Inference, Learning, and Discovery*. Cambridge, MA: MIT Press.

Huerta-Macias, A. 1995. 'Literacy from Within: The Project FIEL Curriculum', pp. 91–9 in *Immigrant Learners and their Families*, edited by G. Weinstein-Shr and E. Quintero. McHenry: Center for Applied Linguistics & Delta Systems Inc.

Human Sciences Research Council. 1995. *Ways of Seeing the National Qualification Framework*. Pretoria: Human Sciences Research Council.

Humphries, Sal. 1997. *Narrative and Interactivity: An Overview of the Story So Far*. <http://www.ngapartji.com.au/research/rosebud/research.html>.

Husserl, Edmund. 1970. *The Crisis of European Sciences and Transcendental Phenomenology.* Evanston: Northwestern University Press.

Imms, W. G. L. 1961. 'Change and Frustration in the Torres Straits', *Quadrant* 5, 75–9.

Ishikawa, K. 1985. *What is Total Quality Control? The Japanese Way.* Englewood Cliffs: Prentice Hall.

Janks, H. 1996a. 'The Research and Development of Critical Language Awareness Materials for Use in South African Secondary Schools', *Education,* University of Lancaster.

Janks, H. 1996b. 'Why We Still Need Critical Language Awareness in South Africa', *SPIL PLUS,* 29: 172–90.

Jernudd, B. 1992. 'Planning English Language Acquisition: Development and Maintenance of Languages in ESL and EFL Societies', pp. 491–530 in *Bilingualism and National Development,* edited by G. Jones and C. Ozog. Bandar Seri Begawan Brunei: University of Brunei Darussalam Press.

Kalantzis, Mary. 1997. 'The New Citizen and the New State: An Australian Case for Civic Pluralism', in *Occasional Paper No. 9.* Sydney: Centre for Workplace Communication and Culture.

Kalantzis, Mary, and Bill Cope. 1993a. 'Histories of Pedagogy, Cultures of Schooling', pp. 38–62 in *The Powers of Literacy: A Genre Approach to Teaching Literacy,* edited by Bill Cope and Mary Kalantzis. London: Falmer Press.

Kalantzis, Mary, and Bill Cope. 1993b. 'Republicanism and Cultural Diversity', pp. 118–44 in *The Republicanism Debate,* edited by W. Hudson and D. Carter. Sydney: University of New South Wales Press.

Kang, H. W., P. Kuehn, and A. Herrell. 1996. 'The Hmong Literacy Project: Working to Preserve the Past and Ensure the Future', *The Journal of Educational Issues of Language Minority Students* 16, 17–32.

Kanter, R. M. 1995. *World Class: Thriving Locally in the Global Economy.* New York: Simon & Schuster.

Kauffman, S. A. 1991. *Origins of Order: Self-organization and Selection in Evolution.* Oxford: Oxford University Press.

Kedourie, E. 1961. *Nationalism.* London: Hutchinson.

Kelly, K. 1994. *Out of Control: The New Biology of Machines, Social Systems, and the Economic World.* Reading, MA: Addison-Wesley.

Kenway, J. 1995. 'Reality Bytes: Education, Markets and the Information Super-highway', *Australian Educational Researcher* 2, 35–65.

Kohl, H. 1973. *Reading: How to.* New York: Dutton.

Koskinen, P., I. Blum, N. Tennant, E. M. Parker, M. Straub, and C. Curry. 1995. 'Have You Heard Any Good Books Lately? Encouraging Shared Reading at Home with Books and Audiotapes', pp. 87–103 in *Family Literacy: Connections in Schools and Communities,* edited by L. Morrow. Newark: IRA.

Kotter, J. P. 1995. *The New Rules: How to Succeed in Today's Post-corporate World.* New York: The Free Press.

Kramarae, C. 1995. 'A Backstage Critique of Virtual Reality', pp. 36–56 in *CyberSociety,* edited by S. Jones. Thousand Oaks: Sage.

Kramarae, C., and H. J. Taylor. 1993. 'Women and Men on Electronic Networks: A Conversation of Monologue?', pp. 52–61 in *Women, Information Technology, and Scholarship,* edited by J. Taylor, C. Kramarae, and M. Ebben. Urbana: University of Illinios Press.

Kress, G. 1990. *Linguistic Process and Sociocultural Change.* Oxford: Oxford University Press.

Kress, Gunther. 1993. 'A Glossary of Terms', pp. 248–55 in *The Powers of Literacy: A Genre Approach to Teaching Writing,* edited by Bill Cope and Mary Kalantzis. London: Falmer Press.

Kress, G. R. 1995. *Writing the Future: English and the Producation of a Culture of Innovation.* Sheffield: National Association of Teachers of English.

Kress, Gunther, and Theo van Leeuwen. 1996. *Reading Images: The Grammar of Visual Design.* London: Routledge.

Kurokawa, Kisho. 1991. *Intercultural Architecture: The Philosophy of Symbiosis.* London: Academy Editions.

Ladson, Billings G. 1995. 'Towards a Theory of Culturally Relevant Pedagogy', *American Educational Research Journal,* 32: 465–91.

Langbridge, J. 1977. *From Enculturation to Evangelisation: An Account of Missionary Education in the Islands of Torres Strait to 1915,* unpublished BA Hons Thesis, Department of Education, James Cook University, Townsville.

Lash, Scott. 1994. 'Reflexivity and its Doubles: Structure, Aesthetics, Community', pp. 110–73 in *Reflexive Modernization: Politics, Tradition and Aesthetics in the Modern Social Order,* by Ulrich Beck, Anthony Giddens, and Scott Lash. Cambridge: Polity Press.

Lash, Scott, and John Urry. 1994. *Economies of Signs and Space.* Beverly Hills: Sage.

Latour, B. 1986. 'Visualization and Cognition: Thinking with Eyes and Hands', *Knowledge and Society: Studies in the Sociology of Culture Past and Present* 6, 1–40.

Lave, J. 1988. *Cognition in Practice: Mind, Mathematics and Culture in Everyday Life.* Cambridge: Cambridge University Press.

Lave, J. 1996. 'Teaching, as Learning, in Practice', *Mind, Culture, and Activity* 3, 149–64.

Lave, J., and E Wegner. 1991. *Situated Learning: Legitimate Peripheral Participation.* Cambridge: Cambridge University Press.

Lee, C. 1993. *Signifying as a Scaffold for Literacy Interpretations.* Urbana: National Conneif of Teachers of English.

Lemke, J. 1990. *Talking Science: Language, Learning and Values.* Norwood, N.J.: Ablex.

Lewontin, R. C. 1991. *Biology as Ideology: The Doctrine of DNA.* New York: Harper.

Liberman, K. 1990. 'An Ethnomethodological Agenda in the Study of Intercultural Communication', in Cultural Communication and Intercultural Contact. Hillsdale. N.J.: Lawrence Erlbaum Associates, pp. 185–92.

Light, P., and G. Butterworth. 1993. *Context and Cognition: Ways of Learning and Knowing.* Hillsdale: Lawerence Erlbaum.

Lipnack, J., and J. Stamps. 1993. *The Team New Factor: Bringing the Power of Boundary Crossing Into the Heart of Your Business.* Essex Junction: Oliver Wright.

Lo Bianco, J. 1997. 'Language Policies: State Texts for Silencing and Giving Voice', in *Difference, Silence and Cultural Practice,* edited by P. Freebody, A. Muspratt, and B. Delvin. Crosskill: Hampton Press.

Lo Bianco, J., and P. Freebody. 1997. *Australian Literacies: Informing National Policy on Literacy Education.* Melbourne: Language Australia.

Lohrey, Andrew. 1995. *Transferability in Relation to the Key Competencies.* Sydney: Centre for Workplace Communication and Culture.

Lopez y Fuentes, G. 1937/1992. *El Indio.* New York: Continuum.

342

Lorentz, E. N. 1993. *The Essence of Chaos.* Seattle: University of Washington Press.

Ludski, H. 1996. 'Distinct Shifts taking Place in the Workplace', in *Cape Times.*

Luke, Allan. 1992. 'When Basic Skills and Information Processing Just Aren't Enough: Rethinking Reading in New Times', pp. 17 in *A.J.A. Nelson Address, Australian Council for Adult Literacy, 1992 National Conference.* Sydney.

Luke, C. 1994. 'Feminist Pedagogy and Critical Media Literacy', *Journal of Communication Inquiry* 18: 30–47.

Luke, C. 1996a. 'ekstasis@cyberia', *Discourse* 17, 187–297.

Luke, C. 1996b. 'Reading Gender and Culture in Media Discourses and Texts', in *The Literacy Lexicon,* edited by G. Bull and M. Anstey. Sydney: Prentice-Hall.

Luke, C. 1996c. 'Media and Cultural Studies', in *Constructing Critical Literacies,* edited by A. Muspratt, P. Freebody, and A. Luke. Crosskill: Hampton Press.

Luria, A. R. 1976. 'Cognitive Development: Its Cultural and Social Foundations', edited by Michael Cole. Cambridge, MA: Harvard University Press.

Lusted, D. 1991. *The Media Studies Book: A Guide for Teachers.* London: Routledge.

MachLachlan, G., and I. Reid. 1994. *Framing and Interpretation.* Carlton: Melbourne University Press.

Marenbon, J. 1987. *English, our English: The New Orthodoxy Examined.* London: Centre for Policy Studies.

Margolis, H. 1993. *Paradigms and Barriers: How Habits of Mind Govern Scientific Beliefs.* Chicago: University of Chicago Press.

Martin, J. R. 1984. 'Language, Resister and Genre', pp. 21–30 in *Children Writing,* edited by F. Christie. Geelong: Deakin University Press.

Martin, J. R., and M. A. K. Halliday. 1993. *Writing Science.* London: Falmer Press.

McCarthy, F. D. 1938. 'Trade in Aboriginal Australia, and Trade Relationships with Torres Strait, New Guinea and Malaya', *Oceania* 9, 405–38.

McFarlane, S. 1888. *Among the Cannibals of New Guinea.* Philadelphia: Presbyterian Board of Publication and Sabbath School Work.

McKie, D. 1994. 'Virtual Fakes and the Future: Cybersex, Lies and Computer Games', pp. 15–28 in *Framing Technology,* edited by L. Green and R. Guinery. Sydney: Allen & Unwin.

McNeill, David. 1992. *Hand and Mind: What Gestures Reveal About Thought.* Chicago: University of Chicago Press.

Mehan, H. 1996. 'A New Reproduction of Inequality under the New Capitalism?', *Organization,* 419–24.

Mehan, H., I. Villanueva, L. Hubbard, and A. Lintz. 1996. *Constructing School Success: The Consequences of Untracking Low-achieving Students.* Cambridge: Cambridge University Press.

Michaels, S., and B. Bruce. 1988. 'The Discourses of the Seasons', Report for the Center for the Study of Reading. Champaign/Urbana: University of Illinois.

Michaels, Sarah, Mary Catherine O'Conner, and Judith Richards. 1993. 'Literacy as Reasoning within Multiple Discourse: Implications for Restructuring Learning', pp. 107–21 in *1993 Restructuring Learning: 1990 Summer Institute Papers and Recommendation.* Washington DC: Council of Chief State School Officers.

Micklethwait, J., and A. Wooldridge. 1996. *The Witch Doctors: Making Sense of the Management Gurus.* New York: Times Books.

Miller, J. D. 1993. 'Script Writing on a Computer Network: Quenching the Flames or Feeding the Fire', pp. 124–37 in *Networked-based Classrooms: Promises and Realities*, edited by B. Bruce, J. K. Petyon, and T. Batson. New York: Cambridge University Press.

Minnick, N. 1993. 'Teacher's Directives: The Social Construction of "Literal Meanings" and "Real Worlds" in Classroom Discourse', in *Understanding Practice: Perspectives on Activity and Context*, edited by S. Chaiklin and J. Lave. Cambridge: Cambridge University Press.

Mitchell, William J. 1995. *City of Bits: Space, Place and the Infobahn*. Cambridge, MA: MIT Press.

Mizell, L., S. Benett, B. Bowman, and L Morin. 1993. 'Different Ways of Seeing: Teaching in an Anti-racist School', pp. 27–46 in *Freedom's Plow: Teaching in the Multicultural Classroom*, edited by T. Perry and J. W. Fraser. New York and London: Routledge.

Moll, L. 1992. 'Bilingual Classroom Studies and Community Analysis: Some Recent Trends', *Educational Researcher*. 20–4.

Morgan, G. 1986. *Images of Organisations*. Newbury Park: Sage Publications.

Morrison, T. 1994. *The Nobel Lecture in Literature*. New York: Alfred A. Knopf.

Mühlhäusler, Peter. 1996. *Linguistic Ecology: Language Change and Linguistic Imperialism in the Pacific Region*. London: Routledge.

Murname, R. J., and F. Levy. 1996. *Teaching the New Basic Skills: Principles for Educating Children to Thrive in a Changing Economy*. New York: The Free Press.

Muspratt, A., P. Freebody, and A. Luke. 1996. *Constructing Critical Literacies: Teaching and Learning Textual Practice*. Crosskill: Hampton Press.

National Center for Family Literacy. 1994. *Family Literacy Program Quality Self-study*. Louisville: National Center for Family Literacy.

New London Group. 1996. 'A Pedagogy of Multiliteracies: Designing Social Futures', *Harvard Educational Review* 66: 60–92.

Nickse, R., A. Speicher, and P. Buchek. 1988. 'An Intergenerational Adult Literacy Project: A Family Intervention/Prevention Model', *Journal of Reading* 31, 634–42.

Nolan, R. 1994. *Cognitive Practices: Human Language and Human Knowledge*. Oxford: Blackwell.

Northern Territory Department of Education. 1986. *Team Teaching in Aboriginal Schools*. Darwin: Northern Territory Department of Education.

Northern Territory Department of Education. 1993. *Getting Going with Genres: Narrative Genre*. Darwin: Northern Territory Department of Education.

Ogbu, J. U., and M. E Matute-Bianchi. 1986. 'Understanding Sociocultural Factors: Knowledge, Identity, and School Adjustment', pp. 73–142 in *Beyond Language: Social and Cultural Factors in Schooling Language Minority Students*. Sacramento: California State Department of Education.

Olsen, David R. 1994. *The World on Paper: The Conceptual and Cognitive Implications of Writing and Reading*. Cambridge: Cambridge University Press.

Ong, W. 1982. *Orality and Literacy: The Technologizing of the Word*. London: Methuen.

Orellana, M. F. 1996. '¡Aquí Vivimos! Voices of Central American and Mexican Participants in a Family Literacy Project', *The Journal of Educational Issues of Language Minority Students* 16, 115–29.

Pattanayak, D. P. 1986. 'Literacy: Some Reflections', in *Aspects of Adult Literacy*, edited by A. K. Pugh and C. Volkmar. Munich: Goethe Institut.

Pennycook, A. 1994. *The Cultural Politics of English as an International Language*. London: Longman.

Perkins, D. 1992. *Smart Schools: From Training Memories to Educating Minds*. New York: Free Press.

Perkins, D. 1995. *Outsmarting IQ: The Emerging Science of Learnable Intelligence*. New York: The Free Press.

Peters, T. 1992. *Liberation Management: Necessary Disorganization for the Nanosecond Nineties*. New York: Vintage Books.

Petre, D., and D. Harrington. 1996. *The Clever Country? Australia's Digital Future*. Sydney: Macmillan.

Pevsner, Nikolaus. 1976. *A History of Building Types*. London: Thames and Hudson.

Phillipson, Robert. 1992. *Linguistic Imperialism*. Oxford: Oxford University Press.

Phillipson, Robert, and Tove Skutnabb-Kangas. 1986. *Linguicism Rules in Education*. Roskilde: Roskilde University Centre.

Piore, M., and C. Sable. 1984. *The Second Industrial Divide*. New York: Basic Books.

Polanyi, Karl. 1975. *The Great Transformation*. New York: Octagon Books.

Polanyi, M. 1962. *Personal Knowledge*. Chicago: University of Chicago Press.

Potts, M. and S. Paull. (1995). 'A Comprehensive Approach to Family-focused Services', pp. 167–83 in *Family Literacy: Connections in Schools and Communities*, edited by L. Morrow. Newark: IRA.

Pratt, M. L. 1991. 'Arts of the Contact Zone', *Association of Departments of English Bulletin*, 33–40.

Reed, M., A. Webster, and M. Beveridge. 1996. 'Mapping the Literacy Curriculum: An Interactive Account of Classroom Literacies', *Changing English*, 3: 189–200.

Reich, R. B. 1992. *The Work of Nations*. New York: Vintage Books.

Rheingold, H. 1994. *The Virtual Community: Homesteading on the Electronic Frontier*. New York: Harper Perennial.

Robertson, R. 1995. 'Globalisation: Time-space and Homogenisation-hetrogenisation', in *Global Postmodernism*, edited by M. Featherstone, S. Lash, and R. Robertson. Beverly Hills: Sage.

Robins, K. 1996. 'Cyberspace and the World We Live In', pp. 1–30 in *Fractual Dreams: New Media in Social Context*, edited by J. Dovey. London: Lawrence & Wishart.

Rodriguez, L. T. 1993. *Always Running: La Vida Loca: Gang Days in L.A.* New York: Simon & Schuster Touchstone.

Rogoff, B. 1990. *Apprenticeship in Thinking*. New York: Oxford University Press.

Rosaldo, R. 1995. 'Foreword', pp. xi–xvii in *Hybrid Cultures: Strategies for Entering and Leaving Modernity*, edited by L. Canclini. Minneapolis: University of Minnesota Press.

Sacks, O. 1996. *Seeing Voices: A Journey into the World of the Deaf*. London: Harper.

Saffo, P. 1993. 'Hot New Medium: Text', *Wired* 1, 48.

Sashkin, M., and K. J. Kiser. 1993. *Putting Total Quality Management to Work*. San Francisco: Berrett-Koehler.

Saxena, M. 1994. 'Literacy among Panjabis in Southall', pp. 195–215 in *Worlds of Literacy*, edited by M. Hamilton, D. Barton, and R. Ivanic. Clevedon: Multilingual Matters.

Scannell, P. 1992. 'Public Service Broadcasting and Modern Public Life', in *Culture and Power*, edited by P. Scannell. Thousand Oaks: Sage.

Schiller, H. 1995. 'The Global Information Highway: Project for an Ungovernable World', pp. 17–34 in *Resisting the Virtual Life: The Culture and Politics of Information*, edited by J. Brooks and I. Boal. San Francisco: City Lights Books.

School Curriculum and Assessment Authority. 1995. *Early Intervention in Children with Reading Difficulties: An Evaluation of Reading Recovery and Phonological Training*. London: School Curriculum and Assessment Authority.

Scollon, R., and S. B. K Scollon. 1981. *Narrative, Literacy, and Face in Interethnic Communication*. Norwood: Ablex.

Senge, Peter M. 1990. *The Fifth Discipline: The Art and Practice of the Learning Organization*. New York: Doubleday Currency.

Seton-Watson, H. 1977. *Nations and States: An Enquiry into the Origins of Nations and the Politics of Nationalism*. London: Methuen.

Shaughnessy, M. P. 1977. *Errors and Expectations*. New York: Oxford University Press.

Shoemaker, A. 1994. 'Selling Yothu Yindi', *Re Publica*, 24–38.

Shore, B. 1996. *Culture in Mind*. Oxford: Oxford University Press.

Solà-Morales, Igansi de. 1997. *Differences: Topographies of Contemporary Architecture*. Boston: MIT Press.

Spender, D. 1995. *Nattering on the Net*. Sydney: Spinifex Press.

Sproull, L., and S Kiesler. 1991. *Connections: New Ways of Working in the Networked Organization*. Cambridge, MA: MIT Press.

Staples, Brent. 1992. 'The War Against Street Gangs'. Editorial page in *New York Times*, May 31.

Stone, S. 1995. 'Split Subjects, Not Atoms; or, How I Fell in Love with My Prosthesis', pp. 393–406 in *The Cyborg Handbook*, edited by C. Hables Gray, H. Figueroa-Sarriera, and S. Mentor. New York: Routledge.

Street, B. 1995. 'Foreword', in *Immigrant Learners and their Families*, edited by G. Weinstein-Shr and E. Quintero. McHenry: Center for Applied Linguistics & Delta Systems Inc.

Street, B. V. 1984. *Literacy in Theory and Practice*. Cambridge: Cambridge University Press.

Taylor, Charles. 1994. *Multiculturalism: Examining the Politics of Recognition*. Princeton: Princeton University Press.

Taylor, D. 1983. *Family Literacy: Young Children Learning to Read and Write*. Portsmouth, NH: Heinemann.

Thibault, P. 1991. *Social Semiotics as Praxis*. Minneapolis: University of Minnesota Press.

Tolson, A. 1991. 'Televized Chat and the Synthetic Personality', in *Broadcast Talk*, edited by P. Scannell. Thousand Oaks: Sage.

Topping, K. 1986. *Parents as Educators: Training Parents to Teach their Children*. Cambridge, MA: Brookline Books.

Toulmin, S. 1992. *Cosmopolis: The Hidden Agenda of Modernity*. Chicago: The University of Chicago Press.

Tufte, Edward R. 1990. *Envisioning Information*. Cheshire, CT: Graphics Press.

Tufte, Edward R. 1997. *Visual Explanations: Images and Quantities, Evidence and Narrative*. Cheshire, CT: Graphics Press.

UNESCO. 1992. *UNESCO Project Design for a Red Book on Endangered Languages*. Paris: UNESCO.

346

Van Leeuwen, T. 1993. 'Genre and Field in Critical Discourse Analysis', *Discourse and Society*, 193–223.

Venturi, Robert, Denise Scott Brown, and Steven Izenour. 1977. *Learning From Las Vegas: The Forgotten Symbolism of Architectural Form*. Cambridge, MA: MIT Press.

Vines, G. 1996. 'Death of a Mother Tongue', *New Scientist*, 24–7.

Virilio, Paul. 1997. *Open Sky*. London: Verso.

Vosniadou, S., and A. Ortony. 1989. *Similarity and Analogy in Reasoning and Learning*. Cambridge: Cambridge University Press.

Vygotsky, L. 1962. *Thought and Language*. Cambridge, MA: MIT Press.

Vygotsky, L. S. 1978. *Mind in Society: The Development of Higher Psychological Processes*. Cambridge, MA: Harvard University Press.

Vygotsky, L. S. 1987. *The Collected Works of L. S. Vygotsky: Vol. 1 Problems of General Psychology, Including the Volume Thinking and Speech*. New York: Plenum.

Wajcman, J. 1994. 'Technological A/genders: Technology, Culture and Class', pp. 3–14 in *Framing Technology: Society, Choice and Change*, edited by G. Green and R. Guinery. Sydney: Allen & Unwin.

Waldrop, M. M. 1992. *Complexity: The Emerging Science at the Edge of Order and Chaos*. New York: Simon & Schuster.

Walkerdine, V. 1986. *Surveillance, Subjectivity and Struggle: Lessons From Pedagogic and Domestic Practices*. Minneapolis: University of Minnesota Press.

Walton, A. R. 1992. *Expanding the Vision of Foreign Language Education: Enter the Less Commonly Taught Languages*. Washington, DC: National Foreign Language Centre, Johns Hopkins University.

Wark, McKenzie. n.d. 'Netlish: English Language on the Internet'. http://www.mcs.mq.edu.au/Staff/mwark/warchive/Other/netlish.html.

Waters, M. C. 1990. *Ethnic Options: Choosing Identities in America*. Berkeley: University of California Press.

Watts, R. 1995. 'Interview: Dr. Ron Watts of Open Learning', *Internet Australasia* 1, 72–3.

Weinstein-Shr, G., and E. Quintero. 1995. *Immigrant Learners and their Families: Literacy to Connect Generations*. McHenry: Center for Applied Linguistics & Delta Systems Inc.

Weishar, Joseph. 1992. *Design for Effective Selling Space*. New York: McGraw-Hill.

Wernick, A. 1991. *Promotional Culture*. Thousand Oaks: Sage.

Wertsch, J. V. 1985. *Culture, Communication, and Cognition: Vygotskian Perspectives*. Cambridge: Cambridge University Press.

Wertsch, J. V. 1996a. *Vygotsky's Two Minds on the Nature of Meaning*. Chicago: Research Assembly of the National Council of Teachers of English.

Wertsch, J. V. 1996b. 'Vygotsky: The Ambivalent Enlightenment Rationalist', pp. 39–62 in *Contemporary Implications of Vygotsky and Luria*, edited by M. Cole and J. V. Wertsch. Worcester, MA: Clark University Press.

Whyte, William H. 1980. *The Social Life of Small Urban Spaces*. Washington, DC: The Conservation Foundation.

Williams, M., and C. Bigum. 1994. 'Connecting Schools to Global Networks: Curriculum Option or National Imperative?', *Australian Educational Computing*, 9–16.

Williams, R. 1973. *The Country and the City*. St Albans: Paladin.

Williams, R. 1977. *Marxism and Literature*. Oxford: Oxford University Press.

347

Williams, R. 1981. *Culture.* Glasgow: Collins.

Worthen, B., L. Van Dusen, and P. Sailor. 1994. 'A Comparative Study of Students' Time-on-task in ILS and non-ILS Classrooms', *International Journal of Educational Research* 51, 25–37.

Yates, Joanne. 1989. *Control Through Communication: The Rise of System in American Management.* Baltimore: Johns Hopkins University Press.

Yule, George. 1996. *The Study of Language.* Cambridge: Cambridge University Press.

Zelasko, N. F. 1993. *The Bilingual Double Standard: Mainstream Americans' Attitudes Towards Bilingualism.* Ann Arbor: University Microfilms International, Dissertation Information Service.

INDEX

Benjamin, Walter 230
bilingualism 92–3, 99
body and identity 85–7

capitalism, new 10–13, 43, 46–50, 61–2, 226
capitalism, old 10, 13–14, 48, 62, 112, 135
capitalism, fast 10–13, 14, 41–2, 43, 46–50, 61–2, 300, 319
citizenship 13–15
civic pluralism 14–15, 17, 18
civic participation, education for 137–40
classrooms: as new communities of practice 50–3; Puente 237, 249–50; traditional 81–2
cyberschooling 81–2
conversationalisation of public discourse 174–80
critical framing 7, 30–2, 34–5, 68, 117–20, 237, 239–42, 246–7, 261, 263–5, 288, 291, 294, 313, 314, 315, 316, 317, 318–20
cyberschooling 81–2

Design 25–7, 25–30, 51, 153–61, 157–8, 159–61, 162, 203–9, 243–8
Design elements 25–30
Design metalanguage 7, 19, 23–5, 31, 99, 243, 313
Designing 22–3, 162–3, 169–70, 203–9; *Redesigned* 23
Designs Available 20–1
Designs of meaning, linguistic, visual, audio, gestural, spatial, multimodal

9, 19–20, 25–8, 152, 162, 169, 180–1, 209–17
Dewey 18, 239
distributed systems 44–7
diversity: *cultural* 3; linguistic 3; local 234; productive 13, 17, 18, 36, 42, 129–31, 146–8, 267, 314; subcultural 5
Domains of Literacy Conference 8, 18, 239, 298

education: *as exclusion* 123; as assimilation 123; for civic participation 131–40; *indigenous* 106–18; as multiculturalism 123–4; as pluralism 124–5

fast capitalism 11–13, 43, 46–50
Ford, Henry 126, 141
Fordism 11, 12, 126–7, 141

ganma metaphor 321–2
globalisation 93–4, 146–8, 165–8

Halliday, M. A. K. 22, 172
Harvard Education Review 8, 292
Husserl 206–8
hybrid textualities 83–5

identity 205; and body 85–7; collective 253–8; kinds of 54–8; people as portfolios 61–2;
indigenous education 106–18
intertextuality 170–4, 180–1

language across the curriculum 14
languages, endangered 98–9

LERN Conference 8, 321
lifeworlds, 15–17, 122–3, 174, 206–9, 241
literacy: critical 4; and designs for social futures 217–23, 234; multimodal 4, 51; pedagogy 3, 5, 7, 9, 106, 157, 223; schooled 142–3; as symbolic capital 121
lives: personal 15–17; public 13–17; working 10–13
Luria, 218

marketisation, 163–5
metalanguage of Design 7, 23–5, 31, 99, 243, 313
mobots 45–6
Morrison, Toni 268–70
multilingualism 92
multimedia 9, 16, 143, 158–9, 182–4; and designs for social futures 223–33
multimodality 52, 153–4, 158–9, 182–4, 187–93

nation state 96–8, 132–40
nationalism 132–40, 204

orders of discourse 18, 20, 170–4, 180–1
Overt Instruction 7, 31–4, 67, 116–20, 237, 239–43, 246, 261–3, 288, 291, 294, 314, 315, 317, 319

pedagogy: definition 9; theories 9, 30–2, 530–53, 87–91
post–Fordism 11, 127–9
productive diversity 13, 17, 18, 36, 42, 129–31, 146–48, 267, 314
Puente 237, 249–58, 327–9

Reading Recovery Program 251–2
red book 98–9

semiotics: theories of 155–6; of visual space 199–202
sharing time 322–7
Situated Practice 7, 31–3, 67, 116–20, 237, 239–45, 261–3, 288, 291, 294, 314, 318, 319
synaesthesia 158–9

technologies 69–77, 223–34
Transformed Practice 7, 30–2, 35–6, 68, 117–20, 237, 239–42, 247–8, 261, 263–5, 288, 291, 294, 314, 316, 317, 319

Vygotsky 32, 44, 52, 218, 252, 261–3

work, education and changing patterns 10–13, 125–31
workplaces 4, 7, 11, 19–20, 35–40, 50, 61–2; new flattened hierarchies 11–13
workplaces, virtual 82–5